Gods of the City

Religion in North America

Gods of the City

of the

Religion and the

American Urban Landscape

edited by Robert A. Orsi

Indiana University Press

Bloomington and Indianapolis

This book is a publication of

Indiana University Press
601 North Morton Street
Bloomington, Indiana 47404–3797 USA

www.indiana.edu/~iupress

Telephone orders   800-842-6796
Fax orders   812-855-7931
Orders by e-mail   *iuporder@indiana.edu*

© 1999 by Indiana University Press

The paper used in this publication meets the minimum requirements of American National Standard for Information Sciences—Permanence of Paper for Printed Library Materials, ANSI Z39.48–1984.

Manufactured in the United States of America

Library of Congress Cataloging-in-Pubication Data

Gods of the City : religion and the American urban landscape / edited by Robert A. Orsi.
        p.   cm. — (Religion in North America)
Includes index.
ISBN 0-253-33499-3 (cloth : alk. paper). — ISBN 0-253-21276-6 (pbk. : alk. paper)
1. Cities and towns—Religious aspects. 2. Cities and towns—United States. 3. United States—Religion.   I. Orsi, Robert A.
BL2525.G63 1999
200'.973'091732—dc21   98-48338

1 2 3 4 5 04 03 02 01 00 99

My city's a location of memory and desire, and I can plot in this neighborhood points of rapture and longing and wonder.

—Mark Doty, *Heaven's Coast: A Memoir*

Contents

Foreword

In this volume, Robert A. Orsi and the essayists he has assembled set out to define, describe, and celebrate the role of urban religion in twentieth-century America. In their collective judgment, this nation's cities have been the site of much of what is most creative in modern American religion. Yet the story of religion in the United States that historians tell is often a narrative that features and even romanticizes rural and small-town values to the exclusion of the urban experience. This volume is a forceful declaration of the shaping role that cities have played in the religious life of our nation.

Orsi, whose earlier award-winning studies have established him as one of America's most instructive observers of urban culture and of ethnic religious devotions, strikes the primary themes of this volume in his opening essay. Collectively, the essayists expand on those themes, giving voice to the religious experiences of city dwellers. Orsi's own concerns with religion on the ground and with theoretical reflection about the lived religion of the diverse inhabitants of the cities carry over into the essays in this collection. For example, the essayists highlight the ways the urban physical environment shapes the sites and modes of religious expression—from storefront churches to backdoor shrines, from fourth-floor apartments to the streets themselves. The sites that become the settings for urban religion expand our understanding of the concept of sacred space and force us to recognize the limitation of confining sacred acts to churches, synagogues, and temples. The rich examples that follow document the ubiquity of the sacred in the geography of the city.

Another theme echoing throughout these disparate essays is the reality and the results of contact among different religious peoples in the urban setting. The density of population in the city means that isolation is not possible; contact among diverse religions is therefore inevitable. Sometimes the results are conflict and strife; other times, as these essayists point out, interacting produces creative religious interchange and fruitful spiritual negotiation. Out of these urban circumstances have arisen some of the most potent and enterprising religious movements in twentieth-century America. The essayists in this collection are confident that the years ahead will yield even more of the same.

That prediction rests in part on the fact that today urban centers are frequently the site of immigrants' first American homes. New arrivals from Asia, Africa, the Caribbean, and Latin America are pouring into the metropolitan centers of the country, bringing with them the wealth of the world's religious traditions. And these transplanted traditions are flourishing here, as the essays in this collection document. America's new religious pluralism includes diverse expressions of Islam, Hinduism, and Buddhism, as well as countless varieties of Jewish, Christian, Afro-Caribbean, and sectarian religion, all of which are finding the city environment to be a congenial location. Priests and priestesses, healers and practitioners, ministers and adepts are able to gather followers and form communities in the cities. There seem to be no natural limits to the creative religious possibilities in the urban world.

In his introductory essay, Robert Orsi provides us with a sweeping assessment of the changing nature of the study of the city, the diverse attitudes that have been generated about the city, and the prospects for a fuller understanding of urban religion. We share his hope that this volume will advance the cause of understanding the religious history of America in a different way. In the past, fear of the city has been a major theme in the literature; we trust that the thick ethnographic details in this collection will serve as a partial corrective to such misplaced notions. We believe that the scholars represented herein make a convincing case for paying more attention to the demography and topography of urban religion. Beyond that, we anticipate that a host of scholarly studies centering on urban spaces, neighborhoods, and landscapes will increase our comprehension of how these contexts have shaped the religious lives and experiences of many Americans. This volume is therefore a step toward rectifying an imbalance in the historiography of American religion.

Catherine L. Albanese
Stephen J. Stein, *Series Editors*

Acknowledgments

Writing is a more collaborative activity than the popular image of the solitary, inward-looking author suggests, and a project such as this is collaborative all the way through. So I want to thank those who have supported this work in one way or another over the years. The "Gods of the City" project emerged out of a conference organized with the financial assistance of the Lilly Endowment, and I am grateful to the officers of the Endowment for their initial enthusiasm and support; my colleague David H. Smith played an important role in directing this funding my way. Karen McCarthy Brown, Joe Sciorra, and Jack Kugelmass participated in the conference, and the idea for this volume first emerged in conversation with them; filmmaker Beth Harrington was there too, and if only the technology were right, we could have included some of her wonderful work on city religion. Indiana University has provided me essential research support along the way at key junctures.

The introduction took longer to write than I had originally anticipated, as its scope and ambitions changed, and for their patience I must thank the contributors to the volume and Robert J. Sloan of Indiana University Press. Different drafts of the introduction were read by Sarah Pike, Stephen J. Stein, Diane Winston, and Catherine Albanese (and a group of her students); struggling with their sharp-eyed and thoughtful criticisms made the final version a much better text than any of my first attempts, although I acknowledge as my own all remaining errors and infelicities of expression. I asked Jon Butler and Colleen McDannell to read over the manuscript, in the final days of writing the introduction, and they kindly agreed. Again, Martha Cooley's support, encouragement, and advice were essential. And, as always, thanks to Jeff Keller, Michael Jackson, Maria Laurino, John Efron, Jeff Isaac, and above all to Claire Harlan-Orsi.

Gods of the City

Introduction

Crossing the City Line

Robert A. Orsi

I was standing, one unusually cool and rainy afternoon in late July ten years ago, on the corner of Third Avenue and 167th Street in the South Bronx, next to a Franciscan Sister whose everyday work was ministering to the spiritual and physical needs of prostitutes in another nearby city. West of us, on the hills sloping down from our feet toward Webster Avenue, one of the Bronx's main commercial avenues, block after block of abandoned buildings dissolved in the gray drizzle. Sister Marty knew all too well the depths of suffering and depravity that could suddenly open up for unfortunate people in contemporary American cities, and she seemed to view the world with compassionate but clear eyes. The great economic revival of the South Bronx (which Jack Kugelmass describes in his contribution to this collection) had not yet begun; there was tremendous vitality in the neighborhoods, but it was not evident from where Sister Marty and I were standing. There were no people around. The empty buildings exhaled an icy breath reeking of urine and rot from doorways ripped open by junkies, tingling my skin even on that cool day.

"When the hookers on the street tell me what happens to them," Sister Marty was saying, "how they get beat up and hurt, I cry with them." Tall weeds and thick undergrowth spilled from vacant lots and over rusted fences in lush green profusion, as nature reclaimed the spaces abandoned by people and their dwellings. As we contemplated the decay and devastation of the place—the same place where I had grown up many years earlier—Sister Marty said, "Something in me comes alive when I come into this area. I feel God's presence more strongly here than anywhere else."[1]

Sister Marty and I had met earlier that morning at a conference on Catholic peacemaking hosted by a Franciscan friary called San Damiano on 167th Street and Franklin Avenue. Monks and nuns began entering the various communities of the South Bronx in the 1960s and 1970s, just when corrupt landlords were burning their South Bronx properties to collect insurance compensation as they abandoned the neighborhoods. It was in one of these years that the New York Yankees, who play in the South Bronx, were in the World Series, and the rest of the country got to see great towers of smoke rising into the air behind the outfield on national television. Catholics had always lived in the Bronx, of course—immigrants and migrants, workers in the city's commerce and industry—second- and third-generation Irish first, decamping from the tough streets of Hell's Kitchen and the Tenderloin in Manhattan, and then Italian immigrants and their children come from East Harlem and the Lower East Side to the cleaner, safer streets of the Bronx, then most recently Puerto Ricans and other Spanish-speaking Caribbean people after the Second World War, along with the priests, nuns, and lay brothers who served these different communities. But the monks and nuns seeking out the most desolate and dangerous areas of the South Bronx in the fire years were migrants of another sort. They imagined the South Bronx to be the deserts of Syria and Egypt, where they would re-create the ancient spirit of Christian monasticism in its purest forms of prayer, sacrifice, and service. The South Bronx—and landscapes like it in other cities around the country—would be the new Scete, and the monks and nuns signs of hope and transcendence amid the devastation.[2]

Many of these religious migrants were reversing the pilgrimage that their parents, the children or grandchildren of immigrants, had made to the suburbs in the 1940s and 1950s; they were dedicating themselves to places their mothers and fathers had struggled to get away from. Among the new pilgrims were Franciscans in brown robes and Mother Theresa's Sisters in white saris hemmed in blue. They reclaimed abandoned buildings, cleared ground, and planted gardens. The two young men who founded San Damiano, Brother Giles and Brother David, had been called to the South Bronx by Mother Theresa herself, who had heard about their desire to live a primitive Franciscan life (meaning a life in strict adherence to Saint Francis's spirit and to the earliest rules of his followers) among poor people. As soon as Brother Giles saw the neighborhood where he would settle, he thought to himself, "This is where I will find God." The friars told me that the South Bronx nourishes and nurtures them, and they meant this literally: the wood and bricks used in renovating the friary all came from surrounding ruins, the flowers in the beautiful garden were transplanted local wildflowers, and the friary was heated with the wood of dead Bronx trees.

At the time of the 1987 conference, the friars at San Damiano had plans to build a park in the lot across the street from the friary where three apartment buildings had once stood. The park design had evolved in conversations between the friars and the local community and included flower beds, benches, and nineteen vegetable plots for neighborhood people to tend. One side of the park was going to be left as it was, littered with garbage and debris from the fallen buildings; according to the friar who was overseeing planning of the site, this side of the park would "speak about death and the bad things of the neighborhood" and, on the level of Christian cosmology, "paradise lost." But then chaos and rubble would give way to flowers and vegetables, a sign of hope and the promise of resurrection for the South Bronx. In the middle of the park—midway between loss and reclamation, despair and triumph, the Cross and Easter morning—the friars wanted to put an immersion tank for baptisms. New Christians would begin their spiritual journeys amid the debris of the old world/lost Eden/the South Bronx in disrepair, and then move through the waters of rebirth to the garden—and a revitalized South Bronx—beyond.

This is one South Bronx story—two, really, the Franciscans' and mine, because on my trips to the Bronx I am always consumed with love and a sense of loss for a world of childhood streets and relatives long gone, and more recently with hope and joy as the borough obviously comes back to renewed life. Here is another story: Just about the time of the peacemaking conference, a young German artist went into an abandoned South Bronx public school building and, on the wet, blistered walls of its vast auditorium two floors below street level, painted (by torchlight) a huge image of the Hulk, the rocky green chthonic hero of Marvel comics. The figure arched up across the ceiling over broken seats. On the night of the work's unveiling, well-dressed downtown New Yorkers picked their way past drunks and drug addicts who had taken up residence in the school, past the carcasses of two dead dogs that the artist insisted be left in the building's courtyard for the occasion, and down several flights of dark steps under dripping ceilings to glimpse, intermittently by flashlight, this figure of primeval power erupting along the walls of the room where the children of immigrants and migrants had recited the Pledge of Allegiance not very long ago, and over the stage to which they had stepped up to be commended for their academic achievements.

A final story: Sister Marty and I continued our walk through the Bronx and eventually met an older African American woman on her way home from grocery shopping who stopped to talk with us. She said she had lived in the neighborhood for thirty-two years, and she wanted us to know that nowadays "there's more bad than good here, more bad than good, and that's the truth."

Excavating the Alien City of Desire and Fear

I offer these tales of the South Bronx in the late 1980s to introduce the intricacy and complexity of religious practice and imagination in contemporary American cities and of the interpretation of urban religious worlds by those who come from outside of them. Sister Marty proposes one account of urban religion. It is here that God is encountered with special intimacy, she says, amid the ravages wrought by the collapse of the old industrial economy, and surrounded by the homes (current and abandoned) of those generations of immigrants and migrants who suffered (and suffer) most from this global restructuring. This is a theological account of the city, on one level, shaped both by the overarching Christian narrative of salvation through suffering and by certain themes in contemporary Catholic thought, specifically liberation theology's affirmation of Christ's special presence among the oppressed, and its insistence on the obligation of the Christian community to maintain a preferential "option for the poor." But some less theologically sympathetic critics might say that Sister Marty's vision is a romantic one, in the pejorative meaning of the term: Marty has transformed other people's suffering into a feeling of spiritual authenticity for herself and remade ruins into the ground of holiness. She appears to have appropriated to herself what anthropologist Victor Turner referred to as the "powers of the weak," by which I understand him to have meant the extraordinary capacities of feeling and being, of spiritual vitality and erotic potency, that those with social power first attribute to the most marginalized populations in their midst and then wrest from them for their own purposes and pleasure (a recurrent impulse in American urban history, as we will see).[3]

What of the artist's view of the South Bronx, then? Again a process of transformation and appropriation seems to be under way. As Sister Marty reaped spiritual benefit from this landscape of suffering, so the artist has mobilized the area's distress for his own aesthetic and political ends. But Sister Marty at least cannot be accused of lacking compassion or responsibility; the German artist, on the other hand, appears to be exploiting the Bronx in order to make a private protest against the downtown art scene as he enhances his status within it. European tourists roamed the South Bronx in these years in air-conditioned tour buses on safari across the blighted tundra of late capitalist urbanism, looking for (and of course finding) confirmation of whatever it was they believed about American society and culture. Are the real troubles of city people so easily annexed by other people's plans, needs, political agendas, and desires? What difference is there between Sister Marty's apprehension of the sacred in the South Bronx, the artist's evocation of the Hulk's primal power in the bowels of an abandoned building, and the tourists' thrill at seeing a bit of urban decay?[4]

Finally, how does the woman who actually makes her home in the South Bronx—the real city woman (But what does *this* mean? Surely Sister Marty, who works with inner-city prostitutes, is as much a city dweller as this other, and who can be more urban than a Soho artist?)—live with these competing visions of her world? Is she aware of them? Does it make any difference to her everyday experience that she lives in a sacred place (according to Sister Marty) or a place of strange and funky subterranean forces (according to the artist)? This woman seems to be the only realistic figure in this account. She stands as a rebuke against the appropriations, delusions, and nostalgia of the rest of us. But what then does *she* make of the spaces through which she moves every day? How does she interpret her world? Can we trust her judgment that there is more bad than good in this place? What did it mean to be "realistic" about the South Bronx in this period? And if she is right about this, is it because the place itself makes people bad, as if the South Bronx were an agent acting upon those who come within its reach, or do places such as the South Bronx (however readers of this volume understand such locales) make goodness—and religious faith—especially difficult, if not impossible?

Ever since the publication in 1938 of Louis Wirth's influential article "Urbanism as a Way of Life," American sociologists and urban scholars have debated whether the conditions of urban life—population density and heterogeneity, for example, or the frantic pace and welter of distractions in cities—give rise to distinct subjectivities. Is there a characteristic city self? Does the city (isolated from other determinants) make people more or less tolerant, more or less nervous? Does the sorry environment of a slum leach into the hearts and souls of the people who must live there and affect their sense of themselves and of what is possible in the world, a complex of influences that sociologist Gerald D. Suttles called the "social order of the slum"? This debate over the social-psychological consequences of urbanism has generated an extensive but ultimately inconclusive literature. That everyone seems to have an opinion about the issue, however, indicates how high the stakes are in setting or erasing the boundaries between city people and everyone else.[5]

This intense boundary work has deep roots in American civilization. For social, historical, topographical, religious, and cultural reasons that will be explored later in this chapter, as the industrial city took shape on the ground, it also emerged as a discursive construction in several overlapping idioms, a charged imaginative creation of fantasy, terror, and desire. For two hundred years, despite (or perhaps because of) the ceaseless urbanizing of the population, the city was cast as the necessary mirror of American civilization, and fundamental categories of American reality—whiteness, heterosexuality, domestic virtue, feminine purity, middle-class respectability—were constituted in opposition to what was said to exist in cities. A revolution in American reading habits and tastes in the first half of the nineteenth century generated a new competitive marketplace for popular reading material, and as secular and religious publishers competed to shape and appeal to the tastes of an emergent mass audience of readers, religious writers were explicitly concerned to arouse and direct emotionally charged moral responses at a time when disestablishment appeared to threaten public religious authority. Accounts of the "mysteries and miseries" of the great cities, described in graphic detail and sometimes illustrated, became a staple of popular reading and moral pedagogy; they amplified the cry of evangelicals for renewed moral authority.

In the feverish imaginations of antebellum anti-Catholic literary provocateurs, city neighborhoods appeared as caves of rum and Romanism, mysterious and forbidding, a threat to democracy, Protestantism, and virtue alike. Journalism, anti-Catholic and anti-immigrant polemics, temperance pamphlets, and evangelical tracts together created a luridly compelling anti-urban genre that depicted the city as the vicious destroyer of the common good, of family life and individual character, and counterposed the city to an idealized image of small-town life. The *National Police Gazette*, with its salacious "true tales" of urban depravity, was first published in 1845. Historian R. Laurence Moore has dubbed this genre of urban writing "moral sensationalism."[6]

The literature of urban moral sensationalism titillated readers at the same time that it appeared to endorse familiar moral and religious judgments. Indeed, prohibition on one level generated desires on another: the constant reiteration of the dangers and otherness of the city re-created the urban landscape as an object of fascination and a fantasied space of freedom from social constraint. Campaigns for the suppression of vice became vehicles of pornographic excitement. The "city"—rendered as the site of moral depravity, lascivious allure, and the terrain of necessary Christian intervention—became from this moment an enduring commodity of American popular culture and the compulsive domain of prohibited desires and unattainable satisfactions. One consequence of the wide circulation of this literature and its direction of desire toward the cities was the complex, multiply fissured, and unstable representation of the "city" that is still characteristic of American public language. The resonance and strange allure of the term "inner city" today in the minds of those with little or no experience of urban life, as well as in Hollywood fantasies, are contemporary products of this history.

So city people in the United States have always had to live in other people's ideas of where they live as well as in real places on the ground, as my interleaved accounts of the South Bronx indicate. Spaces on the urban landscape are both geographical sites where real people live and constructions of terror and desire among those who live elsewhere, including elsewhere in the city. Whatever "the South Bronx," "Harlem," "East L.A.,"

"South Phoenix," and other such culturally marked urban places mean to residents (and they have meant many things over the years to many different groups of people), these locations have been cast by outsiders simultaneously as squalid, dangerous slums and exotic locales of forbidden sensual delights ("therapy for deeper white needs," as critic Nathan Irvin Huggins describes 1920s Harlem, where "the most forbidden was most available"); as secure "urban villages" populated by contentedly domestic industrial peasants; and as fragmented, anomic no-man's lands. City people know this. Moishe Sacks was well aware that almost everyone who did not live in the South Bronx thought of it as a post-apocalyptic moonscape, part bombed-out Dresden, part Fort Apache. Toward the end of his life, Sacks played with this imagery in his own narrative engagement with the place he lived, as Jack Kugelmass describes in his chapter in this volume. Part of the work of city religion is contending with the consequences of such fantasies.[7]

The alienness of the city afforded the opportunity for the projection and satisfaction of needs and desires otherwise denied in the culture and, conversely, the pivot for articulations of the deepest fears and apprehensions swirling at any moment through the wider society—a focusing lens for the prohibited and the wanted, the unimaginable, the denied and feared. Desire is not necessarily either good or bad, positive or negative. This impulse of need and fantasy toward the city has generated tremendous achievements of love, sacrifice, and generosity—evident, for example, in the work of Jane Addams, or the lifelong ministry of Pentecostal minister David Wilkerson to Brooklyn's youth gangs, or Sister Marty's compassionate service to prostitutes. But it has mattered for the fate of American cities that the places outsiders entered to reform or revive, with the best intentions, were always places in the alien city of desire.[8]

The complexity of this encounter and the ambivalence of this desiring can be illustrated by an odd comment Jane Addams makes in *Twenty Years at Hull-House*, her account of the founding and work of the famous Chicago settlement house. It was the impulse of the settlement house movement, Addams writes, "to be swallowed and digested, to disappear into the bulk of the people" moving into American cities. Addams's reference here is to the southern and eastern European immigrants among whom she eventually settled and to whom she dedicated herself. But swallowed and digested? To be eaten by the city and absorbed into its immigrant flesh and blood?[9]

Addams's comment on one level expresses the Christian longing to empty out the self in order to be filled by the other who is Jesus—in Saint Paul's account, to die to the self in order to rise in Christ, a spiritual path and discipline called *kenosis* in Greek. Addams is proposing a distinctly

American Christian urban kenosis here. A spirituality of redemptive suffering deeply informs her account of the settlement house movement (even though her memoir ostensibly records the waning attraction of evangelical piety among her peers and their search for more socially relevant forms of "humanitarian" religion) as well as her understanding of her presence in the city. She says elsewhere that the settlement house movement "undertakes to bear its share of the neighborhood burden imposed by poverty." Social service, she warned idealistic readers, was a "travesty" without this willingness to empty the self and bear the other's cross.[10]

But there are clearly other currents moving through Addams's fantasy of being consumed and digested by the city, not alongside her Christology but within it. Her image of being consumed and digested hints at the self-contempt and humiliation Addams acknowledges that she felt before finally finding her moral and spiritual direction in the settlement house movement. She had been haunted by "a certain sense of shame that I should be comfortable in the midst of such distress" evident in the cities of her age. She fretted that the college education reserved for women in the United States deprived them not only of compassion but of the capacity to connect to others; she was afraid of emotional and spiritual enervation, of the loss of her ability to feel. The opening chapters of *Twenty Years at Hull-House* powerfully and poignantly articulate the loneliness and emptiness of the middle-class self, male and female, in the modern American city. Addams discloses the uncomfortable realization by this isolated self of being surrounded by, but also ineluctably separated from, the vitality, density, and human drama of the immigrant and working-class sections of the city. These pages speak of a terrible absence, distance, and hunger.[11]

So the spiritual metaphor of being consumed and digested also expresses the more earthly longing to escape middle-class emptiness and loss by being filled up by the city and its peoples. This is the local (and social-psychological) meaning of Addams's kenosis: to empty the self in order to be filled by the immigrant other, to complete her humanity by theirs. Addams says she wants to be devoured, absorbed, digested, but her fierce metaphor bespeaks an equally powerful desire to devour the other, to reconstitute the self by absorbing the other; emptying and filling are parallel movements in this impulse into the city. The metaphor of oral absorption is unstable and doubled. Self-surrender and desire, kenosis and eros, sacrifice and possession spin around each other on a spiritual and psychological axis.

Many idealistic young people of Addams's generation and since have gone into the city for such braided spiritual/psychological, self-aggrandizing/self-sacrificial motivations. The city as the domain of primitive vitality and the really real (embodied in its streets and by some of its peoples) became a privileged American site of self-discovery and moral heroism, a place to reach spiritual heights not available elsewhere in an increasingly homogeneous, middle-class society. There was spiritual significance in crossing the border that has separated the "inner" city from the middle-class domains over the last century and a half. Long given moral force by the American discourse of the city, this border almost inevitably acquired cosmic significance. The profane became the ground of the sacred by the inverting logic of desire; the boundary debated by social scientists between city folk and others turned into the charged threshold between the sacred and the mundane for spiritual seekers. As Sister Marty said, the city is where God is encountered; it is holy ground.

The city attracted desire of all sorts, of course, and Americans went there to lose themselves in other kinds of experiences. By the early nineteenth century, middle-class pleasure seekers looking to escape the constraints of bourgeois virtue were already imagining the cities as places where they might explore dimensions of their identities and sexualities that were otherwise and elsewhere religiously and socially constrained or forbidden. Holy for some, the city was sexually charged for others. The possibilities for licentiousness in the city were even thought to have healing capacities in the 1920s: in the cities, so it was said, people could free themselves of the repressions and inhibitions that were doing them such physical and emotional harm, as popular appropriations of Freud had it.

Addams did not search for spiritual vitality along prosperous boulevards and among comfortable citizens; not every place in the city was spiritually compelling (or spiritually terrifying) and existentially real (or culturally threatening) — just the working-class, immigrant, and African American sections. This has been true from the early republic to today. In 1920s Harlem, 125 nightclubs catered to a white clientele "eager to enjoy a little regression back to jungle life," as Ann Douglas characterizes one of the impulses of the jazz age. The "moral underworld" of the cities, in Malcolm Cowley's term for the terrain he and his fellow bohemians roamed in the 1920s, was the world of working-class immigrants and African American migrants transformed by a century of moral opprobrium, reform initiatives, and fear into alluring figures of desire. In Harlem, white middle-class men and women searched for the blackest companions, as Langston Hughes and Malcolm X both recount, and for the roughest working-class trade. Cowley said that it was "virility" his generation sought to acquire from mingling with African Americans, just as in an earlier generation Addams was searching for the actual and the "vital" among immigrants.[12]

It can be seen, then, that for all the many things that separate the sensualist from the settlement house worker, the morally degraded from the morally impassioned, both are gripped by the particular desire aroused by and for the city as the space of the alien other, and for an encounter with the real or the primitive that the circumstances of their respectability occluded. The history of the verb "to slum" or "to go slumming" records the proximity of these two apparently unrelated social enterprises. These "middle-class words," as sociologist Irving Lewis Allen calls them, came into use in the United States and England in the 1880s. Initially, "to go slumming" meant "to visit a slum to do charity work," but the term increasingly and simultaneously acquired the additional meaning of visiting a slum "for fashionable entertainment and to satisfy curiosity about how the other half lived." Slightly before "slumming," in the 1870s and 1880s, the term for prowling around slum and vice quarters was "hunting the elephant," which Allen explains was a "variation of *seeing the elephant*, or seeing 'life' and seeking out shocking and thrilling experiences." Addams's phrase for the elephant (or immigrant) was "the really vital situation spread before our eyes." "Slumming," as word and practice, was given meaning and force by distance: Allen quotes historian Sam Bass Warner Jr.'s, observation that "no one went slumming when the poor lived on the alley behind his or her house." To "go slumming" meant—and still means—to go on a journey across the charged divide between classes, races, and city spaces.[13]

It was not a mere coincidence of city history that just as the vogue of Harlem primitivism was peaking among white slummers, the most popular play on Broadway was Marc Connelly's *The Green Pastures*, which presented an African American cast in modern dress acting out Bible stories transposed to contemporary Louisiana. The play's action was presided over by "de Lawd"—Yahweh as a dignified old black man (Adam Clayton Powell, Sr., was offered the part, but demurred) who smoked "ten cent seegars" with his angels and ate firmament custard—and featured, among other things, a fish fry in Heaven dished out by bustling "mammy angels," rousing spirituals, Pharaoh's palace as a "Negro lodge room," and Babylon as a Louisiana Negro barrelhouse dive. *Green Pastures* was filled with gentle good humor (Connelly recalled in his memoir that he was scrupulously careful not to wring laughs from stereotypes) and ended with a powerful scene of "de Lawd" discovering that his love for the men and women he had created must be tested and tempered by the pain of the Cross. But *Green Pastures*, seen in the context of relations between blacks and whites at this moment in American history, was spiritual primitivism opening up in the space of the other who was also the object of erotic longing. "The beauty of *The Green Pastures*," Huggins writes, "was that, for a moment, it made faith possible and vicariously experienced" to jaded and disillusioned—empty and hungry—white audiences. Just as whites had found erotic excitement in clubs that excluded African Americans, so white audiences found spiritual enrichment not in real exchanges with African American religious practitioners but in a fantasied representation of blacks as a naive, childlike people of simple, premodern faith.[14]

When desire is provoked by the distance authorized by race and class, then desire itself becomes implicated in strategies of power and domination; desire so provoked, in order to sustain itself, contributes in turn to the maintenance of distance. Fantasies born of desire for (and fear of) the alien city overwhelmed the real lives of city people; the latter became figures in other people's dramas and objects of other people's needs. Pleasure seekers did not work for social justice in Harlem, which would have required a real engagement with the lives of local people: as Huggins writes of Carl Van Vechten, one of the great connoisseurs and impresarios of the erotic possibilities of the imaginary "Harlem" of white desiring, "Try as he might to illustrate that Negroes were much like other people, Van Vechten's belief in their essential primitivism makes him prove something else." What good would immigrants and migrants have been to settlement house workers or pleasure seekers if the racial and class distance that established their otherness had been closed by a deep and thorough recognition of a shared humanity?[15]

This alienation or obfuscation is clear in the phantasmagoria of urban pornography, but it is evident too in the popular American genre of Christian narratives of city redemption; indeed, the genre depends on it. Consider one of the best-known and generically influential of these narratives, David Wilkerson's *The Cross and the Switchblade*. Wilkerson begins his account of what he comes to see as his providential mission to the city by emphasizing the radical strangeness of Manhattan and the shock of his discovery of the depths of New York depravity. It is the opening move of the book to establish the necessary otherness of what he calls "the dirty city." "I am a country preacher," Wilkerson tells an audience of rowdy city adolescents, "three hundred miles from home, and I have a message for you."

But the dirty city is also the holy city: by the conventions of the genre, it is precisely into these dark, filthy depths that God comes. The dramatic and spiritual fulfillment offered by these Christian narratives of urban conversion lies in their affirmation of the power of grace to touch absolutely the darkest, most vile, and most inhuman corners of the city's sinfulness.[16]

Urban distress is real, of course, and so may be God's grace, but missing from these Christian stories are other dimensions of city life—the historical experiences of city people, for example; their cultures; the rich array of religious idioms available to them (including various forms of African Caribbean religion and Roman Catholicism); the social complexity of city neighborhoods; and the local political, social, familial, and religious resources for stability and order. Wilkerson's disinterest in the cultures of the young people he has come to save is evident in his persistently calling dark-skinned Puerto Ricans "Negroes." What matters to him is the depravity of these youth, not their histories: the city is so dark in these narratives so that all that can be seen is the light of God's grace. Just as the pornographic thrill could not be found in city neighborhoods understood as the world of complex, recognizable human beings, so the urban holy is not encountered in neighborhoods of hard-working, disciplined people just like the rest of us, but amid images and fantasies of urban desolation, primitivism, alienation, depravity—of emptiness that fills (as it is filled by) the desire that obliterates the lived reality of the other.[17]

At the beginning of my urban religion class, I always ask students to excavate the images, fantasies, and fears of the city they already carry with them, and then to commit themselves to tracking throughout the semester what they discover during this exercise in relation to how they see themselves understanding the particular examples of urban religious practice I show them. This is the challenge of studying urban religion generally: we must read through and across the fantasy of the city as it has emerged over the last two centuries, attending to both the forces that have shaped this fantasy and their impress on the ways in which we construe urban popular experience, religious and secular.

The path to the study of urban religion has to be cleared. The urban world, as Jane Addams's metaphor suggests, is alive with the competing and divergent dreams projected onto it and found within it by outsiders. It is crisscrossed by discrepant narratives and fissured by incommensurable visions of what is possible and good in cities. Before we look at cases of religious engagement with the urban world, then, we have to step back and examine what converges on that world; to see what Moishe Sacks, Mama Lola, and the other religious improvisors who appear in this collection of essays made of the city for themselves, we have to consider first the broad outlines of what was being made of the city for and against them, in the plans and programs of others.

The rest of this chapter falls into two parts. The first sketches with broad strokes a two-tiered story of American cities. It traces the fate of urban spaces and demography since the early nineteenth century, paying special attention to the shifting look of the urban landscape and the arrangement of peoples on it, and describes key moments in the emergence of the discourse of the alien city. These are not distinct processes, of course: religious activists and moral crusaders contributed to the topography of cities, and architects and planners articulated the culture's moral myths and social disciplines in stone and design. The second part of the chapter outlines some of the theoretical orientations to urban religion that guide the essays in the collection. This introduction ends with a brief epilogue orienting readers to the selections that follow.

Cities on the Ground and in the Imagination: The Shaping of the Antebellum City

The United States has been an urban nation since the early years of the twentieth century. The balance between rural and urban populations shifted definitively in 1920, when for the first time more than half of all Americans (51.4 percent) resided in cities; but cities had been on the rise, in population and cultural influence, for a century before that. Nostalgia and dissatisfaction with the qualities of urban life in an industrial and then post-industrial society have created a lasting myth of small towns and family farms as the bedrock of all that is characteristically American (who would talk of the South Bronx—or Detroit or East L.A.—as "the heartland," besides, perhaps, Sister Marty and her fellow Franciscans?); but important as this narrative has been (and remains) for politics and culture, the fact is that the story of this last century in the United States is the story of large numbers of people moving into and then contending with cities.

Nothing seems more solid, more overwhelmingly *there*, than the colossal skyscrapers, huge brick factories, vast department stores, and crowded neighborhoods of tenements and housing projects of American cities, but this solidity is only apparent. Cities have been built and torn down and built again many times over in the United States in the last century and a half. Neighborhoods have risen, prospered or failed (or both), and then disappeared, sometimes right out from under the feet of the men and women living in them. Massive urban environments have dissolved into speed and movement as trolley lines, subways, and then highways were spun across the landscape. Parts of cities that were once distant from each other have been drawn together almost overnight by new lines of transportation and communication, while adjacent places have been rent by unforeseen demographic, architectural, or social forces. The cities into which immigrants and migrants have come over the years have forever been melting into air, to borrow Marx's description of modernity— forever being "developed and redeveloped at quickening rates to keep up with the new tempo and rhythms of accumulation," in the words of contemporary social critic Ira Katznelson.[18]

The urban population of the United States increased 700 percent from 1830 to 1860, from 500,000 to 3.8 million inhabitants. Between 1800 and 1890, the population of the whole country increased twelvefold, and the urban population multiplied by eighty-seven times. Most of the urban growth in the years before the Civil War took place in old eastern coastal towns that were "almost literally demolished and rebuilt," according to historian Paul Boyer, but urbanization became a national phenomenon at this time with the explosive rise of western boomtowns. Trade and commerce created a network of cities connected across the nation by boat, road, and rail (Chicago and New York were connected by train, for example, in 1852). Inland commercial towns such as Cincinnati developed rapidly under the impetus of an "untrammeled commercial life," according to urban scholar Witold Rybczynski, while on the Atlantic Coast, New York City, whose population declined during the Revolution to about 10,000, rose again as the city recaptured trade from other coastal competitors with the completion of the Erie Canal in 1825, making it "the largest and busiest city in the nation." These burgeoning cities were defined by "industrial employment, access to power sources (steam, gas, and eventually, electricity), pollution, literacy, technological innovation, unemployment, social reform," writes Rybczynski.

Space was organized by function, but the chaotic and sometimes catastrophic nature of urban growth was evident in unpaved streets and the absence of zoning regulations. Pigs were not legally prohibited from rooting about in garbage and filth for food within New York's limits until 1867. Water supply, sewage disposal, and street paving did not keep pace with this explosive urban growth, and American cities remained filthy, unhealthy, and unsightly through the 1880s and 1890s.[19]

Mid-nineteenth-century urbanites could still remember a time in the past when they might have climbed an outlying hill to get an encompassing view of the whole cityscape stretched out below them, but this experience of urban space was no longer possible in the industrial cities of the early republic. The first artists' renderings of bird's-eye views of cities were printed at this time, offering city dwellers at least a mediated experience of the comprehensive sense of their environments that they could no longer acquire for themselves. The great industrial cities in Europe and the United States were vast spectacles—"shock cities," in historian Asa Brigg's phrase—unprecedented in scale and scope and movement in comparison with the cities of a century before. "It is impossible," Katznelson writes, "to overstate the radical quality of the urban break of the nineteenth century." The city had become, over only a few generations, visually, spatially, and experientially other. Some observers found in the pandemonium, the human density, and even the squalor of cities a distinctly modern expression of the romantic sublime, evocative of the same emotions of mystery and the uncanny that others found in nature or ancient ruins. Some, such as Whitman, saw the tumultuous city as an exciting festival of democracy and celebrated urban diversity and possibility. But many others were terrified by what was happening in American cities, and by the city itself.[20]

The municipal government of New York in 1811 determined that new streets built north above the narrow, twisting lanes of the old walking city in lower Manhattan would follow a symmetrical grid pattern of parallel lines. The hope was that the grid would impose some order on the city's explosive development as it encouraged further growth and expansion. Other cities soon adopted this innovative and successful plan (first used on this continent in the colonial cities of the Spanish Empire). Grids were imposed on the natural landscapes of developing urban environments around the country, obliterating the natural contours of the land; topography was transformed into an efficient engine for moving goods and workers across the urban terrain. The gridding had implications as well for the kinds of relationships that might take place in cities. There were no central meeting places on the grid, no places to stop and talk, to congregate, or to sit back and watch the spectacle of city life. The grids made American cities, Richard Sennett writes, into "places without centers or boundaries, spaces of endless, mindless, geometric division," a process completed later in the century when the grids rose up into the skies as skyscrapers. People did, of course (and still do), step out of the endless urban street flow, making occasions for meeting and conversation; but after 1811, such encounters would have to happen against the intentions of the grid. One of the challenges for those living in American industrial and post-industrial cities is contending with the social constraints and discipline of geometry.[21]

The early industrial city also witnessed a radical restructuring of social space. The proprietors of small shops and businesses in colonial towns had lived and worked alongside their employees, sharing the same streets, amusements, and even dwelling places. But members of the new urban middle class in the early republic—factory owners, clerks, accountants, and bankers—instituted a sharp ideological and geographical distinction between home and work. They moved out of city neighborhoods crowding up with the workers needed in the new economy to more pleasant and tranquil areas outside the industrial and financial districts just becoming accessible on transportation lines expanding out along the grids. Social distinctions in the emergent industrial city were sharper and more visible than before. The new class mapping of the city carried moral valence: the public world of the center city was characterized as the place of harsh competition, work, and conflict, and as the domain of lascivious, uncontrolled, and dangerous social classes, while the domestic world was the space of nurture, protection, civility, and safety, and of the upright middle classes.[22]

The fearsome otherness of working-class enclaves was further exacerbated by religious difference. The foreign population of the United States increased dramatically between 1820 and 1860; some 600,000 immigrants arrived in the 1830s, well over 1.5 million in the 1840s, and more than 2.5 million in the 1850s. Many of the newcomers were Catholics. Almost a million Germans arrived in the United States between 1850 and 1860, roughly a third of them Catholic; most Germans in this migration settled in rural areas, but substantial numbers took up residence in eastern and midwestern cities. Immigration from Ireland started relatively slowly in the first three decades of the nineteenth century—about 260,000 Irish emigrated to the United States between 1820 and 1840—but between 1845 (when the failure of the potato crop initiated a long period of severe distress in Ireland, which was already suffering from the cruelties of British rule) and 1860, a million and a half Irish arrived, the vast majority of them Catholic. Most Irish settled in eastern cities and took up work in factories and building the new transportation lines. Altogether between 1840 and 1890, 7.5 million Irish and German immigrants arrived in the United States, 5.5 million of them Catholics. The American religious landscape had been permanently altered by these demographics.[23]

At the same time, then, that antebellum cities were becoming more heterogeneous than ever before, they were also becoming ever more fragmented into discrete, homogeneous domains differentiated by function, class, ethnicity, and religion. The spatial history of modern American cities, industrial and post-industrial, begins, in other words, in separation and displacement—of immigrants and migrants from the places they came from, of social classes from each other within the cities, of industrial and working-class areas from middle-class domestic enclaves. One result of these divergent demographic and geographic trajectories was greater anxiety among the middle classes that the spaces from which they had separated themselves, and into which they could not so easily peer anymore, were slipping beyond the reach of their authority. The moral history of the city correspondingly begins in fear occasioned by separation. By the early nineteenth century, the urban population was already divided into "distinct and mutually uncomprehending groups," according to Paul Boyer.[24]

The industrial city seemed out of control to most Americans from the moment of its inception, and since that time Americans have never stopped wondering whether the moral and physical health of their bodies, of their families, and of the nation itself would survive the cities. The beginning of urbanization in the United States coincided with and partially occasioned a crisis of national identity, furthermore, and from this point on, what it meant to be an American—morally, religiously, politically, even physically—was defined in opposition to the cities, even as the nation became increasingly and inexorably urban. In a society that was convinced both of its unique, divinely mandated destiny in world history and that powerful human and supernatural enemies were arrayed against it, the cities became and have remained central locations on the map of American paranoia.

Some among the genteel classes coped with the new cities by enforcing the distance and separation between themselves and the others. From the end of the eighteenth century on, historian Richard Bushman writes, "polite society isolated itself more and more from the coarseness of ordinary city life." Closed carriages first became common at this time to shield middle-class wives and children from the ugly sights of the poorer quarters of the cities. Other American-born whites of all classes responded more directly to what they saw as the challenge of the cities. A mob burned and looted an Ursuline convent outside Boston in 1834. A decade later, Protestants and Irish Catholics fought pitched battles in the streets of Philadelphia in what one historian has called a "brutal ethno-religious war." Earlier in the decade, New York's Bishop "Dagger John" Hughes, an Irish immigrant himself, had warned that he would turn New York City into a "second Moscow" if confronted with anti-Catholic rioters. Twenty people were killed in 1855 in a religious riot between German Catholics and nativists in Louisville.[25]

As social, religious, and economic divisions deepened in the cities and industrial wages declined from the 1830s through the 1850s while immigration rose, security became a prime concern for the propertied classes, and white-collar workers (who made up 40 percent of the antebellum workforce) worried about "lower-class Irishmen unable to cope with urban life." Demands for the institution of new methods of surveillance, supervision, and disclosure multiplied, leading to the creation of municipal police departments (Boston organized the first professional police force in 1838, although it was New York's, founded in 1844, that became the national prototype), vice squads and rescue societies, and aggressive Protestant reform campaigns—all dedicated to eradicating the criminal threat and moral contagion of the cities. Such campaigns, secular and religious, mounted again and again over the next century, were never very successful, either at eliminating the genuine causes of working-class suffering or in transforming working-class men and women into docile, submissive citizens. It is one of the contradictions of American history that as techniques of industrial regulation, regimentation, and supervision were perfected over the century, the capacity of social agencies to supervise and control the lives of workers in the streets and neighborhoods of the cities, which had never been very secure, diminished.[26]

Christian reformers throughout the nineteenth century attempted to contain the danger and risk of the city, especially for those middle-class

Americans who had only recently moved there from the countryside, by enacting in various media—for example, Sunday school classes, revival rhetoric, the decor of reading parlors and rooming houses, and the moral dramas of temperance tracts—an emotionally compelling and ethically authoritative account of small-town life (as small towns were imagined by sentimental Christian reformers preoccupied with urban danger). This was a distinctly Protestant anti-urban poetics in which the pre- or anti-urban became the moral and aesthetic ideal. There was a disciplinary edge to this discourse: pious evocations of the countryside throughout the nineteenth and into the twentieth centuries were meant to re-create, in the city, experiences of shame that middle-class Protestants understood as the necessary condition for good behavior and religious rectitude. The problem of moral life in the city, in the view of many reformers, was that no one was watching.[27]

The performance of the small town in the city (in text, architecture, and rhetoric) and the elaboration there of its strategies of watchfulness and supervision were meant to bring city dwellers to their senses. The city could be a daunting as well as exciting place of unfamiliar sounds, smells, sensations, and opportunities. Revivalists and reformers became adept at exploiting the disorienting effect of all this on newcomers by intensifying the sense of the city as alien and forbidding as they constructed the normative fiction of small-town virtue. The YMCA, which arrived in the United States from London in 1856, labored almost exclusively among native-born Protestants to erect a solid moral barrier of reading rooms, polite amusements, and physical discipline against the temptations of the city, serving for some as a secure haven from the pressures and unfamiliarity of urban life (and for others as a safe context from which to go out and explore what the city had to offer).

Another way of transforming city into village was actually to move the city—or at least its most vulnerable and portable segments: children, women, and the unemployed—out to the country. Secular relief agencies as well as Catholic and Protestant organizations undertook pastoralization campaigns from the early nineteenth century well into the middle years of the twentieth century, sending city people out to farms and ranches (although many of those "returned" to the better life of the country had never lived in rural settings or had been determined to leave them). Both Charles Loring Brace, founder in 1853 of New York City's Children Aid Society, and the leadership of the Salvation Army, which first came to the United States after the Civil War, made plans to transplant city dwellers to the countryside. Catholic prelates and lay intellectuals from the early republic to the Catholic revival in the twentieth century imagined rural life as an antidote to the spiritual decay and physical distress of the cities.[28]

Other reformers were determined to bring the country into the city. Historian Paula Kane argues that the architecture of the American Catholic parish represented for many Irish and German priests and prelates a "miniature form of the medieval pastoral world . . . an enclosed haven" that stood for a "harmonious social ideal against the corruptions of the urban environment." Ernest Thompson Seton, a founder of American scouting, maintained that learning woodcraft and lore at "rooftop campouts" in the city would transform street urchins into upright citizens, and similar ambitions informed Frederick Law Olmsted's designs for Central Park, which he believed would exert a "distinctly harmonizing and refining influence upon the most unfortunate and most lawless classes of the city." Among the motivations for this impulse to de-citify urban populations was simply the wish to provide some relief from the oppressive physical conditions of city life, certainly; but the doubled nature of urban reform pragmatics in the United States is evident here too. Such efforts to bring the country to the city or the city to the country were predicated on and endorsed the assumption that the contrast between city and country was morally significant, a cultural discourse that Paula Kane has referred to as the "gospel of rural goodness." These were rear-guard efforts, however, because the future lay in the cities.[29]

The Urban Nation

American cities grew phenomenally after the Civil War, as did fear and hatred of the city and, inevitably, the city's erotic allure. In the half-century from 1850 to 1900, to cite just some examples of the nation's explosive urban growth, New York's population swelled from 515,500 to 3,437,202, Chicago's from 29,963 to 1,698,575, St. Louis's from 77,860 to 575,238, and San Francisco's from 34,776 to 342,782. Only six American cities had populations larger than 8,000 in 1800; by 1890, 448 did; six had populations of over 1 million. Buffalo, Detroit, and Milwaukee more than doubled in size in the last two decades of the nineteenth century; St. Paul and Denver quadrupled. Census takers identified the United States as an "urban nation" for the first time in 1920.[30]

Immigration and migration were largely responsible for this surge in the urban population—from southern and eastern Europe and Ireland, from the American South as the African American migration commenced, and after 1924, when federal legislation closed the nation's gates to foreign workers, from Mexico. More than 5.2 million immigrants came to the United States in the 1880s, and 3.75 million in the 1890s; 8.8 million came between 1900 and 1910. Most settled in the industrial cities of the North and Midwest. By 1910, 41 percent of the inhabitants of American cities were foreign-born. Some cities were populated largely by immigrants and their children: for example, 90 percent of Milwaukee's population was either born outside the United States or of immigrant parents; the figure for New York and Chicago was 80 percent. There were more Italians in New York City by the end of the nineteenth century than in Naples, more Irish than in Dublin. The Mexican-born population of the United States grew from approximately 400,000 in 1910 to 651,596, according to the 1920 census, and by the end of the latter decade, there were 1,422,533 Mexicans in this country. The Mexican presence in Los Angeles increased dramatically, from 15,500 in 1920 to 39,000 in 1930.[31]

The great black migration from the South lay in the future, but African Americans first began turning away from agriculture and the hopelessness of rural life at the turn of the century, looking to nearby cities and small towns for better economic opportunities. The black population of Birmingham, Alabama, tripled in the first decade of the new century, from 16,575 to 52,305. In Atlanta, the black population grew from 35,727 to 51,902; in Richmond, Virginia, from 32,230 to 46,733; and in Jacksonville, Florida, from 16,236 to 29,293. The direction of this migration soon shifted northward. Between 1910 (when 89 percent of African Americans lived in the South, two-thirds of them in rural areas) and 1940, more than a million and a half African Americans moved into northern and midwestern cities, attracted by the prospects of industrial work (especially during the two world wars) and driven by determination to escape the humiliations and brutality of the Jim Crow system inflicted on them in the last decade of the nineteenth century. Exuberant editorials and industrial promotions in the northern black press and billboard advertisements in southern cities painted a compelling picture of the "great opportunities . . . for my people in the north," as the gospel music pioneer Thomas A. Dorsey recalled of one of the Chicago *Defender*'s campaigns. Factory wages in the North could go as high as $3.00 or $4.00 a day; domestic pay was about $2.50 daily. Between 1910 and 1920, the black populations of northern cities rose dramatically, from 44,103 to 109,458 in Chicago; from 5,471 to 40,878 in Detroit; from 8,448 to 34,451 in Cleveland; from 91,709 to 152,467 in New York; and from 84,459 to 134,229 in Philadelphia. The North became the "spatial synonym for unlimited opportunity" to southern blacks, according to gospel music historian Michael Harris.[32]

A series of technological developments around the turn of the century forever changed the look and feel of the urban landscape. Electric lights came on first in San Francisco and Cleveland in 1879, brilliantly illuminating city streets that until then had fallen at night into the dim shadows cast by gas lamps; and electric-powered urban transit, first introduced in Richmond, Virginia, in 1887, moved people ever more quickly across the brightly lit cityscapes. The erection of skyscrapers boomed in the 1880s; steel frame construction was first used in Chicago in 1888–90 for the Rand McNally Building, designed by Daniel Burnham and John Root, and the following year, the word "skyscraper" appeared in an American dictionary. The telephone switchboard, first installed in New Haven, Connecticut, in 1878, made rapid communication across a city and up and down the new vertical grids possible, and improvements in the technology of elevators removed any limitation that the human heart and lungs placed on the height of buildings. Within thirty years, skyscrapers would come not only to dominate the skylines of the cities that could afford them but to symbolize modern urbanity itself; height became the idiom of city architects and planners, the aspiration of urban visionaries, and the vehicle of the public arrogance of industrialists and financiers.

The skyscraper took the grid form, with all its ambitions for profitable efficiency and order, and drove it vertically, into the air, and this had consequences as profound for the lives of city people—for their relations with each other on the streets and for their experience of space—as had the imposition of the grids half a century earlier. Most European cities imposed limits on the height of buildings, but such restriction was thought to be an abrogation of property rights in the United States. The vertical eclipsed the horizontal in the modern city after the turn of the century, and height eventually drained away the vitality of the local, making it difficult for city people to feel secure or grounded or even present on the streets. Height subdued "those who must live in the space . . . disorienting their ability to see and to evaluate relationships." The neighborhood represents another kind of city life, another way of arranging and inhabiting urban space, but many neighborhoods ultimately could not survive the intense pressures against local space and experience imposed by height.[33]

The fifty-year span from the 1880s to the late 1920s was a time of explosive political, cultural, and artistic innovation in the cities, as working-class immigrants and migrants and their children, artists, entertainers, intellectuals disillusioned with Western civilization after the devastation of the First World War, labor organizers, newspaper and magazine writers, progressive reformers, merchants, entrepreneurs, and musicians together (if not always with common goals and values) shaped a new and exciting popular culture. "The modern world as we know it today," Ann Douglas writes, "all the phenomena that to our minds spell the contemporary, from athletic bodies and sexual freedom for women to airplanes, radios, skyscrapers, chain stores, and the culture of credit, arrived on the scene" in the decade after the Great War. But the war only made more urgent changes in mores, desires, even in the look and movement of bodies in city spaces that had been long under way.[34]

By the turn of the century, young workers of both sexes roamed across a landscape of dance halls, rooftops, alleys, parks, and stoops, constituting an ecology of desire in their search for pleasure, freedom, and excitement. African American migrants experimented in the 1920s with forms of music, art, and literature, sacred and secular, that were both more southern and more urban and that spoke more directly to their experience of migration, loss, and hope than what was offered them by their staid counterparts in the northern black social world, who often complained that the newcomers "didn't know how to act" and so "spoiled things" for everyone. Lynchings and race riots around the nation in 1917 (which were met with silence from Wilson's White House) and the summer of violence that greeted black soldiers returning from Europe in 1919 created a great political ferment in the growing African American urban centers of the North and Midwest. One important expression and source of the new political mood in these neighborhoods was Marcus Garvey's Harlem-based black nationalist movement, which directed the imaginations of struggling working-class men and women (most of them recently arrived in the industrial city) toward Africa, encouraged black entrepreneurship, and offered a powerful message of racial pride.[35]

The folly of Prohibition quickened popular tastes for an edgy nightlife. Entertainers pushed the limits of what was socially and morally acceptable, testing the boundaries of race, class, and gender. African American comedy had taken on a more confrontational tone by the mid–1930s. Working-class and middle-class pleasure seekers encountered each other in the same haunts, and the cabaret performers of New York's tremendously popular "pansy craze" of 1920–33 subverted authoritative representations of masculine and feminine.[36]

The ebullient urbanism of the period forever defined a distinctly American city style that was relayed to the rest of the country (and the world) by new media of mass entertainment and the nascent advertising industry. It was at the turn of the century that New York became a "world city," in Oswald Spengler's phrase; the rise of New York, Spengler said, was "the most pregnant event of the nineteenth century." Commodified representations of city life became national and international objects of desire. Although some argue that the United States was always urban in culture, with city mores and styles transmitted to rural areas by democratic mass media (and, as we have seen, the city as a commodity of popular culture appeared much earlier in U.S. history), it was in the early twentieth century that American, and so also global, popular culture became irrevocably citified. Traveling movie shows brought the new excitements of cinema—and with it visions of the pleasures of urban life—to rural areas; advertising, which became a New York industry in the 1920s, stimulated citified desires across the land. As Laurence Moore comments on the popularity of the "refined thrills" provided by the late-nineteenth-century traveling movie shows of Lyman H. Howe, "the General Conference of Methodist churches went on banning the commercial entertainments of the city, while small-town Methodists were sitting in church basements watching a film showing people enjoying themselves in Luna Park at Coney Island." By the end of the 1920s, one out of three Americans owned a radio and record player, three out of four went to the movies at least once a week, and "virtually no one was out of reach of advertising's voice," which means that no one was out of reach of the city.[37]

Many observers outside the cities (and inside, too) found all this dangerous and frightening. The nation's failure to confront the bitter consequences and unresolved social and cultural challenges of the Civil War amid the deepening industrial crisis of the postwar years provoked what literary historian Andrew DelBanco has called America's "great age of scapegoating." The United States was a "culture in panic," DelBanco writes, and the "source of affliction" was externalized as the alien other in the cities. American intellectuals regarded the city as the realm of chance and accident, where the contingent and unanticipated overwhelmed the planned and purposeful. Theological, ideological, economic, and spatial factors converged to heighten the cultural strangeness of the cities. Older urban Protestant congregations after the Civil War tended to be wealthier than their surrounding populations. Church-sponsored studies in Pittsburgh and Allegheny in the 1880s, for example, found that business and professional men made up less than 10 percent of the populations of these areas but 60 percent of the Protestant congregations. Spatial segregation acquired greater moral resonance than before the war. Protestant churches in the first decades of the modern urban age in the United States remained committed to economic and moral individualism and laissez-faire; in expensively appointed churches, middle-class urban Protestants listened to a complacent "gospel of wealth" from comfortable pastors who reassured them with theology and pseudo-science that their comforts and the sufferings of the poor and working classes were alike justly deserved.[38]

The reorganization of the wartime interdenominational United States Christian Commission into the American Christian Commission at a special meeting in Cleveland in 1865 offers an opportunity to sound the fears of middle-class Americans about the city at a critical juncture in the nation's history and to preview the society's nascent urban agenda. One of the commission's first acts was to survey conditions in thirty-five cities across the United States. The results were predictably alarming. The report emphasized the threat that the increasingly foreign character of cities in the United States posed to American values and politics, pointed to the inadequate response of Protestant churches to the challenge of the cities, and accused fellow Protestants of indifference to social issues. The commission also collected information on the responses of European churches to the industrial city, a sign of an emerging awareness of the city as a global challenge to Christian faith and culture.[39]

The commission's recommendations exemplify the combination of fear, genuine social concern, an eagerness to get to work, and xenophobia that would characterize mainstream American responses to the city over the next half-century. The commission advocated closing the spatial, cultural, and religious distance that had opened in cities between classes and between foreigners and Americans by sending Christian visitors, in particular women church workers, into alien working-class environments, urged the denominations to work together in the cities, and proposed the use of churches for humanitarian purposes in addition to specifically religious activities. These were not new ideas. Secular and religious reform agencies had been sending out "visitors" since the early nineteenth century, and the efforts of antebellum evangelical reformers were often interdenominational. But the immensity of the urban danger in the imagination of postwar Protestants lent a new focus and urgency to these programmatic suggestions, while the social-service role envisioned for city churches by the commission indicates the beginnings of a crucial shift in American social and religious attitudes.

The commission's call for unified action among Protestant denominations would be echoed repeatedly over the next century, indicating not only the pervasive sense among the mainstream churches that they had an urgent responsibility to transcend divisions in order to meet the intensifying challenge of the cities, but also their recognition that the city itself offered the opportunity for such transcendence. Interdenominational enterprises continued to be hobbled by intractable differences among the churches, by theological reservations, and by the suspicion that such efforts offered only a watered-down gospel to city dwellers in need of stronger fare. But changing urban demographics stretched the resources of individual churches, making cooperation unavoidable and imperative. The obvious successes of organizations such as the YMCA and the Salvation Army also made concerted responses attractive. So the city ironically came to be seen as holding the promise of renewed cultural and religious authority among late-nineteenth- and early-twentieth-century Protestant clergy who lacked the formidable social presence of their antebellum predecessors. Interdenominational Protestant urban missions to Americanize and Christianize Catholic immigrants offered Protestant denominations the occasion to "coalesce" into a unified front. Many forces shaped modern American Protestantism, as distinct from separate denominational identities, but one of the most important was the dynamic relationship established between the churches and the cities by the widespread sense of apocalyptic urban crisis provoked by the swelling populations of immigrant Catholic laborers.[40]

These commitments to moral stewardship in the cities inspired a range of religious and ecclesiological innovations in pastoral care, theology, seminary education, and institutional structure. Native white middle-class American Protestants held a conflicted view of the industrial city at this time, writes sociologist Kevin J. Christiano, as constituting both a "diabolical threat" to American life and a "God-given opportunity" for the churches. Historian Jon Butler has referred to the years 1870 to 1920 as the era of "Protestant success" in the city, a time of "remarkable advance in institutional religious commitment" that separated the cities of the United States from the unchurched industrial urban worlds of Europe. Well-established city churches in old and changing neighborhoods were determined to compete effectively with the wider range of social opportunities available in the cities, and to this end they offered congregations a broader menu of social, familial, and recreational services. Middle-class "social congregations" (in E. Brooks Holifield's term) provided diversions for congregants of all ages. The institutional church movement, extending and enlarging the antebellum work of city missions, called for attention to the whole person in his or her environment. The leaders of Wesley Chapel, for example, the oldest Methodist house of worship in Cincinnati, recognized in the early 1890s that the church would survive amid the new conditions of its downtown neighborhood only "by being an institution of all round salvation . . . honeycombed with educational, musical, and industrial work and appliances. . . . It must work as Christ did, healing and helping the temporal condition of man along with its ordinary spiritual work." Four years later, Wesley Chapel included a kindergarten, a day nursery, a young ladies' benevolent society, a legal aid society (called the "bureau of justice"), a home visitation society, and a building society to encourage home ownership in the community. By the end of the twentieth century, there were approximately 170 such centers around the country, according to historian Aaron Abell.[41]

Churches had functioned as social centers in African American communities since before the Civil War; historian Evelyn Brooks Higginbotham has called the black church a "discursive, critical arena" where crucial issues of community life were engaged. "Because blacks were denied access to public space, such as parks, libraries, restaurants, meeting halls, and other public accommodations," she writes, "the black church— open to both secular and religious groups in the community—came to signify public space," housing "a diversity of programs including schools, circulating libraries, concerts, restaurants, insurance companies, vocational training, athletic clubs—all catering to a population much broader than the membership of individual churches." As blacks moved north after the turn of the century, they brought this tradition of community churches with them; they also discovered well-established northern church centers. This tradition of churches as social and political centers as well as sacred spaces remains strong in African American communities today. Bridge Street AWME in Brooklyn, New York, for example, is open from early in the morning until late at night, providing space for some sixty local clubs and self-help groups. Its outreach efforts include a food-distribution program, a résumé-writing service, drug and alcohol counseling, homeless shelters, ministry to local prisons, and night classes for adults working toward high school equivalency degrees. Other churches in the borough have built homes for elderly residents and low-income families. Radical, nationalist theologies have found a sympathetic hearing among black Christian leaders nurtured in this tradition of religiously motivated social activism and public responsibility, and Brooklyn's black churches have produced impassioned city and national leaders. Pentecostals, too, have followed the institutional church model in Brooklyn, overcoming their premillennial reluctance to get involved with the dilemmas of a sinful world.[42]

Service to the city became a way for young Protestant men and women, many of whom had quietly rejected their parents' beliefs, to act in faith with the social covenant they had inherited from Calvinist social teaching. Many chose to leave their comfortable middle-class environs and actually move into the cities. Although evangelical societies and charity agencies had both sent representatives into working-class city neighborhoods, it was not until the turn of the century that living in city neighborhoods alongside the poor became a distinct form of moral witness, social responsibility, and civic education in England and the United States. Henceforth, those who merely visited the homes of the poor would be viewed as moral dilettantes or as agents of outside power by the newer generation of urban activists.[43]

Social Gospel theologians such as Washington Gladden, whose 1886 publication *Applied Christianity* provided a major impetus for this new religious social reform impulse, and Walter Rauschenbusch, who saw the severity of urban distress firsthand as pastor of a German Baptist church on the edge of New York's Hell Kitchen from 1886 to 1897, developed a socially informed biblical hermeneutic that interpreted the meanings and implications of Jesus' announcement that he had come to establish the Kingdom of God in light of the contemporary "social crises." "The kingdom of God," Rauschenbusch wrote, "is . . . a collective conception, involving the whole social life of man. It is not a matter of saving human atoms, but of saving the social organism. It is not a matter of getting individuals to heaven, but of transforming the life on earth into the harmony of heaven." Social Gospelers, who came from different denominations, severed the long-established association of poverty with moral depravity in American Protestant culture and made possible the new kind of Christian engagement with the city.[44]

The first American settlement house was opened in New York City in 1886 by Stanton Coit with the help of Felix Adler and the Ethical Culture Society; three years later, Jane Addams founded Hull House in Chicago. By 1910 there were more than 400 settlement houses in the industrial cities of the Northeast, often associated with universities or seminaries. Called to their mission by complex impulses, as we have seen, settlement house workers, many of whom had grown up in small towns or country areas, discovered in the cities the "basic likenesses" (as Addams put it) among peoples—even though the norm for this likeness was often enough middle-class American Protestantism—and thus contributed to the redefinition of American national identity as one that confidently embraced a diversity of cultures. Settlement house workers came to value the richness and excitement of city life, offering an alternative to the animus against the city that otherwise largely dominated American reform movements. They participated in the Social Gospel's work of ending the collusion between American Protestantism and social Darwinism, denying the belief that starvation, deprivation, and unemployment served to motivate immigrants to endurance and success (a belief that Addams curtly denounced as "fatuous") and emphasizing the importance of environmental reform.[45]

This sojourn in the city was so attractive by the early years of the twentieth century that major Protestant seminaries began to require it of students, an initiative pioneered by Union Theological Seminary in New York. A number of seminaries relocated from the countryside to the cities, and it became common for seminaries to recruit their major professors and administrators from large urban churches. It is thus an irony of American religious history that as the congregations of urban churches shrank in the older, central areas of cities, the prestige of many of these city institutions rose, and the demand for a serious moral engagement with the city was widely acknowledged, at least among socially active denominations. The city, furthermore, was transforming not simply the location of seminary education, but its content and methods as well. Professors of Christian ethics focused on urban issues; some sent their students out into the streets to study social problems empirically, at first hand.[46]

Later in the century, after Catholics had begun to follow Protestants and Jews out to the suburbs, young priests and nuns and Catholic collegians, whose immigrant parents or grandparents had only relatively recently been the objects of national concern and consternation, went to live with the desperately poor in Catholic Worker houses founded by Dorothy Day and Peter Maurin, to work for interracial solidarity in Catherine De Hueck's Friendship Houses, and later, in the 1960s, to play in the streets and playgrounds with inner-city children in "summer in the city" programs. The industrial city served as a moral laboratory and spiritual terrain for clergy and dedicated laity and an opportunity for a season of religious sacrifice that profoundly changed the lives of many who participated in these programs, as indicated by the experience of those who thought they were going into the city for a short time and stayed on for much of their lives.[47]

Religiously motivated responses to the city were gradually supplanted after the turn of the century by a variety of secular efforts inspired by progressive ideals and optimism (and endorsed by Social Gospel Christians). Middle-class women home visitors who had been sent out before and after the Civil War to represent the finest aspects of American domesticity to immigrant populations (its hygienic practices, nutritional choices, ways of public comportment, and moral rectitude), and to exercise an immediate surveillance over the alien city, were replaced by professional social workers. Many in the first generation of social-science innovators, settlement house workers, and progressive activists were children of religious parents, and the new fields and methods of social endeavor and research that they created and entered, such as scientific social work, urban studies, and a morally informed social science, can be considered religious responses to the city, too, in a new register. The Social Gospel and settlement house movements were inspired by and in turn offered additional moral and cultural sanction to the progressive movement in the early years of the twentieth century. Progressivism addressed itself to the social and economic causes of urban distress, proposing (more optimistically than some religious reformers) that urban conditions could be improved by careful planning and structural reorganization based on empirical study. Progressive campaigns resulted in important legislation that eliminated the dangerous, filthy, airless tenements in the most overcrowded working-class areas of cities; built city playgrounds; implemented housing codes; and enforced better sanitation and street lighting.

The Social Gospel, settlement house, and institutional church movements were all vital responses to the crisis and challenge of the city after the Civil War, but they were countervailing impulses. Equally if not more typical of the country's moral and social posture toward the cities were the Charity Organization Societies (COS), founded in 1877 in Buffalo, New

York. Whereas settlement house workers discovered the recognizability of immigrants and migrants and offered a culturally pluralistic model of American society, the charity movement, operating with suspicion and mistrust for city life and poor people, authorized difference and separation. COS doctrine emphasized the moral complicity of poor people and insisted that clients acknowledge personal failings as a precondition for assistance. The use of shame as a disciplinary tool for the poor was common among charity workers, and bureaucratically organized: by the mid-1890s, the Charity Organization Society of New York City had compiled data on 170,000 families and "could supply information by return mail to anyone 'charitably interested' in a particular family." Dossiers compiled by COS visitors, whose ongoing scrutiny of the poor was referred to as "moral oversight for the soul" by one of the organization's leaders, were made available to banks and landlords, in addition to other relief agencies. Visitors were encouraged to befriend clients by way of facilitating the work of supervision and oversight, thus remaking friendship into a vehicle of cultural authority, moral intrusion, and social control.[48]

These impulses of purification, discipline, and surveillance persisted from the Gilded Age into the 1920s, constituting an ongoing parallel tradition to the more sophisticated efforts of progressives and some religious activists to come to terms with the city. The widening discrepancy between white Protestant insistence on cultural and spiritual authority in the nation and an increasingly heterogeneous urban population led to explosions of xenophobic violence, legalized discrimination, and efforts to purify the population by racist and anti-immigrant exclusions and prohibitions. "Scum of creation" was "a standard populist epithet for city dwellers"; immigrant neighborhoods were identified by police and journalists with sobriquets redolent of sulfur—Hell's Kitchen, Satan's Circus. The vicious city remained good copy. Middle-class readers thrilled to urban apocalypses such as Joaquin Miller's *The Destruction of Gotham* (1886) that presented images of "revolutionary chaos and mass destruction" in cities. The popularity of the revived Ku Klux Klan in the 1920s, especially in the growing urban centers of the West and Midwest, was largely a reaction to fear of the cities. "With its whippings of 'loose women,' its raids of speakeasies, and its embittered anti-city bias," Paul Boyer writes, "the Klan became the pathetic residual legatee of generations of accumulated anxiety over the disappearance of a simpler America." Dark-skinned migrants and immigrants to the cities were identified by the specious logic of racial "science" with physical incapacity, criminality, disease, and insanity. Urban entertainments had become more sexualized by the turn of the century, and this served further to intensify both the compulsion and the danger of the city to middle-class guardians.[49]

Characteristic of most reform efforts, however, was a distinct spatial politics: immigrant and working-class neighborhoods would be penetrated, watched, and monitored. New York's moral watchdog Committee of Fourteen sent undercover agents into dance halls and saloons in 1910, trolling the terrain of desire to spy on the working classes at promiscuous play. The YWCA scrutinized the sexual habits of young women who worked in department stores. New York's Committee for the Suppression of Vice and Boston's Watch and Ward Society pursued aggressive campaigns of censorship and surveillance. The Committee on Amusements and Vacation Resorts of Working Girls fretted about how young city women were passing their rare bits of leisure time. All of these were efforts at "regulat[ing] public sociability," in George Chauncey's phrase.[50]

Progressives, Social Gospelers, and settlement workers were not exempt from the culture's broader animus against the city, either. Progressive initiatives to transform urban space were rooted in a "moral environmentalism" and social psychology according to which the alien populations of the cities would be remade into safe and decent citizens by the action upon them of improved spatial conditions. Social Gospeler Josiah Strong called on fellow Protestants to save the cities from foreign domination. Even settlement house workers nostalgically counterposed an idealized and morally resonant picture of rural life—either American or European—to life in the city. Addams saw as her role in part "to preserve and keep whatever of value [immigrants'] past life contained and to bring them in contact with a better type of Americans." She was attentive in furnishing Hull House to model a normative image of middle-class American domesticity. Sometimes she even yielded to the temptation to condemn the "general spirit of bitterness and strife" she imagined filling the city.[51]

The ambivalence toward the city of even the most sophisticated social scientists and progressives is evident in the writing of the pioneering urban sociologist Robert Park. Park, who was based at the University of Chicago, proposed a moral theory of scale: the physical, spatial, and social conditions of the city made possible an aggregation of vice conducive to the satisfaction of obsessions only furtively imagined elsewhere. Cities are made up of a series of "moral regions," Park argued, in which men and women who share a particular vice or antisocial proclivity can congregate with kindred souls to find "moral support for the traits they have in common" in "an unhealthful and contagious intimacy." Such individuals existed in small towns, Park acknowledged, but in moral isolation that prohibited them from indulging themselves. Not so in the cities, where heterogeneity, population density, and anonymity resulted in a "weakening of . . . restraints and inhibitions." Park assumed that the audience for his writings was middle-class people who had little contact with actual city life, and he wrote across the spatial divide separating them from the urban masses—another explorer presenting tales of a hidden realm to astonished and shocked listeners.[52]

In Park's view, immigrants were unenlightened peasants whose abrupt journey from medieval squalor to industrial urbanity left them confused and morally disoriented. (Even the distance separating the immigrants from their homelands could be a source of danger for American culture!) Moral order dissolved in the city, Park told his readers (confirming what they already knew): interpersonal relationships and kinship bonds were attenuated, and other agencies had to intervene and assume the function of family and community. Although he shared the general progressive optimism about reform, Park also worried that such efforts could not be as effective in cities as in smaller, more homogeneous environments. City people do not have as much information about each other as small town folk do, Park noted, echoing the evangelical belief that city people lacked shame. The effects of cities on culture, the Chicago sociologists warned, were "subversive and disorganizing."[53]

"Wear rubber gloves" when dealing with city folk, popular evangelist Billy Sunday warned God in the 1920s, a bit of epidemiological advice that has sadly been heard many times since in a country as preoccupied with the moral contaminations of urbanity as it is with imitating city styles and idioms. Sunday, according to one of his biographers, objected to the "dancing and cardplaying and smoking and gossiping and telling off-color jokes and billiard playing and birth control and undue attention to pets, especially dogs, and novel reading and licentious music and slander and selfishness and the theater and premarital sex and cursing and idleness and lust and greed and vanity [and]. . . LIQUOR" that went on in cities. The preacher was troubled most of all by the blurring of boundaries in cities that elsewhere were taken for granted—between good women and bad women, for example, or between what was to be desired and what feared, even between animal and human (those pampered dogs!). Ambiguity and ambivalence reigned in cities, as Sunday and others like him saw it; city life undermined moral certainty.

It was the irony of Sunday's career, however—and of the careers of other popular anti-urban prophets in the United States, then and since— that while his fulminations against the temptations and depravity of urban life won him enthusiastic audiences, his success on the competitive revival circuit, like Dwight L. Moody's before him and Charles G. Finney's before Moody, reflected the preacher's easy manipulation of the idioms of urban popular culture and mastery of the modern arts of communication, business management, public relations, and self-promotion. Even the success of the Ku Klux Klan depended in large part on the skills of two city-based public-relations experts who used the Red Scare of 1919–20 to market the new organization, and to the widespread popularity of the film *Birth of a Nation*. Like Pentecostals who condemned the cities that provided them with a hospitable environment for their entertaining spectacles of emotion and faith, Sunday was inexorably a product of the modern city culture that he rejected.[54]

The Contemporary Urban Landscape

The years from the Depression through the late 1950s represented the apotheosis of the industrial city and the beginning of its demise. Workers in the cities were doing better than ever before, despite inflation, periodic housing shortages, and intermittent unemployment. Their neighborhoods were controlled by capable men of their own ethnicities, however weak such cultural identities had become over the years, and the sons of immigrants and migrants headed city administrations around the country. Churches and synagogues flourished, presided over by leaders risen from the local communities. The GI Bill allowed many in this generation to attend college after the war, often as the first in their families to do so, and to make their way more confidently into the middle class. American culture, moreover, had become synonymous with city culture. What better represented the ambition, drive, and style of the United States than the skyscraper or the suspension bridge, or the rhythms of its life than the elegant swing of Basie, Ellington, and Fitzgerald and then the hard bop of Dizzy Gillespie, Bud Powell, and John Coltrane or the post-immigrant brio of Frank Sinatra, Louis Prima, Rosemary Clooney, and Dean Martin? These artists defined an adult urban style appropriate for a generation that had survived depression and war. It was a time of "grand expectations," as historian James Patterson has written, and most of these originated with the manufacturers of desire in cities.[55]

The children and grandchildren of European immigrants, lamenting the loss of their familiar urban world in the late 1960s and 1970s, looked back to this time just before and after World War II as the last good days of the old neighborhoods. This was the time, they say, when women walked securely home from work late at night under the watchful gaze of vigilant neighborhood guardians, when people kept their doors open all day long so their neighbors could drop by, when children played safely on clean sidewalks, and the old people who had settled these communities a generation before shopped in markets offering the smells and tastes of the old countries. But the prophets of the "ethnic revival" (as the resurgence of white ethnic self-identification in the 1970s is called) failed to remember, perhaps because they were too young to notice, the changes and troubles already under way in this apparently secure world. The loss of jobs and the decay of housing stock during the Depression had weakened city neighborhoods. The reverse migration out to the expanding belts of suburbs, which were already growing faster than cities by the 1930s, had commenced. Despite the continuing arrival of newcomers, urban population growth slowed to zero by the middle of the Depression decade. Boston began to lose people in the 1930s, and two decades later, New York, Philadelphia, and other smaller cities had stopped growing altogether.[56]

The passing of the ethnic industrial city is most often blamed by the nostalgic on the dark-skinned migrants who moved first to the edge of the old enclaves and then right into the apartments next door (although now the doors were closed) in the decades after the war. It is certainly true that new people were arriving in the cities. The perfection in 1944 of the first successful mechanical cotton picker, capable of doing the work of fifty laborers, resulted in the "great migration" of African Americans from the South, where 77 percent of black Americans still lived in 1940 (49 percent in rural areas). Five million African Americans moved north between 1940 and 1970, the culmination of a century-long process, one of the most important transmigrations of people in North American history. Racist restrictions, sometimes violently enforced, limited where these newcomers could live; older black neighborhoods such as Harlem, Chicago's Bronzeville, and East Saint Louis quickly became overcrowded. The Puerto Rican great migration got underway in 1946, and from that date until 1964, more than 500,000 islanders came to the mainland—the vast majority to New York City, in a relocation of some 40 percent of all Puerto Ricans in the world.[57]

The new migrants were the most visible markers of a broader transformation under way in the cities. But the great lament of many in the old neighborhoods—that "they" took "our" cities away—obscures the more complex reality that many things led to the passing of the old neighborhoods in the 1960s, including decisions made by the children and grandchildren of immigrants and disastrous schemes hatched by politicians they had elected and trusted. Sadly, the enduring mistrust between the races in the United States must be traced at least in part to this ironic moment in American urban history, when things were not nearly as great as memory renders them. (My essay in this collection explores some of the consequences of this misperception.)

Two developments after the Second World War were especially important for the future shape of U.S. cities. The construction within and across cities of vast and intricate networks of highways that literally rose above or rammed right through working-class neighborhoods "wrought physical havoc in the established urban fabric." Effective lobbying by big-city mayors diverted to the cities $50 billion of funds allocated by the Federal Aid Highway Act of 1956. "The distinctive sign of nineteenth-century urbanism was the boulevard," writes Marshall Berman, "a medium for bringing explosive material and human forces together; the hallmark of twentieth-century urbanism has been the highway, a means for putting them asunder." Stable communities were literally demolished to make way for highways and highway approaches; sacred places in the path of the cars were destroyed and their congregations scattered. People who had once shared a common urban world found themselves separated from each other by lanes of speeding traffic. Madeline Duntley points out in her contribution to this collection that the Japanese Presbyterian church, reestablished after the dislocation of wartime internment, was compelled to relocate in 1963 out of the way of Seattle's Interstate 5. The modernist dream of urban speed had created a new space for city folk to contend with—the shadowed, filthy, and dangerous streets underneath highways elevated on massive cement pylons.[58]

The other major structural influence on postwar cities was the plethora of badly designed, federally funded programs that came under the unintentionally ironic heading of "urban renewal." The Housing Act of 1949, calling for "a decent home and suitable housing environment for every American family," mandated the use of federal funds for land acquisition, slum clearance, and the construction of 800,000 units of public housing. As a result, "billions of dollars poured into cities in what was probably the largest burst of construction since the boom period of the late nineteenth century." In a society that had long viewed cities as alien, dangerous places inhabited by foreign populations morally responsible for their own social and economic distress, it was inevitable that "urban renewal" would become the disaster it did, but the extent of the destruction is still shocking.[59]

Working-class neighborhoods, many of them economically viable and socially stable, were torn out to make room for public housing projects that were designed and built with little appreciation, if not with outright contempt, for the distinct fabric of city street life. Blocks of streets were obliterated by city bureaucrats wielding federally funded clout and unaccountable to the populations they were uprooting. Height dominated: public housing was commonly designed as vertical neighborhoods situated on empty islands of space, the unfortunate realization of the modernist vision of "towers in the park" as the future of urban architecture. The buildings, furthermore, faced away from what was left of the neighborhoods, toward internal courtyards that were rarely landscaped or made comfortably inhabitable in any way, despite many promises to do so; these courtyards remained empty, dangerous terrain, another eviscerated modern urban space like the dead zones beneath highways. Inept and corrupt city agencies failed to keep up basic services. Darkened hallways and broken elevators isolated people in their apartments. Racist disdain for the populations of these new buildings was expressed through the absence of windows in some rooms of apartments and the exposure of elevator waiting areas to the weather.

It is hard to avoid the conclusion that much of the housing built under urban-renewal initiatives was meant to confine and segregate certain urban populations. A number of these structures have been demolished in recent years in admission of their inadequacy as decent environments. It has been one of the challenges of contemporary inner-city Protestant and Catholic churches to find ways of reconnecting these environments, in which many of their congregants make their homes, with the life and movement of the cities surrounding them.[60]

The structural transformations wrought in the late industrial city by deindustrialization and the development of the service economy, the reconfiguration of city space by highways, urban renewal, and changing workplaces, and the ongoing out-migration of middle-class residents to the suburbs form the social and environmental setting for the emergence of the post-industrial city. Space in the postmodern city is characterized by displacement, diffusion, and extension. Contemporary downtowns, according to urban historian Mark Girouard, take two forms: the "single high-density downtown, culminating in a burst of skyscrapers," surrounded by a "girdle of motorways, beyond which low-density suburbs stretch to the horizon," and the Los Angeles model of the "low-density multicentre city." Single cities have been replaced by distended tri-state metropolitan zones, "ever expanding regional areas that are amorphous in form, massive in scope, and hierarchical in their scale of social organization." Between 1960 and 1970, more than 8,000 new shopping centers opened in the United States. Another 25,000 opened between 1970 and 1990—an average of one every seven hours. Most of these centers were situated in vast parking lots well beyond the old city centers, where land was scarce and expensive.[61]

The nature of contemporary urban experience has generated a new geographical lexicon beyond the simple bipolarity of "suburbs" and "inner cities": edge cities, metropolitan corridors, world cities, and so on. While industrial cities could no longer be taken in at a glance, to the great disorientation of their earliest inhabitants, the new cities cannot be seen as cities at all. A bird's-eye view of New York today would have to include a sizeable portion of the Atlantic Seaboard to incorporate the whole area populated by people whose lives are oriented—by work, by their choices in entertainment and recreation, and by family and friends—toward that city. Nor is it necessary any longer for people who work in the service industries based in urban centers to actually go to them, since the "there" of contemporary cities now "exists" in a spaceless domain constituted by telecommunications, resulting in the "disarticulation of work from place."[62]

Many cities in the United States today are "world cities" that look to other urban locales around the globe for their primary associations and business. World cities are connected to each other by the constant movement of people into and out of them along circuits of rapid transportation, sophisticated communication channels, and global media conduits that make possible instantaneous transmission of distant events. World cities, as anthropologist Ulf Hannerz writes, are "places in themselves, and also nodes in networks," switching points of "cultural flows" in an "intercontinental traffic in meaning." Roger Sanjek, referring to New York, describes the world city as "heart to a planetary circulatory system of ideas, people, and artifacts." For contemporary migrants and immigrants, the globalization of urban space has rendered the meaning of "home" extraordinarily complicated (an existential reality with profound religious implications, as the first four chapters in this collection discuss). Living in two or more places virtually at the same time, these individuals are transnationals or binationals (more neologisms necessitated by the conditions of contemporary urban life), connected by open and sustainable "channels of communication and exchange . . . between themselves and their families back home," as Maxine P. Fisher writes of the South Asian community in New York City. Karen McCarthy Brown reports in her chapter in this volume that Haitian immigrants in New York and Miami knew what was going on in the streets of Port-au-Prince during the fall of Jean-Claude Duvalier from videos smuggled out on night flights to the United States.[63]

Control of the Streets in White Cities

At stake in all reform efforts, religious and secular, from antebellum temperance campaigns to mid-century harassments of homosexuals, was control of city streets—the definition and delimitation of what sorts of experiences and expressions were possible on streets that had been gridded into efficient conduits of the material and monetary flows of capitalism. Disorderly-conduct legislation was intended (among other things) to discipline the bodies of city people, to regulate their movements and postures. Ministers and social reformers in African American communities likewise set themselves the task of supervising street life and teaching newly arrived southerners how to comport themselves respectably in public. Street performance of all sorts had long been controlled by the bureaucratic tools of permits and licenses, although working-class people found many ways of resisting such restrictions. The god of the American city—and this was the singular deity of a decidedly monotheistic faith—was order, and the rituals of this faith were the control and supervision of the streets. In the sight of this deity (or its representatives), almost everything that happened on the streets in immigrant and migrant communities was profane. The struggle for the streets was a fundamentally religious contest.[64]

No one has served this god better than the architects and urban planners entrusted with the task of designing and refashioning the city landscape. "The idea of using architecture to control public pastimes," Laurence Moore writes, was throughout the second half of the nineteenth century "a standard way to judge the success or failure of any large public project." Much of modern urban planning in England and the United States was characterized from its inception by an anti-urban sensibility rooted in the familiar contrast between corrupt urbanity and virtuous rural life, and this ethos has subsequently governed many urban rehabilitation programs. One of the most important influences on both city planning and the design of American suburbs was the Garden City movement, founded at the end of the nineteenth century in England by Ebenezer Howard. The Garden City ideal, deeply influenced by Western millennial imagery of the New Jerusalem and by the anti-industrial spirit of English social critics such as John Ruskin and William Morris, envisioned small, village-like environments with limited populations and ample space devoted to gardens and lawns as the alternative to the industrial city. The Garden City agenda was warmly embraced by American planners: it confirmed their own deep prejudices against the city and complemented an indigenous design tradition going back to William Penn's plans for Philadelphia, which sought to dissolve the boundary between the city and nature by surrounding urban dwellings with lawns and gardens for moral as well as aesthetic reasons. This arrangement, planners from the seventeenth to the twentieth centuries agreed, would provide city people with the salubrious physical, moral, and spiritual benefits of regular contact with the natural world.[65]

Garden city advocates believed, as Mark Girouard points out, that cities were terrible places that could be made "bearable" through the intervention of architects and planners. (This contrasts, of course, with the belief that cities are already good places for what they offer in the way of diversity, complexity, and spontaneity, so that the goal of planning should be to enable cities to function better *as cities*—a position characteristic of the work of Jane Jacobs and William Whyte.) Those responsible for marketing Los Angeles at the close of the nineteenth century trumpeted, in true Garden City style, the "kindly, helpful, natural, and innocent" quality of life in the booming city, in contrast to the "corrupt, diseased, cruel and artificial" world of eastern and midwestern industrial cities; oranges became the obsessively reiterated symbols of this distinction and beacons of the American dream of a non-urban urban future. The latent animus against the city that was present from the beginning in the Garden City movement came out clearly in its American incarnations.[66]

A signal moment in the history of American urban planning came at the World's Columbian Exposition in Chicago in 1893 with the construction of a planned model urban environment by some of the nation's most prominent architects and landscape architects, including Chicago's Daniel Burnham (who was director of works for the exposition), Louis Sullivan, and Charles Follen McKim. Frederick Law Olmsted was responsible for the master plan of the exposition. "The planners conceived of the fair," writes Witold Rybczynski, "as an explicit exercise in forward-looking urbanism." The open vistas of the White City, its formal groupings of buildings designed with the full "classical architectural vocabulary—fluted columns, capitals, and entablatures," and its elegance, order, and restraint deeply impressed visitors. Rybczynski, who admires the White City as a "potent and realistic vision of a new direction for the American city" on a scale in keeping with the American landscape, notes that "for the public, the experience of the Exposition was an eye opener": "Only seven miles from the Loop's undisciplined commercial downtown choked with traffic, [visitors to the Exposition] could walk around enjoying water pools, the lake view, landscaping, and public art. It was like going to Europe, which is to say that for most people it was their first experience of the pleasures of ordered urbanism." The White City generated an enthusiasm that was millennial in its excitement and intensity.[67]

But much of the loveliness of the White City in the eyes of its admirers was in explicit contrast to the darkness of the immigrant city: it was the chiaroscuro of the culture's fears of foreignness, of the working class, of dark-skinned others, and of the alien city that lent the buildings on the fairgrounds their compelling luster. Middle-class observers marveled at how respectful and well-mannered working-class visitors to the White City showed themselves to be—evidence of the moral influence of the planned landscape, and a contrast to the behavior of these same people in their own environments. The White City seemed to be the alternative Americans had long sought to the threatening messiness of the immigrant city.

While one sympathizes with this era's hopes for more decent urban environments, it is obvious that what appeared so promising about the scale, imposing classicism, and orderliness of the White City's design was its capacity to dominate, overawe, and organize the foreign masses just then flooding American cities. "The White City might be a sign of a new Pentecost and the New Jerusalem," theologian Harvey Cox writes in a thoughtful comparison of this projection of the urban future, and the way of being it envisioned, with the roughly contemporaneous birth of Pentecostalism in very different city conditions on Azusa Street in Los Angeles, "but it was a Pentecost in which proper English would be spoken and a Jerusalem in which refinement and decorum would prevail." The White City was "safe because empty; safe because clearly marked," to borrow Richard Sennett's more generally applicable assessment of American Christian visions of the good city.[68]

Among the lasting impacts of the White City was its contribution to the rise and flourishing of the City Beautiful movement, which drew together urban reformers, politicians, landscape architects, community workers, city planners, and architects in a common enterprise of urban reform. Although advocates of the City Beautiful were more benevolently inclined toward cities than Garden City planners, they too lacked a full appreciation of the possibilities of the diversity and density of urban street life, preferring instead monumental public buildings and squares that were meant to both express and inculcate civic pride and social order. Daniel Burnham's plan for Chicago, never realized but influential in shaping the future of the city, proposed broad tree-lined boulevards, wide streets of multiple traffic lanes, and grand classical buildings. (Jane Jacobs acerbically dismissed this manner of organizing city space as "decontaminated islands of monuments.") The aesthetic of the City Beautiful movement was one of "bigger places for use by fewer people," in Mark Girouard's words—as it had been at the White City.[69]

Both major influences on American urban planning, the Garden City and the City Beautiful movements, used space "less so that something would happen in it than for its own sake," Girouard says, "either as a symbolic representation of national or civic dignity and power, or as a symbolic rejection of the congestion of 'unnatural' cities." The crowds in Burnham's Chicago were not encouraged to linger within the city, Richard Sennett notes, but were pushed out by design toward the edge in avoidance of "the otherness concentrated at the center." The presence of lots of different kinds of people interacting in unpredictable ways in the streets, which has long characterized American urban life (and urban religion, as we will see), and which is what some actually value about city life, was identified by planners as the problem to be solved by design. Already by 1920, some three hundred American cities had planning commissions inspired by the principles of these movements.[70]

But it was the grid driven up into the heavens by the powers of finance, commerce, and manufacturing that became the true harbinger of the international urban future; other visions of possible cityscapes necessarily had to contend with the triumph of height. American architects had been designing skyscrapers since the 1880s, of course, but the poet and pitchman of the form was Charles-Édouard Jeanneret, better known as Le Corbusier, a Swiss theorist who came to the United States via Paris in the early twentieth century. Le Corbusier's dream of the urban future centered on immensely tall, freestanding towers set down in green spaces, surrounded by elevated highways of speeding cars and connected high off the street by pedestrian walkways. He proposed for Manhattan block after block of massive apartment-house slabs through which people would move in elevators and along interior streets. Le Corbusier was a prophet of a cool modernism for whom speed and efficiency mattered most in the experience of cities.[71]

Although there are clearly profound differences between Le Corbusier's urbanism and the urbanism of Burnham, Olmsted, and others, the life lived on the ground in the cities, the specificity and diversity of urban cultures, and the exciting contingencies of city streets were eclipsed in all of them. Marshall Berman refers to this process as the "flattening out of the urban landscape." The environments envisioned in these idioms, however one assesses them — and all have admirers and detractors — were simply not intended to be the habitations of immigrants and migrants or places where these foreign people of strange customs could make lives for (or public spectacles of) themselves; for these populations, the environment at best could function as an agent of assimilation and acculturation. The language used to describe the "Olympian" (in Jane Jacobs's word for them) views of the city characteristic of all these various planning idioms contrasts strikingly with the language used in newspaper accounts of the dwellings and bodies of immigrants and migrants: lovely, harmonious, elegant, natural cities, on the one hand; sweaty, smelly, dirty, disorderly immigrants, on the other. As Le Corbusier put it, "The street wears us out. And when all is said and done we have to admit it disgusts us." The American ideology of the city thus acquired the authority of a platonic hierarchy of essential opposites — spirit/matter, soul/body, beautiful/ugly, good/bad. It was hoped that the control of the urban other, who had vexed the American imagination since the early republic, through geometry, monumentality, and exposure to carefully cultivated nature in the city could bring order out of chaos, unity out of diversity, whiteness out of color.[72]

Religion in the Spaces of the City

The religious idioms studied in this volume consistently confronted — and continue to confront — both the modernist dreams of a pure, orderly, white city and the efforts of Christian and secular reformers to remake cities into idealized, homogeneous small towns. By turning apartments into abattoirs (as the practitioners of Santería do), the basements of housing projects into venues of the spirits, the streets into penitential pilgrimage routes, city water flows into receptacles for sins or the resting places of Hindu gods, and intersecting street corners into vectors of spiritual power, immigrants and migrants dramatically re-placed themselves on cityscapes that had been explicitly designed to exclude them or to render them invisible or docile. By acting upon the urban environment in these different ways, immigrants and migrants denied the arrangements of space, the understanding of poverty, the marginalization or ostracism of the foreign, and the alienation of the streets built into the urban landscape by law, architecture, and religion. Into every space hollowed out by contempt for the city and its peoples—the bleak apartments of public housing, streets dwarfed and dominated by massive towers of stone and reflecting glass or overshadowed by highways, parks intended for the polite refreshment of people who behaved the way reformers and landscape designers thought they should—or the demands of capital, migrants and immigrants have inserted themselves, making themselves present, indeed at times over-present, usually on their own terms. This is the persistent subversive impulse of popular urban religions in the United States, the counter-story to the narrative inscribed by architects, planners, and reformers on the streets and in the skies of American cities.

Religious practice was not the only way in which immigrants and migrants enacted this presence, of course: there were also parades and street fights, sidewalk games and conversations, riots, political rallies, labor marches, and so on. Throughout the twentieth century, there has been an ongoing struggle over power relationships in industrial urban society and a steady intensification of demands from those on whom this society has borne down the hardest—workers, women, racial and ethnic minorities— to participate fully and equally in social, political, and cultural life. One of the challenges in the study of urban religion is to attend to the relationships between religious practices and other forms of urban popular culture, to discern the place of religion in the history of power in the cities, and to set religious idioms in their place amid the routines of everyday life. But as we will see, religions occupy a distinct place in the engagement of immigrants and migrants with cities.

Until recently, the phenomenology of city religions was not a specific field of scholarly inquiry. This reflects the wider cultural occlusion of strangers in the cities. The very idea of "city religion" struck many as an oxymoron, and the term has been absent from major encyclopedias and dictionaries of American religion. Mircea Eliade, the great historian of religions and a lifelong resident of cities himself, argued that what passed for religion in contemporary Western urban settings were degraded and impotent "survivals" of real religiosity, which necessarily existed in intimate and ongoing connection to the rhythms and revelations of the sacred in nature. Modern men and women, whose lives are governed by function, speed, efficiency, and novelty, have been alienated from the ontological grounds of human experience, said Eliade—from being itself, as being is disclosed and experienced in the hierophanies (or self-disclosures) of the sacred in nature: in the rhythms of the moon, for example, or the pulse of the oceans. The modern city, by this account, is the end product of a long history of spiritual alienation and decline, the outcome of processes of secularization. As moral philosopher Alasdair MacIntyre explained, "When the working class were gathered from the countryside into the industrial cities, they were finally torn from a form of community in which it could be intelligibly and credibly claimed that the norms which govern social life had universal and cosmic significance, and were God-given. They were planted instead in a form of community in which the officially endorsed norms so clearly are of utility only to certain partial and partisan human interests that it is impossible to clothe them with universal and cosmic significance." The task of the study of urban religion, then, if one follows these theorists, becomes either to chart the progress of this decline or to identify isolated pockets of resistance to it.[73]

The strongest theoretical work on urban religions has concentrated on the traditional cities of Asia, Meso-America, and South Asia, carefully explicating the relationships among the plans and architecture of these ancient cities and their respective cosmologies, social hierarchies, and ritual calendars. Although this scholarly tradition reminds us that city culture is not a product of the last two centuries in the West, it has largely ignored the religious lives of people in the turbulent, chaotic industrial city, where cosmology, ritual, architecture, and demarcations of space are not so carefully and intentionally synchronized, if at all. Indeed, it is often precisely the disjunctures between environment and religious idiom that occasion crises, cultural creativity, and religious innovation.[74]

The belief that religion is not natural to cities is pervasive in contemporary American culture. The religious ethos of white middle-class Americans at the end of the twentieth century is dominated by a spirit of "expressive individualism," according to the authors of *Habits of the Heart*, a romantic sensibility akin to Eliade's that is more likely to identify mountaintops and ocean beaches as places evocative of religious feelings than street corners and the basements of housing projects; and religion, in this common understanding, is a matter of feeling rather than of practice, authority, discipline within a tradition, or of feeding the spirits. If there is religion in the cities—"real" religion, that is—then it is either the courageous faith of those who go and live and serve among the poor, or the alluring vitality, spiritual exoticism, and primeval powers of the other. The history and phenomenology of urban religions remain so little explored in large part because of the authority of the narrative of urban religious decline and alienation and of these variant strains of romantic religion in American culture.[75]

Yet the truth is that much of what is characteristic of modern American religion has developed in cities. Pentecostalism, settlement houses, Christian Science, the various modern forms of American Judaism, gospel and soul music, immigrant street shrines and festivals, and the American encounter with the many religious traditions of Asia and Africa, to cite just a few examples, are all phenomena of the cities. Important international religious movements either found indigenous expression in U.S. cities, as with Hasidic Judaism in Brooklyn (where Chagall-like rebbes float above red-brick Brooklyn tenements in paintings sold in galleries on Eastern Parkway), or were recast into more vital forms here before being transplanted back to their cultures of origin, as happened with Swami Prabhupada's Hare Krishna movement. African spiritualities and religious practices took complex urban forms in Vodou and Santería in the spaces and traffic between New York and Port-au-Prince and between Miami and Havana, respectively. Familiar idioms of popular Protestantism assumed new shapes as the rural white population moved into cities, as we have seen; much of what constitutes the distinctive character of modern American Protestantism arose in response to the cities.

Are there distinctly urban religious experiences and practices? The authors represented in this collection think so. It is the shared contention of these essays that industrial and post-industrial cities have been the ground of a unique religious creativity. "Urban religion" does not refer simply to religious beliefs and practices that happen to take place in cities (and that might as well take place elsewhere). Urban religion is what comes from the dynamic engagement of religious traditions (by which I mean constellations of practices, values, and beliefs, inherited and improvised, in ongoing exchanges among generations and in engagement with changing social, cultural, and intellectual contexts) with specific features of the industrial and post-industrial cityscapes and with the social conditions of city life. The results are distinctly and specifically urban forms of religious practice, experience, and understanding.

The spaces of the cities, their different topographies and demographics, are fundamental to the kinds of religious phenomena that emerge in them. Relevant geographical factors include the arrangement of ethnic neighborhoods in relation to each other; the location of markets, schools, different sorts of recreational sites, and workplaces; the possibilities for and forms of intersection of neighborhoods; and the architectural details of different urban landscapes—including stoops, fire escapes, rooftops, and hallways. In the new post-industrial world cities, other factors are the displacement, diffusion, and even erasure of determinate, particular space by recent developments in telecommunications and transportation technologies, the intensification of global traffic in ideas and artifacts, and the extension of city boundaries over such vast terrain as to obliterate the meaning or necessity of an urban "there." This has all made for complex and contradictory experiences of place for those who travel these new pathways and live in these new "placeless places," and new challenges to their religious creativity.

These specific features of the urban (and perhaps post-urban) landscape, which differ from city to city, are not simply the setting for religious experience and expression but become the very materials for such expression and experience. City folk do not live *in* their environments; they live *through* them. Who am I? What is possible in life? What is good? These are questions that are always asked, and their answers discerned and enacted, in particular places. Specific places structure the questions, and as men and women cobble together responses, they act upon the spaces around them in transformative ways. This is the architectonic of urban religion. Religion is always, among other things, a matter of necessary places, sites where the humans and their deities, ancestors, or spirits may most intimately communicate; religious practice in city and countryside alike engages the vicissitudes of the environments that humans find themselves thrown into and makes meaningful places out of contingent spaces. We examine how religious practice in the cities recasts the meanings of the urban environment as the city re-creates religious imagination and experience.[76]

The young James Baldwin, for example, constantly scanned the horizon of avenues, temples, bars, beauty parlors, churches, and candy stores of Harlem for clues to who he was; in the process, he created a distinctly religious sense of the city for himself. His fears and desires shaped what he saw, and what he was seeing in turn oriented his fears and desires. The conflicting South Bronxes in the tales with which I opened this introduction existed as ideas *and* places: as the products of the interaction of understanding, experience, and imagination. Urban religion is the site of converging and conflicting visions and voices, practices and orientations, which arise out of the complex desires, needs, and fears of many different people who have come to cities by choice or compulsion (or both), and who find themselves intersecting with unexpected others (and with unexpected experiences of their own subjectivities) on a complex social field and in a protean physical landscape that insists on itself with particular intensity.[77]

Consider what becomes of Harlem's Lenox Avenue when it is seen through the eyes of the recently converted boy John Grimes in Baldwin's autobiographical novel, *Go Tell It on the Mountain*: "And the avenue, like any landscape that has endured a storm, lay changed under Heaven, exhausted and clean, and new. Not again, forever, could it return to the avenue it had once been. Fire, or lightning, or the latter rain, coming down from these skies which moved with such pale secrecy above him now, had laid yesterday's avenue waste, had changed it in a moment, in the twinkling of an eye, as all would be changed on the last day, when the skies would open up once more to gather up the saints." Likewise, Moishe Sacks, the leader of a South Bronx synagogue that forms the center of Jack Kugelmass's essay in this volume, describes his Sabbath walks through the neighborhood thus: "Every Saturday when I walk to shul, particularly as I get to the area around the shul where all the buildings are gone, even with all the garbage and rubble, it reminds me of the area around the *kotel maravi*, the Western Wall, in Jerusalem. To me this place is my holy place. It's my kotel maravi."[78]

Life in the industrial and post-industrial city demanded (and demands) constant resourcefulness, flexibility, creativity, and existential inventiveness. Modernist intellectuals and artists of the nineteenth century believed that the vitality, pace, and complexity of the industrial city would give rise to distinct art forms capable of bringing the "explosive forces" of urban society to life in art—an aspiration that resulted in a series of formal experiments that included "cubist painting, collage and montage, the cinema, the stream of consciousness in the novel, the free verse of Eliot and Pound and Apollinaire, futurism, vorticism, constructivism, dada, poems that accelerate like cars, paintings that explode like bombs," in Marshall Berman's words. So it has been with urban religious creativity: the world of the modern city has necessitated, encouraged, or simply made possible a tremendous explosion of religious innovation and experimentation.[79]

If this association of urban religions with an exuberant (even if sometimes ambiguous) modernism strikes readers as strange, this may be because in American discourse the dominant metaphors for the cultural experience of city-dwelling immigrants and migrants have tended to be horticultural. Newcomers to the city are "uprooted" or "transplanted" chthonic peasants who pine for their lost earth and re-create their "villages" and shtetls in the cities. But migrants and immigrants to American cities, many of whose journeys to the United States took them not only through farmland or rural areas, but through other cities around the globe, showed themselves to be skilled in the arts of cultural and especially religious improvisation—as resourceful as their ancient counterparts in Rome, Athens, Benares, and Jerusalem. They were makers of their religious worlds of meaning and practice.

African American migrants from the South, for example, built a complex religious culture in northern cities that included Pentecostal practice and experience, New Thought and other metaphysical schools, vernacular healing idioms, the revitalization and reorganization of long-established Protestant denominations touched now by the rhythms and ways of southern migrants, cosmologically derived dietary regimes, African nationalisms, and new faiths such as the Black Jews of Harlem or the Nation of Islam, which drew eclectically on other religious traditions (to name only some of the idioms available in African American city neighborhoods). Such rich environments encouraged a continual, explosive religious creativity, for when "migrants reestablished religious practices and asserted new identities, their experience and exposure to other belief systems altered their religious traditions," as historian Jill Watts writes of the circumstances surrounding Father Divine's movement. The great migration of African Americans northward was, among other things, the occasion for an outpouring of religious creativity.[80]

There is no single urban religious style or idiom; just as there are many different urbanisms reflecting particular economies, demographics, politics, histories, and topographies, so there are many different kinds of urban religions. What people do religiously in cities is shaped by what kinds of cities they find themselves in, at what moment in the histories of those cities, and by their own life experiences, cultural traditions, and contemporary circumstances. Miami's religious history is not like New York's or San Antonio's or Chicago's (although they share common features). The labor histories of migrants and immigrants to Miami, the worlds they left, and the social and physical environments they encountered in Florida are all specific to that city and to those people, as are the forms of religious improvisation and response that have emerged on this ground.

Some city faiths draw individuals into a shared common world through discipline and ritual, while others sanction the radically individualistic quests possible in cities. Some connect migrants and immigrants to the places they came from; others heighten the distance between here and there, now and then. Particular urban religious idioms, such as the Nation of Islam, forcefully proclaim themselves to be new expressions of ancient faiths, while others insist on their identities as ancient and "traditional" faiths. Many urban religious are ambivalently situated among the divergent and competing possibilities available to city dwellers, alternately mitigating and exacerbating the dilemmas of immigrant and migrant experience. They offer not resolution, but creative engagement and response.

Anthropologist Kyeyoung Park, for example, suggests that the Korean Christian conversion experience, *pangŏn*, frees immigrants from the "trivial considerations and secular desires" that weigh so heavily on them while at the same time providing the very prestige and sense of achievement that these immigrants aspire to in the city. *Pangŏn* simultaneously assuages and provokes anxiety (since immigrants worry that they will not have the conversion experience they long for and that they are urged to have). "Urban religion" in the singular is a convenient misnomer; the term should be understood to refer to the complex, contradictory, polysemous range of religious practices and understandings shaped by different groups of urban residents in engagement with the conditions of specific urban environments at particular moments in the environmental, political, and social histories of cities.[81]

City people have acted on and with the spaces of the city to make religious meanings in many different ways. They have appropriated public spaces for themselves and transformed them into venues for shaping, displaying, and celebrating their inherited and emergent ways of life and understandings of the world. They have remapped the city, superimposing their own coordinates of meaning on official cartographies. Certain westside corners in midtown Manhattan, as David Brown points out in his chapter, are considered especially efficacious spiritual crossroads by practitioners of Santería. Flushing Meadow Lake has been appropriated by South Asian immigrants from the tri-state area (New York, New Jersey, and Connecticut) as the home of Ganesh. Neighborhood artists use the sides of abandoned buildings to create memorials to friends who have fallen to violence and drugs. City people have also played upon urban space with the instruments of irony, juxtaposition, contrast, and inversion. Malcolm X used the stark and startling incongruity between the squealing of pigs being butchered next door to Detroit's Temple Number 1 and the calm poise and self-possession of the men and women within the temple precincts over whom the awful sound washed (and who did not eat pork by dietary restraint) to emphasize the dignity of Elijah Muhammad's path in a racist society and to draw and authorize the boundary between the pure and the contaminated. New arrivals to the cities have taken over the sacred spaces of other groups and absorbed signs and symbols on the walls and doors into their own experience of these places, creating a distinctly urban religious palimpsest.[82]

Michael Harris writes that Thomas Dorsey, the progenitor of gospel music, spoke the old tongue of southern black experience in the new land of the northern cities, first in the "grievous, grieving tempo" of the blues and then in gospel. To this I would add that in speaking thus, Dorsey created a new religious language for African American migrants' experience of the city. The religious practices that concern us are, like Dorsey's songs, new creations, crafted within and in response to the everyday experience of city dwellers. These are not syncretic forms but creative "recombinations" (to borrow Diana DeG. Brown's and Mario Bick's description of Umbanda ritual in urban Brazil) of inherited, found, and improvised idioms.[83]

African American sacred quartet rehearsals offer a paradigm of the nature of urban religious creativity. Younger singers raised in the cities, some of whom have had no experience of the South, meet to prepare new songs and movements with older performers possessed of rich stores of southern idioms in their memories and in their bodies. The generations work cooperatively and competitively, commenting on each other's efforts, trying out new things as they acknowledge and mutually enforce the authority of a "tradition" that itself is always fluid and changing. Movements and sounds learned in the South are inflected with the rhythms and styles of northern popular culture. The resulting performances belong not to the South or the North, not to the young or the old, but are new creations on the ground between generations and places—like urban religion generally: between memory and contemporary experience, tradition and innovation. They belong neither to the time and place before the city nor to the city itself, but to both.[84]

It was through their religious displays that urban people announced in their own voices the heterogeneity of cities. Studies of religious practices in specific city neighborhoods that ignore the broader ideological and architectural contexts within which urban religions take shape may fail to recognize that it was through public religious practice—by bringing the Madonna out into the streets, for instance, or transforming apartments in neglected housing projects into ebullient domains of the spirits—that immigrants and migrants staked a claim to living in a particular kind of nation. It has been by their religious practice as much as their politics that migrants and immigrants joined the national debate about pluralism, multiculturalism, and heterogeneity.

Urban street life is a spectacle of recognizable signs, a semiotics of place, that divides the initiated from the uninitiated. Even apparently chaotic street patterns mask "a highly organized street culture, whose boundaries and conventions were well-known to the initiated." This is one of the reasons that style is so important to urban people and to urban religion— why people dress themselves, their gods, and their children so carefully for public display during religious events. It is through style—

through the intricate intentionalities of public self-representation, and especially through style in religion—that city people have made meanings and impressed those meanings on themselves and others, have met and contested the gaze of reformers and bureaucrats, and have presented themselves at the borders and junctures of adjacent urban social worlds.[85]

The spaces of the city are not simply venues of display, however. Rather, urban people negotiate a delicate balance between revelation and self-effacement, display and concealment, in their use of the cityscape. The Vodou practitioners described by Karen McCarthy Brown, for example, and the Santería adept in David Brown's essay are profoundly sensitive to the dangers of too much visibility, and they remain constantly in tension between declaring themselves present in the city as they serve the spirits with sound, color, tastes, and smells, and removing themselves from the gaze of others (especially from those who would prevent them from serving the spirits by legal restriction). The cities allow for play with the possibilities of concealment and revelation.

Outsiders have consistently mistaken the vitality and heterogeneity of city streets for disorderliness, neglecting the ways that these streets are spaces of an indigenous moral watchfulness and order. Jane Jacobs understood that neighborhoods police themselves through finely woven and carefully sustained webs of interpersonal connections, bonds that are often constituted, disclosed, celebrated, and negotiated in public religious events. Jacobs represented this dimension of urban culture with a domestic image: the streets raised children. This phrase has been used by others, of course, to register the familiar unease with the mores of the inner city and to issue a dire pronouncement: left to the streets, children will be corrupted by the city. But Jacobs means just the opposite, because she understood that it was in the streets of neighborhoods not destroyed by the many forces converging against the modern American city that people acknowledged and accepted responsibility for their world. This is why the diminution of the streets by height and by urban renewal programs was so destructive to the communities on which they were inflicted. It is in the streets that urban people have encountered themselves as moral agents and as makers of their cultural worlds. Streets are "conduits of sociability." The streets were prooftext for Malcolm X's religious message: Just look around you, he urged his listeners on Harlem afternoons, to see what the white man has done to you. People have studied the streets to learn what was possible and what not; children have discovered here the temptations of transgression but also the reach of authority.[86]

The streets are not simple spaces, then. If they were, there would be no need to take the gods out into them. Migrants from the Spanish-speaking Caribbean revealed a deep apprehension of *la calle* as well as a deep fondness for it in conversations with a *New York Times* reporter in 1980. *La calle* taught their children to be cold, they said, to be disrespectful to their elders, to value material goods over family connectedness. As they spoke, *la calle* took shape as an agent in their stories of life in New York. These men and women understand the spaces of the city as their inevitable partner in making a moral world for themselves and their children; their response to this inevitability was ambivalence. The streets were to be contended with, encountered, rendered part of the moral universe of families and neighborhoods.[87]

Religious figures of all sorts—clergy with established congregations, upstart leaders of new religious movements trying to build followings by raiding the flocks of others, Pentecostal street preachers, Vodou practitioners, and so on—have long understood the importance of making their presence known in the spaces of the city, to keep an eye on those in their care, to establish and maintain their own authority, and most of all to listen to the voices of these spaces, to attend to what is going on, and to catch the signs and portents offered up by the urban landscape. In the 1940s and 1950s, for example, Harlem's streets, parks, stoops, and churches buzzed with unhappiness and disappointment, a palpable political and moral atmospherics that the editors of a memoir by Malcolm X's assistant minister, Benjamin Karim, describe as a pervasive "street-corner discontent." Harlem was being created in this way as a community of concern and protest; issues of human rights and economic justice were being debated and the nature of religious truth was contested, all in the flow of conversation, gesture, and presence in its spaces. By moving attentively through these spaces, walkers on the sidewalks joined the neighborhood discourse.[88]

African American ministers and Roman Catholic priests have been especially connected to the urban environment, interacting with their respective flocks (and with those who were not but who could be part of their flocks) and establishing links between their congregations and the necessary powers within and beyond the neighborhoods. Malcolm X was a master of the art of street presence. He loved moving through the spaces of Harlem. Catholic urban experience in the cities of the industrial North and Midwest was so thoroughly articulated to place that Catholics identified their neighborhoods by the names of their churches: they came from "St. Stan's" or "St. Bridget's." Catholics "used the parish to map out—both physically and culturally—space within all of the northern cities," creating disciplined moral worlds in which "neighborhood, parish, and religion were constantly intertwined." They celebrated this Catholic ecology in an annual round of processions, carnivals, and block parties. Catholic priests and nuns roamed these city worlds in their distinctive garb, extending the moral authority of the church into saloons, parks, and candy stores. It was one of the intentions of the Franciscans in the South Bronx, for example, to cause a stir on the streets by appearing in their unfamiliar medieval garb, which the friars hoped would so startle and intrigue local people that it might be a step toward shattering the dreadful isolation and givenness of their local world. The environmental authority of African American and Roman Catholic religious figures is particularly evident during community crises, when ministers and priests circle through the neighborhoods to calm the crowds in the streets.[89]

The city comes alive for immigrants and migrants as they move through its emptied spaces in a dynamic fundamentally different from the city's allure in the experience of missionaries, pilgrims, and sexual voyagers. These latter encounters have depended on the absence or occlusion of the other. In contrast, to take one example, Frank Bartleman, a pioneer of Pentecostalism, understood the area around Azusa Street in Los Angeles to be a charged and active terrain: people on their way to the revival found themselves already overcome by God's spirit present in the streets surrounding the chapel and fell into trances on the sidewalks. The city itself comes alive in this imagining and in other experiences of urban religion—suffused with the energies of the sacred. But this is the result of presence, not absence—the presence of divinities and of the people who engage them in the city's spaces.[90]

Urban Religious Cartographies: Maps of Being

Contemporary urban cultural theory, challenging an earlier generation's view of the city as socially and psychologically anomic, argues that metropolitan regions comprise complex networks of "pathways" that city people travel in their daily rounds, which connect them with others across the cityscapes. It is along such pathways that city people construct durable and dependable networks of association. A few of these networks constitute a way of life for any city dweller; together, they make up the social order of the city.[91]

Many of these life-making and -sustaining urban pathways are in fact pilgrimage routes. Urban religious idioms have responded to the spatial dilemmas created by the circumstances of diaspora and dislocation, by urban real-estate markets that make it nearly impossible for families and friends to choose to live near each other, and by the spatial upheavals of mid-century. The experiences of the African American diaspora are again instructive. On Sunday mornings, African American Christians of all denominations visit from church to church, driving across the city in buses bought by congregations at considerable sacrifice and clearly, proudly, and publicly identified as the property of the churches. Many African American neighborhood churches have extensions in other communities, off-shoots founded by members of the main body. These extensions can be quite distant, with some as far away as the area in the South from which the founders of the mother church migrated, and so on Sunday morning, buses marked with the language of the Lord circulate across neighborhoods and between the South and the North—a circulatory system of regional friendship and spiritual association. Urban landscapes are also mapped by African American Christians through citywide schedules of gospel concerts. A concert in one neighborhood is announced in others by posters stapled to telephone poles, handbills taped to store windows, and notices in local papers and church bulletins, all linking the different African American neighborhoods in a gospel network. Family connections and friendships are thus maintained by religious practice amid constant urban spatial reconfigurations.[92]

George Chauncey uses the phrase "sexual topography" to describe the mental maps that told gay men earlier in the century which parts of New York City were safe for them and which not, where they might find pleasure and companionship, and where they had to be careful to hide themselves. Borrowing this phrase, it is possible to talk about urban religious topographies—a Santería map of the city, for example, or a Southern Baptist or Pentecostal map. These are not the only maps practitioners have of their worlds, of course: urban experience is complex, and city people live with multiple, competing, and conflicting maps. A gay Roman Catholic, for example, knows not only the sexual topography of the city but the Catholic one as well; if he works in a bank or brokerage house, he knows the city's financial topography, too. People must contend with intrusions upon their religious topographies, with the efforts of others to control, reorient, redistrict, or even obliterate their distinct experience of the city, and with conflicts and disjunctures in their own mappings. But the social and religious life of American cities is constituted by overlapping cultural cartographies—variant mappings reflecting complex histories, ideologies, spiritualities, and personal experiences and needs.[93]

Urban religious maps do not mark only local coordinates, moreover. The East Coast Santería urban map, for example, connects the Bronx, Newark, Miami, Jersey City, Havana, and Manhattan. It is plotted around the homes of prominent ritual specialists, well-stocked botanicas, and the annual calendar of celebrations. Urban religious idioms are not best studied exclusively as local phenomena, a matter of neighborhood gods, but as practices of making connections, real and imaginary, within neighborhoods, across the city, and around the globe. The Sikh *gurudwara* (temple) in Queens, New York, for instance, draws on the tri-state area for its congregation, bringing far-flung devout down the northeast corridor for weekly worship. The followers of Father Divine's Peace Mission Church in the 1930s traveled across the country in buses emblazoned with the church's name. Sacred spaces in particular city neighborhoods serve as centers of national and international religious affiliation: Chicago's South Side for the Nation of Islam, for example; Harlem for Marcus Garvey's Pan-African millennial movement in the 1920s; Brooklyn's Crown Heights for Lubavitcher Hasidism; the Catholic Worker's House of Hospitality, on New York's Lower East Side, where the movement's newspaper is still produced.[94]

Cities are also places of diverse religious ontologies. Religious maps constitute as they disclose to practitioners particular ways of being in the world, of approaching the invisible beings who along with family members and neighbors make up practitioners' relevant social worlds, and of coordinating an individual's own story with an embracing cultural narrative. Santería cartography, for instance, provides information about where the spirits are best encountered; within these coordinates, a Santería adept can expect a different kind of experience of reality from that available at other sites on other pathways that he or she follows through the city. The maps that people of different cultures have in their heads and in their bodies articulate space and being to each other.

There is nothing necessarily liberating about the alternative worlds constituted or disclosed by these urban religious maps. African American Pentecostal mappings of the city, for example, constitute a disciplinary cartography, marking out forbidden places and revisioning places of secular entertainment as sites of evil, transgression, and damnation. All religious reconfigurations of urban space make some experiences possible, encourage and satisfy some desires and aspirations, while disallowing others. "It was the roar of the damned that filled Broadway," James Baldwin's autobiographical character, young John Grimes, muses on a trip downtown from the ambivalent security of his father's Pentecostal Harlem. "Broadway: the way that led to death," the young man continues, "*was* broad, and many could be found thereon; but narrow was the way that led to life eternal, and few there were who found it." John's father's religious imagination recasts the topography of the city for the boy, and Baldwin's autobiographical character must eventually free himself, as Baldwin did, from the crushing coordinates of his father's mapping of the city in order to live as he himself wishes.[95]

One of the relatively overlooked dimensions of the spatial practice of urban and suburban religious history in the United States, finally, has been the dedicated commitment by middle-class suburban Protestant, Catholic, and Jewish congregations to establish and maintain bonds of connection with their urban counterparts. Sometimes these ties are to neighborhoods in which the suburban congregations originated; at other times, particular suburban churches have established supportive relationships with inner-city churches of more limited economic resources. Bonds of this sort reveal a serious moral commitment to the city, countering the regrettably more insistent imperative to move away from troubled city environs. Our sense of urban religious maps must include these ties of responsibility, spiritual partnership, and personal affection across the barriers and dislocations of race and class prejudice.[96]

Religious practice and imagination thus continually rework urban landscapes that are themselves forever in upheaval. Religious practices have served as media for creating and sustaining bonds among people scattered across the city and between people in the city and others beyond its borders, and for constituting a meaningful sense of space on intersecting neighborhood, urban, national, and global levels. Religious cartographies disclose the coordinates of alternative worlds for practitioners, remaking the meanings of ordinary places and signaling the locations of extraordinary ones, establishing connections between the spaces of the city and other spaces, real and imaginary, between humans and invisible sacred companions of all sorts. American cities are composed of complex topographies of interleaved, sometimes incongruous domains of experience and possibility, knowledge of which is borne in the bodies and senses of city people who move through multiple urban worlds in their everyday lives.

Religion and the Making of City Selves

"In America," playwright Anna Deavere Smith has written, "identity is always being negotiated." City people have been challenged to make identities for themselves at the intersection of communities, between their experiences of the world and the accounts that outsiders give of them, at the meetings of generations, between this land and others. Urban subjectivities are situational, fashioned from the city's "multitude of activities, alignments, and perspectives," as Ulf Hannerz observes, and the situations are interstitial. Urban subjectivities take shape in the fissures created by multiple conjunctures and separations. The "diversity" of selves in the cities, Hannerz continues, means that the self-awareness of city people "may be intensified by the observation of the difference between self and other," a distinctly urban dialectic of self-constitution. This process of looking for oneself in the mirror of the other can often be tense and aggressive; city people experience themselves in each other's eyes, with the inevitable risks of misperception and hate—or, worse, of not being seen at all.[97]

City people think with each other, furthermore. They tell complicated stories about their neighbors that are also stories about themselves, about their own fears, hopes, needs, and desires. These narratives, which arise at the borders between groups, are another form of urban creation, and they become an inescapable dimension of the reality with which urban people must live. Italian Americans and African Americans, Haitians and African Americans, Jews and Italians, Mexicans and Colombians, Salvadorans and Chinese, and so on, must live with the stories they tell about each other and about themselves in the idiom of the other, within the broader context of American racial and ethnic ideologies. The identity politics of city streets, or what I refer to below as the cultural strategy of alterity, are volatile, and violence and high emotion in the streets point to the fluidity of urban subjectivity and its origination at the borders. As Deavere Smith writes, "American character lives not in one place or the other, but in the gaps between the places, and in our struggle to be together in our differences."[98]

Religious spaces have been essential locations of self-reflection and self-constitution in cities. Urban selves have been and are still constituted, displayed, sanctioned, affirmed, and rendered recognizable in religious settings such as those described in the essays in this collection. The men and women who brought their lives into these spaces were very often in crises occasioned by the separation, loss, and alienation of migration and immigration, or by the tensions and emotional consequences of life in the cities—of overcrowded housing, unemployment, overwork, or the dangers posed to the younger generation by the streets. The religious idioms improvised in cities responded to such dilemmas, offering healing and reorientation by linking the individual both to a larger community and to a shared narrative about the nature of the world. African American churches in the North, for example, often formed clubs of congregants from the same southern states, surrounding northern newcomers with others holding memories like theirs.

The self becomes recognizable to itself in the familiar stories others tell in familiar accents in such settings. In the cities, where the grounds on which people stand are literally always moving, where conditions of work and family are beset by manifold social and psychological pressures, and the inherited structures of selfhood are under tremendous pressures, the remaking of selves in religious practice proceeds with particular intensity. This is why religious events in cities can be as volatile and unpredictable as the life of the streets on which they occur.

Migrants and immigrants to American cities have been responsible for loved ones living in other places, and accountable for duties and identities—as fathers and sons, for example, or godmothers and aunts—associated with bonds made in other environments. Immigration historians have noted how important the financial remittances sent back from the United States by emigrants have been to the economies of other places, but just as important have been their remittances of self. This is one of the material conditions for the complexity and difficulty of urban subjectivity. To live such an existentially and geographically dispersed life demands complicated psychological strategies. The strains of this effort become evident in the religious rituals described in this volume.

The identities of migrants and immigrants constructed and disclosed in religious ritual were not recapitulations of who they were in the places they left, however, or were never only this. Urban religions have offered occasions for new possibilities of selfhood to be crafted, discovered, assayed, and represented, and for contesting customary gender arrangements, racial understandings, ethnic affiliations, and cultural expectations. When they enacted the various cultural possibilities of the self, real and hoped for, in religious settings, city people often enough found ways both to be recognizable to themselves and to dissolve or extend the boundaries of the expected and familiar. African Caribbean spirit service, Italian street festivals, the Pentecostal language of spiritual kinship, and Korean conversion experiences have offered participants opportunities to share their stories of coming to and living in the cities with others who they knew would witness to the truth of these accounts from their own experiences—an intimate commingling of lives and narratives. Other religious practices set up barriers against the fluidity of urban subjectivities. Going door to door in city neighborhoods represents for Jehovah's Witnesses, for example, a rigorous subjective discipline meant not really to convert others but to organize the lives of church members and to curtail the chaotic play of self in the cities. Urban religious idioms must be studied carefully to understand the distinct sacred politics of subjectivity they offer, what each allows and disallows the self.

Religious environments in the cities have been crucial sites, too, for the assimilation of children into their parents' habitus, sociologist Pierre Bordieu's term for the structures of feeling, physical experience, cognitive categories, and communicative idioms through which persons of particular social worlds develop into persons and experience and communicate the world. "In church," folklorist Ray Allen writes of gospel quartets, "youngsters absorbed the basic elements of pitch, rhythm, harmony, vocal techniques, and body movement simply by watching, listening, and eventually repeating the behaviors of older singers." Likewise among Italian immigrants and their children, essential idioms of comportment—the necessary gestures of the Italian American self—were embodied in children at *feste*, where they were called upon to perform themselves as they were expected to be in the eyes of others. The self is constituted at such occasions by a kind of religious kinetics in the full gaze of the community. The younger generations are not passive at such events. The ties that form between immigrant or migrant adults and their children in the space of religion have been fraught with tensions because one way that the older folk have attempted to negotiate their own conflicted relationships with the places they came from is by reenacting these other worlds—or idealized versions of them—in the experience of their children at religious celebrations. Such events often have become the loci of intense generational contestation as well as of familial intimacy.[99]

The "communities" that have encountered each other at urban boundaries—the African American community or the Italian American community, for example—have themselves been fictions, constructed provisionally and extemporized in specific political and social circumstances. There has never been one Harlem, for example; no urban community is as homogeneous as designations such as "Little Havana" and "Chinatown" pretend. The "Italian" of Italian American is a creation of life in the cities, not a reference to some essential ethnic or historical identity. Pan-Indian identity took shape in the United States among immigrants from the subcontinent; it was not brought over with them. Ethnic identity is labile and situational in the United States. Men and women from the Dominican Republic identify themselves as "Puerto Ricans" when they feel they have to, for example, and people are more Italian or Jewish or Irish in some circles than others. Urban life is a matter of protean selves in protean communities encountering each other; hence, tense issues of personal and communal identity have been at stake in many racial, ethnic, and religious conflicts in cities over the last several decades. This should not be misread as suggesting that ethnicity does not matter for the construction of selves or for life on the streets; indeed, the more labile ethnicity is seen to be, the clearer the intensity, and sometimes violence, of the strategies for sanctioning it.

No aspect of urban experience is impermeable to others. Urban religions do not exist in a sacred space apart, but in the midst of social life: all the currents of life in the cities flow through the religious spaces discussed in this collection. Urban selves take shape across a variety of domains of experience, real and imaginary, and there is a continual contest or commentary among the various possibilities of experience and being in a man's or woman's life. City peoples must contend with considerable discrepancies among dimensions of their experience, and it is one of the challenges of the study of urban religion to understand how practitioners live with such existential multiplicity. Theories of the power of slums over people's minds and hearts fail to appreciate the heterogeneity of even the most restricted and isolated urban worlds.

A Review of the Chapters Ahead

"How could the spirits [of Vodou] be active in New York," Karen McCarthy Brown asks, "if they were tied to the particular spaces and places of Haiti?" The first four chapters in this volume are concerned with the religious response of recent immigrants to American cities to this "cosmo-logistical problem," as Brown calls the spiritual and existential challenges confronting immigrants in the cities. Immigrants recrafted inherited traditions, invented new ritual practices, and reconfigured the meanings of cities with improvisatory religious practices of stone and space. They re-created particular spaces in the cities to better serve their religious needs. The cities had to be transformed into suitable environments for communicating with spirits, gods, and ancestors whose identities were fundamentally linked to other places. And in the process of working on the city, religious idioms were transformed as well: readers should take note of what becomes of Vodou, Hinduism, Cuban Catholicism, and Santería as practitioners of traditions use them to engage the cities.

Brown writes about Haitian immigrants looking for ways to feed the spirits, whose nourishment usually comes through the soil and water of Africa and Haiti, in their new homes on top of the "concrete, metal pylons, water and sewer pipes" of Brooklyn. Joanne Punzo Waghorne, describing the construction of the Sri Siva-Vishnu Temple in Lanham, Maryland, by highly mobile, middle-class Indian immigrants, points out that the temple (which was located on a site chosen for its convenient access to adjacent highways and not for any traditional coordinates) is poised between the spiritual geography of "India," envisioned by emigrants as sacred and unchanging, and "America," the land of action, work, and material success to which the emigrants have journeyed. The design and construction of the spaces of the temple became the occasion for a reworking of Hindu identity and practice, of gender and relationships between generations, in this complex intersitial space.

The Cuban migrants who come to the Shrine of Our Lady of Charity, discussed in Thomas Tweed's essay, are exiled from a homeland that is tantalizingly close. They have remapped Miami in the image of the "Cuba" of their desire in a distinctly diasporic mimesis: Miami becomes Cuba. The shrine is one pivot of this religious and nationalistic re-imagining. "Cuba and the Virgin are the same thing," a shrine visitor told

Tweed. The rituals that take place at the shrine—which is constructed around a cornerstone made from sand from each of the Cuban provinces mixed with water from the bottom of a raft on which fifteen people died making the crossing to Miami—dissolves the distance between here and there, desire and memory, to "unite the Virgin's devotees in Miami with other Cubans" in "an imagined moral community."

None of the religious practices discussed in this volume are univocal; it becomes clear that it is impossible to talk about a singular Cuban American or Haitian religious culture. All practices are fissured by conflict and dissent and by discrepant desires, memories, and ambitions. Immigrant urban religions are inevitably unstable and polysemous. Tweed shows, for example, that Cubans of different religious and political affiliations, social classes, and generations sharply contest the meanings of the site.

One of the sources of conflict at the Shrine of Our Lady of Charity has been the appearance in this place of practitioners of Afro-Cuban religions, which, although widely practiced among all social classes in Cuba, are prohibited by the Catholic Church. This Afro-Cuban religion forms the subject of David Brown's essay. Brown begins by detailing the extraordinarily intricate cosmology, ritual idioms, symbolic language, and visual semiotics of Afro-Cuban religions (which draw on both Roman Catholic and Yoruba sources). Then he turns to a consideration of the aesthetic practices by which city spaces are made into homes for the spirits and altars for their celebrations. He is especially concerned with the redesign of apartment interiors by Santería priests. Serving the spirits entails constant work in a yearly cycle of rituals. The necessary materials for these redecorations are obtained from *botanicas*, special markets serving as local outlets in an international circulation of ritual objects moving among Africa, the Caribbean, and American cities.

Brown's essay closes with an examination of some recent efforts to curtail Afro-Cuban religious practices on the part of animal rights advocates, city and state government officials, Cuban emigrants disdainful of these idioms, and American Christians who fear them as Satanic. Santería is represented in these hostile campaigns, Brown notes, as "a malign growth infecting assimilated middle-class urban cultural space." This is a recent example of the metaphorical discourse of disease that has lent the urgency of the body at risk from disease to campaigns of social and religious discipline since the late nineteenth century.

Descendants of earlier generations of immigrants to the United States are the focus of the next four chapters in the volume. We turn from streets and buildings to urban religious narrative practice in Jack Kugelmass's presentation of Moishe Sacks's Scriptural and Talmudic rendering of the South Bronx landscape. My chapter traces the negotiation of the meanings of ethnicity and race on the unstable borders among Italian Americans, Puerto Ricans, and Haitians at the annual feast of Our Lady of Mount Carmel, within the broader context of American racial ideology. Madeline Duntley describes how a heterogeneous Asian Christian Presbyterian congregation in Seattle, internally divided by ethnicity, generation, and language, has created and re-created its Christian, Asian, and American identities in ritual and in the building and rebuilding of its church structure. Finally, Joseph Sciorra details the rich world of Italian American street festivals in Brooklyn and discusses how these neighborhood events both inscribe and transgress neighborhood and ethnic boundaries.

Urban street performances—the mapping and remapping of city space by religious procession—are the topic of the final two chapters of this collection as well. Wayne Ashley writes about the Good Friday procession developed in the 1970s and 1980s at St. Brigid's Church on New York's Lower East Side. The pilgrimage of Stations of the Cross began as the combined efforts of clergy and their mostly Puerto Rican congregants. But over time the interests of the two parties diverged, and the annual Holy Week event turned into an occasion of bitter conflict. The clergy of St. Brigid's Church imagined the local populace as a community of resistance; they also incorrectly thought that their working-class congregation had the same interests as the neighborhood's homeless population. Operating under this misapprehension, as Ashley understands the situation, the priests took the annual Stations of the Cross in political directions that outraged and alienated the community.

Another kind of religious movement through space occupies Diane Winston: the Salvation Army's processions and parades across New York City in the nineteenth century. While the ubiquitous red kettle nostalgically evoked the nurture and plenty of idealized frontier homes, the Army's turn to parades and spectacles as a way of both confronting and co-opting the city's riotous secular entertainments represented a creative innovation in city work that reflected its leadership's recognition of the "need for latitude in saving souls," as Winston writes. The Army's presence on the streets built a "cathedral of the open air" out of the city, and challenged the distinction between sacred and profane that inhibited, as Army thinkers saw it, the efficacy of the mainstream churches in meeting the crisis of the industrial city. The point, they said, was to "sanctify the commonplace."

Back to Genesis Garden

A number of contemporary scholars of the post-industrial city have issued dire warnings about the moral and cultural implications of the peculiar spatial configurations of these environments. The segregation of generations and classes is more pronounced now. Elderly persons, children, adolescents, and poor people are stranded by the necessity of automobiles in the vastly dispersed new metropolitan regions. The bonds of social responsibility and accountability become attenuated in this spatial context, some theorists claim, and the invisibility of the classes to each other leads to deepening social callousness, alienation, and irresponsibility among elites, and to passivity and helplessness among the poor. There is no place in the spaceless city, moreover, for individuals to stand and take stock of themselves. If human interiority is constituted by engagement with others in a recognizable and spatially situated social world over which residents have some reasonable influence—the "where I come from" with which people respond to queries about who they are and what they value—then the spread-out, centerless cities of today make it all but impossible to anchor values, create new cultural practices, and establish existential priorities. How do contemporary migrants to the city, the people who live in between two places, ground a secure sense of themselves? These issues became pressing amid the spatial arrangements of the industrial city, and they persist amid those of the post-industrial city.[100]

Clearly, city people, many of whom have come to the cities from elsewhere, have had to contend with the social, psychological, and cultural implications of the arrangements of space in and through which they have lived. The specific configurations of urban landscape reviewed in this introduction, from the division of social classes that begins in the early industrial city to the environmental revolutions of the turn of the century to the transformed experience of space in the post-industrial city, have represented real challenges to the quality of human life in cities and to the kinds of worlds people may make for themselves in these environments. The emphasis in this collection is on the active engagement of city people with the conditions and implications of their environments. The essays provide a series of soundings into the cultural creativity and religious improvisations of city people over the last fifty years. The authors hold in tension an awareness of the forces bearing down on city people with a perception of the cultural resources, specifically religious, with which contemporary city dwellers have met these challenges and explored new possibilities of meaning and being.

It is not enough to say that the dispersal of families across the extended urban terrains of the post-industrial city threatens to undermine the sort of kinship connections that helped earlier generations of migrants and immigrants prosper in the industrial city. We have to ask how people respond to the challenge of distance by generating new cultural forms. The friendships that anchor and endorse cultural and religious values may be more difficult to sustain on this landscape; many factors beyond the control of individuals or communities are changing the nature of urban interpersonal bonds. But space does not simply act on people; city people contend with space, and it is in their religious practice that they struggle with the most intimate dimensions of spatial challenges. As Anthony Cohen writes, *"People enculture the city,* rather than responding passively to its deterministic power."[101]

Religious imaginings have taken up the life of the city—its spaces, pains, and dangers as well as its hopes, excitements, and possibilities—and have made life in the daunting and exciting conditions of industrial and post-industrial cities not simply possible but enjoyable and meaningful. The city is compelling—and pleasing—to its inhabitants, those there by birth or circumstance as well as those there by freer choice. This is not romanticism; it is a fact of urban life.

A good part of this introduction has been devoted to establishing a distinction between the religious practices of working-class immigrants and migrants in the industrial and post-industrial city and the experience of the city as a realm of desire, fear, fantasy, and "sacrality." Encounters with the urban holy, as I call the charged fantasy of the city in the imaginations of religious activists and seekers, have been fundamentally shaped by the realities of race and class in American culture. There was spiritual power in crossing the line drawn by intense and incessant cultural activity—the line that divided neighborhoods where poor people, foreigners, Catholics, Jews, and blacks lived, and those where "Americans" lived. Across the line one could approach and appropriate the spiritual and existential vitality of populations and spaces designated as other; one could dream of being consumed by the city, as Jane Addams did—of emptying oneself out to be filled by it. But the power of the complex desires directed toward the compelling city obscured the lived experience of the working-class, immigrant, and migrant peoples there, and still does. So we had to begin our approach to urban religions with a social history of the processes by which the city became alien.

But I want to return now, at the end, to Genesis Garden in the South Bronx. From my first meeting with Marty and the Franciscans, I was troubled both by what I understood to be the religious romanticism by which they construed the city, on the one hand, and by the coincident and unavoidable fact that it was just this way of imagining the city that led these men and women to lives of tremendous sacrifice and generosity in the most dangerous city neighborhoods inhabited by the most destitute and needy populations. The same might be said of Jane Addams, David Wilkerson, Dorothy Day, and other pilgrims to the city, of whom I would ask the same critical questions framed by the history outlined in this chapter. Against this way of thinking of the city, the essays in this volume offer a rigorous, self-critical, analytical, historically conscious empiricism, which itself is both an intellectual and a moral orientation.

Yet it is clear that the line between the work of the Franciscans in—and on—the South Bronx and the remaking of the meanings of metropolitan space by Italian street *feste*, for example, or Moishe Sacks's narrative activity, Santería ritual, or Vodou practice, is not absolute. The interplay of stone and imagination, realism and hope, city space and religious narrative that characterized Genesis Park is evident in the religious workings and reworkings of the city by immigrants and migrants, too. Although they come to their city work from very different starting points, the migrants and immigrants and the Franciscans, who can stand in here for all religious pilgrims to and servants of the industrial and post-industrial city, meet on the shared ground of the religious imagination at work on the city. This is the ground that the essays in this collection explore.

Notes

1. I first told this story in "Reimagining the World: Franciscans Find God in the South Bronx," *Village Voice*, August 4, 1987, 25–26.

2. The best account of this period in the history of the Bronx is Jill Jonnes, *We're Still Here: The Rise, Fall, and Resurrection of the South Bronx* (Boston and New York: Atlantic Monthly Press, 1986).

3. Victor Turner, *Dramas, Fields, and Metaphors: Symbolic Action in Human Society* (Ithaca: Cornell University Press, 1974), 152, 231–71.

4. For a provocative discussion of the complicated and finally tormented relationship between an artist and the South Bronx neighborhood he set out to represent in his art, see Jane Kramer, *Whose Art Is It?* (Durham: Duke University Press, 1994). Perhaps I should note here that other interpretations of the artist's underground mural/performance are possible than the one I advance in the text.

5. Louis Wirth, "Urbanism as a Way of Life," *American Journal of Sociology* 44, no. 1 (July 1938): 1–24; see also Georg Simmel, "The Metropolis and Mental Life," in *The Sociology of Georg Simmel*, trans. and ed. Kent H. Wolff (New York: Free Press, 1950), 409–24. An important entry in the long debate prompted by Wirth and other urbanists of his generation is Herbert Gans, "Urbanism and Suburbanism as Ways of Life: A Reevaluation of Definitions," in Arnold M. Rose, ed., *Human Behavior and Social Processes: An Interactionist Approach* (Boston: Houghton Mifflin, 1962), 625–48; see also Claude S. Fisher, "Toward a Subcultural Theory of Urbanism," *American Journal of Sociology* 80, no. 6 (1974): 1319–41. For a classic statement of the moral power of slum environments, see Gerald D. Suttles, *The Social Order of the Slum: Ethnicity and Territory in the Inner City* (Chicago: University of Chicago Press, 1968).

6. R. Laurence Moore defines and discusses "moral sensationalism" in relation to antebellum accounts of the city in *Selling God: American Religion in the Marketplace of Culture* (New York: Oxford University Press, 1994), 12–39; my understanding of the ideological conflicts of this period are informed by, among other works, Jenny Franchot, *Roads to Rome: The Antebellum Protestant Encounter with Catholicism* (Berkeley and Los Angeles: University of California Press, 1994); David S. Reynolds,

Walt Whitman's America: A Cultural Biography (New York: Knopf, 1995); and Robert H. Wiebe, *The Opening of American Society: From the Adoption of the Constitution to the Eve of Disunion* (New York: Knopf, 1984).

7. Nathan Irvin Huggins, *Harlem Renaissance* (New York: Oxford University Press, 1971), 91; Huggins notes that after World War I, "Afro-Americans and Harlem could serve a new kind of white psychological need" (89).

8. For Wilkerson's story, see David Wilkerson, with John and Elizabeth Sherrill, *The Cross and the Switchblade* (Old Tappan, N.J.: Fleming H. Revell, 1979; orig. pub. 1963).

9. Jane Addams, *Twenty Years at Hull-House* (New York: New American Library, 1981; orig. pub. 1910), 218.

10. Ibid., 118, 187. Addams herself identifies the kenotic dimension of her quest when she reflects that the struggles to survive of the poor among whom she has gone to live are an embodiment of the Christian hope of "dying to live" (105).

11. For Addams's expression of a "certain sense of shame," see ibid., 186; Addams contrasts the emptiness of middle-class women's higher education in the United States, which she says puts them at risk of losing "that simple and almost automatic response to the human appeal" (64); for Addams's sense of loss and the compensatory attraction of immigrants, see pp. 92–93. A few years into her new Chicago life, Addams wrote that "subjective" motivations as well as the "objective" circumstances of the life of the poor had led to the rise of the American settlement house movement (Allen F. Davis, *American Heroine: The Life and Legend of Jane Addams* [London: Oxford University Press, 1973], 38). Davis emphasizes that Addams's discovery of social work at the moment when she was desperately trying to find a guiding purpose and meaning for her life (and to avoid the destiny of becoming a "maiden aunt") does not make her decision to found Hull House a purely personal one. The young woman had been inspired by developments in British social service, which she had observed firsthand in 1888, in particular by the examples of Toynbee Hall and the People's Palace (a philanthropic institute that provided working-class people with clubrooms, meeting rooms, and workshops), and by her reading of John Ruskin and Walter Besant (ibid., 48–52). As the idea of Hull House took clearer shape in her mind, Addams also familiarized herself with similar efforts in American cities, such as the Neighborhood Guild in New York City and the plans of a group of Smith alumnae to open a settlement house on the Lower East Side. Nevertheless, as Davis reports, psychological appeals were crucial in Addams's efforts at recruiting young people to work with her. She and her companion, Ellen Gates Starr, appealed to the pervasive sense of "uselessness and frustration" among middle-class college graduates to whom they spoke about Hull House; these young people, as Davis summarizes Addams's view, had led "overcultivated and undernourished lives" (ibid., 38). Starr wrote her sister in 1889, "Jane's idea which she puts very much to the front and on no account will give up is that it is more for the benefit of the people who do it than for the other class" (ibid., 56). Addams described Hull House to prospective participants as "a place for invalid girls to go and help the poor" (ibid., 64). On this period in Addams's life, see also Daniel Levine, *Jane Addams and the Liberal Tradition* (Madison: State Historical Society of Wisconsin, 1971), esp. 24–41, and James Weber Linn, *Jane Addams: A Biography* (New York: Appleton-Century, 1936).

12. Ann Douglas, *Terrible Honesty: Mongrel Manhattan in the 1930s* (New York: Farrar, Straus and Giroux, 1995), 74; Cowley on "virility" is quoted on p. 80. See Malcolm Cowley, *Narrative of Ideas* (New York: Norton and Co., 1934). On this period, see also Gilbert Osofsky, *Harlem: The Making of a Ghetto—Negro New York,*

1890–1930 (New York: Harper and Row, 1971); David Levering Lewis, *When Harlem Was in Vogue* (New York: Vintage, 1982); and Jervis Anderson, *This Was Harlem: A Cultural Portrait, 1900–1950* (New York: Farrar Straus Giroux, 1981).

13. Irving Lewis Allen, *The City in Slang: New York Life and Popular Speech* (New York: Oxford University Press, 1993), 230–31; for the use of "slumming" in reference to white visitors to Harlem in the 1920s, see pp. 74–75; Addams, *Twenty Years*, 63.

14. Marc Connelly, *Green Pastures* (London: Delisle, 1963; orig. pub. 1929). This edition contains a fascinating symposium of prominent Protestant theologians on the enduring power of the play's simple and concrete representations of sacred things to speak to moderns uncertain of their faith. In the theological reflection that opens the volume, Vincent Long tells readers, "We appear to be sharing, perhaps with indulgent condescension, the colorful life of some naïve negroes of the Deep South. We soon find, however, that we are entering into an experience of real religion" (ix). John Macmurray understood this reprinting of *Green Pastures* and the appearance of Bishop Robinson's *Honest to God* as "early skirmishes in the fight for the rediscovery of Christianity and the renewal of living religion" (111). Such are the hopes brought to the Other (Huggins, *Harlem Renaissance*, 300). Huggins concludes his discussion of *Green Pastures* with "Here, again, it was the qualities that whites had invested the Negro with, qualities that they had insisted on through the perpetuation of the stereotype, that made the emotional and spiritual experience possible. The black mask again was a way to psychic peace" (300). For a harsher expression of this psycho-social dynamic, see James Baldwin, *The Fire Next Time* (New York: Laurel, 1985; orig. pub. 1962), 129. Connelly reports in his autobiography that Broadway producers were initially unenthusiastic about a "play in which God was depicted as a Negro," fearing public disapproval; he also had trouble finding a theater that would book a black cast. A direct link between *Green Pastures* and the wild Harlem nightclub scene was established by the scores of black performers, trained in the latter ambience, who found parts in the play (*Voices Offstage: A Book of Memoirs* [New York: Holt, Rinehart and Winston, 1968], 165).

15. Huggins, *Harlem Renaissance*, 111. Malcolm Cowley tells a story at the end of his memoir about a friend's experience in Harlem on New Year's Eve, 1930: "After attending four successive parties he found himself in a sub-cellar joint in Harlem. The room was smoky and sweaty and ill-ventilated; all the lights were tinted red or green, and, as the smoke drifted across them, nothing had its own shape or color; the cellar was like somebody's crazy vision of Hell; it was as if he were caught there and condemned to live in a perpetual nightmare" (293). "Harlem" here becomes a medium for the articulation of a white man's self-disgust, and self-disgust, not surprisingly, is all this man can see around him in "Harlem" when he surfaces onto the morning street.

16. Wilkerson, *The Cross and the Switchblade*, 7–34; the phrase "dirty city" is on p. 83, Wilkerson's introduction of himself as a "country preacher" on p. 57. For other examples of and variations with this genre, in relation to New York City, see C. Kilmer Myers, *Light the Dark Streets* (Garden City: Doubleday, 1957); Dan Wakefield, *Island in the City: The World of Spanish Harlem* (Boston: Houghton Mifflin, 1959); and Bruce Kenrick, *Come Out the Wilderness: The Story of East Harlem Protestant Parish* (New York: Harper and Row, 1962).

17. This dynamic of obliterating social realities by a vision of urban holiness characterized, at least in part, and eventually undermined Monsignor Robert J. Fox's "summer in the city" programs in New York. Fox, a handsome and charismatic priest, organized the program in the mid–1960s as a means for bringing young Catholics

studying to be priests and nuns, many of whom had grown up in suburbs, into mostly black and Puerto Rican inner-city neighborhoods for a period of service, political awakening, and personal growth. According to historian and theologian Ana Maria Diaz-Stevens, in a thoughtful and quite positive review of Fox's work, "Fox made the Puerto Rican culture into a kind of sacrament; it was to be venerated as a sign of something sacred. Those who recognized the human values of Puerto Rican customs and traditions were placed in the presence of God's work among the poor of this earth" (*Oxcart Catholicism on Fifth Avenue: The Impact of the Puerto Rican Migration upon the Archdiocese of New York* [Notre Dame: University of Notre Dame Press, 1993], 151). Fox's programs accomplished much good, and by their own accounts the experiences of the young religious who spent time in city neighborhoods they might otherwise never have seen were transformative. But this had less to do with the everyday lived experience of Puerto Ricans than with images of Puerto Rican culture as "sacramental." The limits and intolerance of this sacral perspective were soon disclosed in Fox's growing alienation from Puerto Rican Catholics who refused to acknowledge the authority of his vision of their religious world. The divergence reached a crisis over Fox's efforts to transform the popular Puerto Rican fiesta de San Juan into a showpiece for his political and religious values (see Diaz-Stevens, *Oxcart Catholicism*, 158–60). "The mirth and frivolity of the crowds of people who annually came to picnic at the fiesta were seen as inimical to the higher purposes Fox had set" (162). Diaz-Stevens concludes, "The people, their needs, and their response were never completely or adequately understood" (173). Wayne Ashley traces a very similar conflict in his contribution to this collection.

18. Ira Katznelson, *Marxism and the City* (Oxford: Clarendon Press, 1993), 111.

19. The figures in the first sentence of these two paragraphs are from Paul Boyer, *Urban Masses and Moral Order in America, 1820–1920* (Cambridge: Harvard University Press, 1978), 67, and "The Urban Society," in John Blum, Edmund S. Morgan, Willie Lee Rose, Arthur M. Schlesinger, Jr., Kenneth M. Stampp, and C. Vann Woodward, *The National Experience*, 4th ed. (New York: Harcourt Brace Jovanovich, 1977), 443; see also Howard Chudacoff and Judith E. Smith, *The Evolution of American Urban Society*, 4th ed. (Englewood Cliffs, N.J.: Prentice-Hall, 1994), 37–77. The phrase "untrammeled commercial life" is from Witold Rybczynski, *City Life: Urban Expectations in a New World* (New York: Scribner, 1995), 95, as are the statistics and descriptions of New York City in this paragraph, pp. 99–100; the quote from Rybczynski in the preceding paragraph is from p. 49; this paragraph also relies on Katznelson, *Marxism and the City*, 193–99.

20. Asa Briggs is quoted in Katznelson, *Marxism and the City*, 143; Katznelson's reflection about the "urban break" is on p. 193. Mark Girouard discusses the increasing difficulty of getting a view of the whole industrial city in *Cities and People: A Social and Architectural History* (New Haven: Yale University Press, 1985), 343; see also Boyer, *Urban Masses*, 68.

21. On the gridding of cities, see Rybczynski, *City Life*, 44–46, 99; Rybczynski quotes John W. Reps on the New York innovation: "As an aid to speculation the commissioners' plan was perhaps unequaled, but only on this ground can it be justifiably called a great achievement" (99; from Reps, *The Making of Urban America: A History of City Planning in the United States* [Princeton: Princeton University Press, 1965], 132). Richard Sennett, *The Conscience of the Eye: The Design and Social Life of Cities* (New York: Knopf, 1990), 55; the grid plan "neutralizes the environment," Sennett writes, stripping away the "character of a place" (48, 51). For a wonderful

examination of how city people live on and against the grid, see William H. Whyte, *City: Rediscovering the Center* (New York: Anchor, 1988).

22. My understanding of this period in U.S. urban history owes a great deal to Paul Johnson, *A Shopkeeper's Millennium: Society and Revivals in Rochester, New York, 1815–1846* (New York: Hill and Wang, 1978); Charles Sellers, *The Market Revolution: Jacksonian America, 1815–1846* (New York: Oxford University Press, 1991); Elizabeth Blackmar, *Manhattan for Rent, 1785–1850* (Ithaca: Cornell University Press, 1989); and Wiebe, *Opening of American Society*. A useful survey is "Urban Life in the New Nation, 1776–1860," in Chudacoff and Smith, *Evolution of American Urban Society*, 37–77; see also Katznelson, *Marxism and the City*, 14–15, 203–56.

23. I draw the figures in this paragraph from a number of sources: Blum et al., *National Experience*, 288; Chudacoff and Smith, *Evolution of American Urban Society*, 114–15 (for the total of Irish and German immigrants between 1840 and 1890); Jay P. Dolan, *The American Catholic Experience: A History from Colonial Times to the Present* (Garden City: Doubleday, 1985), 128–30 (for the numbers of Irish immigrants between 1820 and 1840, and for the estimated percentage of Catholics among German immigrants in the 1850s); and Boyer, *Urban Masses*, 67 (on Irish immigration). The specter of the "strangeness of non-Protestant immigrants" in the nation's "teeming cities," writes George M. Marsden, was one of several factors contributing to the suspicion by the end of the nineteenth century that the "Christian era" in the United States had come to an end; *Fundamentalism and American Culture: The Shaping of Twentieth-Century Evangelicalism, 1870–1925* (Oxford: Oxford University Press, 1980), 102.

24. Boyer, *Urban Masses*, 55.

25. Richard L. Bushman, *The Refinement of America: Persons, Houses, and Cities* (New York: Knopf, 1992), 84, quoted in Rybczynski, *City Life*, 108, which is also my source for the detail about closed carriages. The comment about ethno-religious war is from Michael Feldburg, *The Philadelphia Riots of 1844: A Study of Ethnic Conflict* (Westport, Conn.: Greenwood, 1975), quoted in Charles R. Morris, *American Catholic: The Saints and Sinners Who Built America's Most Powerful Church* (New York: Times Books/Random House, 1997), 60 (without page reference); Morris also cites Hughes's remark about Moscow. On anti-Catholic violence in this period, see James Hennesey, S.J., *American Catholics: A History of the Roman Catholic Community in the United States* (New York: Oxford University Press, 1981), 116–27; Ray A. Billington, *The Protestant Crusade, 1800–1860* (New York: Quadrangle, 1962); and Franchot, *Roads to Rome*.

26. As Laurence Moore argues, although the assaults on working-class culture, especially working-class entertainments, by middle-class moral reformers persisted throughout the nineteenth century, their efforts succeeded only when the working class itself apprehended the value of reform; *Selling God*, 200–201. The comment on middle-class anxiety over "lower-class Irishmen" and the statistic on white-collar workers are from Steven A. Reiss, "The City," in Mary Kupiec Cayton, Elliot J. Gorn, and Peter W. Williams, eds., *Encyclopedia of American Social History*, vol. 2 (New York: Scribner, 1993), 1263. This paragraph is also indebted to Lori D. Ginzburg, *Women and the Work of Benevolence: Morality, Politics, and Class in the Nineteenth Century United States* (New Haven: Yale University Press, 1990), and Boyer, *Urban Masses*.

27. This paragraph is based on Boyer, *Urban Masses*, 30–32, 40, 51, 113–19, and 248; Kathy Peiss, *Cheap Amusements: Working Women and Leisure in Turn-of-the-*

Century New York (Philadelphia: Temple University Press, 1986), 180–82; and Colleen McDannell, "Christian Retailing," in *Material Christianity: Religion and Popular Culture in America* (New Haven: Yale University Press, 1995), 222–69. George M. Marsden notes that Dwight L. Moody emphasized "motherhood and domesticity" in his revival preaching, a reflection of "the widespread evangelical conviction that stability in the home was the key to the resolution of other social problems"; *Fundamentalism and Culture*, 37.

28. On the Salvation Army, see Aaron Ignatius Abell, *The Urban Impact on American Protestantism, 1865–1900* (Hamden, Conn.: Archon, 1962), 128–29; an excellent discussion of twentieth-century American Catholic anti-modernist agrarianism can be found in Peter A. Huff, *Allen Tate and the Catholic Revival: Trace of the Fugitive Gods* (New York: Paulist Press, 1996), 50–71; for a very sharp reading of Catholic homesteading, see James Terence Fisher, *The Catholic Counterculture in America, 1933–1962* (Chapel Hill: University of North Carolina Press, 1989), 119–25; for another example of Catholic anti-urban sentiment in the twentieth century, see Alden V. Brown, *The Grail Movement and American Catholicism, 1940–1975* (Notre Dame: University of Notre Dame Press, 1989).

29. Paula M. Kane, *Separatism and Subculture: Boston Catholicism, 1900–1920* (Chapel Hill: University of North Carolina Press, 1994), 111, 113; Kane uses the phrase "gospel of rural goodness" to describe the anti-modernist preaching of Boston's William Cardinal O'Connell, who exemplifies in her view the broader "anti-urban tradition among American bishops" in the twentieth century (110–11). "The theories and designs of Boston's Catholic architects," Kane writes, "can be viewed in part as an apologetic, an aesthetic, and a social critique of urbanism" (114). Olmsted is quoted in Alexander von Hoffman, *Local Attachments: The Making of an American Urban Neighborhood* (Baltimore: Johns Hopkins University Press, 1994), 82. Ernest Thompson Seton's "rooftop campouts" were the subject of a paper by Philip J. Deloria, "'He Said the American Pioneers Were Scalawags and Low Types': Daniel Carter Beard, Ernest Thompson Seton, and the Transformation of Scouting," American Historical Association meetings, Chicago, 1995.

30. The figures in this paragraph are taken from Blum et al. *National Experience*, 443; Douglas, *Terrible Honesty*, 4; and Reiss, "The City," population table on p. 1273.

31. The numbers here again are drawn from Blum et al., *National Experience*, 446; Reiss, "The City," 1267. Figures for Mexican migration are from Jay Dolan and Gilbert M. Hinojosa, eds., *Mexican Americans and the Catholic Church, 1900–1965* (Notre Dame: University of Notre Dame Press, 1994), and from George J. Sanchez, *Becoming Mexican American: Ethnicity, Culture, and Identity in Chicano Los Angeles, 1900–1945* (New York: Oxford University Press, 1993). Sanchez comments on the dramatic increase in the Mexican population of Los Angeles on p. 90. See also Rodolfo Acuña, *Occupied America: A History of Chicanos*, 3d ed. (New York: Harper and Row, 1988).

32. The population figures for southern and northern cities come from Evelyn Brooks Higginbotham, *Righteous Discontent: The Women's Movement in the Black Baptist Church, 1880–1920* (Cambridge: Harvard University Press, 1993), 171–72. On the great migration more generally, see Carole Marks, *Farewell—We're Good and Gone: The Great Black Migration* (Bloomington: Indiana University Press, 1989); Jacqueline Jones, *Labor of Love, Labor of Sorrow: Black Women, Work, and the Family from Slavery to the Present* (New York: Random House, 1985); Nicholas Lemann, *The Promised Land: The Great Black Migration and How It Changed America* (New York: Knopf, 1991). Dorsey's comment is taken from Michael W. Harris, *The Rise of Gospel*

Blues: The Music of Thomas Andrew Dorsey in the Urban Church (New York: Oxford University Press, 1992), 47; for a moving account of Dorsey's encounter with Jim Crow humiliation, see p. 48; the final comment in the paragraph is from p. 50.

33. Sennett, *Conscience of the Eye*, 60; the comparison with European cities is from Thomas S. Hines, *Burnham of Chicago: Architect and Planner* (New York: Oxford University Press, 1974), 47.

34. Douglas, *Terrible Honesty*, 192.

35. My understanding of the ecology of desire is informed by Peiss, *Cheap Amusements*, and more generally by Lewis A. Erenberg, *Steppin' Out: New York Nightlife and the Transformation of American Culture, 1890–1930* (Chicago: University of Chicago Press, 1981); Roy Rosenzweig, *Eight Hours for What We Will: Workers and Leisure in an Industrial City, 1870–1920* (Cambridge: Cambridge University Press, 1983); John F. Kasson, *Amusing the Million: Coney Island at the Turn of the Century* (New York: Hill and Wang, 1978). The complaints against recent southern arrivals by northern African Americans are from St. Clair Drake and Horace Cayton, *Black Metropolis: A Study of Negro Life in a Northern City*, vol. 1 (New York: Harper and Row, 1962; orig. pub. 1945), 73–74, quoted in Harris, *Gospel Blues*, 49, and see also 119. Harris writes that from 1920 forward, "old-line religion [in the North] was shaped by the mounting socio-cultural impact of migrant southerners" (121). On Marcus Garvey, see Rupert Lewis and Patrick Bryan, eds., *Garvey: His Work and Impact* (Mona, Jamaica: Institute of Social and Economic Research and Department of Extra-Mural Studies, University of the West Indies, 1988); Rupert Lewis, *Marcus Garvey: Anti-Colonial Champion* (Trenton: Africa World Press, 1988); and Robert A. Hill, ed., *The Marcus Garvey and Universal Negro Improvement Association Papers* (Berkeley and Los Angeles: University of California Press), esp. vol. 1 (1983), vol. 2 (1983), vol. 3 (1983), vol. 4 (1985), and vol. 5 (1986).

36. On African American comedy, see Mel Watkins, *On the Real Side: Laughing, Lying, and Signifying—The Underground Tradition of African-American Humor That Transformed American Culture from Slavery to Richard Pryor* (New York: Simon and Schuster, 1994), 384; on the "pansy craze," see George Chauncey, *Gay New York: Gender, Urban Culture, and the Making of the Gay Male World, 1890–1940* (New York: Basic Books, 1994), 257–58, 302–29.

37. Spengler is quoted in Douglas, *Terrible Honesty*, 4; the argument that Americans, including those living in rural areas, were "culturally speaking" urban is made by Rybczynski, *City Life*, 112–15. Rybczynski writes, "Because many new settlers [on the frontier] were themselves former townspeople and because Americans were inclined to move from place to place, the line between town and country—rural and urban—blurred. Life on plantations and country estates, especially in the South, could be as mannerly as life in the city, and life in small country towns and on prosperous farms was only slightly less refined. As a result, the United States is the first example of a society in which the process of urbanization began, paradoxically, not by building towns but by spreading an urban culture" (113–14). Moore's description of Howe's Coney Island film is from *Selling God*, 161; the final comment about the range of advertising's voice is from Douglas, *Terrible Honesty*, 20; on the history of advertising generally, I have learned from Jackson Lears, *Fables of Abundance: A Cultural History of Advertising in America* (New York: Basic Books, 1994), and Roland Marchand, *Advertising the American Dream: Making Way for Modernity, 1920–1940* (Berkeley and Los Angeles: University of California Press, 1986).

38. Andrew Delbanco, *The Death of Satan: How Americans Have Lost the Sense of Evil* (New York: Farrar, Straus and Giroux, 1995), 163, 164; for Delbanco's discussion

of the culture's preoccupation with the triumph of chance in cities, see pp. 141–53; the Pittsburgh and Allegheny church studies are cited in Abell, *Urban Impact*, 62. Abell makes it clear that middle- and upper-class Protestant urban congregations in these years found the cities ever more alien spaces (96); see also Boyer, *Urban Masses*, 133–42.

39. This discussion of the American Christian Commission relies on Abell, *Urban Impact*, 11–26, 55–56. Abell writes of the commission, "Its plan and philosophy of action were so comprehensive that all kindred subsequent movements could be but elaborations or specializations. Of special importance for its guidance of 'Christian work' in the early days, it created a tradition of religious and social sympathy which influenced all later social movements in American Protestantism" (26). On this period, see also Sydney E. Ahlstrom, "Urban Growth and the Protestant Churches," in *A Religious History of the American People* (New Haven: Yale University Press, 1972), 735–48. Ahlstrom notes that "large elements of the new urban population had no contact with any Protestant churches . . . [and] urban growth had created a serious cleavage in city population in relation to religious affiliation. The people who could afford churches were well churched; those who could not were unchurched—and hardly cared, or even regarded church people as their economic oppressors" (738).

40. Kevin J. Christiano uses the word "coalesce" in his discussion of Protestant responses to the Catholic urban presence in *Religious Diversity and Social Change: American Cities, 1890–1906* (Cambridge: Cambridge University Press, 1987), 135; see his general discussion of this dimension of urban religious history, 134–49.

41. Details about Wesley Chapel are from Abell, *Urban Impact*, 158–59. Robert H. Bremner points out that "by 1880 there were at least thirty undenominational societies supporting missions in the slums of different cities"; *From the Depths: The Discovery of Poverty in the United States* (New York: New York University Press, 1956), 58. On the evangelical impetus to the institutional church movement, see Marsden, *Fundamentalism and Culture*, 80–85. Marsden concludes, however, that the "evangelical endorsement and confirmation of the prevailing values of middle-class America" was "more prominent" in the holiness revival than social work. Evangelicals in this period were "dedicated first to saving souls, greatly occupied with personal piety, and held pessimistic social views" (85). Jon Butler challenges the standard narrative of the religious history of American cities, according to which Protestantism collapses in the face of the urban crisis, in "Protestant Success in the New American City, 1870–1920: The Anxious Secrets of Rev. Walter Laidlaw, Ph.D.," in Harry S. Stout and D. G. Hart, eds., *New Directions in American Religious History* (New York: Oxford University Press, 1997), 296–333; the quotations in the text are on p. 313. Christiano, *Religious Diversity and Social Change*, 13.

42. Brooks Higginbotham, *Righteous Discontent*, 7. On contemporary Brooklyn, see Clarence Taylor, *The Black Churches of Brooklyn* (New York: Columbia University Press, 1994), 191–234; details about Bridge Street AWME are on pp. 202–203. Samuel Freedman offers a moving portrait of a Brooklyn black church in *Upon This Rock: The Miracles of a Black Church* (New York: HarperCollins, 1993).

43. My understanding of this period is indebted to Robert M. Crunden, *Ministers of Reform: The Progressives' Achievement in American Civilization, 1889–1920* (Urbana: University of Illinois Press, 1984), esp. 3–38, 64–89, and John Patrick Diggins, *The Promise of Pragmatism: Modernism and the Crisis of Knowledge and Authority* (Chicago: University of Chicago Press, 1994). Addams warned that Hull House would be a "mere pretense and travesty of the simple impulse to 'live with the poor,' so long as the residents did not share the common lot of hard labor and scant fare"; *Twenty Years*

at Hull-House, 187. The point of the settlement house movement was to "settle!" an exasperated English movement pioneer exclaimed to a society lady who just could not seem to get it. "The essence of the settlement house" movement, writes Daniel Levine, was that "residents came to reside, and the institution developed in accordance with the personalities and perceptions of the residents confronting the situation of the neighborhood"; *Jane Addams and the Liberal Tradition*, 42.

44. See Ahlstrom, "The Social Gospel," in *Religious History*, 785–804. Charles Howard Hopkins, *The Rise of the Social Gospel in American Protestantism, 1865–1915* (New Haven: Yale University Press, 1940), is still useful. Hopkins identifies the period 1900–1915 as the time of the maturation of the movement (203). See also Martin E. Marty, *Modern American Religion*, vol. 1: *The Irony of It All* (Chicago: University of Chicago Press, 1986), 290–95. Marty offers an acerbic reading of the movement, especially with reference to the issue of race, pointing out that many Social Gospelers were "uncritical of Anglo-Saxon racist claims" (294). The quotations from Rauschenbusch in the text are from Sydney E. Ahlstrom, ed., *Theology in America: The Major Protestant Voices from Puritanism to Neo-Orthodoxy* (Indianapolis: Bobbs-Merrill, 1967), 557.

45. Addams, *Twenty Years at Hull-House*, 89, 104.

46. This paragraph relies on Abell, *Urban Impact*, 225–31.

47. On Dorothy Day, Peter Maurin, and the Catholic Worker movement, see William D. Miller, *A Harsh and Dreadful Love: Dorothy Day and the Catholic Worker Movement* (New York: Liveright, 1972); idem, *Dorothy Day: A Biography* (San Francisco: Harper and Row, 1982); Mel Piehl, *Breaking Bread: The Catholic Worker and the Origin of Catholic Radicalism in America* (Philadelphia: Temple University Press, 1982); and Fisher, *Catholic Counterculture*, 1–129. On Baroness de Hueck's interracial efforts, see Catherine de Hueck, *Friendship House* (New York: Sheed and Ward, 1947). For a moving firsthand account of Monsignor Robert J. Fox's "summer in the city" programs, see Mary Cole, *Summer in the City* (New York: R. J. Kenedy, 1968).

48. On the investigative efforts of the COS, see Boyer, *Urban Masses*, 150. Robert H. Bremner places a somewhat different emphasis on the charity organization movement's means and purposes. The Charity Organization Societies, he says, "sought to foster a better administration of private charities," by coordinating the work of separate philanthropic agencies and collecting necessary information about needy persons. Persons seeking assistance were subject to "rigid examinations" for certification as worthy poor, writes Bremner, and the COS volunteers who went out to visit the needy were "expected to be combination detectives and moral influences." Their work was premised on the assumption that "some personal weakness of character, intellect, or body ordinarily redounded to the distress of the poor." But the apparent harshness of COS visitors and officers "was simply the result of a sincere effort to do a difficult task in a competent manner." The information they gathered made possible "a fund of more reliable and comprehensive data on the economic and social problems of the very poor than had been available since the days of the close-knit village economy." They treated poverty as an "abnormal," "unnecessary," and "curable" condition, and their case study method emphasized an "objective and factual" approach to the problem. Bremner concludes that while the charity organization movement had begun as "the expression of a somewhat narrow, moralistic, and individualistic attitude toward poverty," the direct experience of the conditions of poverty by case workers induced "many" COS representatives to shift their understanding of the roots of poverty from personal to industrial causes. Bremner, *From the Depths*, 51–57. For a brief comparison of settlement house workers and charity organization society visitors

more akin to the one I offer here, see Levine, *Jane Addams and the Liberal Tradition*, 47.

49. Boyer, *Urban Masses*, 218; the reference to "scum of creation" is from Delbanco, *Death of Satan*, 165; the description of urban apocalypses is from Boyer's *Urban Masses*, 131. Kenneth T. Jackson estimates that the Invisible Empire enrolled some 2,030,000 persons between 1915 and 1944 (about 1,500,000 of whom were active at any time), and fully half of them resided in "metropolitan areas of more than 50,000 persons." Thirty-two percent (650,000) lived in metropolitan areas containing more than 100,000 persons in 1920. The leadership at the Imperial Palace, furthermore, was dominated by men of urban backgrounds or experience. As Jackson concludes, "These grand dragons may have occasionally denounced the iniquities of urban politics or offered lip service to the virtues of farm and country, but they chose the city for themselves and thereby set the pattern for the Invisible Empire." *The Ku Klux Klan in the City, 1915–1930* (New York: Oxford University Press, 1967), 237–38.

50. Peiss, *Cheap Amusements*, 98, 104, and 50, on the Committee of Fourteen, the Committee on Amusements and Vacation Resorts of Working Girls, and the YWCA, respectively. On the Watch and Ward Society and the Committee for the Suppression of Vice, see Kane, *Separatism and Subculture*, 66–67, 306–307. See also Chauncey's discussion of state liquor licensing authorities, *Gay New York*, 336–37; the phrase quoted at the end of the paragraph is on p. 347.

51. The phrase "moral environmentalism" is from von Hoffman, *Local Attachments*, 73; on Strong, see Ahlstrom, *Religious History*, 849–50; Addams, *Twenty Years at Hull-House*, 169, 299.

52. For Park's awareness that he was shocking "average readers" with his accounts of the city, see Robert E. Park, "The City: Suggestions for the Investigation of Human Behavior in the Urban Environment," in Robert E. Park and Ernest W. Burgess, eds., *The City: Suggestions for Investigation of Human Behavior in the Urban Environment* (Chicago: University of Chicago Press, 1967; orig. pub. 1925), 1–46. The phrase "average reader" is on p. 3; "moral regions" are discussed on pp. 43–46; "weakening of the restraints and inhibitions" appears on p. 25.

53. For Park's social psychology of the city, see ibid., 40–41; also Ernest W. Burgess, "The Growth of the City: An Introduction to a Research Project," in Park and Burgess, *The City*, 47–72; and Robert E. Park, "Community Organization and Juvenile Delinquency," ibid., 99–112. The final comment in this paragraph is from Ernest W. Burgess, "Can Neighborhood Work Have a Scientific Basis?" ibid., 153. Geographer Paul Wheatley comments on the negative orientation of the Chicago School toward the city in the broader context of what he sees as the "predominantly anti-urban sentiment" in British and American intellectual traditions of cultural geography, in *City as Symbol* (London: Lewis, 1969), 7.

54. Sunday's advice to God is quoted in Roger A. Bruns, *Preacher: Billy Sunday and Big Time American Evangelism* (New York: Norton, 1992), 147; Bruns discusses Sunday's objections to the city on p. 140. On the role of "two enterprising promoters," Edward Young Clarke and Mrs. Elizabeth Tyler, in reviving the KKK, see Jackson, *The Ku Klux Klan in the City*, 9–23. Edith L. Blumhofer writes that Aimee Semple McPherson's revivals in Los Angeles "gave transplanted, entertainment-starved, working-class people a rich sampling of theatrical skill. At a time when Pentecostals shunned theaters, McPherson offered an appealing substitute"; *Restoring the Faith: The Assemblies of God, Pentecostalism, and American Culture* (Urbana: University of Illinois Press, 1993); 166. See also Blumhofer's discussion of another Pentecostal sensation, Edith Mae Pennington, on pp. 168–69.

55. James T. Patterson, *Grand Expectations: The United States, 1945–1974* (New York: Oxford University Press, 1996).

56. On the ethnic revival, see Richard D. Alba, *Ethnic Identity: The Transformation of White America* (New Haven: Yale University Press, 1990); Perry L. Weed, *The White Ethnic Movement and Ethnic Politics* (New York: Praeger, 1973); Jonathan Rieder, *The Jews and Italians of Brooklyn against Liberalism* (Cambridge: Harvard University Press, 1985); and Andrew M. Greeley, *Why Can't They Be Like Us?* (New York: Dutton, 1971). A text that defined and shaped the revival as it exemplified it was Michael Novak, *The Rise of the Unmeltable Ethnics* (New York: Macmillan, 1971). The pace of suburbanization from the 1930s forward is discussed in Rybczynski, *City Life*, 173–96; by 1935, Rybczynski notes, "suburban living was a well-established fact of American life" (175). See also Kenneth T. Jackson, *Crabgrass Frontier: The Suburbanization of the United States* (New York: Oxford University Press, 1985). For a representation of nostalgia for the old neighborhoods, treated in a different way than I am doing here, see Alan Ehrenhalt, *The Lost City: Discovering the Forgotten Virtues of Community in the Chicago of the 1950s* (New York: Basic Books, 1995).

57. Statistics on the Puerto Rican "great migration" are from Diaz-Stevens, *Oxcart Catholicism*, 12–13; see also Joseph P. Fitzpatrick, *The Meaning of Migration to the Mainland* (Englewood Cliffs, N.J.: Prentice-Hall, 1971); figures on African American migration are from Lemann, *The Promised Land*, p. 6.

58. The comment about the impact of urban renewal on the social fabric of cities is from Rybczynski, *City Life*, 161, as is the figure on the funds directed to cities by the Federal Highway Act. The contrast between boulevard and highway is from Marshall Berman, *All That Is Solid Melts into Air: The Experience of Modernity* (New York: Simon and Schuster, 1982), 165. My thinking about modernist dreams for the city was informed by, among other sources, Sennett, *Conscience of the Eye*; Peter Jukes, *A Shout in the Street: An Excursion into the Modern City* (Berkeley and Los Angeles: University of California Press, 1990); Elizabeth Wilson, *The Sphinx in the City: Urban Life, the Control of Disorder, and Women* (Berkeley and Los Angeles: University of California Press, 1991); Jane Jacobs, *The Death and Life of Great American Cities* (New York: Vintage, 1961); Douglas, *Terrible Honesty*.

59. Rybczynski, *City Life*, 160.

60. The modernist dream of "towers in the park" is discussed in Wilson, *Sphinx in the City*, 95–96; Sennett, *Conscience of the Eye*, 57–62. This paragraph also relies on Rybczynski, *City Life*, 149–72. Robert A. Caro, *Power Broker: Robert Moses and the Fall of New York* (New York: Vintage, 1975), shaped my thinking about this period, as did Jacobs, *Death and Life*.

61. Girouard, *Cities and People*, 380. The comment on "ever expanding regional areas" is by Mark Gottdiener, *The Social Production of Urban Space* (Austin: University of Texas Press, 1985), 4, quoted in Katznelson, *Marxism and the City*, 287. The information about shopping centers is from Rybczynski, *City Life*, 203, 207.

62. Katznelson, *Marxism and the City*, 285. Jacobs refers to all this as the "murder" of city downtowns; *Death and Life*, 171.

63. Ulf Hannerz's comments on world cities are drawn here from two sources: "The Cultural Role of World Cities," in Anthony P. Cohen and Katsuyoshi Fukui, *Humanising the City? Social Contexts of Urban Life at the Turn of the Millennium* (Edinburgh: Edinburgh University Press, 1993), 67–81, quotation from pp. 68–69; and idem, "The World in Creolization," *Africa* 57, no. 4 (1987): 546–59, quote from p. 547. Roger Sanjek, "Urban Anthropology in the 1980s: A World View," *Annual Reviews in Anthropology* 19 (1950): 151–86, quote from p. 159; Maxine P. Fisher, *The*

Indians of New York City: A Study of Immigrants from India (Columbia, Mo.: South Asia Books, 1980), 78.

64. On the issue of control of the streets in African American neighborhoods, see Brooks Higginbotham, *Righteous Discontent*, 204–205. Higginbotham writes, "The competing images of the church and the street symbolized cultural divisions within the mass of the black working poor" (204).

65. Moore, *Selling God*, 103; see also von Hoffman, *Local Attachments*, 73. On the Garden City movement, I have been helped by Girouard, *Cities and People*, 350–51; Rybczynski, *City Life*, 183–94; Wilson, *Sphinx in the City*, 100–105, 123–27. For the classic statement of the movement's vision, see Ebenezer Howard, *Garden Cities of To-morrow*, ed. F. J. Osborn (London: Faber and Faber, 1945).

66. Girouard, *Cities and People*, 355, 370. Jacobs has a strong critique of the Garden City movement in *Death and Life*, 205–206, 17–22.

67. Rybczynski, *City Life*, 128–29. On the white city, see also von Hoffman, *Local Attachments*, 202; Boyer, *Urban Masses*, 182–84. On Olmsted's participation, see Elizabeth Stevenson, *Park Maker: A Life of Frederick Law Olmsted* (New York: Macmillan, 1977), 395–99, and Melvin Kalfus, *Frederick Law Olmsted: The Passion of a Public Artist* (New York: New York University Press, 1990), 303–308. "Fusing moralism, class biases, and a desire for administrative efficiency," von Hoffman writes, municipal reformers "pursued a vision of a city unified by civic virtue. Nothing symbolized the urban reformer's vision more than the World's Columbian Exposition" (221). Burnham and his associates, Kalfus writes, insisted on a "uniformity of theme" in their commissions for the fair (304). In an oddly prophetic coincidence, one of the "common laborers" on the White City was Walt Disney's father (Hines, *Burnham of Chicago*, 74).

68. Episcopal churchman William S. Rainsford, who was a leader in the institutional church movement, reflected in his autobiography, *The Story of a Varied Life* (Garden City: Doubleday, Page, 1922), on his experience of the White City: "If things looked dark in New York . . . there was another city whose white, classic loveliness stood, for one summer"; quoted in Boyer, *Urban Masses*, 182. Olmsted caught another spirit in the working-class visitors making their way through the ordered environment. In a letter to Burnham while the fair was still under way, Olmsted lamented that there was a "melancholy air" in the crowd and that people's faces remained "too *business-like, common, dull, anxious and careworn*"; Kalfus, *Frederick Law Olmsted*, 306–307. Harvey Cox's reflection on the White City is from *Fire from Heaven: The Rise of Pentecostal Spirituality and the Reshaping of Religion in the Twenty-First Century* (Reading, Mass.: Addison-Wesley, 1995), 29; Sennett's comment is from *Conscience of the Eye*, 37.

69. Girouard, *Cities and People*, 355. Girouard emphasizes that Olmsted and Burnham did not share a single approach to the city: "Olmsted's schemes were all conceived in terms of people," and of the influence of landscape on subjectivity. Jacobs's comment is from *Death and Life*, 169. On City Beautiful, see also the warmer evaluation by Rybczynski, *City Life*, 133–48; on Burnham's Chicago Plan, see Hines, *Burnham of Chicago*, 312–45.

70. Girouard, *Cities and People*, 355; Sennett, *Conscience of the Eye*, 95; von Hoffman, *Local Attachments*, 221–22. The figure on the number of cities with planning commissions is from Boyer, *Urban Masses*, 268.

71. Rybczynski, *City Life*, expresses the contrast between the City Beautiful movement and the skyscraper as a "clash between horizontal ideals and vertical aspirations," and the triumph of the "city profitable" over the city beautiful (144, 147). On Le

Corbusier, see also Wilson, *Sphinx in the City*, 95–97; Jukes, *Shout in the Street*, 181, 193, 196, 202, 227; Sennett, *Conscience of the Eye*, 169–76; Girouard, *Cities and People*, 360.

72. Jacobs, *Death and Life*, 437. Le Corbusier is quoted in Sennett, *Conscience of the Eye*, 172. See also Berman, *All That Is Solid*, 167–69; the comment about the "flattened" urban landscape is on p. 169. Sennett notes that Le Corbusier changed his thinking after World War II in the direction of a more human-scale urbanism, but his prewar writings were the more influential in the development of contemporary cities. Le Corbusier, Berman argues, was at least interested in healing the wounds of modern urbanism, essentially by effacing the city, whereas "more typical of the modernist movement in architecture was an intense and unqualified hatred for the city, and a fervent hope that modern design and planning could wipe it out" (169). For a complex and deeply moving tour of this flattened landscape, see ibid., 290–312.

73. Alasdair MacIntyre, *Secularization and Moral Change* (New York: Oxford University Press, 1967), 14–15, quoted in Christiano, *Religious Diversity and Social Change*, 122; Christiano offers a helpful discussion and incisive critique of the secularization thesis on pp. 118–33. For a review of the current state of religious historical scholarship on urban religion, with useful bibliographies, see Butler, "Protestant Success in the New American City, 1870–1920."

74. Mircea Eliade, *The Sacred and the Profane: The Nature of Religion*, trans. Willard R. Trask (New York: Harper and Row, 1961; orig. pub. 1957), 13, 24, 51, 116–59, 178–79, and 201–13. Eliade writes, "The religious sense of urban populations [in industrial societies] is gravely impoverished. The cosmic liturgy, the mystery of nature's participation in the Christological drama, have become inaccessible to Christians living in a modern city. Their religious experience is no longer open to the cosmos" (178–79). For a discussion of the continuing centrality of some version of the secularization thesis to the study of urban religions, see Callum G. Brown, "Review Essay: Religion in the City," *Urban History* 23, no. 3 (December 1996): 372–79. Influential studies of religion and ancient cities include Wheatley, *City as Symbol*; idem, *The Pivot of the Four Quarters: A Preliminary Enquiry into the Origins and Character of the Ancient Chinese City* (Chicago: University of Chicago Press, 1971); idem and Thomas See, *Form Court to Capital: A Tentative Interpretation of the Origins of the Japanese Urban Tradition* (Chicago: University of Chicago Press, 1978); Eliade's discussion of "city-cosmos" in *Sacred and Profane*, 47f.; Jonathan Z. Smith, *To Take Place: Toward Theory in Ritual* (Chicago: University of Chicago Press, 1987); Johanna Broda, David Carrasco, and Eduardo Matos Moctezuma, *The Great Temple of Tenochtitlan: Center and Periphery in the Aztec World* (Berkeley and Los Angeles: University of California Press, 1987); David Carrasco, ed., *To Change Place: Aztec Ceremonial Landscapes* (Niwot: University Press of Colorado, 1991). For an attempt to apply this theoretical orientation to the modern city, see Ira G. Zepp, Jr., *The New Religious Image of Urban America: The Shopping Mall as Ceremonial Center* (Westminster, Md.: Christian Classics, 1986).

75. Robert N. Bellah, Richard Madsen, William M. Sullivan, Ann Swidler, and Steven M. Tipton, *Habits of the Heart: Individualism and Commitment in American Life* (New York: Harper and Row, 1986), 32–35, 48–50, 333–34; on the enduring power of nature in American religious imaginings, see Catherine L. Albanese, *Nature Religion in America: From the Algonkian Indians to the New Age* (Chicago: University of Chicago Press, 1990).

76. My understanding of spatial "architectonic" and of the relationship in general between religious creativity and environment was influenced by James W. Fernandez,

Bwiti: An Ethnography of the Religious Imagination in Africa (Princeton: Princeton University Press, 1982); Gaston Bachelard, *The Poetics of Space*, trans. Maria Jolas (Boston: Beacon, 1969; orig. pub. 1958); Henry Glassie, *Passing the Time in Bally-menone: Culture and History of an Ulster Community* (Bloomington: Indiana University Press, 1995; orig. pub. 1982); Henri Lefebvre, *The Production of Space*, trans. Donald Nicholson-Smith (1974; reprint, Oxford and Cambridge, Mass.: Blackwell, 1991), esp. 169–228; and Tony Hiss, *The Experience of Place: A New Way of Looking at and Dealing with Our Radically Changing Cities and Countryside* (New York: Vintage Books, 1990).

77. Baldwin engages the meanings of the spaces of Harlem in many of his writings; for an especially powerful example, see the opening pages of "Down at the Cross: Letter from a Region in My Mind," in *The Fire Next Time* (New York: Dell, 1985; orig. pub. 1962), 27f.

78. James Baldwin, *Go Tell It on the Mountain* (New York: Dell, 1977; orig. pub. 1953), 215–16; Jack Kugelmass, *The Miracle of Intervale Avenue: The Story of a Jewish Congregation in the South Bronx* (New York: Schocken, 1986), 173.

79. Berman, *All That Is Solid*, 145.

80. Jill Watts, *God, Harlem USA: The Father Divine Story* (Berkeley and Los Angeles: University of California Press, 1992), 110; see also Milton C. Sernett, *Bound for the Promised Land: African American Religion and the Great Migration* (Durham: Duke University Press, 1997).

81. Kyeyoung Park, "'Born Again': What Does It Mean to Korean-Americans in New York City?" *Journal of Ritual Studies* 3, no. 2 (Summer 1989): 287–301; the phrase quoted is on p. 294.

82. The celebration of Ganapathy referred to here is from Fisher, *Indians of New York City*, 65–67. On memorial walls, see the powerful collection by Martha Cooper and Joseph Sciorra, *R.I.P.: Memorial Wall Art* (New York: Holt, 1994). Malcolm X refers to the pigs in *The Autobiography of Malcolm X* (New York: Grove Press, 1965), 194.

83. Harris, *Gospel Blues*, 60. The phrase "grievous, grieving tempo" is Dorsey's; "recombination" from Diana DeG. Brown and Mario Bick, "Religion, Class, and Context: Continuities and Discontinuities in Brazilian Umbanda," *American Ethnologist* 14 (February 1987): 73–93, p. 74; see also Diana DeG. Brown, *Umbanda: Religion and Politics in Urban Brazil* (New York: Columbia University Press, 1994).

84. This paragraph relies on Ray Allen, *Singing in the Spirit: African-American Sacred Quartets in New York City* (Philadelphia: University of Pennsylvania Press, 1991), esp. 50–74.

85. The phrase in the text is from Chauncey, *Gay New York*, 191. Jacobs refers to an "underlying order of cities," *Death and Life*, 15.

86. Jacobs, *Death and Life*, 74–88. "Conduits of sociability" is from Peiss, *Cheap Amusements*, 57.

87. David Vidal, "Hispanic Residents Find Some Gains amid Woes," *New York Times*, May 12, 1980.

88. Benjamin Karim, with Peter Skutches and David Gallen, *Remembering Malcolm* (New York: Carroll and Graf, 1992), 44.

89. The phrases in the text on Catholic parishes are from John T. McGreevy, *Parish Boundaries: The Catholic Encounter with Race in the Twentieth-Century Urban North* (Chicago: University of Chicago Press, 1996), 15, 22; see also Eileen M. McMahon, *What Parish Are You From? A Chicago Irish Community and Race Relations* (Lexington: University Press of Kentucky, 1995). Benjamin Karim writes that "walking,

mostly, kept Malcolm fit, and the many people he knew or would meet on Harlem's streets—the storekeepers, businessmen, mothers and children, the clergy, panhandlers—kept his spirits high"; *Remembering Malcolm*, 71.

90. Frank Bartleman, *How Pentecost Came to Los Angeles, As It Was in the Beginning: Old Azusa Mission—From My Diary* (n.p., 1928), 53. Bartleman writes, "When men came within two or three blocks of [Azusa Mission] they were seized with conviction."

91. For example, A. L. Epstein, "The Network and Urban Social Organization," *Rhodes-Livingstone Inst. Journal* 29 (1961): 28–62; Sanjek, "Urban Anthropology," 176; Ulf Hannerz, *Exploring the City: Inquiries towards an Urban Anthropology* (New York: Columbia University Press, 1980), 163–201, 233–35.

92. See, for example, Allen, *Singing in the Spirit*, 21, 76–94. Enduring pathways between northern and southern African American congregations are described in several essays in Clifford J. Green, ed., *Churches, Cities, and Human Community: Urban Ministry in the United States, 1945–1985* (Grand Rapids, Mich.: Eerdmans, 1996), especially Luther E. Smith, Jr., "To Be Untrammeled and Free: The Urban Ministry Work of the CME Church: 1944–1990," 52–76, and Robert Michael Franklin, "'My Soul Says Yes': The Urban Ministry of the Church of God in Christ," 77–96.

93. Chauncey, *Gay New York*, 195. This way of thinking about the city is indebted, whether consciously or not, to the innovations of humanistic geography in the 1960s and 1970s; for a useful review of this movement that is a provocative contribution in its own right to the human meanings of cities and space, see Steve Pile, *The Body and the City: Psychoanalysis, Space, and Subjectivity* (New York: Routledge, 1996), especially parts I and III. The notion of mapping I am developing here is akin to Barbara Kirshenblatt-Gimblett's "sense of the city," which she introduced in an important article on urban cultural studies, "The Future of Folklore Studies in America: The Urban Frontier," *Folklore Forum* 16 (Winter 1983): 175–234, esp. 185–90.

94. Fisher, *Indians in New York*, 70–71; Watts, *God, Harlem USA*, 111; on Brooklyn's Hasidim, see Jerome R. Mintz, *Hasidic People: A Place in the New World* (Cambridge: Harvard University Press, 1992), and Israel Rubin, *Satmar: An Island in the City* (Chicago: Quadrangle Books, 1972).

95. Baldwin, *Go Tell It on the Mountain*, 34.

96. Nancy T. Ammerman discusses this briefly in "Golden Rule Christianity: Lived Religion in the American Mainstream," in David D. Hall, ed., *Lived Religion in America: Toward a History of Practice* (Princeton: Princeton University Press, 1997), 196–216; for another example, see Richard Luecke's discussion of Chicago's Bethel Church (LCA), "Themes of Lutheran Urban Ministry, 1945–1985," in Green, *Churches, Cities, and Human Community*, 131–32.

97. Anna Deavere Smith, *Fires in the Mirror* (New York: Anchor, 1993), xxxiii; Hannerz, *Exploring the City*, 222.

98. Smith, *Fires in the Mirror*, xli.

99. Allen, *Singing in the Spirit*, 53.

100. For example, Aidan Southall, "Towards a Universal Urban Anthropology," in Ghaus Ansari and Peter J. M. Nas, eds., *Town-Talk: The Dynamics of Urban Anthropology* (Leiden: Brill, 1983), 7–21; Katznelson, *Marxism and the City*, 285–308; Cohen and Fukui, *Humanising the City*.

101. Anthony P. Cohen, "Introduction," in Cohen and Fukui, *Humanising the City?* 1–18, quote from p. 5. Cohen's hopes for the contemporary city are modest; fortunately, he says, politicians and planners fail, leaving it to city people to "take their destinies in their own hands, at least so far as their identities are concerned" ("The

Future of the Self: Anthropology and the City," in ibid., 201–20, comment on p. 217). The authors in the present collection, however, insist, on seeing city people in engagement with the social and physical environments—not simply on their subjectivities. On the other hand, because we insist that there have been many forces in the cities over which immigrants and migrants had little or no control, our approach differs from that proposed by the great geographer Emrys Jones, who in a more optimistic spirit declared, "We fashion our cities and are not fashioned by them" and "Men and women [in cities] move and live in an environment which they themselves have created." One of the major points of my introduction has been precisely to show how this is not true of American cities, or not simply so. This collection shares neither Cohen's pessimism nor Jones's optimism but instead examines the tension between environment and religious creativity. Jones's comments from "The City in Geography," inaugural lecture, London School of Economics and Social Science, May 3, 1962 (London and Southampton: Camelot Press, 1962), 23, 25. Likewise, we do not assert that urban religions are simply subversive or counterhegemonic, either; again, the emphasis is on the complexities of engagement.

Staying Grounded in a High-Rise Building

Ecological Dissonance and Ritual Accommodation in Haitian Vodou

Karen McCarthy Brown

Approximately 500,000 Haitians—about 8 percent of all Haitians—live in greater New York, an area that includes New York City as well as the New York and New Jersey communities that participate in the life of the city.[1] The majority of these Haitians serve the Vodou spirits. "Serving the spirits" is the more common expression among Haitians for what journalists and academics, as well as increasing numbers of Haitians themselves, call Vodou.[2]

Mama Lola, a Brooklyn Vodou priestess I have worked with for more than fifteen years, originally thought that her move away from Haiti would be a move away from the Vodou spirits as well. At that time, she said, "I don't think I'm going to need no spirit in New York." Yet whenever she tells this story, she quickly adds, "And I was wrong!"[3] Mama Lola found that the same pain and struggle that required the help of Vodou spirits in Haiti were present in New York, although in different forms, and if the problems were there, the spirits had to be there too. But how could the spirits be active in New York if they were tied to the particular spaces and places of Haiti? Mama Lola's solution to this cosmo-logistical problem is, on the surface at least, deceptively simple: "The spirit is a wind," she says. "Everywhere I go, they going too . . . to protect me."

There is another, perhaps more important, way in which Mama Lola and many other Haitians living in New York remain in touch with the spirits: they return to Haiti. While Haitians in New York may suffer the melancholy that comes from being away from home, they do not suffer the trauma of cosmic proportions that their African ancestors did when they realized that home was irrevocably lost. Even the sizeable number of Haitians in New York City who are undocumented aliens, and therefore cannot at the present time travel back and forth between New York and Haiti, have reason to hope that this will not always be their condition.

The ability of U.S. immigrants to go back to Haiti has important religious ramifications. Unlike the Africans forced into slavery in Haiti,

Haitians in the second diaspora have not lost contact with their ancestors. Those who return home regularly, like Mama Lola, often make a trip to the cemetery one of their highest priorities. (Once when I was traveling with Mama Lola, we actually stopped at her mother's grave on our way from the airport.) More significantly, for Haitians in New York, the Vodou spirits remain accessible. It is often possible to go back to Haiti for important Vodou ceremonies, but in more routine ways, the spirits can be well served in New York City partly because there is such frequent contact between the diaspora community and Haiti itself. The stream of arrivals from Haiti enriches the community's memory of songs, dances, and rituals. New arrivals and frequent travelers carry herbs from Haiti to be used in treatments in New York. They bring beads, icons, and ritual implements. They even carry bits of the soil of Haiti. All kinds of Vodou ritualizing goes on in New York, from acts of daily devotion to major ceremonies involving one or two hundred people.

The Haitian immigrant community in New York functions like an outpost of Haiti in North America. In fact, Haitians living in the United States portray themselves in this way. They like to call themselves the Tenth Department—that is, the tenth and last of Haiti's administrative districts. Thus Haitians living and practicing their religion in New York City are not so much immigrants, in the traditional sense of that term, as they are transnationals:[4] people with emotional, social, political, economic, and spiritual commitments in two places, and with the ability to move back and forth between these two places in order to make use of each to compensate for what the other lacks.

Transnationalism is a phenomenon of the second half of the twentieth century. In a general way, it is a condition made possible by affordable air travel, fax machines, and computers, as well as by the decreasing significance of nation-states and the increasingly enmeshed global economy. For Haitians, transnationalism is a particularly apt label, because so many of those now living in New York were driven to emigrate from Haiti by economic and social processes that originated far closer to New York than to Haiti. In order to understand how transnationalism affects the Haitians' experience of immigration in general, and specifically the religious dimensions of their experience, it will help to look even more closely at the contrasts between the Haitian migration to North America that began in the late 1950s, and the forced migration beginning in the seventeenth century that originally brought Africans to Haiti.

Migration as the Loss of Home

John Berger, writing about European immigration to the United States in the *Village Voice*,[5] captured the significance of the home immigrants left behind by calling on one of the simplest and most familiar images for the organization of space, two mutually bisecting lines. "Originally," Berger said, "home meant the center of the world—not in a geographical but in an ontological sense."

> Home was the center of the world because it was the place where a vertical line crossed a horizontal one. The vertical line was a path leading upward to the sky and downward to the underworld. The horizontal line represented the traffic of the world, all the possible roads leading across the earth to other places. Thus, at home, one was nearest to the gods in the sky and to the dead in the underworld. This nearness promised access to both. And at the same time, one was at the starting point and, it was hoped, the returning point of all terrestrial journeys.

Once cut off from home, Berger suggests that the immigrant

> never finds another place where the two lifelines cross. The vertical line exists no more: there is no longer any local continuity between [that person] and the dead, the dead now simply disappear; and the gods have become inaccessible. The vertical line has been twisted into the individual biographical circle which leads nowhere but only encloses. As for the horizontal lines, because there are no longer any fixed points as bearings, they are elided into a plain of pure distance, across which everything is swept.

Berger's image, intended to depict an Old World European point of view, somewhat surprisingly, also does an elegant job of describing the cosmology of Haitian Vodou.[6] I will use Berger's image of intersecting lines to explore some of the cosmological dimensions of the two Haitian diasporas.

The Religious Crisis Posed by Slavery

When those who serve the spirits in Haiti want to call their ancestral spirits up from the watery subterranean world they call Ginen, Africa, they draw a *veve* on the earth floor of the Vodou temple. Since each of the different *veve* is associated with a particular Vodou spirit, these transitory, mostly abstract, cornmeal drawings can be thought of as private passageways between the spiritual African homeland under the earth and the everyday world in which people walk upon the earth.

Almost all the *veve* begin with a simple Cartesian grid, two mutually bisecting lines. Most *veve* would fit in an area from two to three feet square, and they are often drawn around the *poto-mitan*, the sacred center pole of a Vodou temple. (If the *veve* are individualized roads leading up from Ginen, the *poto-mitan* is the highway on which all spirits can travel.) The vertical line of the *veve*, the first of the delicate lines of cornmeal laid down on the earth, radiates out from the *poto-mitan*, as if it were its shadow. The first line drawn in a *veve* is thus a horizontal reiteration of the vertical *poto-mitan*, the road that stretches between subterranean Africa and the sky (home to a particular group of the Vodou spirits, as well as to Bondye, god). The second line, which bisects the first, becomes a transformation of the surface of the earth. The point of intersection of these two lines in the *veve*, where a lighted candle is often placed, offsets and reiterates the point where the *poto-mitan* pierces the earth on its way from the land of the living to the land of the dead and of the spirits. The straightforward little cross that is the basic armature of almost all *veve* is one of the simplest forms in Vodou sacred geometry, yet once it is drawn on the floor of a Vodou temple, its rich polyvalence becomes immediately apparent. It is both a crossroads,[7] the ritually accented place where two roads meet at right angles, and a map of the cosmos itself; both a reference to an intimate corner of human-scale space and a cosmogram.[8]

The Earth, Where the Horizontal and Vertical Lines Cross

Africans enslaved in Haiti knew they could not return to their home-land. This realization was traumatic for many reasons. High on the list was loss of contact with the land, literally with the earth of the homeland, and therefore with the protection of the ancestors buried in that earth. The profundity of the loss may help to explain the significant cosmological shift that accompanied it: Africa was "spiritualized" and transposed to the New World, where it became an invisible but directly accessible parallel world lying beneath the feet of displaced Africans. It is a matter of some impor-tance that, with Africa lodged there, both the Vodou spirits and the ancestors could once again receive the libations poured for them. In contemporary Haiti, people use the word "Ginen" to refer both to the continent of Africa that lies across the Atlantic and to the home of the spirits and the ancestors that is found in the water beneath the earth on which they stand. Most frequently they use "Ginen" to refer to the latter.

There was precedent for such a maneuver in the traditions of the peoples of Africa represented in Haiti's slave population. For example, among the Fon of Dahomey, there was (and is) a belief that the dead reside under the water. The Fon still use common euphemisms for death that include reference to water (e.g., "He returned to the sea"; "She put her hair in the water"). What was new about the Haitian construction was the conflation of the ancestral homeland with the place of the dead. Perhaps there was no other way to solve the cosmo-logistical problems created by the loss of contact with continental Africa.[9]

Regardless of how much commercial traffic there might have been between Africa and Haiti, the inability to go back was the overwhelming emotional truth about the African homeland. For virtually all people brought from Africa during the period of slavery, travel across the Atlantic was in one direction only. It was this sense of profound loss, not confusion about geography as some have argued, that caused "Africa" to come across the Atlantic and lodge beneath the feet of Haitians.

Several Vodou songs indicate a preoccupation with the loss of contact with Africa. For example, a simple Vodou song, one announcing that "the family is gathered" and a ceremony is about to begin, ends with the words "Se Kreyol nou ye / Pa genyen Ginen anko" ("We are Creoles / Who have Africa no longer"). Two songs that follow this one in the ceremonial order can be heard as responses to such a raw statement of loss. The first is a sad, defiant boast: "Janme, janme / M'pa bliye Ginen ray-o" ("Never, never / I'll not forget the ranks of Africa"). But it is the second song that reveals a solution to the problem. In this song, the cosmos realigns itself.

> Depi anwo, jouk anba,
> Nan Ginen, tande la.
> Mezanmi, tout sa m'ape fe-a
> Nan Ginen tande.
> Bo manman mwen,
> Bo papa mwen,
> Nan Ginen tande.
>
> From up here, to down there,
> In Ginen they hear.
> My friends, everything I am doing
> Is heard in Africa.
> The family of my mother,
> The family of my father,
> In Africa they hear.

Once Africa is transposed to the bottom of domestic bodies of water, the ancestors (on both sides of the family) are within earshot, and also within range of prayers and supplications. As a result of the transposition of Africa into the New World, the souls of the dead in Haiti can be called back from the depths of local rivers and streams,[10] and the spirits also are within hailing range, hovering just below the surface of the waters. Witness the words of one of the best-loved Vodou songs: "Anonse o zanj nan dlo / Bak odsu miwa . . ." ("Announce to the angels [spirits] down in the water / back beneath the mirror . . ."). Offerings to Agwe, the sea spirit, placed on small rafts and floated in the ocean just off the coast of Haiti are said to sink suddenly when Agwe reaches up to claim his tribute. None of this would be possible if Africa had not dissolved into water and swept across the Atlantic to surround the colonies with protection.

Berger suggested that when the emigrant leaves home, the dead disappear and the gods become inaccessible. Something quite different actually happened for the African people who were taken as slaves to what would eventually become Haiti.[11] For them, history became archaeology; the homeland became the subterranean base of the new land.[12]

The second migration, the one to North America, involving perhaps as many as one million Haitians, poses different cosmo-logistical issues. For reasons that may already be obvious, Haiti could not simply be relocated beneath New York, as Africa had once been slipped underneath Haiti; and neither could Africa "move over" one more time. For Haitians of the second diaspora, Haiti is a very real and concrete place, about four hours away by airplane. Nevertheless, in New York, the loss of immediate access to Haiti is keenly felt, and this feeling is laid over top of the long-familiar sense of loss that surrounds Africa. In New York, the two deprivations become almost interchangeable themes. For example, some of the African people forced into slavery managed to carry away small bags of soil from Africa, when they could bring nothing else. In New York, charms and talismans used in healing are manufactured with pinches of Haitian soil that have been secreted in travelers' suitcases and carried to North America: a pinch of earth from in front of the family home, a pinch from the center of the market, or a pinch from the Port-au-Prince cemetery. A sense of yearning for contact with hallowed earth, African and Haitian, resonates through the ceremonies performed in North American cities.[13]

The reinstitution of peasant agriculture as a result of Haiti's successful slave revolution (1791–1804) means that the land itself has become a powerful symbol in Haitian politics and religion. The ritually accented role of the earth in Vodou is the result of ties to the land that are two centuries deep, and these resonate with ties to the land of Africa that are considerably deeper than that.[14]

The significance of the earth is, in the final analysis, its ability to connect human beings with their ancestors and with the Vodou spirits. The soil, which contains both the bones of the ancestors and the seeds of the next harvest, provides the context for exchange among the living, the dead, and the spirits. The living need the spirits to come from Ginen, the watery world below the earth, and to possess their "horses" in order for those spirits to gain voice and body. The living need the blessings, advice, and protection that only these embodied spirits can give. The spirits and ancestors, in turn, need to be nourished by the praise, the gratitude, and, most of all, the libations and food offerings that only the living can provide.

Pouring Libations in New York

Pouring libations, a common means of saluting the spirits in Vodou, provides a ritual arena in which to examine more closely the subtle cosmological shifts going on within the second diaspora community as a result of loss of contact with the Haitian soil—and at times in New York City, loss of contact with any soil at all. The routine practice of feeding spirits and ancestors by pouring a few drops of liquor, water, or perfume on the earth becomes highly problematic in New York City. Once, when I asked Mama Lola to talk about the differences between serving the spirits in Haiti and serving them in New York, the first thing she thought to mention was libations. "In Haiti, you got this big yard, and you pour the rum on the earth for the spirit," she said. "But here you pour it on the floor—and you have to be careful not to pour too much." It is far easier to imagine that libations poured onto the earth of Haiti make their way to Africa than it is to imagine that libations nourish spirits in any way when they are poured onto concrete, linoleum, or carpet, the most common types of flooring in New York apartments.

The loss of direct contact with the earth is not, however, the sort of dilemma that presents itself to Haitians in the abstract. The sense of loss is more likely to grow slowly. It is impossible to say how many times and in how many different ways the people who serve the Vodou spirits have to experience the impenetrability of the ground in New York City before they begin to feel that the spirits are starving, and they themselves are slowly being drained of life energy; in New York it is hard to keep believing that "from up here to down there, in Ginen they hear," when Ginen is so palpably inaccessible.

Yet I do not want to leave the impression that Haitians are literalistic and need to believe that the very liquid they pour out in libations finds its way into the dry throat of a subterranean spirit. Such literalism is hardly typical of those who serve the Vodou spirits. Rather, I want to speak of a subtler and more elusive process by which the physical spaces in which we live either reinforce our cosmological assumptions or grate against them.

What are the cosmological implications of living on top of a mass of concrete, metal pylons, and water and sewer pipes? How can a person feel rooted when the vibrations of subways can be detected beneath the streets and sidewalks? How can anyone stay grounded in a high-rise building?

I know a Vodou priestess who responded to the latter challenge by hauling a garbage pail full of earth up to her apartment on the thirty-seventh floor of a low-income housing project in Bedford Stuyvesant, Brooklyn. During rituals, she and the others who were serving the spirits in her small living room poured their libations there. Mama Lola found another, more subtle, solution to the dilemma posed by libations. For everyday ritualizing, she was careful to pour economical little dollops of liquid which were allowed to evaporate. But when she had a sizeable ceremony, she, like many other priests and priestesses in New York, placed an enamel basin in front of the altar to collect the accumulated rum, water, perfume, and other liquids offered to the spirits in the course of an evening's ritualizing. What was unusual about Mama Lola's approach was what she sometimes did with the resulting brew. She poured it into several small bottles, calling them "good-luck baths," and parceled them out to those who served the spirits at her home. These people then spread the "bath" over their bodies and went without a regular wash for three days so their skin would thoroughly absorb the liquid. This is an ingenious solution, even if the sheer volume of libations makes it an impractical one. The spirits in Vodou are as much in the person who inherits them as they are out there in the world. In theory, at least, one could feed them as well through the skin as through the earth. As a matter of fact, traditional Vodou initiations choreograph such double-track feedings of the same spirits, both inside the devotee and outside in the world. What is not entirely clear is whether recycling libations as baths does not foster, in spite of the good intentions, what Berger pictured as the twisting of the cosmogram's vertical line into "the individual biographical circle which leads nowhere but only encloses."

In New York, it is also possible to stay in touch with the land metaphorically by continuing the practice of the agricultural rituals that are central to Vodou in Haiti. Here the significance of the actual earth is condensed into the taste of yams, supposedly recently dug from that earth.

An Agricultural Feast in New York City

One of the most interesting Vodou rituals in the North American repertoire is the three-day *bouye yam*, "cooking the yams." Occurring at the beginning of fall, usually in early October, this Vodou ceremony was originally a harvest celebration. Except for initiations—and some priests and priestesses will perform those only in Haiti—the *bouye yam* is the longest and most elaborate of the New York Vodou rituals. Some families spend hundreds of dollars just to acquire the proper kind of yams in sufficient quantity to put on a good *bouye yam*. For most Haitians living in New York, even one hundred dollars is a significant expenditure, and the cost of the yams is only a part of the money required to stage these elaborate rituals. In Haiti the *bouye yam* costs considerably less because it works with the products of the land at the time when they are most abundant. The cost of the *bouye yam* ceremonies and the amount of energy required to pull them off in New York could be read as signs of a subtle lack of harmony between the religion and its current locus—that is, as a kind of ecological dissonance.

On the first night of a typical New York yam ceremony, the night known as the *kouche yam*, "putting the yams to sleep," a small number of people gather to pray over the large, hard, white yams, and later to install them on a leafy bed beneath a decorated altar table prepared for this event. Because it is almost always impossible to find the preferred *mombin* leaves, central to so many rituals in Haiti, New York ritualizers pull branches from neighborhood trees, or purchase decorative greenery from the florist. Almost any kind will do. Thus, in New York City, the agricultural dimension of the *bouye yam*, once both the context and the content of the festival, is reduced to a handful of anomalous leafy branches and a pile of yams.

Vodou yam feasts in New York are mainly about family. The second day of the *bouye yam* demands full attendance from the Vodou "family" of the priest or priestess staging the event. A dense, interdependent social network grows around a typical Haitian religious leader. These persons are not all blood kin, but they relate with one another as if they were; they expect the same privileges and take on the same responsibilities as members of a blood family. These New York Vodou communities are centers for the circulation of goods, services, and information essential for the survival of immigrants in New York. Mama Lola, for example, has a closet stocked with winter coats and warm clothing for recent arrivals from tropical Haiti. And on several occasions over the years, I have known her to give food and shelter to members of her Vodou community temporarily down on their luck. Given that most Haitians living in New York experience periodic unemployment, and when they are employed occupy jobs toward the bottom end of the economic scale, the survival strategy represented by participation in a New York Vodou community can make the difference between succeeding and failing. Vodou "families" thus function as safety nets for Haitian immigrants struggling to make it in the city.

On the second day of the *bouye yam*, people gather in the early evening for a celebration that may last until sunrise the next day. This large feast is the main event of the ritual cycle and the time when family, in both a literal and a figurative sense, is "gathered up," much as the yams are gathered up from the fields—both family and yams in the largest numbers possible. This is a time to exhibit and celebrate abundance. A particularly lively song sung on the second day of the *bouye yam* emphasizes the point about assembling family in force: "m'pral cheche layeh-a pou ramase zanfan-yo" ("I'm going to get a basket to gather up the children").

Sometime after midnight, the yams, along with a number of large dried fishes that have been "put to sleep" next to them, are raised from their slumbers and joyously paraded around the dancing area in front of the altar. In Haiti these ceremonies are exhibitions of the fruit of the farmers' labor, and therefore of the wealth and security of the family. Yams for the ritual are piled high on family land in rural Haiti, perhaps within sight of the fields from which they were harvested. In New York the yam rituals are confined to small living rooms and cramped basement quarters. As a result, the dance of the yams and fishes is often quite a boisterous scene verging on the chaotic, as fish, yams, and dancers circle around and around the room. The sheer human density of the *bouye yam* creates its own feeling of abundance, a type of human relational plenitude worth more in New York City than a mountain of yams.

What is constant in all Vodou rituals from Haiti to New York is that while service to the spirits is the main ritual agenda, a great deal of social commentary and social play goes on in and around the rituals. Loko, the Vodou spirit who is the patron of priestcraft, usually arrives to cut the yams. But before he has blessed the yams and sent them off to be cooked, he holds court with the people gathered to honor him. Every person there, if they all so choose, can line up for an audience with the spirit. I remember Loko at one such ceremony in 1986. As he dealt with each person — hugging and holding, chastising, giving advice — key information was simultaneously handed over to the community. Someone was about to go to Haiti to be initiated as a priestess; several were mourning the death of a young Brooklyn priest from AIDS; and one young woman feared for her children, who were being raised by her mother in politically volatile Port-au-Prince. After Loko left, Gede, spirit of death, sex, and humor, arrived to entertain the guests with his practical advice and raunchy humor while the food was being prepared.

During another yam feast, Marie, a diligent worker and faithful servant of the spirits, was called away from the kitchen when the group began to sing an appreciative song to Gede, a song that included a line describing Gede as "moun solid-o," a solid person. Praise for Gede became simultaneously praise for the hardworking Marie as people "threw the song" in her direction.

The climax of the yam ceremony is a sumptuous feast of peasant fare — boiled firm white yam and salted fish that has been soaked and then boiled. Traditionally, both are dipped in oil as they are eaten. It is plain peasant food served in copious amounts. The minimum definition of family in rural Haiti is "those who eat together," and the success of the yam feast is measured in the amount of food consumed and the number of people who leave no trace of yam or fish on their plates.

On the third and final day of the *bouye yam*, the spirits will be called again to direct the dismantling of the altar constructed for the event. Loko will also be asked whether he is content with the service offered to him. More important, this is a day for family and close friends, providing an occasion for them to process intimate problems with the spirits and to claim more of the spirits' time and attention.

It is no small undertaking to reproduce an African-Haitian agricultural holiday in late twentieth-century New York City. The ritually established parallel between the gathered yams and the gathered "family" may go a long way toward explaining the expenditure of time, money, and energy necessary for the *bouye yam*. That an agricultural festival would be the most potent and appropriate context in which to articulate and strengthen family ties speaks to the same connection between land and family that we have already considered from several other angles. But now the connection is entirely metaphoric. While the harvest festival is the occasion for the gathering, the ritual work in these rites is focused on surfacing issues in the community and on healing and strengthening people and relationships within that community.

Vodou-Catholic Pilgrimage in New York City

Several distinct African religious traditions blended with one another and with French Catholicism in Haiti to produce Vodou. About 80 percent of the Haitian population serves the Vodou spirits, and all of these people also consider themselves good Catholics. Each year in Haiti, there are half a dozen pilgrimages officially hosted by the Catholic Church, which are at the same time important Vodou events for most of the people who attend. The July pilgrimage to the Church of Our Lady of Mount Carmel at Saut D'Eau, near the town of Ville Bonheur, in the mountains northeast of Port-au-Prince, is one of the most popular of these Catholic-Vodou events.

Vodou spirits have both African and Catholic names, and Our Lady of Mount Carmel is also Ezili Danto. There are several Ezili sisters; Danto is the dark-skinned one. The stories about Danto (she has children but no mate; she is poor and struggles to support her family; she works tirelessly and is occasionally given to fits of rage) sketch a fairly accurate portrait of the average poor Haitian woman. As a strong, loyal, and hardworking mother, Ezili Danto has resonance for Haitian men and women alike. She is among the most popular of the Vodou spirits, and her annual Saut D'Eau pilgrimage attracts as many people as any religious event in Haiti.

Pilgrims usually spend several days in Saut D'Eau for the July celebration of Mount Carmel's feast day. They rent a room or sleep outdoors. Their days are packed full of activities that fall into two tiers. Many attend mass each morning; virtually everyone at least once follows that Stations of the Cross up a neighboring hill to the little chapel at its top where there is a large statue of Christ on the cross. These are largely Catholic events, but the same pilgrims also follow a parallel Vodou route. They go to a sacred waterfall that gives its name to the little town, and at this site many enter trance or communicate with the spirits through those who do. Pilgrims also go to a wooded area close to the church where the Virgin Mary is said to have appeared. Here, amid almost constant drumming, singing, and dancing, they await further apparitions of the spirits, especially of Our Lady of Mount Carmel (Ezili Danto) and of Saint James (Ogou, the warrior spirit who has fathered children with Danto).

People dressed as the Vodou spirit Azaka, a peasant farmer, wander the streets of the village, practicing humility through ritual begging, something the spirits command people to do. Others, in light Gede possessions, frolic in the streets with their faces covered in white powder, swigging on bottles of rum, and joking with passersby.

The two-tiered nature of the event, both Catholic and Vodou, is a form of semipublic deception in which almost everyone participates with a shrug and a wink. Pilgrims packed into the colorful painted buses that struggle up the narrow mountain road to Saut D'Eau sing lively Vodou songs to Ezili Danto until the bus takes the last curve and the church comes into view. Then they switch to more stately Catholic hymns addressed to Our Lady of Mount Carmel. The resident Catholic priest at Saut D'Eau gives daily homilies suggesting that those who serve the Vodou spirits will go to hell, and members of the Vodou hierarchy observe, without seeming very bothered by it, "That is the way priests talk." Everyone is together for the climax of the pilgrimage, when the statue of the Virgin is taken from the church and paraded in a circular route around the village.

Haitians in New York City feel their loss of access to Saut D'Eau and to the annual pilgrimage for Ezili Danto. They compensate in various ways. Some make pilgrimages to the Doylestown, Pennsylvania, shrine of Our Lady of Czestochowa, a Polish black Virgin and a manifestation of Mater Salvatoris. It is this black Madonna's image that usually represents Ezili Danto in Vodou settings. But Our Lady of Mount Carmel is also used to represent Ezili Danto because, like Mater Salvatoris, she holds a child on her arm. Only this Vodou connection explains why, in July, around the time of the feast of Our Lady of Mount Carmel, chartered buses to the Doylestown shrine of Our Lady of Czestochowa can be seen idling on more than one street corner in Brooklyn's Haitian areas. The priests who maintain the shrine in Doylestown knew nothing about the many Haitians who visit there until the summer of 1993, when the revelation of a possible Vodou connection caused quite a stir. So it is necessary for the Haitians who go there to keep their multiple religious allegiances well hidden.

Other Haitians go to the Church of Our Lady of Mount Carmel at 115th Street in East Harlem for the annual celebration. Here they spend the better part of a day performing, in extremely concentrated space and time, the nostalgic rituals of Saut D'Eau. A trip around the inside of the church, where small plaques of the Stations of the Cross can be found, substitutes for a trip up the hill next to the Saut D'Eau church. In Vodou, Gede is conflated with St. Gerard, who is pictured wearing a priest's black robe, so a few coins or a small food offering slipped into the hand of one of the black-clad clerical figures in a side chapel of the East Harlem church substitutes for looser exchanges with Gede on the streets in Saut D'Eau. Everyone comes together for the procession of the statue of the Virgin around the streets of East Harlem. This group includes a mixed staff of Catholic priests, mostly white Euro-American; Hispanics, currently the largest ethnic group in the area; Italian families who moved out of Harlem long ago but come back each year for the feast of Our Lady of Mount Carmel; and Haitians who do not regularly attend the church and usually come only on the day of the procession.[15] At this New York version of the Saut D'Eau pilgrimage, Haitians have to keep their Vodou allegiances much more carefully disguised than they do in Haiti.

The Transposition of Space

Mama Lola combines different techniques for acknowledging the Haitian roots of the Vodou spirits she serves. As we have seen, she returns to Haiti frequently, and there are some rituals she will perform only in Haiti. But Mama Lola and others who serve the Vodou spirits also re-create Haiti in New York, by transposing Haitian places onto New York spaces. Brooklyn's Prospect Park, for example, sometimes functions as Mama Lola's local Gran Bwa (Big Wood), a sacred forest where a key part of the Vodou initiation rites takes place and where routine healing rituals occur.

A more familiar yet related process goes on outside of religious contexts. Giving the unknown the name of the known is the most primal of responses to being dissettled. (This is, after all, how New York got its name.) So it is not surprising that Haitians in Brooklyn have named two local markets after major markets in Port-au-Prince: Marche en Bas and Marche Salomon. (It is more complexly ironic that one part of a notoriously bad Port-au-Prince slum is known as Brooklyn.) These latter examples, though less momentous, are nevertheless related to the transposition of Africa from across the Atlantic to comfortable proximity beneath Haiti, and to the condensation of the Saut D'Eau pilgrimage site into the space of a Catholic church on 115th Street in East Harlem.

The transposition of sacred spaces—African onto Haitian,[16] rural Haitian onto urban Haitian, and, finally, Haitian onto the U.S. urban landscape—is a continuous fluid process that results in a wide range of cosmological configurations that share an inner logic. People play with space in an effort to express the meaning of place—ultimately of *their* place—in the world. African religious cultures are particularly suited to this type of "play" because they are characterized by great flexibility. Africa enters the New World in the form of streams of changing continuity, religious habits of orientation within space that are articulated in terms of geography and architecture, but are not necessarily attached to particular spatial incarnations of these habits.

The simplest and most powerful example of such fluid habits of orientation is the crossroads, a central image for Haitians and for the various groups of African people represented in Haiti's slave population. Every crossroads, because it is the place where two opposed paths meet, refers to an encounter with otherness. When actual crossroads are treated as sacred space, ritualizing creates the possibility for such an encounter. In virtually all Vodou rituals, crossroads appear in a steady stream of shape-shifting transformations. To give just a few examples: the *veve* are based on a crossroads image; the opening salutations for a spirit move a devotee's body through a crossroads pattern; and in the opening prayers, the so-called sign of the cross is traced on the upper body again and again through fluid hand gestures. Once the ritualizing body has absorbed the crossroads, it has no trouble concluding that the place where Nostrand Avenue crosses Empire Boulevard in Brooklyn is an appropriate spot to leave a parcel intended for the Vodou spirits.

The Socialization of the Cosmos

The trauma of slavery apparently occasioned a shift in the religious sensibilities of those enslaved, a shift I have referred to elsewhere as the socialization of the cosmos.[17] Many of the spirits or deities of Africa have survived in clearly recognizable forms in Haiti, but there is a subtle and pervasive change among them. Their connections to natural powers of wind and rain, storms and lightning have not disappeared, but they have receded to the background. In the meantime, the social powers of these spirits have emerged as stronger and more embellished than before. Perhaps this happened because people became the most enigmatic and dangerous forces in the world of the African in Haiti. The Vodou spirit Ogou is an example of a particular kind of shift of character. Elsewhere I have discussed at length the changes that the African *orisa* Ogun underwent in Haiti.[18] These were changes in which his connections to metal and metalsmithing, for example, were subsumed in various military personae.

The refocusing of Ogun's character that went on in Vodou should be set in the context of the central and highly problematic role the military played in Haiti's history, and continues to play in its daily life. The Vodou spirits appear to be drawn like magnets to the most problematic and challenging of existential arenas.

The earlier discussion of the *bouye yam* illustrates another aspect of socializing the cosmos. In this ceremony, references to the land were attenuated through layers of displaced signification. Vodou images drawn from the natural world are not as helpful in New York as they were in Haiti in sorting out the challenges of life; they have little depth and resonance for those who have grown up in urban settings. In the living rooms, basements, and bedrooms where New York Vodou ceremonies are held, social dimensions, specifically the personalities of the Vodou spirits, now carry more and more of the weight of signification.

A Hidden Religious Identity

In significant ways, the experience of Haitians coming to the United States has not been like the experience of European immigrant groups, and there are few reasons to believe that with time it will come to parallel the Euro-American experience any more than it does now. Ever since Haitians succeeded in liberating themselves from slavery, they and their religion have been feared and reviled. Moreau de St. Mery, a Caribbean planter writing in the midst of the Haitian Revolution (1791–1804) who many believe provides the earliest description of Haitian Vodou practice, painted a portrait of the religion replete with blood, lust, and violence.[19] He also characterized its trance states as out of control and, worse, potentially contagious for outsiders who stumble on such rites. Others writing somewhat later made the point more directly: all a civilized person had to do was look at Haitian religion, and it would be clear that blacks were not capable of governing themselves.[20] Contagion, sex, violence, lack of civilization—these are constant themes in the larger world's image of Haiti.

In the sixteenth century, Haiti was accused of being the source of syphilis in Europe. In the nineteenth century, Haitians were accused of introducing tuberculosis to the United States. Then it was AIDS. In the early 1980s, when it was not yet clear that HIV infection had come into Haiti from the United States rather than the reverse, I heard many stories about New York Haitians losing jobs, apartments, and friends because someone connected them to AIDS or to Vodou or—on more than one occasion—to the overweighted combination of the two. The relentlessly racist stereotypes of Haiti and of Vodou affect the lives of Haitians in New

York City almost as much as their often precarious economic circumstances do. Those who serve the spirits respond by secreting their religious allegiances behind a fabric of half-truths, outright denials, and defensive maneuvers. Even young Haitian children in the United States know that there are two ways of talking: one within the Vodou family and one outside it. For example, Mama Lola's son once crowed with delight when I affirmed his intuitive decision that it was probably not a good idea to discuss Papa Gede with the Catholic priest who was conducting his First Communion classes. When another child in the family had her First Communion, Mama Lola actually staged a two-tier celebration. Upstairs was the Christian event. There was a huge table loaded with food, and in the midst of it, a family Bible placed next to a cake baked in the shape of an open Bible. To acknowledge the diversity among her guests, Mama Lola arranged to have both Catholic and Protestant prayers offered before the meal. But only some of the people upstairs were invited down to the basement, where a smaller table allowed the Vodou spirits to share in the day's feast. The concrete evidence of Vodou practice in New York is kept carefully segregated within the private corners of Haitian homes, often behind closed and locked doors.

When I first met Mama Lola in the summer of 1978, her altars were in a tiny room in the back of her townhouse basement, a room that she could close and lock when someone came to read the electric meters. Inside the room, however, her altar for the sweet-tempered Rada spirits was out in the open on a big table. The fiery Petwo spirits had their altar on a similar table placed at right angles to the first, and the Gede's low-to-the-ground, stair-step altar was in a corner of the same room. Yet by 1982, both the Rada and Petwo altars had disappeared behind closed doors. First, the Petwo altar went into a closet in the small basement room. Some months later, a tall metal cabinet with locking double doors was purchased to house the Rada altar. With this arrangement, Mama Lola could lock up her altars before she locked the altar room itself.

In 1984 Mama Lola moved from that house because one of the neighbors had started to complain about her being "a Vodou Lady." She moved again in 1987 for a similar reason. Recently, however, things have shifted back toward more openness. I do not know what all the reasons are for this, but I suspect that one is the publication in 1991 of our book, *Mama Lola: A Vodou Priestess in Brooklyn*. In the last few years, Mama Lola has had a great deal of positive response to her religion and to herself as a professional healer within that tradition. So the curtains have recently come down from the latest incarnation of her spirit altars, and she has expanded the size of her altar room and taken great care in redecorating it. Yet her altars are still located in a basement room that can be safely locked against those who are too curious or too judgmental. Upstairs in Mama Lola's home — on the living room walls, on her bedside table — the only things an outsider sees are devotional objects for the Catholic saints.

Mama Lola's children and grandchildren knew from the time they were very young that the Vodou spirits who counseled and comforted them in the rituals that took place in their homes were not to be acknowledged in their larger social worlds. The habit of having a public and a private religion, and admitting to the first only, is deeply ingrained in the Haitian community. It fits with a larger sense of secretiveness (routinely using more than one name, for example) born of a feeling that Haitians are neither respected nor welcome in the United States. These habits of hiding speak to the power issues that shape Haitian life and religion in New York City in the late twentieth century. Any attempt to describe Vodou in North American cities that does not give a central place to power questions distorts the Haitian experience.

New York Vodou

Several of the characteristics of New York Haitian Vodou that have emerged in this discussion actually have their roots in earlier developments in Haiti. This is further reinforcement for the admonition that Vodou is best understood as a transnational phenomenon shaped by forces that transcend any one particular nation-state or culture.

It is important to note that, by and large, it was not migration to New York that caused Haitians to lose contact with the land. For most of them, that process had started one, or even two, generations earlier. Significant rural out-migration began more than fifty years ago in Haiti, and it has continued up to the present. The forces that caused the shift of population from the countryside to the cities are poverty, soil erosion, overpopulation, local political corruption, and, not insignificantly, zealous foreign investors who have periodically tried to amass large tracts of land for business ventures. The majority of Haitians in New York come from Haiti's cities. In many cases, it was the parents or grandparents of these people who left the countryside in search of a better way of life. Port-au-Prince, the launching pad for much of the second diaspora, has seen a steady and rapid growth in its ghettos as a result of the influx of rural population. Most Haitians now living in New York therefore encountered urban life, and inevitably also North American culture, well before they emigrated.

New York City turns up the volume and intensifies these processes, but many Haitians come to the United States already quite urbanized and Americanized. Indeed, exposure to things that for a long time were available only in Haiti's cities—U.S. popular music and television, Bruce Lee movies, blue jeans, and Johnny Walker scotch—is what started many young people dreaming of life in New York. It should not be overlooked, however, that more sober reasons for coming to the United States go hand in hand with such fantasies. Often one emigrant represents the survival strategy of an entire family. A black-market tourist visa can cost a lot of money in Port-au-Prince, so frequently entire families have to invest in the enterprise, and they expect a return on that investment.

What I have described here as the socialization of the Vodou cosmos also began long before the Haitian immigrants' first encounter with New York City. Perhaps even before their arrival on the island of Hispaniola, it may have proven necessary for Africans to refocus the lenses of their various religions in order to address the hellish social system that was chattel slavery. This abrupt shock may well be the originating point for Vodou's extreme sensitivity to the social drama and the various roles within it.

Finally, New York badgers Haitians with racism, an especially virulent form of which singles out their religion for self-righteous and vitriolic attacks. But even this is not an unknown for Haitian immigrants. Haiti's mulatto elite and the Catholic Church hierarchy have periodically tried to destroy the popular African-based religion called Vodou. During the worst of the so-called anti-superstition campaigns in Haiti, Vodou withdrew discreetly behind temple walls. The habit of maintaining a secret religious life intensifies and becomes more elaborate in New York City, but the need for it does not come as a rude shock to most Haitians.

Religious Transnationialism

One thing, however, is quite different for Haitians involved in the second diaspora. This time around they *chose* to come, more or less. And this time they can and do go back—sometimes for visits and sometimes to stay. Furthermore Haitians in New York City remain in touch with friends and families in Haiti; they even participate in Haitian politics. These are the reasons why Haitians in New York are more accurately called transnationals than U.S. immigrants. As was said earlier, Haitians living in New York City are people whose identity is rooted in two places and who simultaneously sustain cultural, familial, and financial ties in both countries.

Some examples will make the significance of this transnational condition more apparent. During the upheaval that followed the 1986 departure of President Jean-Claude Duvalier, Haitians in New York were kept well informed about what was happening in Haiti by video news cassettes. Tapes covering important developments could be purchased in shops on both Nostrand and Flatbush avenues in Brooklyn, often within twenty-four hours of the events they depicted. This informal news network was able to provide much more extended and visually graphic news coverage than any of the television networks. The tapes, some made by amateurs, were flown in on the daily American Airlines flight from Port-au-Prince and duplicated in a studio in New York.

Direct immigrant participation in Haitian politics provides another example of this transnationalism. The so-called Tenth Department raised a significant percentage of the money expended on the candidacy of Father Jean-Bertrand Aristide. Aristide came to New York during his campaign for office, drawing crowds that numbered in the thousands. In December 1990, Aristide became the first president in Haiti's history who could make an honest claim to having been democratically elected. When he was ousted in a coup in September 1991, the Tenth Department became a financial supporter of his government in exile.[21]

The spiritual life of the Tenth Department is also enmeshed with that of Haiti. Haitian Vodou has become a transnational religion in the second diaspora. The label "transnational religion" is intended to call attention not only to the parallel Vodou ceremonies being performed, following the same ritual calendar, in both Haiti and New York, but also to the more interesting circumstances that make Vodou a key player in the exchange of people, goods, and money between Haiti and the continental United States.

The Tenth Department pumps a substantial amount of money into the local Haitian economy, approximately $100 million per year.[22] Unlike other monies circulating in Haiti, a significant amount of this money goes directly to poor people. It follows that much of the elaborate Vodou ritualizing in Port-au-Prince would probably not be possible without the money Haitian exiles send to friends and family members back home.

Some New York Vodou leaders, furthermore, who are either U.S. citizens or resident aliens and therefore are free to travel, insist on going to Haiti to perform particularly important ceremonies. Mama Lola is one of them. She will not initiate anyone in New York City because, she says, initiates need to be able to put their bare feet on Haitian soil during these ceremonies. Some prominent diaspora Vodou leaders will initiate people in New York and take on just about any cure there as well, but part of Mama Lola's authority in the diaspora community stems from her willingness to travel.[23]

Once initiated into a Vodou lineage based in Haiti, a person acquires lifelong connections to a family-like network of temples there. Many people think that rituals that take place on Haitian soil are more powerful than ones that do not. So some U.S. priests and priestesses send money to their "brother" and "sister" priests and priestesses in Port-au-Prince, asking that ceremonies be performed in Haiti for New York clients. Occasionally items of clothing are sent through the mail as surrogates for the people who need healing or, perhaps, controlling.

Trips to Haiti are sometimes occasioned by Mama Lola's healing practice. When she has reached a dead end in an attempt to help one of her clients, Mama Lola may decide to travel to Haiti for one last effort. She had some "work" to do in the early 1990s, for instance, for a client about to go on trial for a serious crime. When a volatile political situation and a U.S. embargo on flights to Haiti prevented her from going there, she flew instead to the Dominican Republic, which shares the island of Hispaniola with Haiti. She picked her herbs and performed her rituals in a location as close to Haiti as she could get.

The elaborate eight-day cycle of rituals for ancestors and family spirits that Mama Lola performed in Haiti in the summer of 1989 would also fall into the category of ceremonies that would not be as effective if performed in New York City. Mama Lola spent several thousand dollars on these rites, the first ancestral ceremonies on such a scale that she had been able to stage since she emigrated in 1963. On an economic level alone, these 1989 rites had a significant impact on the downtown neighborhood where her mother's house is located and in whose backyard she performed her family rituals.

Vodou also generates a number of small-scale international markets for herbs, religious images, beads, and other Vodou paraphernalia. Travelers to Haiti often bring back hard-to-find herbs, discreetly tucked into their luggage. But when informal means of keeping Haitian healers supplied with the tools of their trade are insufficient, there are commercial solutions. In large cities such as New York and Miami, *botanicas*, general supply stores of African-based religions in North America, carry a wide selection of fresh and dried herbs from Haiti. One Miami *botanica* provides shopping carts for its clients to use as they browse the aisles of refrigerated cases holding herbs and roots from all over the world, including several countries in West Africa, as well as Haiti.

John Berger described the experience of immigration with simple geometry. Home was the "center of the real" and the place where two lines intersected, the vertical "path leading upward to the sky and downward to the underworld" and the horizontal line representing "the traffic of the world." For Berger, immigration is synonymous with the loss of home and the attendant loss of contact with ancestors and gods. With no "fixed points as bearings," the traffic of the world dissolves into meaningless wandering. Berger's sense of home as the center of the real has deep resonance in Vodou; the crossroads image, omnipresent in Vodou, is basically the same as Berger's intersecting lines. But at least in the Haitian case, and one suspects in others as well, Berger's analysis of the consequences of immigration could not be more wrong.

The key factor for the people of Haiti's second diaspora is that they did not lose Haiti when they left Haiti. In the late twentieth century, the continuous movement of people, money, goods, and information between New York City and Haiti traces and retraces the horizontal line of the crossroads figure, anchoring it solidly in place. Spiritual cargo also flows along this horizontal line and unites Haitians in New York with the *potomitan*, the sacred center pole, that is Haiti itself—and from there with God in heaven and the spirits and ancestors below in Ginen, Africa.

Yet it is necessary to add that life in New York is not always a thoroughly comfortable fit for Haitians and their religion. Haitian Vodou is a religion, like the several African traditions out of which it was born, that is characterized by flexibility and a certain natural, unstrained hospitality toward other religious traditions, other cultures, and other value systems. Nevertheless, it is not hard to see Vodou in New York stretching and straining to accommodate new, and often alien, spaces. Most of this strain is felt at the level of ecological dissonance, a lack of natural harmony between the religion and its adopted socio-ecological niche. Ceremonies condense and twist themselves around to accommodate the more confining spaces of New York. Some dimensions of Vodou's symbol system become attenuated, distant; others intensify and undergo greater embellishment. Vodou rituals, which are always about the lives of the people staging them, become yet more articulate in New York about the fine points of the human capacity for love and treachery. And there is ambivalence visible within the religious system. On the one hand, Vodou ceremonies in New York exhibit a longing for contact with the earth; on the other, the earth becomes little more than a metaphor for family and family roots. Thus Vodou accommodates itself to life in New York, refuels itself through contact with Haiti, and, on the whole, thrives.

When Mama Lola tries to account for the transnational character of her spirits, she says, "The spirit is a wind. Everywhere I go, they going too . . . to protect me." By casting her spirits in the image of wind, she makes them movable, dynamic, powerful. She also lifts them above the boundaries of states and cultures. Intuitively, she knows what comes next for the Vodou spirits. Her metaphor points in the direction of what may well be Vodou's biggest challenge in the future.

The increase of Protestantism and of Protestant missionaries in Haiti has heightened Haitians' awareness of the power and utility of transcendent worldviews that attempt to account for the whole world and to assign each group of people to their respective place within it. When home was "the center of the real," it was not necessary to have a worldview that accounted for everything and everybody that fell outside that reality. But cities are by definition made up of many realities. Even a city the size of Port-au-Prince, which has approximately one million people, contains enough human diversity to put a strain on a unified understanding of the world. A city the size and complexity of New York puts considerably more pressure on the local spiritualities that its immigrants bring. The felt need is greatly intensified for a universal scheme that not only accounts for one's own self and one's own beliefs but also places that self in relation to others and accounts for the larger reality that encompasses the two. How those who serve the spirits respond to this pressure will be determined by how they come to understand and to use power in the modern world, how they relate to their neighbors, and how they negotiate morally across the spaces between Haiti and New York and between generations.

Notes

1. A precise number is difficult to come by. Apparently some Haitians were not counted in the last census, many of them undocumented aliens.

2. The word comes from the Fon *vodun*, meaning god or spirit. In Haiti, the word *Vodou* (the correct spelling according to the official Haitian Creole orthography) originally referred to one style of drumming and ritualizing among many such styles. It was outsiders who first applied the word *Voodoo* to the entire complex of religious action and belief in Haiti.

3. For a fuller story of Mama Lola's immigration, see Karen McCarthy Brown, *Mama Lola: A Vodou Priestess in Brooklyn* (Berkeley and Los Angeles: University of California Press, 1991), 70–78.

4. See, for example, Linda Basch, Nina Glick Schiller, and Christina Szanton Blanc, *Nations Unbound: Transnational Projects, Postcolonial Predicaments, and Deterritorialized Nation-States* (New York: Gordon and Breach, 1994).

5. John Berger, "Homegrown," *Village Voice*, July 3, 1984, 53. Berger's article takes no particular group as its focus but begins with a quote from Whitman and is illustrated with a depiction of a white family in a comfortable, although not wealthy, European home. For these reasons I conclude that the context for his musings is European immigration to the United States.

6. The only significant difference is that in Haitian Vodou, it is not always possible to make hard and fast distinctions between the ancestors and the Vodou spirits; furthermore, some of the spirits or *lwa* live "up there" in the sky and some "down there," in Ginen or Africa.

7. In all the various cultures of Africa represented in the Haitian slave population, crossroads are sacred, ritually accented places where the ordinary world and the world

of the spirits intersect. Thus it is not surprising that the crossroads image should be pervasive in Haitian Vodou as well.

8. See Robert Farris Thompson, *The Four Moments of the Sun: Kongo Art in Two Worlds* (Washington, D.C.: National Gallery of Art, 1981).

9. Scholars of the African diaspora are increasingly aware of the significance of actual contact between the slave colonies and Africa. In the mid-eighteenth century, Haiti had one of the busiest ports in the world. Ships went back and forth between Haiti and Africa frequently and in large numbers. Newly arrived slaves brought information from the homelands and, on occasion, probably even information about the families of slaves already there.

10. These ceremonies are called *rele mo nan dlo*, "calling the dead from the waters." They are generally performed for Vodou initiates.

11. No doubt something quite different happened among the communities of European immigrants in the United States. One good example is found in Robert Orsi's study of southern Italian Catholics in East Harlem. See Orsi, *The Madonna of 115th Street: Faith and Community in Italian Harlem, 1880–1950* (New Haven: Yale University Press, 1985).

12. There are lingering reminders of other attempts to compensate for the loss of direct access to Africa. For example, there is a Vodou sacred town called Vil-o-Kan (Ville-aux-camps) in the northwestern part of Haiti. Several times I have heard those who serve the spirits talk about it as a sort of "embassy" in the New World for the African spirits.

13. After the success of Haiti's slave revolution in 1804, a significant percentage of the land in the new republic was turned over to ex-slaves. Most Haitians have since lived on the land, and many still own the small parcels of earth on which they engage in subsistence farming. The family dead are usually buried on a part of the family land that is jointly owned. No matter how many times the larger tract of land is divided among members of subsequent generations, the *heritaj* is kept intact. The small building that houses the altars and ritual accoutrements of the spirits is often found on the same small, indivisible parcel of earth. The fact that peasant agriculture had a rebirth in Haiti makes for significant differences between Haitian Vodou and the African-based religions of other former slave colonies. Cuban Santería and Brazilian Condomble, by contrast, have largely urban roots. Cities were influential in the development of Vodou, but always in relation to rural extended-family compounds.

14. In Haitian Vodou, for example, there is a general class of rituals called *pye-pa-te* ("feet-on-the-earth") rituals. In these rites, those who serve the spirits have to be barefoot; only the priest or priestess wears shoes. The sacerdotes' shoes give them the leverage in relation to the spirit realm that they need to act as intermediaries between the spirits and the living. If priests and priestesses had bare feet, they would be in direct contact with spiritual energy that could overwhelm them. When the lively singing and dancing are successful in attracting a spirit who possesses the priest or priestess, the priest's shoes are immediately removed. But at the same time, the *asson*, the calabash rattle signaling priestly authority, is taken from the priest and given to another, who is then in charge of the ceremony. While those whom the spirits "ride" in New York City also have their shoes quickly removed, there is no possibility of putting their feet, or the feet of the other *serviteurs*, for that matter, in direct contact with the earth.

15. See chap. 6 of this volume "The Religious Boundaries of an In-between People: Street *Feste* and the Problem of the Dark-Skinned Other in Italian Harlem, 1920–1990."

16. The Vodou ceremony that is traditionally said to have started the Haitian slave

revolution took place in Bois Cayman, the Crocodile Forest. There are no such animals in Haiti, and there apparently never have been. But there is a locally famous and purportedly ancient Bois Cayman in one of the Mahi towns in central Benin, an area from which many people were taken to be sold as slaves. It seems not unreasonable to suggest that the Haitian Bois Cayman is an African transposition.

17. See, for example, Karen McCarthy Brown, "Systematic Remembering, Systematic Forgetting: Ogou in Haiti," in Sandra T. Barnes, ed., *Africa's Ogun: Old World and New* (Bloomington: Indiana University Press, 1989).

18. Ibid.

19. M. L. E. Moreau de St. Mery, *Description Topographique, Physique, Civile, Politique, et Historique de la Partie Française de l'Isle de St Domingue* (Paris: Libraire Larose, 1958; orig. pub. 1797).

20. See Robert Lawless, *Haiti's Bad Press: Origins, Development, and Consequences* (Rochester, Vt.: Schenkman Books, 1992).

21. President Aristide made the Tenth Department official. During his initial short tenure in office, he appointed Gerard Jean-Juste, director of the Miami Haitian Refugee Center from 1980 to 1991, as the first director of the Tenth Department.

22. Jean Jean-Pierre, "The Diaspora: The Tenth Department," in James Ridgeway, ed., *The Haiti Files: Decoding the Crisis* (Washington, D.C.: Essential Books/Azul Editions, 1994).

23. Mama Lola goes to the place where problems manifest—a plot of land, a car, or a house—in order to treat them directly. In addition to Haiti, her healing work in recent years has taken her to Canada, Jamaica, and Belize (on two occasions), as well as to Boston and several small towns in the southern United States.

The Hindu Gods in a Split-Level World

The Sri Siva-Vishnu Temple in Suburban Washington, D.C.

Joanne Punzo Waghorne

A "country" mailbox, metal encased in wood, stands on the road in front of an archetypal suburban split-level house. Wrought iron letters read SSVT. Behind this symbol of American family life rise the ornate *vimanas* or spires of the largest Hindu temple in the United States. The temple stands on fourteen acres of former Maryland farmland at the edge of the sprawling suburbs of the nation's capital. Its congregation is made up of the first generation of a new wave of immigrants. Neither tired nor poor nor huddled masses, the technological and scientific elite of India began coming to the United States in the late 1960s and early 1970s, when changes in the immigration laws removed odious restrictions against Asians. Unlike immigrants from the past who began their life on American shores far lower on the occupational hierarchy, these educated newcomers quickly prospered and chose to settle in the suburbs, new cities, and edge cities, among their colleagues from major technological corporations, hospitals, and universities.

The Sri Siva-Vishnu Temple is located on Cipriano Road, the local route to the NASA Goddard Space Center less than a mile away. It shares the road with two churches. Just next door is another split-level used by a gospel study group, the Victory World Outreach. Another house, now used as a Hindu temple for those devoted more exclusively to the god Murugan, is in the vicinity. Homes in this neighborhood range from the modest 1950s ranch styles typical of the first suburban inroads onto this once-virgin Maryland farmland to newer and larger split-level subdivisions. A garden apartment complex and modern new industrial buildings now impinge on the large tracts of farmland that remain within two miles of this fast-growing outpost of metropolitan Washington. On Saturday mornings, East Asian Americans, African Americans, and European Americans can be seen mowing their lawns. Cipriano Road reflects a multilayered suburban community with an economic, racial, and ethnic mix that reflects its layers of growth. Lanham, Maryland, is united only, it seems, by its middle-class ethos marked by good fences, good houses, and the good jobs that make home ownership a reality.

Indians around Washington, as in other parts of the country,[1] have not settled in any one neighborhood, although Arlington and Silver Springs do have a larger proportion of South Asians than other areas. The only temple located near a "little India" is, not surprisingly, in New York City. The Hindu Temple Society of North America created the first temple in the United States in the early 1970s by reconstructing an old Greek Orthodox church in Flushing, now down the road from an Indian shopping center that functions less as a residential neighborhood than as a center of commerce. The larger Hindu temples built in the last two decades, however, rise from suburban landscapes convenient to major interstate highways in Pittsburgh, Houston, Boston, Chicago, and Nashville. The Sri Siva-Vishnu Temple, like other major American Hindu temples, is in many ways both more incongruous with its particular environment and yet more a part of the generic mainstream American landscape than older religious centers in the many Little Italies, Little Polands, and Chinatowns that anchor ethnic space in the inner cities.

Unlike the earlier waves of immigrants at the turn of the century, many of these recent arrivals left urban environments in India that better prepared them for life in the United States. Many Indians came here from middle-class homes—not affluent, but fluent in English and familiar with the business-suit world of modern urban commerce inherited from two hundred years of British rule. The parents or even the grandparents of migrants especially from South India who make up the majority of the trustees and devotees of the Sri Siva-Vishnu Temple belonged in India to the mobile and multilingual civil service, university, and scientific communities. The traditional ties that bound persons to particular places in India had been severed, then, a generation earlier in the families of many of the new Indian Americans. In urban centers such as Madras and Bangalore, *enka ur*, "our town," is usually somewhere away from *enka vitu*, "our house." Many Indians, certainly many of those most active in the SSVT, came to the United States already "twice-migrated,"[2] with a history of dis-placement: a heritage of multiple meanings for "our land," "our home," and "our place" in the world.

This pattern of "double migration," however, is complicated by the two decades of rapid technological change (1960s–1980s) that brought many of the earliest Indian immigrants to the United States, often as agents of that change. They moved with their degrees from India's institutes of technology and schools of medicine to highly specialized jobs at institutions such as NASA, at university research institutes and hospitals, or at large corporations such as IBM and Burroughs-Wellcome.[3] But in this postmodern era, the technology that lured them from India at the same time holds them close to each other and to the mother country through a global network of telephones, modems, jetliners, and now international newspapers, including *Hinduism Today, India Today, Accent,* and *The Indian-American.* Under the headline "Trend to Watch," *Hinduism Today,* published in California, proudly quoted Joel Kotkin's forecast in *Tribes: How Race, Religion and Identity Determine Success in the New Global Economy:* "The more than twenty million overseas Indians today represent one of the best-educated, affluent groupings in the world. . . . The Indian may prove to be the next diaspora to emerge as a great economic force."[4] This newspaper, which proclaims its task as "Recording the Modern History of Nearly a Billion Members of a Global Religion in Renaissance," touted the suggestion that a tight network of the Indian "tribe" in the new global village may be the key to its success in this age of transnational economics.

But as prepared as Indian Americans may be to take up their role as the newest diaspora, an ideology of journey and wandering was never at the heart of their ancient culture. Unlike the Jews, who are often mentioned by Indian Americans as a model for economic acculturation with continuing community cohesion,[5] Indians have been conquered but never forcefully driven from their soil. The gods of the Hindus, unlike the Lord God of Israel, have no strong tradition of moving about in a tent for their dwelling[6] or of residing solely inside their holy word: they live in temples. Thus over the last decade, many of the most successful of the new "tribe" of overseas Indians—many now American citizens—have given the money derived from their great success along with their boundless energy to once again construct "authentic" Hindu temples that nonetheless stand on a highly complex space that is at once American, Indian, and global, but at the same time also middle-class and suburban. The Hindu gods of metropolitan Washington, D.C., like the Hindu gods of the cities of Houston or Pittsburgh or Nashville, live in a substantive holy house that nonetheless *is* and yet *is not* at home on the land on which it stands.

Middle-Class and Hindu: An Indian Matrix, a Global Context, an American Venue

Indian Americans at the Sri Siva-Vishnu Temple, like others in this new diaspora, express a continuing bond to the mother country. Some equation of their Hinduism with India always remains. But at the same time, these diaspora Indians openly acknowledge that they felt forced to leave this mother as too old, too tired, and too slow to nurture the ambition and the skills that so many possessed. When they differentiate America from India, India is the "spiritual and unchanging" place, while America is the land of "material" success, recently given the Sanskrit name *karma-bhumi*, meaning "the land of action, the place of work."[7] At a classical Indian dance recital in Raleigh, North Carolina, in the early 1990s, a prominent Indian guru now settled in the United States told his largely Indian American audience that they should combine "the East with the West." From the West, said the guru, they could learn "punctuality and how to succeed materially." Implied, of course, was that the East held all the cultural riches. Yet in spite of the continued sense of deep kinship with family and old colleagues left behind, the particular character of the interconnection between India and its diaspora is, as Amitav Ghosh points out, "a very peculiar, almost inexplicable phenomenon."[8]

In an article written in 1989, Ghosh points to the curious lack of any real institutional structures that could unite India with overseas Indians. The economic links are insubstantial, the marriage ties weak, the political connections fragmented. Pointing to the international fame of diaspora writers such as V. S. Naipaul, A. K. Ramanujan, and Salman Rushdie, Ghosh instead suggests that the strongest cultural bonds are "lived within the imagination" in the space of literature. And, indeed, the construction of a "spiritual India" among many Indian Americans echoes the broad, often mystified sense of the homeland developed by the most famous of India's long-absent sons, Mahatma Gandhi, who spent his early career among Indian migrants in Africa. This imagined India is the *Area of Darkness* that Trinidadian V. S. Naipaul so stunningly contrasted with the shocking reality of his first "return" to the country he had never seen.[9]

However, very recent evidence of the rapidly developing institutions that now mediate between diaspora Indians and India, including political parties and organizations with a conservative religious message, suggests the rise of a more structured solidarity with the motherland. Conspicuously active in the United States is the VHP (Vishwa Hindu Parishad, "World Hindu Council"), the religious wing of India's right-wing party, the BJP (Bharatiya Janata Party, "the Indian People's Party"). The VHP in 1993 sponsored "Global Vision 2000" in Washington, D.C., to celebrate Swami Vivekananda's famous presentation of Hinduism before the World Parliament of Religions in 1893.[10] The event drew Indo-American enthusiasts, but also others protesting the disguised conservative agenda.[11] These same organizations are part of an increasing popular Hindu "fundamentalism" within India that defines Indians—over and against the "foreign" Christians and Muslims—as citizens *native* to the soil who put no other gods, no other holy places, before Bharat Mata, mother India. The *India Times*, published in Washington, D.C., has become a voice for this new strident nationalism of some Indians, permanent residents of the United States and sometimes citizens, who nonetheless write editorials urging an electoral platform for the BJP that would create "India as a strong economic power . . . India as a strong military power . . . India as a nation with an unwavering sense of identity with the secular Vedic-Hindu civilization."[12]

This very visceral attachment to the land arises from a definition of India as *the* Hindu nation whose "Vedic Hindu" civilization emanates so naturally from the soil that it should not be called "a religion" like the foreign-made Islam. Hence Hinduism is truly the "secular" civilization of India. This Hindu mother India now exists as another model of the home country among diaspora Indians alongside the more easily portable, less controversial "spiritual India" of art and sacred literature. So difficult and dense are these questions defining the place of so many of the world's most recent immigrants in this new age of global migration and multiple identities that the problem precipitated three new academic journals: *Diaspora: A Journal of Transnational Studies; Transition: An International Review;* and *Public Culture: Bulletin of the Center for Transnational Cultural Studies.*

This ambiguity involved in defining a place for "India" in the Hinduism of the diaspora has much to do with the equally puzzling problem of defining the place of "Hinduism" within modern India, especially for the mobile, middle-class professionals who were the parents and are often the stay-at-home brothers and sisters of the new Indian Americans. While the BJP tries to forge an unbreakable link between Hinduism and India as a nation, the urban middle class has a history of a different solution to the sense of religious and personal dislocation felt in a new urban environment. The problem is complicated by the paucity of studies on religion among the urban middle class, whose workday habits in Bombay offices or Madras bureaucracies could never attract the anthropological eye away from the exotic and more dazzling bells and smoke-filled rituals of their country and tribal cousins. The available studies of modern trends in religion within India have tended to stress the ways that the modern middle class in India's new industrial cities adapted older forms of Hinduism to their own needs through what Max Weber first identified as the intensive emotional surrender to the charismatic guru, the divine teacher, which he assumed "quite naturally became the primary form of holy seeking for the aliterary middle classes."[13]

In *Redemptive Encounters,* Lawrence Babb investigated three modern religious movements in India's capital city of New Delhi that centered on founding saints. Babb found that disconnection between person and the daily place of residence or place of work in these movements was so radical that "interactions with deities and deitylike persons" became "a way in which a very special sense of self and the world, which has little basis in the experience of everyday life, can be assimilated to a devotee's inner life."[14] In describing the sense of community in one such movement formed around this common ethos of a split between inner and outer life and absolute belief in the founding spiritual teacher, Babb doubts if it can be called "a community in any normal sense because its territorial dispersion mitigates against the formation of anything resembling corporate ties. The group is probably best conceived as a loose 'congregation.'"[15] The contemporary middle class in India, then, are not strangers to social and economic factors that demand a relocation — often a radical relocation — of the self in a seemingly fragmented world.

Several of these same guru-centered organizations have become international, and their "congregations" spread over the globe.[16] For many middle-class Hindus in the United States, these guru-centered global communities continue to provide a sense of relocation and re-identification of the self with a spiritual network that connects — sometimes by telepathy or telephone, letter, or fax — the devout with the guru while transcending national boundaries.[17] To fully understand where "India," "America," and "Britain" are on the map of their spiritual life is difficult, but one thing is certain: Where the guru is, there is holy space. However, the temple builders in Lanham, Maryland, or Flushing, New York, or Houston, Texas, by envisioning and constructing temples they consider authentic, have chosen to center their religious life in the temple itself, and therefore to adopt/adapt a tradition that has connected making a holy house with sanctifying the land.

Amid all the complexity of the place of "India" within diaspora Hinduism and the place of "Hinduism" within middle-class India stands the new Hindu temple in America as a marker of what John Fenton, in a study of South Asian immigrants to the United States, calls "the process of becoming at home (having a *desh* or place where one belongs) on the foreign soil of America."[18] Other scholars of contemporary temple building in America verify the almost literal sense of the "transplantation" of Hinduism into American soil,[19] and of the process that makes God "immediate; this land, holy."[20] But amid this process of implantation (the ceremony to consecrate a Hindu temple creates strong analogies between planting a seed and "planting" a temple) remain the shifting borders of modern life — the transfers and new assignments and career advances that necessitate continued mobility. The Hindu temple is in "America" and stands as a marker of the acceptance of a new place for the growth of Hinduism; but at the same time, this holy house cannot be easily associated with a new stable group of people now permanently (re)tied to this land. "America's" place in the temple and the temple's place in America is a far more complex issue than the traditional place of the temple in India—even in modern India.

In *Space and Place*, Yi-Fu Tuan reminds his readers that "the original inspiration for building a city was to consort with the Gods." Gods live in traditional Hindu temples quite literally embodied in iconic form and firmly fixed in a specific locality. The most common words for temple in classic Sanskrit texts, according to Stella Kramrisch, are *vimama*, "measured out," and *prasada*, "seat." Both words emphasize the fixing, seating, settling of the divine in a constructed abode.[21] The most familiar contemporary words for "temple" in both Sanskrit and vernacular languages translate as "palace," "house of God," "place of God," "abode of God." As S. S. Janaki puts it, "synonyms like *alayam, mandiram* and *grha* are in a general way applicable to the dwelling place of both human beings and divinities."[22] The Indian city then continues as a place where humans and divine inhabitants share the same space—each in their own respective houses. Stella Kramrisch, in her now-classic study of the Hindu temple, quotes texts which state that the installation of divine icons in temples should be made "in forts; in auspicious cities, at the head of shop-lined streets."[23] And indeed in many of the still-living temple cities of South India, the most exclusive shops are located on the four streets that surround the urban temple complex, the *mada* streets. Here the finest silk weaving, the best brassware and jewelry can be found.

The Sri Siva-Vishnu Temple, however, is not defined by the patterns of interconnected yet bounded communities that historians of modern India have described as characterizing Indian cities even at the turn of the century. The model of little villages within a larger urban corporation marked Indian cities until the mid-nineteenth century, when British residents of colonial port cities such as Madras began to move their personal residences from the trading and governmental centers to new garden suburbs.[24] The rising middle-class Indians in Madras city, for example, began to build new neighborhoods like their British overlords, but they always re-created an older Indian sense of urban space: a central temple surrounded by a combination of houses and stores. The Mylapore area of Madras is a perfect example of this older urban model that continues even today.[25] Only after independence in 1947 did Madrasis begin to create purely residential suburbs in the American sense of bedroom communities. In the Indian context, the oft-quoted maxim "Do not live where there is no temple" is taken seriously in the new suburbs, which have seen the rise of small temples built by new multi-caste and multi-ethnic constituencies that are within residential neighborhoods but no longer at their literal center.

2.1. The Kapaleeswara Temple in Mylapore, Madras city. The complex is enclosed by a wall with grand gopora or gates, which are visible in front of a large water tank used for festivals.

In the new American context, devotees of the Sri Siva-Vishnu Temple have built and now maintain a multi-million-dollar temple complex that is even less the center of a new neighborhood than its Indian counterparts. They have moved one step beyond the Indian urban middle class. Their temple is not even contiguous to their residential neighborhood. The temple takes on even greater importance, then, as the only concrete embodiment of the community. Ironically, it rests on land in a non-Hindu neighborhood and yet remains the focal point for a Hindu community that itself has no clear edges except its sprawling middle-class suburbanness. There is as yet no obvious—visibly created and theoretically formulated—relationship between the space of the temple and the land of Maryland and the life that it supports. The "space" of the Sri Siva-Vishnu Temple exists somewhere amid the concreteness of the traditional temple, the ethereal space of "spiritual" India, the newer creation of an ideological motherland, and the shifting space of the everywhere/nowhere/every-body's/nobody's split-level world of the migrating international middle class. Without acknowledgment and understanding of that conundrum, the *place* of the temple among Hindu Americans would be lost.

Suburban areas such as Lanham, Maryland, must not be ignored as an important environment for building newer dimensions to modern Hinduism. New Hindu temples in Boston, Los Angeles, Pittsburgh, Chicago, and Nashville rise up at the very edge of urban centers in the same way that new temples now complete the suburban landscape of Madras, Bangalore,[26] New Delhi, London,[27] Singapore,[28] Sydney,[29] and Durban.[30] Indeed, the same English-speaking and highly articulate architects trained at government-sponsored schools of religious architecture in Mahabalipuram outside Madras city and in the famous temple city of Tirupati in Andhra Pradesh have provided designs and guided the construction of new temples in suburban India and the United States. Thus the sacred homes built for these Hindu gods of the American city are at the same time a part of strongly contested definitions of an emerging global Hinduism. The questions of what is India-Indian, what is America-American, where *is* the temple and who belongs there are all written, I will argue, on the walls, into the design, and throughout the ritual life of this temple. Rather than debating the definition of Hinduism in a public forum, as does the VHP, or quietly setting aside a place in their minds or spirits for a new internalized Hinduism, as do many middle-class Indians, the patrons and devotees of this temple are finding and founding a place to shape their answers to this new "world of crisscrossed economies, intersecting systems of meanings, and fragmented identities," as an advertisement for the new journal *Diaspora* describes it.

Inside/Outside: The Modern Hindu Temple
in a Suburban World

A carefully designed brochure used to solicit donations in 1989 for the first permanent building of the Sri Siva-Vishnu Temple provided a brief history of the temple along with construction plans, estimated costs, and an explanation of the organization of the Sri Siva-Vishnu Temple Trust:

> The dream of setting up a Hindu Temple, in the Nation's Capital, where religious services are performed in the time-honored tradition, was conceived in January, 1980. The SRI SIVA-VISHNU (SSVT) TRUST was formed and registered in the state of Maryland for religious, educational and charitable purposes. The primary aim of the trust is to build and maintain an authentic Hindu temple for performing various religious functions.

The establishment of the trust was followed four years later by the purchase of a modest split-level house on four acres. The split-level became the first temple with the installation of the *balalaya*, literally the "baby" images—the wooden prototypes of the gods that would eventually be remade in stone and housed in the permanent temple. When the trust purchased the ten adjacent acres, plans for construction began in earnest under the direction of a famous *sthapati*, a traditional temple architect, Sri V. Ganapathi Sthapati, from an ancient center of traditional Hindu artisans, Mahabalipuram near Madras city. By September 26, 1990, the basic structure was finished and the final round of inspections completed on the very eve of this major celebration, as the November 1990 temple newsletter later divulged.

The first stone images of three of the fourteen gods and goddesses that the SSVT planned to install in the new temple had made the long journey from the sculptors in Madras to arrive in Lanham for the elaborate rituals of consecration—also, as I was later told, at the last moment. Priests from other Hindu temples in Albany, Los Angeles, and New York joined the resident priest on Cipriano Road for the four-day *pranapratistha* rituals which "fix" (*pratistha*) the "life breath" (*prana*) into the stone sculpture, transforming it from a work of art into a visible embodiment of a God.

I first saw the temple and met the trustees at this point as part of a visual documentation of contemporary temple rituals that my husband, photographer Dick Waghorne, and I had started in Madras two years earlier. We have returned each summer since then to photograph and participate in a series of consecration rituals that have marked the growth of this temple.

On July 3–7, the first *mahakumbabhisekam* was carefully performed. The *vimanas*, the ornate spires that covered the sanctum of the major god Siva and his son Murugan, were sanctified along with the divine images of these deities by the pouring of holy water (*abhisekam*, "sprinkling") from a sacred vessel (*kumba*, "pot") simultaneously over the gold finial of the *vimana* and the divine image fixed in the chamber just below. On July 9–12, 1992, a second *mahakumbabhisekam* consecrated the *vimanas* and a monumental reclining stone image of Vishnu in his form as Padmanabha, the deity awaking from rest at the moment of creation. A new wing was added to the temple and dedicated to the God Venkateeswara in the summer of 1993. The consecration ceremonies in 1993 were on Memorial Day weekend, May 28–30. Fundraising was already moving quickly to build a new wing on the temple to house an image of the God Aiyyappa. The cost of this temple in this early period exceeded two million dollars, as not only the deities but also extensive external ornamentation has been added by sculptors who have come and gone from Madras to Lanham in

2.2. The chief priest pours water from a holy pot onto the top finial of the temple, which covers the main shrine at the moment. This is the final ritual act that consecrates the new temple.

continual rotation so that the bare cinderblock is now fully dressed in unmistakable Indian garb.

To anyone familiar with Hindu deities, the particular selection of gods and the general style of the temple would immediately reveal the South Indian origins of most of the trustees and the devotees of SSVT. Thus I, like the majority of the trustees, came to this temple from the context of the urban temples I have known in South India. As a steady migrant in the opposite direction over the last twenty years, I have lived in or near the neighborhoods from which many of the SSVT devotees came,

2.3. The main entrance to the temple, with the new plaster ornamentation that now covers the modern construction. The stairs are covered with flowers to mark the day of the consecration ceremonies.

and I know families like theirs as neighbors and friends in Madras with cousins, brothers, sons, and daughters in America. We are all part of a generation of crisscrossings and multiple heres and theres. The detailed description that follows is grounded in this shared experience on two continents, the numerous conversations I have had here and there, and observations of similar rituals in suburban Madras and suburban Washington, D.C.

On the first day of the scheduled activities for the week of July 4, 1991, when the second of the four-year cycle of consecration rituals occurred, the front yard in Lanham still held several crates containing the sacred stone sculptures of the temple's major deities, which had been transported from the hands of their *silpis* (sculptors) in southern India to their new guardians in America. Several *silpis* had come from Madras prior to the sculptures' arrival to complete their installation in the temple as part of this five-day-long *mahakumbabhisekam* ritual, which would fully consecrate the images. The details of this July 4 week when the Hindu gods were fully manifest near the U.S. capital will serve as the text for a careful consideration of the nature of the space that was first sanctified that day.

The temple at this point still lacked its exterior decoration, thus exposing the basic form of its architecture. The temple's base unit is the traditional square, in this case 90 by 90 feet. The two stories, however, are

2.4. The traditional architect of the temple, the famous Ganapathi Sthapati, wears the three marks of the god Shiva on his forehead during the ceremony that honored his work.

very untraditional. The upper floor, which is actually on the ground level at the rear, houses the divine images; the lower story, which opens from the side to the parking lot in the front, contains a large auditorium for cultural performances, the dance and music that has long been part of Hindu temple practice. This central auditorium is ringed by a modern kitchen, restrooms, classrooms, a library, an office, and meeting rooms. Families gathered on the first day of the consecration week in the auditorium, eating lunch while keeping an eye on the video monitor that carried every moment of the ongoing five-day ritual in progress upstairs.

The board of trustees of this impressive religious institution expressed great pride that this temple was designed by one of India's leading temple architects, Sri Ganapathi Sthapati. "Sthapati" is a title borne by certain families who, like priests, know and control a special set of sacred texts that give careful guidelines as to the proper forms and methods of their work.[31] Within these formal parameters, however, there is always latitude for change, provided the architect himself commands respect for his own knowledge and personal religiosity, since in Hindu traditions authority ultimately rests with authoritative people, not books. Thus devotees can rightly claim that this temple is thoroughly "authentic" in spite of the considerable and obvious innovations.

The most striking distinctions between this modern American temple and its older urban counterparts in India are its use of levels and its manner of enclosing space. The Kapaleeswara Temple, for example, in the Mylapore section of Madras not twenty miles from Mahabalipuram, where Sri Ganapathi Sthapati works, has no basement level. The idea of a basement would normally be unthinkable because the deities should always be in unbroken contact with the ground. During the consecration rituals, the stone images are literally glued to their base, and the base is firmly fixed into the temple floor and thus to the earth. When I asked Ganapathi Sthapati about this seemingly unorthodox practice in building the temple in Lanham, he explained that under each of the images is a separate hollow pillar that is filled with dirt. From the basement level these look like supporting pillars, but in fact they serve fundamentally to provide each image the requisite contact with earth. The columns allow the temple to remain orthodox, with a basement.

In the Kapaleeswara Temple in Mylapore, all functions occur at ground level, but not under one roof as in the temple in Lanham. The Madras temple is actually a walled courtyard enclosing many smaller structures. Musicians often perform under the *mandapam*, the pillared pavilions. They do not use an auditorium with a stage but perform close to the gods in their holy sanctums; their music is directed to the gods and only overheard by devotees. The gods' several shrines can be recognized by their ornate domes. The kitchens and the business offices, which are built onto the inner walls of the temple, are where the temple's daily routine occurs. Outside, the four surrounding streets are lined with shops, but on festival days the streets become the gods' royal roads when the divine images are processed around the temple borders. Thus the Kapaleeswara Temple, like the Sri Siva-Vishnu Temple, provides space for music, for daily officekeeping chores, and for preparing the *prashad* (sanctified food that is offered to the gods, then eaten by devotees). However, while the Sri Siva-Vishnu Temple divides these functions from the actual seats of the gods in one two-storied building, the Kapaleeswara Temple remains a single-level complex of buildings.

Climatic differences alone cannot account for this change in architecture from a walled compound in India to a single structure in America. The design of the Sri Siva-Vishnu Temple openly articulates theological changes that have occurred in the transplanting of India's gods to America. The community of devotees in the Washington area chose to construct a temple that would unite the two major Hindu traditions, Vaishnavism and Shaivism, "under one roof," as one member of the board of trustees aptly put it. Thus the Gods Siva and Vishnu are each housed in their own shrines, but within this single building. Other deities associated with each tradition have smaller shrines along the sides and the back of the first floor. A large shrine to Lord Murugan is at the center of the temple. The cupola over his image seems to blossom out of the temple's roof. He is flanked on the right and left by shrines of Siva and Vishnu respectively. The *vimanas* of their shrines likewise burst through the roof. The *vimanas* of other shrines are confined to the interior of the building.

A member of the board of trustees explained to me that the temple was carefully designed to exactly balance the two cosmic forces embodied in Siva and Vishnu. Thus, while the divine image of the powerful Goddess Durga rests on the north wall of the temple next to the Siva shrine, an image of the powerful Rama, an incarnation of Vishnu, was to balance her power on the east next to Vishnu's shrine in the original plans. Now Hanuman stands in this place as a deity of dimensions expansive enough to balance the goddess's own staggering force. These stone images of Durga and Hanuman were the first to be consecrated, on September 27–30, 1990.

The choice of the divine occupants for these shrines was much discussed by the trustees and community of devotees here and remains in flux. The original plans for the temple included in the early fundraising brochure called for a shrine to Rama, an incarnation of Vishnu, to be placed next to another shrine housing Nataraja, Siva as the cosmic dancer. Now Hanuman occupies the place next to Rama, as is traditional. The large wing dedicated to Lord Venkateeswara was proposed by a committee formed within the larger congregation, who then gained the support of the trustees. The board of trustees announced in the temple newsletter that "in response to the overwhelming desire of the devotees," it had decided to build a Sri Venkateeswara shrine as another extension to the present temple at the cost of $240,000. I received notice of the formal proposal to raise $300,000 to construct a shrine to Ayyappa as "an extension of the existing structure with the traditional 18 steps."

These decisions to include certain images reflect the creation of what could be called a new American Hindu pantheon. While traditional temples in South India often house several deities, and some major temples have substituted or subordinated one major deity for another in their thousand-year history, the choice of such an eclectic mix of deities from different regions in India and from once more distinct theologies is a phenomenon of modern times—especially of the rapid pace of temple growth in America. This new model is crucial because in America all the gods live in the same house.

This new model of a single enclosed space holding a group of different shrines is yet another architectural innovation within the boundaries of authenticity. The changes were explained to me by the member of the board of trustees who served as liaison between the board, Ganapathi Sthapati, his Indian crew, and the American contractors who actually built the basic structure. What appears in Lanham to be the outer wall of the temple actually functions like the outer wall that normally surrounds the open courtyard of a Hindu temple in South India. Thus inside this enclosure each deity continues to occupy his or her own shrine. The cupolas of the shrines of the three major deities actually protrude from the roof, and it is these three ornate *vimanas* that neighbors in Lanham see as they pass the temple. There are plans to put the *gopara*, the traditional massive gates at the cardinal directions in a temple's surrounding wall, onto the walls of this temple. But in the American context, these gates will appear as doors into this enclosed space. Hence the plurality of gods here live under the same roof, but nonetheless in their own rooms. Devotees tell me that this conglomerate space allows them either to see the temple as a unified divine area or to concentrate their devotion on one deity. As one said, "I can feel as though I am with only one god if I want, or with all."

The curious feature of this great effort at unity within the diversity of Hinduism, however, is the concomitant separation of sacred from secular in the use of two levels. Music, eating, office work, and education are now "downstairs" functions, while upstairs is reserved for the holy rituals and ceremonies. Further, no festival actually spills out into the streets of this quiet suburban neighborhood. When the gods are first processed, they are carried inside around the first floor. During important rituals, such as the recent consecration rites, the priest carries holy water in sacred pots around an outer promenade which forms a railed porch circling the entire first floor and opening out onto a grand staircase leading down to the lower parking lot. Processions around this outer promenade are the only public display of Hindu rituals that Lanham, Maryland, will normally see.

The only god whose eyes turn to Cipriano Road is Ganesa, who can be seen looking out from his niche in the exterior wall. Ganesa, as the divine guardian of doors, is by his very nature a border-ward and thus looks out to the world. The other deities will live their lives, on the upper level, within these cinderblock walls. And more important, the devotees have chosen to demarcate the holy life of the gods above from the music, education, and business carried on below. Thus dance and education will not be conducted in front of the very eyes of the gods, as is the case in India. The Hindu gods in America truly live in a split-level suburban world, with its inside/outside, upstairs/downstairs dichotomies.

The transplantation of Hinduism to America in the case of the Sri Siva-Vishnu Temple is not just a matter of finding a home and feeling at home, as John Fenton so well describes; it is a matter of building and maintaining a house. The crucial clue revealed in the design of the temple and its place on Cipriano Road is that ultimate marker of the American dream—home ownership. In India, ancient temples were built and maintained by kings. During the colonial period, this royal function passed to the new British government, which created a system of temple trusts both independent of and yet part of the state governments, a system, much like our federal reserve, which remains today. In modern India the very wealthy build temples, and the state still has a hand in their maintenance and construction. In Lanham, on the other hand, the devotees own the temple as a joint trust. Several members of the board of trustees pointed out that the model of administration by elected and appointed trustees supported by hundreds of individual contributions is new. They would agree with the way the chairman of the board of trustees of a Hindu temple in Nashville described the situation: "We found ourselves, a bunch of amateurs, trying to manage the complexities of a religious institution." Through their trustees, devotees pay the mortgage each month, and all the other problems of home ownership must be met without fail.

But this house belongs to the whole community and marks the true rise of the middle-class Indian. As they moved close to the deity, or climbed up on the roof to see the *vimanas*, or sat right next to or even entered the sanctum during the rituals, members of the board of trustees and many devotees said to me, "We could never get this close to the ritual in India; we could never see such things there; we could never take such an important part in this ritual." In owning a temple, thus, the middle class has thrown down the rights of kings, the rights of the British Raj, and the rights of the state over such structures. It was not lost on devotees that as the fireworks blasted above Washington on July 4, 1991, the Sri Siva-Vishnu Temple was installing its gods! In 1993, I heard a legend that a famous psychic at the turn of the century had predicted that Hindu temples would come to America on a Fourth of July holiday.

But what does this phenomenon of home ownership have to do with the issues of the universality and particularity of the Hindu temple that began this essay? The point here can be stated simply: The mobile middle class in the world now goes from house to house, not place to place! The temple stands amid other houses, but it is not related to them in any way other than that this suburban world allows such a temple to exist as a house among houses. Even the zoning laws in such areas recognize such houses of god as residential and not commercial property. In this sense, only such neutral areas that are not bounded neighborhoods could so easily tolerate such diversity. The Indian community at the temple takes great care not to disturb its close neighbors and those whose houses border the temple. Devotees have invited their neighbors to participate in important activities, and a few of these folks do drop by as good but somewhat bewildered neighbors. I found myself explaining the rituals to an African American neighbor who had come by to see her new neighbors. She quietly asked me the pressing question for her as a Muslim: "Do they believe in God?" When I said yes, she left satisfied, saying that was all that really counted.

Suburban land on the borders of the metropolitan area remains segmented into plots. Like their neighbors, the devotees of the Sri Siva-Vishnu Temple do not bring their private religious life out into the streets. Religious practice is carried on within the confines of their own castle — in a very middle-class sense of that term. Here is one structure that is to hold the new Hindu family in America under one roof, separate but equal with the other religions of America. The gods of India have a new home, a foothold on the western shore, a life beyond the borders of India but yet a life confined to a house. Is this not the quintessential characteristic of the suburban home? Family on the inside facing out. Diversities living side by side but never infringing on the other — a patchwork quilt, a cut-and-paste world of multiculturalism that is stitched together by neighborliness and good fences. Yet within the walls of each square exists a private world, my blue heaven, as the old song goes, "with a plot of, not a lot of land."

Thus as a house, the Sri Siva-Vishnu Temple becomes a very particular and concrete entity, while as a place, Lanham, Maryland, remains seemingly neutral — the location a plot on a surveyor's chart of streets and houses. But this American Hindu holy house also contains two levels.

What are the upstairs and downstairs of this world? Certainly the downstairs is not completely situated in Lanham, Maryland, but it is also not identical to the orthodox upstairs where the priests imported from India do their holy work. Ultimately, the split-level world of this suburban Washington temple provides an apt image for the cultural world of the affluent Indian American community here. In America, Indians live in a split-level universe that is "traditional" above but with a lower floor that is the space of the worldwide modern middle-class family life—from which Indians came in India, but which is now enhanced by their move to America.

Upstairs/Downstairs:
Negotiating Gender and Generations

In the attractive brochure introducing the temple to prospective donors, the temple lists its services as "religious," "cultural," and "philosophical." The category "religious" is confined to the celebration of festivals, group worship, the performance of weddings and other life-cycle rites, and classes on "Sanskrit, Vedas, and Hindu rituals." The term "religious," in other words, now belongs only to the ritual performances of the priests. These are the upstairs activities. Philosophical talks and discussions—the preaching activities of Hinduism—now belong downstairs with such teaching activities as summer camps for youth and adults, yoga classes, dance classes, and lessons in the various vernacular languages of India. Although such an upstairs/downstairs division of the temple (reserving the word "religion" for the upstairs) is quite out of step with Hindu tradition, the division makes sense in America. Sacred is not really divided from secular here, and middle-class family life has actually invaded what were once professional and priestly realms. The family is now on the lower floor of the temple. The middle-class world has been reconstructed within the temple as it is known in the homes of recent immigrants. These are not sanctuaries *from* America, because the suburban outside has been integrated into both floors of the temple, though as an Indo-American, not a Euro-American, phenomenon.

The case of dance is instructive here. Until the early part of this century, dancers in India were temple servants who worked alongside the priests to provide comfort and pleasure to the gods embodied in the temple. A rigorous reform movement accused these *devadasis*, slaves of god, of being nothing more than glorified prostitutes and corrupting the temple, and they were soon expelled. But within two decades, Indians realized that they had thrown out an important cultural performance in the name of an ostensible moral purity. Dance was revived outside the

2.5. The two levels of the temples are clearly visible, with very American picnic tables just outside the kitchen areas.

temple as an art to be cultivated by the daughters of the rising upper-middle class, and so it remains in performance halls in India. But in America it has returned to the temple, while acquiring much the same place that ballet lessons have in the Euro-American home, as a matter of family pride in the accomplishments of a daughter who, nonetheless, is rarely encouraged to become a full-time professional dancer.

Pride in the "culture" of the homeland frequently marks the middle-class first and second generation's most permanent tie to the mother country in the American context. For the secular Indian, the categories of "culture" and "philosophy" have become neutral terms with few religious overtones. A great Carnatic vocal performed in the common room is like the Ave Maria sung in a concert hall, not at the altar in a Catholic church. Similarly, discussions of the meaning of religious texts are "philosophy" and fully congruent with the modern rational world, whereas the same text chanted in ritual might seem an embarrassing incantation. There are many in the Indian American community who are not supportive of religious ritual, but they do want to keep up family values and to retain Hinduism as a moral and aesthetic force in their life. The lower-floor auditorium is for them.

The lower floor is also for the second generation, for whom the activities upstairs often seem as confusing as for any American youth. John Fenton summarizes the dilemma for the generation who pledged much of their lives and even their fortune to help build this temple: "The irony of Hindu temple-building activity in America is that it emphasizes that aspect of Hindu religion that so far has the least meaning and that is the most opaque to second generation Indian immigrants."[32] "We have built this for the sake of our children," said one older devotee while pointing to this grand edifice in the nation's capital. "Are we building it for nothing?" A telling scene in the movie *Mississippi Masala* shows two young second-generation children playing cowboys and Indians (the Native American variety) in the midst of the celebration of the holy Hindu wedding rites in a small town in Mississippi. Several young boys with baseball bats in hand, ready to "play ball," can be spotted outside the holy *yagasala*, the tent constructed to build the sacred fires needed to awaken the gods during the great installation rituals in July.

Such "youths," at quite a loss on the upper floor, are more at home in the classrooms below. In the first National Indian-American Students Conference, hosted by Sangam, the Indian students' association at the University of North Carolina/Chapel Hill, Indian American college students from almost fifty institutions articulated their discomfort with religion "as a show" and with ritual that they could not and were not asked to understand.[33] An essay in *Sanyog: South Asian Expressions* poses the dilemma of ritual for the second generation: "You can't give god a granola bar."[34] Here in Washington, those families who chose to watch the ritual on video downstairs sat in congenial groups, as mother-father-children, while upstairs the South India proprieties were tacitly observed, with gender-segregated seating. An active group of young people who were trying to get into the spirit of things during this *mahakumbhabhisekam* ritual nonetheless did not remain upstairs for the rituals but sold "Om Shanti" t-shirts on the lower floor, while their mothers cooked a phenomenal amount of food, which they sold downstairs at nominal cost to raise money for the temple.

Women in the kitchen downstairs and men carrying out priestly functions (now defined as "religious") upstairs is the source of low-level, but palpable, tension in the temple. This gender dichotomy in part reflects traditional Indian society, but it also is created by the upstairs/downstairs spatial division. There are some real ironies here. For American feminists, women in the kitchen marks gender segregation and subordination, but these South Asian women work in the temple kitchens, a task that in India is reserved for Brahmin men, whose ritual purity was a prerequisite for handling the holy food which was always served first to god. When women now make this *prashad*, sanctified meals eaten by devotees as a sacrament, they are assuming a priestly role; their domestic task has expanded in America into temple service. The downstairs of the temple now has become a true home where the housewife cooks and serves the larger family of devotees. Sharing this home-space with young people, women find their status at once enhanced by their greater role but also diminished because that role is no longer on a level (literally) with the other ritual functions of the temple. In American fashion, food, now only vaguely sacralized as the *prashad*, is served as "lunch" on Styrofoam plates by exhausted volunteers and eaten with plastic spoons.

Women grumble about this aspect of the new split-level world. Many of these women work and succeed in America, as do their spouses. Yet here in this space, the division could be seen as even more segregated than in the "control" temple Kapaleeswara in Madras, where the cooking is left to the Brahmins and women are not behind kitchen walls. I heard discontent in the American temple; women mentioned to me that they have no real say in serious decision making. Yet women were forceful and very active not only in cooking but also in decorating the temple upstairs and in organizing fundraising; most important, I heard a number of women chanting in Sanskrit along with the priest as they sat "listening." I suspected a desire for an increased ritual role, and my suspicions were realized late on the last holy night of the installation rituals that July. After a long, quite beautiful marriage ritual for the god Murugan and his wives while the congregation chanted the wedding vows for the divine couples, the lovely palanquins with the bronze images of the deities inside were lifted by male devotees for the ride around the borders of the interior of the temple. When they reached the shrine of the goddesses Sarada and Parvati, however, the two palanquins apparently changed hands—for when the procession came out the other side of the temple, they were being carried by some joyous women. I asked one female palanquin bearer if it was usual in India for women to do this. She replied immediately, "In India they are male chauvinists, but this is America." As the palanquins turned the corner, one middle-aged woman grumbled about seeing women behave in this manner, but the faces of the hijackers revealed the glee of women taking their first steps toward a new role in their ritual and managerial positions in the temple.

Upstairs/downstairs may be solid architectural space, but it is not, then, stable social space. The more domesticated the temple becomes, the more its overarching model becomes the family, the more the tensions in middle-class family life will explode through the seemingly solid floors. By adopting the suburbs as the location of the temple, by opting for the suburban split of domestic life from public life, the founders of the Sri Siva-Vishnu Temple sought to create a Hindu family within the American world of family life and family values. American life has not been factored out; it has been invited in to rest right under the Hindu holy sanctums. But as the women here have already shown, the space between the floors is not airtight.

Between Upstairs and Downstairs: Technology as the Third Space

The moment when the priests awakened the gods to their new life in America by pouring the holy waters, the *abhisekam*, over the stone images was viewed by many devotees on video monitors carefully placed alongside each sanctum. In the earlier *pranapratistha* ceremonies which awakened Durga, Hanuman, and Ganesa, the *abhisekam* for each deity was performed in rapid sequence in each sanctum. Devotees sat facing the deity whose rituals they had sponsored through donation. The video monitors allowed devotees to get the closest view of the ritual in front of them and to witness each of the consecutive consecrations; the chief engineer for this complex technology switched from camera to camera to catch the crucial moments at each shrine. A telling moment in this conflation of ancient ritual with advanced technology occurred when I was seated with a large group of devotees in front of Hanuman, with another group of devotees at our rear facing the Durga shrine in the opposite direction. At the moment when the holy waters awakened Durga, my Hanuman group raised their folded hands in the sign of devotion to the image on the video monitor in front, when a simple twist of the head would have revealed Durga in the flesh just behind. The image on the video monitor was an acceptable double for the image to the rear.

In the consecration ritual, this video system operated by an African American crew and director became an ever-present symbol of the modernity of these rituals. Although few non-Indians participated, the video crew was afforded the clearest vision of the holiest of sights by virtue of their skill in the new medium of imaging. This use of video cameras is by no means new to the Hindu temple. The cameras now have the first view of the holiest of rituals in the sanctums of major temples in India when there is no other way to accommodate the desire of the vast crowd of devotees to share in these holy sights. But new in America was the choice to put these cameras in non-Hindu hands. The crew remained patient and respectful through the long days of these rituals. The remark of one tired "grip" showed how well the presence of the video cameras had made the translation of this temple ritual to an American idiom: "This is the longest church service I ever attended," he sighed on the fifth straight day of the rituals.

The non-Hindu community was again directly incorporated into the ritual at the point of another technical skill. The African American mason who carefully cut and fixed the marble on the walls of the interior of the sanctum, the very place where the divine images would reside, became an important participant in the consecration ritual. On the first day of the rituals in July, this mason found himself standing with his shirt and shoes removed in front of the sacred fire. Minutes later, with a turban on his head, this obviously serious but delighted mason pulled a burning straw man through each of the interiors of the new sanctums in the temple. His was the final act of purification to make the sanctums ready for their divine residents. His work as mason had taken on its full ritual significance.

The Sri Siva-Vishnu Temple lives with its doors open to its neighbors. No one is excluded; an announcement of the consecration rituals in July invited "all Hindus and non-Hindus alike to join in this unique event." Some non-Hindu Indians, some non-Hindu Americans, and some Hindu Euro-Americans came. But they were not as openly representative of the greater American community as the mason who was seen to stand for the many non-Hindus who had a hand in constructing the temple.

There are non-Hindus who now figure in the stories told about the monumental five-year task of constructing this temple. I heard particular praise for the Italian American master stonecutter who worked with his Indian counterparts, the *silpis* from Madras. Their common love of stone led to an exchange of ideas and techniques. The American stonecutter introduced the *silpis* to the ideas of laser cutting and developing computer patterns for their decorative work. He marveled at their style and the skill of their work. These exchanges took place on the level of seeing and doing, because many of the *silpis* know little English. Another much-praised non-Hindu company were the movers who successfully brought the two-ton stone sculpture of Vishnu into his sanctum inch by inch without harming a speck of his body. Their technical skill, but also their quiet and innate sense of the sacredness of the piece, impressed the Indian crew. It is in such stories of a shared love of craft and the technology of construction, the mutual awe at skills and design, that Hindus and non-Hindus meet in this temple, just as it is in front of the video that families of all generations are able to sit together. Technology, in this temple, is the third space where

2.6. The African American stonemason works in the interior of a main shrine, while a traditional mason from India completes the exterior ornamentation.

differences of generation and even of ethnic and religious origins are increasingly able to find a meeting ground.

Conclusion: A House with Many Rooms

Trustees and devotees of the Sri Siva-Vishnu Temple live with and talk openly about the many tensions in their new lives in the United States. Husbands and wives worry about the loss of Indian culture in their children. The "children" who are now adults in college wonder about the meaning of this Hinduism that they see reconstructed in front of them. At a time of rising Hindu nationalism in India, these Hindus away from India wonder how to react to the new Indian political-religious parties now coming here for their support. Men remain worried about their chances for ultimate success in a highly competitive global market. Discussion of an economic "glass ceiling" are part of the ethos of those who also worry about the economics of keeping a roof over the gods. But this congregation has built the dialogue, the tensions, and the uncertainty of their lives into the space of a temple in suburban Washington, D.C. In a move that was at once as characteristically American as it was Indian, they offered their prosperity as a down payment, mortgaged their fears, and built a house.

This temple as a *house*, however, has fixed nothing for these Indian Americans—and, I would argue, was never meant to *fix* anything. This building made of concrete, these gods formed from stone, are not inanimate objects that are riveted motionless. The temple and the gods are "vibrating," as Ganapathi Sthapati told the devotees at the moment of the consecration of the temple in July 1991. Once the houses—of the gods and of humanity—are freed from their status as inanimate things, their power to transform and to re-create their creators becomes clear. In this sense of the *power* of space, the American home and the Hindu holy house live as analogues in the modern world.

In a dramatic statement in *The Poetics of Space*, Gaston Bachelard declares, "The house remodels man."[35] David Knipe, in a striking conclusion to a volume of cross-cultural essays on the temple in society, also ends with the suggestion that temples are ultimately places for and models of "transformation" both for the self and for an entire culture.[36] In these approaches to constructed space, the human house and the divine temple are alive with power; those who associate the construction of buildings only with finding security or with engraving meanings in stone do not understand the tensile, active, "vibrating" nature of holy stones or sacred rocks or even houses. Bachelard's houses are built out of wood and stone and imagination to re-place the human soul into a built life in this world.

But just as Bachelard constructed his musings on space in the middle of this century out of his experiences with the house, so the house in the contemporary world may be the primary model and space for middle-class imaginings of the saved. "The City" as a place of dreams may well have been replaced by "the house." Certainly children "grow up" in houses, and old people hope to "pass away" in the heart of their own homes; the magazine rack at the grocery store is filled with photos of "dream houses." The Sri Siva-Vishnu Temple in America may prove to be the kind of contemporary house—with enough rooms, staircases, twists, and turns— to hold a very diverse family made up of gods and humans, men and women, parents and children, Indians and Americans, while giving them all space enough to grow.

Notes

1. Surinder M. Bhardwaj, "Asian Indians in the United States: A Geographic Appraisal," in *South Asians Overseas: Migration and Ethnicity*, ed. Colin Clark (Cambridge: Cambridge University Press, 1990), 195–217.

2. See Parminder Bhashu, "New Cultural Forms and Transnational Women in the Diaspora: Culture, Class, and Consumption among British Asian Women," paper presented at "The Expanding Landscape: South Asians in Diaspora," sponsored by the Independent Scholars of South Asia and Southern Asian Institute, Columbia University, March 5–6, 1993.

3. Raymond B. Williams, *Religions of Immigrants from India* (Cambridge: Cambridge University Press, 1988), 14–23.

4. New York: Random House, 1993. Quoted in *Hinduism Today*, September 1993, 27.

5. Priya Agarwal, *Passage from India: Post 1965 Indian Immigrants and Their Children* (Palos Verdes, Calif.: Yuvati, 1991), 67–68.

6. Bible, 2 Sam. 8:6.

7. Vasudha Narayanan, "Creating South Indian Hindu Experience in the United States," in *A Sacred Thread: Modern Transmission of Hindu Traditions in India and Abroad*, ed. Raymond Brady Williams (Chambersburg, Penn.: Anima, 1992), 164.

8. Amitav Ghosh, "The Diaspora in Indian Culture," *Public Culture* 2 (Fall 1989): 76.

9. V. S. Naipaul, *An Area of Darkness* (London: Andre Deutsch, 1964).

10. Richard Hughs Seager, ed., *The Dawn of Religious Pluralism: Voices from the World's Parliament of Religions, 1893* (La Salle: Open Court, 1993), 421–32.

11. *India Today*, North American edition, August 31, 1993, 48C.

12. *India Times*, June 30, 1993, 4.

13. Max Weber, *The Religion of India*, trans. Hans H. Gerth and Don Martindale (Glencoe, Ill.: Free Press, 1958 [1921]), 309. See J. N. Farquhar, *Modern Religious Movements in India* (reprint; Delhi: Munshiram Manoharlal, 1977 [1914]); Stephen Fuchs, *Rebellious Prophets: A Study of Messianic Movements in Indian Religions* (Bombay: Asia Publishing House, 1965).

14. Lawrence Alan Babb, *Redemptive Encounters: Three Modern Styles in Hindu Religion* (Berkeley and Los Angeles: University of California Press, 1986), 186, 224–25.

15. Ibid., 18.

16. Raymond B. Williams, *A New Face of Hinduism: The Swaminarayanan Religion* (Cambridge: Cambridge University Press, 1984); Williams, *Religions of Immigrants from India*, 129–85; Mark Juergensmeyer, *Radhasoami Reality: The Logic of a Modern Faith* (Princeton: Princeton University Press, 1991).

17. Williams, *Religions of Immigrants from India*, 173–85.

18. John Y. Fenton, *Transplanting Religious Traditions: Asian Indians in America* (New York: Praeger, 1988), 171.

19. Fred W. Clothey, "The Construction of a Temple in an American City and the

Acculturation Process," in *Rhythm and Intent: Ritual Studies from South India* (Madras: Blackie, 1983).

20. Narayanan, "Creating South Indian Hindu Experience in the United States," 18.

21. Stella Kramrisch, *The Hindu Temples*, 2 vols. (Delhi: Motilal Banarsidass), 131–44.

22. S. S. Janaki, "Dhvaja-Stambba: Critical Account of Its Structural and Ritualistic Details," in *Siva Temple and Temple Rituals*, ed. S. S. Janaki (Madras, 1988), 122.

23. Kramrisch, *The Hindu Temples*, 5.

24. Susan Lewandowski, "Changing Form and Function in the Ceremonial and the Colonial Port City in India: An Historical Analysis of Madurai and Madras," *Modern Asian Studies* 2 (1974): 183–212.

25. Joanne Punzo Waghorne, "Mylapore," in *Temple Towns of Tamil Nadu*, ed. George Michell (Bombay: Marg Publications, 1993), 114–28.

26. Philip Lutgendorf, "My Hanuman Is Bigger Than Yours," *History of Religions* 33 (February 1994).

27. Kim Knott, "Hindu Temple Rituals in Britain: The Reinterpretation of Tradition," in *Hinduism in Great Britain*, ed. Richard Burkhart (London and New York: Tavistock, 1987); Robert Jackson, "The Shree Krishna Temple and the Gujarati Hindu Community in Coventry," in *Hinduism in England*, ed. David G. Bowen (Bradford, West Yorkshire: Bradford College, 1981); Steven Vertovec, "Community and Congregation in London Hindu Temples: Divergent Trends," *New Community* 18 (January 1992): 251–64; Susan Nowikowski and Robin Ward, "Middle Class and British? An Analysis of South Asians in Suburbia," *New Community* 8 (Winter 1978–79): 1–10.

28. Fred W. Clothey, "Rituals and Reinterpretations: South Indians in Southeast Asia," in *A Sacred Thread: Modern Transmission of Hindu Traditions in India and Abroad*, ed. Raymond Brady Williams (Chambersburg, Penn.: Anima, 1992).

29. Purushottama Bilimoria of Deakin University is working extensively on new Hindu temples in Australia.

30. Paul Mikula, Brian Kearney, and Rodney Harber, *Traditional Hindu Temples in South Africa* (Durban: Hindu Temple Publications, 1982).

31. V. Ganapathi Sthapati, "Symbolism of Vimana and Gopura," in *Siva Temple and Temple Rituals*, ed. S. S. Janaki (Madras: Kuppuswami Sastri Research Institute, 1988), 114.

32. Fenton, *Transplanting Religious Traditions*, 179.

33. Research Triangle Park, August 6–9, 1992.

34. Anuradha Mannar, "You Can't Give God a Granola Bar," *Sanyog: South Asian Expressions* (Durham, N.C.) 3 (Fall 1992): 28–29.

35. Gaston Bachelard, *The Poetics of Space*, trans. Maria Jolas (Boston: Beacon, 1969), 47. The study of space was introduced to American scholarship by Yi-Fu Tuan, *Space and Place: The Perspective of Experience* (Minneapolis: University of Minnesota Press, 1977).

36. David M. Knipe, "The Temple in Image and Reality," in *Temple in Society*, ed. Michael V. Fox (Winona Lake: Eisenbrauns, 1988), 132–33.

Diasporic Nationalism and Urban Landscape

Cuban Immigrants at a Catholic Shrine in Miami

Thomas A. Tweed

> Diasporas always leave a trail of collective memory about another place and time and create new maps of desire and attachment.[1]

Fidel Castro's revolutionary army victoriously entered Havana on January 8, 1959, and thereby transformed the cultural landscape of Miami. In 1960, only 29,500 Cubans lived in Miami, where they constituted only 3 percent of the local population. Jews had migrated earlier, and they had some public power. Yet the region was still largely southern and Protestant in character. By 1990, however, more than 561,000 Cubans had arrived, and they made up almost 30 percent of the local residents.[2]

The Cubans who have so abruptly and radically altered the cultural landscape of Miami have viewed themselves above all as members of an exiled community, citizens of a dispersed nation. Yet collective identity becomes especially problematic for exiles. Most immigrants experience disorientation, and most retain fondness for their native land. For exiles, however, those feelings are intensified. As the geographer Yi-Fu Tuan has suggested, "To be forcibly evicted from one's home and neighborhood is to be stripped of a sheathing, which in its familiarity protects the human being from the bewilderments of the outside world." The diaspora's sense of meaning and identity is threatened because it has lost contact with the natal landscape, which is "personal and tribal history made visible."[3]

As political exiles, Cubans have experienced the expected disorientation and shown a single-minded passion for their homeland. As Cuban Americans boast, and some non-Latino blacks and "Anglos" complain, the diaspora tenaciously holds to the Cuban past and continually plans its future. In voting, most ask first about the candidate's stance toward Castro. Musicians and singers who have visited Cuba have been banned from performing in the city. Even those who are not as consumed with these issues scan the news for signs of instability in Castro's government or for stories about the latest *balsero*, or rafter, found bobbing in the Straits of Florida. Spanish-language radio stations hold contests to guess the date that Castro will fall; and paramilitary groups, as well as associations of business and education leaders, plan for the future in a democratic and capitalist Cuba. According to recent surveys, less than one-quarter of exiles say they definitely would return to Cuba to live if democracy and capitalism were restored. But even those who might not return to a "liberated" homeland still repeat the expression commonly heard at Christmas Eve family gatherings: "¡La próxima Nochebuena nos comeremos el lechoncito en Cuba!" (Next Christmas Eve, we shall eat the traditional roast pork dinner in Cuba).[4]

This attachment to homeland, or nationalism, has a distinctive character for exiles in general and Cubans in particular. For them, "nation" cannot refer to a state or territory: Castro's socialist government is seen as the main problem, and the displaced live outside their homeland's political boundaries. Yet exiles in Miami continue to refer to themselves as part of the Cuban "nation." Nation, in this context, becomes an imaginative construct, even more than is usually the case. The exile group's identity is created, not given; dynamic, not fixed. Relying on memories of the past and hopes for the future, exiles define themselves. In the process, they deterritorialize the nation. For them, nation becomes a supralocal or transregional cultural form, an imagined moral community formed by the diaspora and the oppressed who remain in the homeland.[5]

Diasporic nationalism, then, comes to mean attachment to the traditions and geography of the homeland, but with a twist. Cuban exiles are attached to the utopia of memory and desire, not to the dystopia of the contemporary socialist state. On the one hand, diasporic nationalism entails "geopiety," or an attachment to the natal landscape. This includes feelings for the natural terrain, the built environment, and the mental map of neighborhood, town, province, and country. Diasporic nationalism also involves attachment to the imagined contours of the liberated homeland as well as affection for the remembered traditions. In this case, it means passionate concern for democracy, capitalism, and various components of Cuban culture, including its music, fashion, architecture, language, and food. Some of these cultural components remain only slightly altered in contemporary Cuba; others exist now only in the exilic imagination.[6]

As part of the imaginative process of creating collective identity, diasporas often shape their new environment in the image of the old. Most Cuban exiles, like other immigrants, have lived in cities; so it is in urban spaces—alleys, streets, stores, apartments, and parks—that the imaginative processes linked with diasporic nationalism have taken place. In Miami, where most Cuban immigrants live, exiles have transformed the built environment. Cuban restaurants and businesses dot the landscape, and streets and parks named after Cuban leaders define space in the predominantly Cuban neighborhoods that spread out in a V-shaped pattern from the port of Miami. One small park in Little Havana that fills with older men playing dominoes, smoking cigars, and discussing politics is named after Antonio Maceo, a hero of the Cuban war for independence. Two blocks east of that park is a monument that has the emotional power for Cuban Americans that the Vietnam War Memorial holds for other Americans. The cylindrical stone monument remembers the men of Brigade 2506 who died during the failed Bay of Pigs invasion.[7]

At the same time, exiles also have drawn new mental maps. They imaginatively have mapped the history and geography of the homeland onto the new urban landscape. For instance, prerevolutionary Cuba had been divided into six provinces and 126 municipalities or townships. In Miami, local organizations called Cuban Municipalities in Exile preserve and intensify old regional and local affiliations. There are 110 officially recognized *municipios en el exilio.* Twenty of them have permanent buildings. Two of the larger ones, Havana and Santiago de Cuba, list almost a thousand members and hold monthly meetings. Most have a few hundred members and meet a few times each year. In their official headquarters, or in rented halls or restaurants, those who hail from the same Cuban township regularly are invited to congregate to sip Cuban coffee and converse about Cuban politics.[8]

Religion has played an important role in the process of transforming the cultural landscape and creating collective identity. In this chapter I explore the role of religion in the construction of "national" identity among Cuban immigrants in their new urban setting. For reasons that will become clear, I focus on devotion to Our Lady of Charity, the patroness of Cuba, at the shrine erected in her honor in Miami. I suggest—and this is my main point—that exiles struggle over the meaning of symbols, but almost all Cuban American visitors to the shrine see it above all as a place to express diasporic nationalism. There, exiles map the landscape and history of the homeland onto the new urban environment through architecture and ritual. Through symbols at the shrine, the diaspora imaginatively constructs its collective identity and transports itself to the Cuba of memory and desire.[9]

I divide this chapter into four sections. I first describe my method and sources and then offer a brief history of devotion to Our Lady of Charity, in Cuba and Miami. Next I consider some of the ways that the meanings of symbols are *contested.* Finally, I explore the *shared* meaning of the architecture and ritual.

3.1. The Bay of Pigs Memorial on Cuban Memorial Boulevard in Little Havana. The inscription reads "Cuba: To the Martyrs of the Assault Brigade, April 17, 1961." The monument memorializes the failed attempt by United States–trained Cuban exiles to overthrow the government of Cuba.

Method and Sources

I use a combination of historical and ethnographic methods. I have analyzed contemporary and archival written sources. As a means of tracing changes over time, I also have reviewed statistical information on the religious life of Cubans before and after Castro's revolution. I have studied the exile community's material culture as well—architecture, yard shrines, murals, holy cards, and statues.

To understand the contemporary situation, I relied on observation and interviews. Most important, I conducted 304 structured interviews in which shrine visitors answered twenty questions on a questionnaire. I conducted research at all days and times. I stood outside the steps near one of the three exits. As pilgrims left, I told them that I was writing a book about devotion to the Virgin at the shrine, and I asked if they had time to answer some questions. This method did not ensure a random sample, of course, even though it yielded responses from a diverse group in terms of gender, region, and age. But it did provide rich detail about how some visitors understood devotion at the shrine. Most of those who spoke to me were middle-aged, and slightly more women than men visited the shrine. Yet often, especially on weekends, extended families would arrive together, kneel at the altar, buy a souvenir, take group photographs, stroll the grounds, and pile back into the minivan for the ride home.

Half of the twenty questions that visitors answered were open-ended. I asked, for example, not only about their arrival date and native region, but also about their impressions of the mural and the reasons for their devotion. Most of the questionnaires were self-administered, but occasionally those who were infirm, aged, or illiterate asked me to read the questions to them. In either case, I stood beside them as they answered. This allowed me to clarify ambiguities in the questions and encouraged them to explain their answers. It also led to a very high response rate. As we went along, I often asked them for elaboration or clarification, and often they volunteered more than I requested, sometimes telling long, and usually sad, stories about their life in Cuba and their exile in America. After they answered the standard questions, I asked visitors if they had time to talk further. Many did. Although I encountered the members of the Confraternity of Our Lady of Charity often, I spoke with most pilgrims once, and the conversations lasted approximately thirty minutes. Some were shorter, as devotees rushed home to make dinner, scurried to gather relatives, or hurried back to the office. Other conversations lasted much longer, even several hours. Except when pilgrims requested otherwise, the interviews were in Spanish. Even when some visitors would begin in English, they would return to their native tongue to express a deeply held belief—and, I learned, many Cuban pilgrims had deeply held religious beliefs.[10]

Our Lady of Charity and the Shrine

Prerevolutionary Cuba was a relatively unchurched nation, especially in rural areas. In 1954, a few years before Castro's revolution, Cuba had the lowest percentage of nominal Catholics and practicing Catholics in Latin America. There were relatively few priests. In a 1957 survey of four hundred rural heads of families, only half identified themselves as Catholics. The vast majority (88.8 percent) never attended services, and only 4 percent attended three or more times a year. In fact, only slightly more than half (53.5 percent) had ever seen a priest.[11]

All this is not to say, of course, that Cubans were not religious. They simply were not linked closely with formal religious institutions. It was the church and the priests with whom many were not familiar; they felt quite comfortable with the Christian God and the Catholic saints, many even with the African *orishas* of Santería. Folk Catholicism was vigorous. The home and the streets were the preferred places of worship. As in other regions of North and South America, religious festivals played a significant part in devotional life. Many of the older exiles I interviewed told me that they had rarely gone to mass: they lived too far away from the churches. But they reported attending the primary public celebrations—on Good Friday, on the Epiphany, and on the feast days of the three main objects of popular veneration: Saint Barbara, Saint Lazarus, and Our Lady of Charity. They also recalled fondly the religion of the home. One sixty-four-year-old man from a rural township who had rarely gone to church as a child told me, trembling with emotion, that his strong devotion to Our Lady of Charity began with the family and in the home. Each night before bedtime, as his mother had instructed, he knelt to kiss the feet of the statue enshrined in their living room.

Cuban devotion to Our Lady of Charity has a long history, and especially since the nineteenth century she has been linked with national identity. "Cuba and the Virgin are the same thing," explained one shrine visitor. This middle-aged woman, who was born in Havana and arrived in Miami in 1960, expressed a common feeling among immigrants, laity and clergy. One exiled Cuban priest, for instance, suggested that "to look at [the image of] the Virgin of Charity is to think about Cuba, because she has been inexorably linked with our nationality and our history." The connection goes back to the beginning of the seventeenth century, when, according to popular legend, three laborers paddling in a small boat found the statue of the Virgin floating in the sea off the eastern coast of the island. This image later was enshrined in Cobre, a town in the easternmost province, Oriente. For two centuries, devotion was intense in that region, and over time it spread westward to the five other provinces of Cuba.[12]

It was during the late-nineteenth-century wars for independence from Spain that the Virgin became almost inseparable from the land and nation. A number of the soldiers who fought for independence (*los mambises*) adopted her as their patroness. Some carried her image with them into battle; others wore it on their shirts. Still others simply asked her to intercede for them and their nation. Because of her participation in the fight for freedom, the people still refer to her as *la Virgen Mambisa*.[13]

The nationalistic elements of devotion to Our Lady of Charity escalated still further after independence was won in 1902. Indeed, it was the veterans of the wars for independence who successfully petitioned the pope in 1915 to name her the patroness of Cuba, and the Virgin's link with national identity and political resistance reemerged clearly just after the socialist revolution. In 1961, when government officials tried to undermine Havana's traditional procession on the feast day of Our Lady of Charity, thousands of devotees defiantly filled the streets near the church. The spontaneous religious procession developed into a political protest, and violence broke out, with one young leader of the protest being shot. The government, sensing the Virgin's significance and the concomitant political threat, prohibited religious processions. One hundred and thirty-two priests were arrested and expelled from the island a week later. Many of the exiled priests landed in Miami, and the Virgin emigrated as well. Although the original statue remains in Cobre, a replica was secretly transported from Havana to Miami on her feast day in 1961. The Virgin, now an exile herself, finally found a new home in Miami when the shrine was dedicated twelve years later.[14]

Exile has preserved and intensified devotion to Our Lady of Charity. The number of pilgrims to the shrine in Miami has risen over the years. By the 1990s, the urban shrine, the sixth-largest Catholic pilgrimage site in the United States, attracted hundreds of thousands of visitors annually. The large number who make the journey, the vast majority of whom are Cuban, attest to its importance to the diaspora.[15]

The shrine, which was dedicated December 2, 1973, rests on an acre of land on the shore of Biscayne Bay, a short distance south of the skyscrapers of downtown Miami. It is hidden from the view of motorists driving to and from the downtown area; only a small sign by the road, in Spanish, announces its location. As you turn down the winding road that leads from the main street, you pass a parish church and youth center. To the right is the parking lot of a Catholic hospital. Two rows of palm trees and a small sign, again in Spanish, mark the entrance. The wide brick path between the palms leads to the steps of the conical shrine. As you face the shrine, picnic tables and a convent/administrative building sit to the left. A few hundred yards to the right is the hospital. Behind the shrine, the cobalt blue of Biscayne Bay stretches toward the horizon. The shrine itself, with a white base and bronze cap, stands ninety feet high and eighty feet wide. Its verticality is emphasized not only by the cross on its peak but also because its foundation rests fourteen feet above sea level. Inside, hovering in front of the mural, the statue of Our Lady of Charity is raised on a pedestal at the center of the altar.

Several priests and nuns, almost all of Cuban descent, help Agustín A. Román, auxiliary bishop of Miami, oversee the shrine's activities. Román, the director of the shrine, was a moving force in building the edifice, and he remains one of the most beloved leaders of the exile community. One woman in her forties repeated what many others had told me: "He's a saint."

The members of the confraternity, and the other visitors, come at all times; but there are three main public rituals. First, there are weekday masses. On Monday, Wednesday, and Friday evenings masses are scheduled, in turn, for each of the 126 Cuban municipalities or townships. Also,

3.2. The Shrine of Our Lady of Charity in Miami.

3.3. Interior of the Miami shrine, with the small statue of Our Lady of Charity in the center. Behind the Virgin's image is the mural, which rises thirty-six feet from the sanctuary floor.

once a year the former residents of each of the six Cuban provinces are invited to return for a *romería*, a festival in which residents from a particular region journey to the local shrine. On the day of the *romería*, exiles from the same Cuban province eat, drink, chat, and worship together. The day, usually a Sunday, begins just after noon with lunch and ends with a rosary and procession around the shrine in the early evening. Finally, on September 8 thousands of exiles also take part in the annual feast day activities. They last all day and into the night. The most important part of those activities is the rosary and mass. Before Hurricane Andrew damaged the structure in 1992, this event usually was held in Miami Marine Stadium, only a short distance from the shrine. Those in the outdoor stadium, which overlooks the downtown skyline, say the rosary first. Later, as darkness falls, the mass begins. A flotilla of boats, all privately owned by exiles, escort the boat carrying the icon on her journey by water from the shrine. At the climax of the mass, that boat motors slowly to the side of the stage by the water's edge. Then several men balancing on the bow reverently lift the Virgin to others standing on the stage. They place the image near the right front of the stage. When the mass concludes, the same men carry the icon up the steep aisles of the stadium so that everyone can get a closer look. Finally, the clergy, choir, and lay readers file off the stage, led by the Virgin. The statue is then placed on the back of a flatbed truck in the parking lot. Devotees crowd close, encircling the unpretentious vehicle, to get another glimpse and to gather the fallen flowers as souvenirs. The truck, with the image secured by several male members of the confraternity, drives the three and a half miles over Rickenbacker Causeway and down a main street to the shrine. Most pilgrims go home as the Virgin leaves the stadium parking lot, but some follow her back to the shrine and remain for an hour or more, praying, singing, and talking.[16]

Contested Meanings

I highlight the shared nationalistic significance of the symbols connected with the shrine; but first it is important to acknowledge that their meaning is, to some degree, contested. There are, for instance, differences in interpretation and attitude between the Cuban American clergy and laity. Even though the exile community feels more positively toward the clergy—and especially Bishop Román—than prerevolutionary Cubans did, "religion as practiced" is partly in tension with "religion as prescribed."[17]

When I asked Bishop Román about the main problem facing the Cuban Catholic community in Miami, he said that it was "evangelization." He elaborated by drawing three concentric circles on note paper.

3.4. Male members of the Confraternity carry the Virgin through the crowd during the feast day mass. Photograph © by Michael Carlebach.

The smallest circle at the center, he explained, represented the minority of exiles who are devoted members of the "liturgical community" and attend mass regularly at their parish. The next-larger circle represented those who were nominal Catholics, the majority of Cuban Americans. The final circle, farthest from the center, represented those who were not officially Catholic. Bishop Román's concern was with the second group, the nominal Catholics who were not active and orthodox members of their parishes.[18]

I thought that I understood, until he explained further: The real challenge, he said, was to eliminate the "confusions." He suggested, "Those evangelizing the Cubans need to realize that one zone in need of purification is that in which the influence of Santería is significant." "Deficiencies in evangelization" have allowed the *orishas* of Santería to be confused with the saints of Catholicism. The number of officially initiated adherents is, he argued, rather small. But many, he claimed, dabble: "What is rather numerous is the amount of people belonging to the baptized multitudes of our Church who sporadically visit the *santero* or minister of that religion looking for good luck, health, protection, or wanting to know the future."[19]

The shrine, the clergy believe, provides the means of "purifying" nominal Cuban Catholicism of the residue of Santería. In the bishop's words, it offers a "pedagogical opportunity." He admitted, indeed, that "the shrine of Our Lady of Charity has been designed with this pedagogical idea in mind." Cubans, who were never as fully integrated into the liturgical community as the clergy would have liked, have had an intense devotion to Our Lady of Charity. So the clergy hoped to use the Virgin to reach the unchurched masses, especially but not exclusively those influenced by Santería. Once they got their attention, they could begin to "catechize," as another Cuban American exiled priest told me.[20]

That catechetical concern is clear in the clergy's attempts to distinguish Our Lady of Charity from Ochún, the Yoruba goddess of the river, with whom she sometimes is "confused." Both are affiliated with water, yellow, and love. Santería initiates, especially devotees of Ochún, still sometimes come to the Miami shrine, even though clerical and lay officials occasionally ask them to leave. One prominent member of the confraternity told me that when they encounter initiates at the shrine, usually dressed in white and throwing pennies, they "chase them off." Yet those Santería followers still find much that is familiar and affirming at the shrine. It is, after all, by the water. Like Ochún, the Virgin is associated with fertility and love, and prayer cards on the souvenir table in the back petition her for a safe and successful pregnancy. Finally, yellow rosebushes and painted yellow stones encircle the left side of the shrine's exterior. For those who know the references, all these elements link the Virgin and the *orisha*. Yet the clergy do their best to separate the two. In these and other ways, Catholic clergy and some laity struggle over the meaning of symbols.[21]

There also is significant diversity among those in the pews: Cuban lay followers struggle among themselves over the meaning of symbols. Gender, class, and race differentiate devotees of Our Lady of Charity, and age seems to be one of the most decisive distinguishing factors. Most studies of urban immigrants have found intergenerational differences in the practice of religion. Cubans seem typical in this regard. The intensity of devotion to Our Lady of Charity declines slightly among those who were born in exile or who came here as young children, those under forty years of age. There seems to be a still more precipitous drop in devotion for those under twenty. One devotee, who arrived at age thirty-three in 1963, put it this way when discussing those who had been born in America or had arrived as young children: "The young people do not believe as we do because they don't know the Virgin of Charity as the patroness of Cuba."[22]

Age was not the only factor dividing Cuban American pilgrims, and nationalistic sentiment was not the only element in their devotion. Respondents of all ages indicated, for instance, that "personal devotions" were more important to them than any scheduled rituals connected with the shrine. Most of the shrine visitors I spoke with suggested that the Virgin provided some sort of spiritual reward: they used words such as "peace," "strength," "confidence," "faith," and "hope." Some of my informants claimed that the Virgin provided material comforts of one sort or another. Pilgrims offered various instrumental prayers, which seek a response about a particular problem. One lower-class woman who arrived from Havana in 1991 did not elaborate but said only that Our Lady "grants me miracles." Many others were more specific. A twenty-eight-year-old woman claimed that the Virgin heals her children when they are sick. Some claimed that the Virgin helped them financially.[23]

Instrumental prayers to the Virgin often are linked with vows that specify the reciprocal action the pledger will take in the event of a favorable outcome, and many shrine visitors come to express gratitude or fulfill a vow. That is what drew one middle-aged man born in Oriente, who traveled all the way from Los Angeles. I first encountered his daughter, aged twenty-four, in the parking lot that Monday afternoon. After talking with her for twenty minutes or so, I was puzzled. She confessed to a complete lack of piety, but that made her presence at the shrine inexplicable. It turned out that she was waiting, not very patiently, by the rental car for her father to emerge. When he did, I asked him the usual questions. But this was no ordinary interview. He was fighting back tears the whole time. I asked if he had come to fulfill a vow. "Yes, I had some kind of problem with her," he said pointing to his daughter, who by now had turned on the car radio to pass the time as she waited in the white convertible. His eyes filled with tears again, and he indicated that he had to stop the interview. Whatever the problem, the Virgin had resolved it, and now this man had expressed his gratitude and kept his promise. Tomorrow they would fly back to Southern California.[24]

Shared Meaning: Diasporic Nationalism

As with this Cuban American from California, devotees' petitions often concerned not only their fate and that of their family but also that of their homeland. The pilgrim from Los Angeles, for example, also forcefully expressed his attachment to his native country. He, like most visitors, reported that his devotion to the patroness of Cuba had increased in exile, and he summarized the significance of that devotion this way: "It is that which maintains my hope to see my country free, and to return to it is very important." The nationalistic significance of the symbols was central for him and the other pilgrims. This is the shared meaning of the symbols. Through artifacts and rituals at the shrine, the diaspora maps the history and geography of the homeland onto the landscape of Miami and imaginatively constructs the moral community that constitutes the "true" Cuban nation.[25]

Architecture

Exiles express personal attachment to their homeland and create collective identity in and through the natural landscape and built environment of the shrine. Some of the nationalistic elements are clear and available to most Cuban American visitors. A Cuban flag—in red, blue, and white—has been painted on stones on the left exterior of the shrine. At the rear are busts of José Martí, the leader of the fight for independence from Spain, and Félix Varela, one of the most important Cuban religious leaders.[26]

Both figures also appear on the huge mural, called *La historia de Cuba en una mirada*, which is painted in brown and covers the area behind the altar. The central place in that painting by Teok Carrasco is reserved for the Virgin herself and the rowboat with the three laborers. The shrine's statue of the small dark-haired Virgin, with her cloak of white, is elevated on a pedestal just below the much larger painted image and immediately in front of the boat. From the traditional Cuban chairs that fill the shrine's interior, the statue appears to be standing in the painted boat, so that through *trompe l'oeil* the recovery of the statue at sea is vividly and three-dimensionally re-created.[27]

Martí is joined on the mural by other Cuban military, cultural, and political leaders. His portrait, which is the largest, rests immediately to the right of the painted Virgin. Just below him is Jesus Rabí, major general of the war for independence, who also presided at the important veterans' reunion in Cobre in 1915, when the former soldiers decided to petition the pope. Above and to the right of Martí is another general of the war for independence, Máximo Gómez. In the top right-hand corner, the painter placed the author of the Cuban national anthem, Pedro Figueredo. At the zenith of the mural, two angels ascend to heaven through clouds, wrapped in the Cuban flag. There is nothing subtle about all this, and few Cuban

American visitors to the shrine fail to notice the links established between the Virgin and Cuban soil.[28]

There are less explicit but still powerful expressions of attachment to homeland embedded in the shrine's natural and built environment. The shrine stands only yards from the bay, and water recalls both the geography of their island nation and the legend of their patroness. The shrine also was designed so that the statue of the Virgin would stand in a direct line with Cuba. Many of the visitors told me they noticed these more subtle messages.[29]

Bishop Román explained to me and his people other symbolic dimensions of the building. The cornerstone beneath the altar contains sand from the different Cuban provinces that was mixed with water found in a raft on which fifteen people died before they could find American shores. The triangular shape of the building's exterior re-creates the contours of the Virgin's cloak, so that the shrine is an architectural expression of a popular Cuban prayer: "Virgen Santísima, cúbrenos bajo tu manto" (Most Holy Virgin, cover us with your mantle). The shrine, then, offers protection to the exiles who gather under her cloak. The Virgin's enveloping care is extended to all Cubans, as another architectural feature signifies. The six evenly spaced buttresses that run down the exterior walls of the conical shrine represent the six Cuban provinces.[30]

A few pilgrims noted the symbolic significance of the six columns and the building's shape. One woman, who was born in Cuba in 1937 and has lived in Miami since 1966, repeated the bishop's interpretation: "It is the mantle of the Virgin which protects her sons." Other visitors remained unaware of these meanings, although they still reported in large numbers that they liked both the site and the building. Some even found other, unintended, significance there. One sixty-six-year-old man, for example, used an analogy that no one else mentioned. "For me," he said, "the shrine is like the Statue of Liberty." A woman from Oriente, the province of the original shrine, offered another distinctive interpretation: "It is symbolic. Since we are not able to have a temple on a mountain as in Cobre, the architecture of the shrine is like a symbol of elevation." Like other visitors, she linked the architecture with the landscape of her homeland.[31]

Ritual

The meanings and feelings evoked by the architectural space arise, in part, from the practices associated with it, and Cuban exiles also form their national identity as they map the natal landscape onto the new urban environment through ritual. The nationalistic significance is clear in the three primary collective rituals connected with the shrine—*las peregrinaciones*, the weekday masses for the townships; the annual *romerías*, which are organized around provincial rather than municipal affiliation; and *la festividad*, the annual festival on the Virgin's feast day, September 8.[32]

Because space is limited, I discuss only the latter here. The pilgrims I interviewed indicated that the annual festival was the most important collective act of devotion, even though many managed to attend only "occasionally." The festival, and especially the mass, is important for the exile community because it allows for the fullest expression of their diasporic nationalism.

The festival's location has changed over the years, but the ceremony and its nationalist significance have not. For example, consider the 1991 festival. As the clergy reminded the audience, it was the eve of the five-hundredth anniversary of the "evangelization" of the New World. More important to those in the stands, the date also marked the thirtieth anniversary of the Virgin's arrival in Miami. At the same time, the recent transformation of Communist nations in Eastern Europe added a millennialist fervor to the proceedings, and many in the crowd and on the stage seemed to believe that democracy and capitalism soon would be restored in Cuba. At various times that night, clergy repeated the familiar prediction that the exiles would "spend next Christmas in Havana."[33]

The usual large and animated crowd filled the stadium on the bay. All 6,536 seats were filled. The head of security for the stadium estimated that the crowd actually numbered 10,000. As far as I could tell, there were few, if any, Anglos there, and as I walked among the participants, I heard no English spoken. This also was true during the other, smaller events at the shrine. I had thought that the festival might draw a wider audience, maybe even some visitors from outside the local Cuban community, but this seems not to have been the case. It was a Spanish-speaking crowd; and, as their passionate responses to the patriotic messages of the evening indicated, it was overwhelmingly Cuban.[34]

The nationalistic significance of the evening's rituals was as obvious as that of the shrine's mural. This theme was expressed clearly on the program I was handed as I entered the stadium. On the top left of the printed page was the phrase "Virgen de la Caridad"; on the right was a petition, "Salva a Cuba!" (Save Cuba). At the center of the blue program cover was an image of the Virgin. Below her, five *balseros* floated on the sea in a makeshift raft, their arms raised to the Virgin. The message seemed to be that as the Virgin had brought the exiles safely to American shores, she also can help those who remain in Cuba. Most important—and this theme was emphasized throughout the evening—she could help "liberate" Cuba from communism. As one woman told a local reporter before activities began, "The Virgin is the patroness of Cuba, and above all we want to petition her to make Cuba free."[35]

Exiles expressed their attachment to homeland in other ways. Several of the songs and prayers—including "Plegaria a la Virgen de la Caridad," "Caridad del Cobre," and "Virgen Mambisa"—recalled the Virgin's historical connection with Cuban land and history and repeated the call for the liberation of contemporary Cuba. Later, after the Virgin's image had been lifted from the boat and onto the stage, some in the crowd waved Cuban flags, and all stood to sing the Cuban national anthem.

During the evening's activities, which were broadcast to Cuba by federally funded Radio Martí, the clergy led the participants in several chants—all of which expressed nationalist sentiment. Perhaps most surprising (at least to me), Father Luis Pérez, a Cuban American parish priest, stopped in the middle of the rosary to urge all to chant "Our Lady of Charity, Save Cuba." At his prompting, the crowd jubilantly shouted it three times. Then, like a cheerleader at a sporting event or a keynote speaker at a political convention, the priest asked the crowd over and over, "What do we want?" "Save Cuba!" was the loud reply each time. The same sort of chants erupted, again encouraged by the clergy, during the sermon. The speaker, another exiled Cuban priest, skillfully stirred the crowd with a poetic and passionate homily filled with patriotic references, interrupting his remarks several times so that he, and most of the participants, could chant "Cuba será libre" (Cuba will be free). He ended his sermon, to the most thunderous applause of the evening, with a prayer to the Virgin: "Our Lady of Charity, save Cuba and bring liberty."

This collective ritual and the natural and built environment of the shrine have both a vertical and a horizontal dimension; and the latter is especially important for the exiles' construction of national identity. On the one hand, the rituals and architecture create a vertical opposition between superior and inferior and lift the Cuban community to another, transcendent dimension. The Virgin, for all her accessibility to devotees, still resides in a realm beyond this world. She can approach us, and we can approach her. Some movement, however, is necessary to establish contact; and the shrine and the devotions held within it provide that, as they also elicit the accompanying emotions—humility, gratitude, and reverence.[36]

More important for visitors to the shrine, the symbolic spaces and practices also have a horizontal dimension. They highlight, and finally overcome, opposition between here and there, us and them. In this sense, exiles are propelled horizontally, not vertically. They move out, not up. The shrine's rituals and architecture unite the Virgin's devotees in Miami

3.5. The Reverend Pedro Luís Pérez, a Cuban-born parish priest, waves to the crowd during the feast day celebration as he leads the chants petitioning Our Lady of Charity to "save" Cuba. Photograph © by Michael Carlebach.

with other Cubans, in exile and on the island, creating an imagined moral community and generating feelings of nostalgia, hopefulness, and commonalty. The symbols bridge the water that separates exiles from their homeland and transport the diaspora to the Cuba of memory and desire. By appropriating the Cuban flag at the shrine, narrating Cuban history in the mural, placing Cuban sand in the cornerstone, organizing devotions by Cuban regional affiliation, and ritually aligning the Cuban patroness with their cause, the displaced community simultaneously reclaims Havana and re-maps Miami. Although Cuban American pilgrims struggle to some extent over the meaning of rituals and artifacts, the symbols' shared nationalistic significance allows exiles to imaginatively construct their collective identity as they map the history and geography of their homeland onto the new urban landscape.

Notes

I gratefully acknowledge the support of the National Endowment for the Humanities. A number of scholars offered helpful comments on earlier drafts, including Ruth Behar, Matthew Glass, Robert Levine, Robert Orsi, and Yi-Fu Tuan. Of course, it is not their fault if errors remain.

1. Carol Breckenridge and Arjun Appadurai, "On Moving Targets," *Public Culture* 2 (1989): i.

2. By the term "Miami" I refer to the greater metropolitan area, or Dade County. Thomas D. Boswell and James R. Curtis, "The Hispanization of Metropolitan Miami," in *South Florida: Winds of Change,* ed. Thomas D. Boswell, prepared for the annual conference of the Association of American Geographers (Miami, 1991), 140–61.

3. Yi-Fu Tuan, *Topophilia: A Study of Environmental Perception, Attitudes, and Values* (Englewood Cliffs, N.J.: Prentice-Hall, 1974), 99; Yi-Fu Tuan, *Space and Place: The Perspective of Experience* (Minneapolis: University of Minnesota Press, 1977), 157.

4. Two surveys in 1992 reported on Cubans' attitudes about returning to their homeland. The first was conducted by pollsters with Bendixen and Associates for a local Spanish-language television station (WLTV). The second was designed by sociologist Juan Clark of Miami Dade Community College and conducted under the auspices of the Archdiocese of Miami. The first survey found that 24 percent said they would return to a free Cuba. The second reported that 45 percent were unsure, and only 10 percent said they definitely would do so. "Poll: Optimism Dips over Quick Castro Fall," *Miami Herald,* May 5, 1992, B1–2; "Sumario de la encuesta de la reflexion Cubana en la Diaspora," *Ideal* 261 (1992): 4–5. The expression about Christmas dinner was mentioned by my consultants and is discussed briefly in María Cristina Herrera, "The Cuban Ecclesiastical Enclave in Miami: A Critical Profile," *U.S. Catholic Historian* 9 (Spring 1990): 212.

5. As far as I can tell, the term "diaspora nationalism" was coined by Ernest Gellner. See Ernest Gellner, *Nations and Nationalism* (Ithaca: Cornell University Press, 1983), 101–109. My understanding of nation and nationalism has been shaped by that work and several others. Benedict Anderson, *Imagined Communities: Reflections on the Origin and Spread of Nationalism* (London and New York: Verso, 1983); Liisa Malkki, *Purity and Exile: Violence, Memory, and National Cosmology among Hutu Refugees in Tanzania* (Chicago: University of Chicago Press, 1995). Several articles in a special issue of *Cultural Anthropology* also were useful, including Akhil Gupta and James Ferguson, "Beyond 'Culture': Space, Identity, and the Politics of Difference," *Cultural Anthropology* 7 (February 1992): 6–23; Liisa Malkki, "National Geographic: The Rooting of Peoples and the Territorialization of National Identity among Scholars and Refugees," *Cultural Anthropology* 7 (February 1992): 24–44.

6. Breckenridge and Appadurai, "On Moving Targets," i. My understanding of attachment to homeland has been shaped by the writings of cultural geographers. The geographer John Kirkland Wright coined the term "geopiety" to describe the religious dimension of this attachment. See John K. Wright, "Notes on Early American Geopiety," in *Human Nature in Geography: Fourteen Papers, 1925–65* (Cambridge: Harvard University Press, 1966), 250–85. Others have modified and applied the concept. See, for instance, Yi-Fu Tuan, "Geopiety: A Theme in Man's Attachment to Nature and Place," in *Geographies of the Mind: Essays on Historical Geosophy,* ed.

David Lowenthal and Martyn J. Bowden (New York: Oxford University Press, 1976), 11–39; and Tuan, *Space and Place*, 149–60.

7. Thomas D. Boswell and James R. Curtis, *The Cuban-American Experience: Culture, Images, and Perspectives* (Totowa, N.J.: Rowman and Allanheld, 1983), 89–96. On immigrants' experiences in American cities, see John Bodnar, *The Transplanted: A History of Immigrants in Urban America* (Bloomington: Indiana University Press, 1985), and Bayrd Still, ed., *Urban America: A History with Documents* (Boston: Little, Brown, 1974), 116–26, 194–203, 392–405. On the role of ethnicity in shaping the American landscape, see Michael P. Conzen, "Ethnicity on the Land," in *The Making of the American Landscape*, ed. Michael P. Conzen (Boston and London: Unwin Hyman, 1990), 221–48. Latino Catholics have received some attention in recent years. Only one history of the Latino church in the United States has been published, but two new book series help fill some gaps. Half of one of those volumes focuses on Cuban American Catholics, but for the most part Cubans remain understudied. The book series on Latino religion are the Notre Dame History of Hispanic Catholics in the U.S. Series, which is associated with the University of Notre Dame Press, and the Program for the Analysis of Religion among Latinos (PARAL) Studies Series, which is sponsored by the Bildner Center for Western Hemispheric Studies at the Graduate School and University Center of the City University of New York. The former has published three books, and the latter, four. Two edited volumes in these series offer useful perspectives on the larger issues that arise in the study of Latino religion: see Anthony M. Stevens-Arroyo and Gilbert R. Cadena, eds., *Old Masks, New Faces: Religion and Latino Identities*, Program for the Analysis of Religion among Latinos (New York: Bildner Center for Western Hemispheric Studies, 1995); and Jay P. Dolan and Allan Figueroa Deck, S.J., eds., *Hispanic Catholic Culture in the U.S.: Issues and Concerns*, Notre Dame History of Hispanic Catholics in the U.S. Series (Notre Dame: University of Notre Dame Press, 1994). The contribution on Cubans in the Notre Dame series was written by a Cubanist who was trained in sociology, Lisandro Pérez, not a specialist in Roman Catholicism or U.S. religion. Lisandro Pérez, "Cuban Catholics in the United States," in Jay P. Dolan and Jaime R. Vidal, eds., *Puerto Rican and Cuban Catholics in the U.S., 1900–1965* (Notre Dame: Notre Dame University Press, 1994), 147–207. The only book-length study of Latino Catholics devotes less than three pages to Cubans: Moises Sandoval, *On the Move: A History of the Hispanic Church in the United States* (Maryknoll, N.Y.: Orbis, 1990), 87, 106–108. Some useful information about Cuban American Catholicism appears in Michael J. McNally, *Catholicism in South Florida, 1868–1968* (Gainesville: University Press of Florida, 1982), 127–66. On immigrants' transformation of the Miami social landscape, see Alejandro Portes and Alex Stepick, *City on the Edge: The Transformation of Miami* (Berkeley and Los Angeles: University of California Press, 1993).

8. Recent information on the municipalities in exile has been published in Boswell and Curtis, "Hispanization of Miami," 54.

9. For a fuller account, see Thomas A. Tweed, *Our Lady of the Exile: Diasporic Religion at a Cuban Catholic Shrine in Miami* (New York and Oxford: Oxford University Press, 1997).

10. I had help with some of the interviews. My research assistants included two Cuban American students at the University of Miami, Ivonne Hernandez and David Sosa. Two other Cuban American assistants, Emilia Aguilera and Ada Orlando, helped in countless ways. In a related project, one of my students, Roxanna Sosa, conducted interviews with yard shrine owners. I am grateful for their aid.

11. The comparison with other Latin American countries and a summary of the 1957 survey are found in Margaret Crahan, *Religion and Revolution: Cuba and Nicaragua*, Working Paper No. 174, Latin American Program, Wilson Center (Washington, D.C.: Smithsonian Institution, 1987), 4. For a historical overview of Cuban Catholicism that includes primary sources, see Ismael Testé, *Historia Eclesiastica de Cuba*, 3 vols. (Burgos: Editorial El Monte Carmelo, 1969). See also Conferencia Episcopal Cubana, *Encuentro nacional eclesial cubano* (Havana: Conferencia Episcopal Cubana, 1987), 33–49. A solid overview of Cuban religion before 1959 appears as the first two chapters in John M. Kirk, *Between God and the Party: Religion and Politics in Revolutionary Cuba* (Tampa: University of South Florida Press, 1989), 3–62. At least ten dissertations on religion in Cuba were written between 1945 and 1991, but only two focused on Catholicism. The others analyze Protestantism or Santería. See Jesse J. Dossick, *Cuba, Cubans, and Cuban-Americans, 1902–1991: A Bibliography* (Miami: University of Miami North-South Center, 1992), 80–81.

12. On national Virgins, see Victor Turner and Edith Turner, *Image and Pilgrimage in Christian Culture: Anthropological Perspectives* (New York: Columbia University Press, 1978). On the history of Cuban devotion to Our Lady of Charity, see Testé, *Historia Eclesiastica*, vol. 3, 346–411, and José Tremols, *Historia de la devoción de la Virgen de la Caridad* (Miami: Album de America, [1962?]). See also Delia Díaz de Villar, "Historia de la devoción a la Virgen de la Caridad," in *Ermita de la Caridad*, n.p., n.d. [Miami: La Ermita de la Caridad], 12–20; and Olga Portuondo Zúñiga, *La Virgen de la Caridad del Cobre: Símbolo de cubanía* (Santiago de Cuba: Editorial oriente, 1995). For evidence of the continuing influence of Our Lady of Charity in the homeland, see the recent pastoral letter from the bishops: Conferencia Episcopal Cubana, *Encuentro nacional eclesial cubano*, 43–45, 265–66. The testimony of Juan Moreno, one of the three laborers who claimed to have found the statue in the sea, has survived. Archivo General de Indias, Sevilla, Audiencia de Santo Domingo, legajo 363. This document was rediscovered by Leví Marreo and published in his *Cuba: Economía y sociedad: El Siglo XVII*, vol. 5 (Madrid: Editorial Playor, 1976), 92–93. Interview #83, August 1, 1991, female, age 51, born Havana, arrived 1960. Eduardo Boza-Masvidal, "Una imagen que es un símbolo," in *Ermita de la Caridad*, 9–10.

13. One interesting sign of the increased nationalistic significance of the Virgin after the war for independence comes from two novenas to Our Lady of Charity published in Havana in 1880 and 1950. The second, published after she had officially become patroness, reprinted exactly the novena of 1880, but the editors affixed a thirty-one-page historical overview that emphasized her ties with the veterans and her link with the nation. Compare the two: *Novena a la Virgen santisima de la Caridad del Cobre* (Havana: Pedro Martinez, 1880) and *Nuestra Señora de la Caridad del Cobre, Patrona de Cuba: Historia, Devocion, Novena* (Havana: Liga de Damas de Acción Católica Cubana Consejo Nacional, 1950). Other Virgins, so important in Latin American cultures, have played a similar role. Our Lady of Guadalupe, for instance, has been associated with rebellions and revolutions. See David Carrasco, *Religions of Mesoamerica: Cosmovisions and Ceremonial Centers* (San Francisco: Harper and Row, 1990), 135–38.

14. The letter to the pope has been reprinted in several works. See "Petición de los veteranos de la independencia de Cuba," in *Ermita de la Caridad*, 42–43. Juan Clark, *Religious Repression in Cuba* (Miami: University of Miami North-South Center, 1986), 10–12. Augustín A. Román, "The Popular Piety of the Cuban People," master's thesis, Barry University, 1976, 81.

15. A German geographer has discussed the shrine in a survey of Catholic pilgrim-

age places in the United States. On the number of annual visitors and other matters, see Gisbert Rinschede, "Catholic Pilgrimage Places in the United States," in *Pilgrimage in the United States, Geographia Religionum*, Band 5 (Berlin: Dietrich Reimer, 1990), 69, 82–83. The number of visitors in 1992, as estimated by the confraternity, was 750,000: T.N., confraternity member, interview with the author, Miami, Florida, June 23, 1992. Of course, without further study it is difficult to assess the accuracy of these figures. There can be no doubt, however, that the shrine attracts large numbers of visitors and that it is a crucial pilgrimage site for Cuban Americans.

16. The feast-day masses have been held at various sites since 1991: Bayfront Park (1992), Dinner Key Auditorium (1993), and Hialeah Racetrack (1994–97). Wherever they are held, the ceremonies are very similar.

17. William A. Christian, Jr., made the distinction between "religion as practiced" and "religion as prescribed." See William A. Christian, Jr., *Local Religion in Sixteenth-Century Spain* (Princeton: Princeton University Press, 1981), 178. For reasons I have noted above, Cuban Americans do talk about the "humanity" of the clergy, but they display somewhat less "anti-clericalism" than the subjects of other studies of "popular" Catholicism in Europe. Compare Ruth Behar, *Santa María del Monte: The Presence of the Past in a Spanish Village* (Princeton: Princeton University Press, 1986); Eric R. Wolf, ed., *Religion, Power, and Protest in Local Communities: The North Shore of the Mediterranean* (Berlin and New York: Mouton, 1984); and Ellen Badone, ed., *Religious Orthodoxy and Popular Faith in European Society* (Princeton: Princeton University Press, 1990).

18. Agustín A. Román, interview with the author, July 15, 1991, Shrine of Our Lady of Charity, Miami.

19. Román, "Popular Piety," 78, 48, 46, 47. On Santería, see Lydia Cabrera, *El Monte* (Miami: Ediciones Universal, 1975); George Brandon, *Santeria from Africa to the New World: The Dead Sell Memories* (Bloomington: Indiana University Press, 1993); David Hilary Brown, "Garden in the Machine: Afro-Cuban Sacred Art and Performance in Urban New Jersey and New York," 2 vols., Ph.D. dissertation, Yale University, 1989; and Joseph M. Murphy, *Santería: An African Religion in America* (Boston: Beacon, 1988). There are no full-length studies yet, but on Santería in Miami, see Stephan Palmié, "Afro-Cuban Religion in Exile: Santería in South Florida," *Journal of Caribbean Studies* 5 (Fall 1986): 171–79, and Diana González Kirby and Sara Maria Sánchez, "Santería: From Africa to Miami via Cuba—Five Hundred Years of Worship," *Tequesta* 48 (1988): 36–48.

20. Román, "Popular Piety," 57, 98. Father Romeo Rivas, interview with the author, February 3, 1992, Shrine of Our Lady of Charity, Miami. The concern to "purify" Cuban Catholicism of the influences of Santería is evident in periodicals published by the Archdiocese of Miami for Spanish-speaking laity and clergy. For example, see Eduardo Boza Masvidal, "Conservemos la pureza de nuestra fe," *Cuba Diáspora* (1978): 13–14. One priest, Juan J. Sosa, has addressed the issue many times. For an example, see Juan J. Sosa, "Devociones Populares: Santa Barbara and San Lazaro," *Cuba Diáspora* (1976): 101–103.

21. Román, "Popular Piety," 41. Murphy, *Santería*, 42–43, 67. T.N., interview with the author, June 23, 1992, Miami. *Verdades de la fe Cristiana*, pamphlet (Miami: Ermita de la Caridad, n.d.).

22. Interview #104, February 4, 1992, female, age 22, born U.S.; Interview #136, March 3, 1992, female, age 60, born Hoguín, arrived 1965; Interview #43, March 1, 1992, female, age 17, born Cuba [municipality not given], arrived 1980; and Interview #44, March 1, 1992, female, age 16, born Spain, arrived 1991; Interview #1, January

26, 1992, female, age 63, born Guanajay, arrived 1949; Interview #114, February 15, 1992, female, age 62, born Havana, arrived 1963.

23. William A. Christian, Jr., *Person and God in a Spanish Valley* (New York and London: Seminar Press, 1972), 118–19. Interview #89, January 18, 1992, male, age 24, born Havana, arrived 1991; Interview #115, February 15, 1992, female, age 28, born Colombia, arrived 1980; Interview #20, February 3, 1992, male, age 33, born Havana, arrived 1967.

24. Interview #17 (the daughter), February 3, 1992, female, age 24, born U.S.; Interview #18 (the father), February 3, 1992, male, age 48, born Cienfuegos, arrived 1961. As William A. Christian, Jr., has noted, the vow is the prototypical prayer of Mediterranean Roman Catholicism. Christian, *Person and God,* 119.

25. Interview #18; Interview #20; Interview #1. Note that half of those who answered the question indicated that their devotion to Our Lady of Charity had increased in exile. Only two said that it had declined.

26. José Martí apparently had some devotion to Our Lady of Charity, since he wrote a poem in her honor. That poem has been reprinted: "Un Poema de Martí a la Virgen," *Cuba Diáspora* (1978): 77–78. He also approved of worshiping "God-*Patria.*" But as one biographer has argued, he was very suspicious of religious institutions and their tendency to assume secular control. He had strong "anti-clerical" impulses. For these reasons, it is not clear how Martí would have felt about being enshrined. John Kirk, *José Martí: Mentor of the Cuban Nation* (Tampa: University Presses of Florida, 1983), 119–25. Varela, on the other hand, probably would have been pleased. Some of Varela's philosophical and religious writings have been translated into English. See Felipe J. Estévez, ed., *Félix Varela: Letters to Elpidio* (New York: Paulist Press, 1989).

27. The title of the mural in English is "The History of Cuba in a Glance." For a description of the contents and history of the mural, see the pamphlet published by the shrine, *El mural de la Ermita* (Miami: Ermita de la Caridad, n.d.). For the artist's account, see Teok Carrasco, "Descripción del Mural," in *Ermita de la Caridad,* 38–41.

28. Interview #84, July 31, 1991, female, age 48, born Havana, arrived 1955.

29. When asked if the site had any special significance for them, a quarter of those who answered mentioned that it was situated by the sea. Others noted that the site had some link with Cuba, and a surprising number of informants even mentioned that the shrine was situated in a line with their homeland. The majority of visitors who answered the question found some nationalistic significance in the site itself.

30. Agustín A. Román, "La Virgen de la Caridad en Miami," in *Ermita de la Caridad,* 6–8.

31. Interview #48, March 1, 1992, female, age 52, born municipality of Trinidad (Cuba), arrived 1971; Interview #109, February 11, 1992, female, age 55, born Guanajay, arrived 1966; Interview #69, January 3, 1992, male, age 66, born Santiago de las Vegas, arrived 1962; Interview #137, March 3, 1992, female, age 51, born Puerto Padre, arrived 1960.

32. I refer here to the "architectonics" of the building, as anthropologist James W. Fernandez has used the term in his study of religion among the Fang in Equatorial Africa. James W. Fernandez, *Bwiti: An Ethnography of the Religious Imagination in Africa* (Princeton: Princeton University Press, 1982), 377, 408–12. Rinschede has reported that "around 10% of all pilgrimage places are visited exclusively by one specific ethnic group only." Besides the shrines in Miami and Doylestown, he mentions four others, two associated with Ukrainian Americans, one with Hungarian Americans, and one with Mexican Americans. Rinschede, "Catholic Pilgrimage Places," 91.

33. For an analysis of later festivals, see Tweed, *Our Lady of the Exile*, 116–18, 125–31.

34. "Miles aclaman a la Caridad del Cobre," *El Nuevo Herald*, September 8, 1991. See also "La aparición de 'la Virgen mambisa' a los cubanos," *El Nuevo Herald*, September 8, 1991; "La Ermita de la Caridad: el sexto santuario más importante de EU," *El Nuevo Herald*, September 8, 1991; and "Exilio reafirma fe en la Caridad," *Diario Las Americas*, September 10, 1991.

35. "Virgen de la Caridad: Salva Cuba!" Program for the Festival of Our Lady of Charity, September 7, 1991 (Miami: La Officina de Liturgia y Vida Espiritual de la Arquidiócesis de Miami, 1991). "Miles aclaman a la Caridad del Cobre," 1B.

36. My analysis of the vertical and horizontal dimensions of the shrine's architecture and ritual has been informed, in part, by Fernandez's discussion of the architectonics of the *Bwiti* chapel and Catherine Bell's treatment of the spatial dimensions of ritualization. Fernandez, *Bwiti*, 371–412. Catherine Bell, *Ritual Theory, Ritual Practice* (New York: Oxford University Press, 1992), 125.

Altared Spaces

4

Afro-Cuban Religions and the Urban Landscape in Cuba and the United States

David H. Brown

The *candomblés*, with the temples, the *pegi* [altars], the groves of sacred trees, the houses of the dead, the spring of Oxalá, represent a reconstruction of the sacred topography of the lost Africa. . . . [S]omething analogous to what happened to Christianity when it left Palestine happened here too. The ecology was transformed into symbolism. In our cathedrals the Israel of the time of Christ is recreated. The church building traces on the ground the Cross of Golgotha; at its center stands the table where Jesus once shared with his disciples the bread and wine of communion. The sacristy or a lateral chapel shelters the manger of Bethlehem; the stations of the Passion are depicted on the walls. But these geographic localities now form a single mystic space. Henceforth the Jerusalem pilgrimage will take place in a compacted, telescoped ecology, which, while retaining its structure intact, will be reduced in format, in which history will become simply an invitation to prayer. (Bastide 1978:248)

The Madonna was taken out into this world [Harlem] . . . of . . . parks, stoops, alleyways, hallways, fire escapes, storefronts, traffic, police, courtyards, street crime, and streetplay . . . and asked to bless it. . . . Only as the inner meanings of the urban landscape become clear does an analysis of urban religious ritual and myth become possible. (Orsi 1985:xxi)

A sense of the city is something accomplished rather than discovered, something constituted rather than uncovered. (Kirshenblatt-Gimblett 1983:185)

The color photographs were spread out before Steve Smoger and he didn't like what he saw. The Atlantic City prosecutor looked at a baby resting on a bed with bloody, white lambs on the floor beside it, their curly fur stained red; pails filled with blood from chickens and ducks; entrails stuffed into plastic bags sitting in a bathtub, and feathers everywhere. (Proctor 1985:69)

Barbara Kirshenblatt-Gimblett revises two received notions about the status of urban folk groups by positing a fruitful middle ground: urban folk groups neither succumb to the homogenizing pressures of alienating and depersonalizing city life, nor retreat conservatively into "folk enclaves," merely "selecting" what they need to maintain essential traditions brought from the outside.[1] Instead, they struggle to constitute their own "sense of the whole city," actively transforming their environment in "choosing the ways they want to live." Against "authoritative images of the city" and lifeways reinforced by law and dominant convention, urban groups pose alternative or oppositional images and adopt solutions and strategies that can be culturally subversive, possibly illegal. Kirshenblatt-Gimblett encourages urban folklorists and ethnographers to ask several questions that are relevant to a study of urban sacred space and geography: "What is the relationship between peculiar features of urban settings and the expressive forms found there?" "How do people use expressive behavior to personalize and humanize the urban environment?" "How do they appropriate and rework mass-produced commodities and shape the built environment?" "How do the inhabitants of a city form images of the larger whole and their place in it?" (Kirshenblatt-Gimblett 1983:183–85).

Priests of the Afro-Cuban Santería, Palo Monte, and Spiritist religions use and rework urban domestic space, landscape, and material culture to serve their ritual needs. Priests fabricate huge, complex altars from ready-made and "customized" mass-produced commodities (see Kirshenblatt-Gimblett 1983:214–17). Interior domestic spaces, originally constructed for private and conventional purposes—kitchens, living rooms, bedrooms, bathrooms—are reorganized according to alternative socioreligious requirements to accommodate multiple altars and large congregations. Private homes become the habitations and spiritual centers not only for immediate and extended natural families, but also for extended ritual families of "godchildren" and proliferating legions of spiritual personages, called *orichas, eguns, palos,* and *muertos.*[2] Domestic arrangements, routines, and budgets constantly shift and change with the challenges of daily healing work and the annual cycle of semipublic religious festivals.

Folklorist Henry Glassie reads American vernacular architecture in order to uncover its "rules" and "grammar." Glassie considers "how a house is thought," the "architectural competence" with which it was produced, and the cultural context of its emergence (Glassie 1975:20–21). Because Afro-Cuban religions have developed predominantly in urban settings so that ritual practices are realized within preexisting infrastructures, my interest lies in how a house is *re-thought.* John Vlach usefully combines Glassie's reading of vernacular architecture with Edward Hall's concept of "proxemics" to demonstrate how creolized Afro-American house-building preserved and reworked African notions of spatial form, with implications for social interaction and identity (Vlach 1978:122–23).

Hall's concept of proxemics turns on the idea that the "use of space [is] a specialized elaboration of culture," and that "people from different cultures . . . inhabit different sensory worlds" (Hall 1966:1–2). Given the syncretic nature of many Afro-Cuban religious practices, however, including conflicting pantheons of spirits that require different kinds of treatment, domestic spatial reorganization must accommodate significant cultural heterogeneity. Indeed, because urban groups do not typically conform to Robert Redfield's ideal anthropological model of small-scale, face-to-face, socially bounded and geographically territorialized folk societies, Kirshenblatt-Gimblett insists that the concept of culture itself be revised. "[S]cholars working in complex societies must conceptualize culture in relation to extreme social heterogeneity" (1988:403; see Redfield 1947). The cultural practices of some groups, particularly creolized Caribbean peoples who build their cultures from diverse sources, may consist in exercising options that crosscut the lives of single individuals and interlocking subgroups. Thus, a useful urban proxemic study would have to consider the ways in which people from such complex and pluralistic cultural groups "shift" or "switch" between different performative codes and frames of experience (see Marks 1974, 1982). To revise Hall's notion, people from the same culture can inhabit different sensory worlds all in the same domestic space.

The cultural work of migrants, refugees, and exiles does not involve merely the simple implementation of original, traditional, and bounded cultural contents on unproblematic urban frontiers. Some groups must patch together remembered and encountered cultural resources and devise strategies and tactics of cultural reterritorialization in order to "transform space into place," including the invention of new "homelands" (Tuan 1977:6, 149–60; Kirshenblatt-Gimblett 1988:551; de Certeau 1984; Shammas 1996a, 1996b). For example, Puerto Rican migrants clear urban lots of rubble by hand and build little rustic *casitas* in the most unlikely places in the Bronx. "I feel like I'm in my country," one such Puerto Rican *casita* dweller declared (Sciorra 1990; Alvarez 1996). But the status of the "original" country or homeland is itself unstable in the contemporary world. Puerto Rico balances between the status of state and independent nation, and the central experience of many Puerto Ricans is a "commuting" relationship between the island and New York City.[3] A majority of Cuban Americans, on the other hand, cannot or will not visit or return to the island of Cuba, which exists for them not as the contemporary socialist state in the Caribbean, but as the imaginary *Cuba de Ayer* (the Cuba of Yesterday).

Such transformations of new spaces into places often proceed in urban arenas fraught with cultural, political, and economic conflict (see Kirshenblatt-Gimblett 1988:551–62). Puerto Rican *casita* dwellers have fought city authorities and private interests for years to maintain their plots (see Sciorra 1990; Alvarez 1996). In the Afro-Cuban case, the ritual use of urban private and public space by Afro-Cuban practitioners became highly controversial in the New York metropolitan area and in south Florida in the 1980s. Religious practice challenged laws and dominant mores when apartments and homes became sacrificial abattoirs and when city spaces became sites for ritual propitiations.

According to Mircea Eliade, founding and living in religious worlds requires "the elaboration of techniques of *orientation* which, properly speaking, are techniques for the *construction* of sacred space." Boundaries and divisions inscribed in space and architecture have cosmogonic value in Eliade's understanding. They effect "breaks" in otherwise homogeneous profane space and constitute the significant and experiential distinction between "sacred" and "profane" space. Thresholds, along with pillars and openings (*axis mundi*), enable communication with other worlds above and below, and between the visible and invisible worlds (Eliade 1959:35–65). The ritual use of space in Afro-Cuban religions, however, particularly in heterogeneous and condensed urban settings, blurs distinctions between "sacred" and "profane." The multitude of artfully arranged objects and images owned by spirits or dedicated to the protection of the house, and the ritual work conducted in relation to them, coexist with the mundane use of domestic objects, such as beds, toilets, stereos, and toasters. The religions of the African Diaspora are immediate, humanistic, and practical. Priests have intimate personal relations with the various pantheons of spirits and the dead (see K. Brown 1991). And insofar as the *orichas* and *palos* are the masters of the house, including its most mundane activities, one can conclude that either everything is sacred or nothing is sacred, in the conventional sense. Indeed, the ancestors and spirits of the dead (*egun* and *muertos*) inhabit the house as social persons, not as rarefied and distant beings. "There is no worship," John Mason writes, "there is only a continuing effort to maintain an ongoing relationship between those who have departed and those who remain. What we are describing would better be labeled the carrying on of familial duties" (Mason and Edwards 1985b:2). The most creative and critical urban spatial work consists in accommodating all of these distinct spiritual personages, in addition to the tenants whose names appear on the lease. In short, domestic spatial organization and differentiation revolve less around distinctions between the categories of "sacred" and "profane" than around specific contextual "separations" that enable the practice of multiple syncretic religions and the managing of heterogeneous social and spiritual communities (see Glazier 1985).

Africa Condensed: The Creation of Afro-Cuban Society, Space, and Religion

The establishment of African-based religions in the New World, most strongly in urbanized coastal and island centers, involved processes of social rearticulation, cosmological selection, and spatial condensation. Religions embedded in the social and political frameworks of global societies in Africa, observed Roger Bastide, became the religions of class subcultures of blacks in the Americas. During the slavery period, black religion articulated with the "new social frameworks" of the system of African "nations" and their respective mutual aid societies, institutions under Catholic patronage called *cabildos* in Cuba and *irmandades* in Brazil (see Bastide 1971, 1978:109–25; Ortiz 1921; Deschamps Chapeaux 1968). In Cuba the principal nations carried the ethonyms Lucumí (Yoruba), Congo (Kongo-Angola), Arará (Dahomey), and Carabalí (Ibo/Ibibio, Efik, Ejagham), and in Brazil they were Nagô and Ketu (Yoruba), Gêgê (Dahomey), and Congo and Angola (see Ortiz 1988 [1916], 1921; Lachatañeré 1961; Bastide 1978:46, 195).

The ethnically based nations of the slavery period served as "incubating cells" (Palmié 1993:341) for the emergence of the Afro-Brazilian and Afro-Cuban religions, whose principal criterion of membership would be ritual initiation, and whose constituencies would become heterogeneous as the religions spread among the black, mulatto, and white working classes in the twentieth century (Palmié 1993; Bastide 1971, 1978; López Valdés 1985). In Cuba, the religions of the distinct African nations (*naciones*) became known as *reglas* (rule, order, domain; see Murphy 1988:33). The Lucumí religion was called La Regla de Ocha (a contraction of the Lucumí term for deity, *oricha*) or Santería, "the way of the *santos*," and the Congo religion was called Palo Monte, after the medicinal "sticks of the forest" with which its fierce spirits work (Cabrera 1986b).[4] Single individuals could, through multiple, sequential initiations, practice La Regla de Ocha and Palo Monte, belong to the Carabalí-derived Abakuá secret society (males), and, as baptized Catholics, take communion in the church. Many have incorporated elements of Masonry and Rosicrucianism into their multifaceted practices as well.[5]

Afro-Cuban religious practice in the evolving *reglas* of Ocha, Arará, and Palo Monte centered around semi-underground "houses" or "house-temples" (*casa, casa-templo*). The "house" of each initiated priest would contain a set of shrines and represent a hub or link in a system of ritual kinship and mutual support. Through *apadrinación*, elder priests, as "god-parents" (*padrinos*), would sponsor the initiation of "godchildren" (*ahijados*) into the religions. The fictive kinship principle of *apadrinación* would organize relations of ritual descent in all of the *reglas*, the Abakuá society, and Spiritism, as well as in the Catholic church. In many cases, single houses would contain interlocking ritual kinship systems of Ocha, Palo, and Spiritism.

Each *regla's* cosmology and ritual system represented a reworking and condensation of regional West African religious principles. For example, the most prominent kingdom-based deity clusters from the various Yoruba-speaking ethnic subgroups were organized into a single, hierarchically organized Cuban Lucumí pantheon of *orichas*. The *minkisi* medicines (singular: *nkisi*) of the decentralized forest villages of Central West Africa (presently Congo-Brazzaville, Lower Republic of Congo, and northwestern Angola) were also shaped into nine or more principal archetypes within Palo Monte. The Ocha and Palo pantheons were cross-indexed with each other and with a selected roster of prominent local Cuban Catholic saints. The Dahomean-derived *foduces* (*voduns*) of the Regla Arará—confined principally to the Matanzas Province—were cross-indexed with the Lucumí *orichas*, as well as with the Catholic saints (see Castellanos and Castellanos 1992:138, 221; Galzagorry Madan 1983). Although orthodoxies have attempted to keep the *reglas* separate, many houses have blended and borrowed attributes from among the several systems, leading to highly syncretic or "crossed" (*cruzado*) practices. Practitioners of all the *reglas* drew on and modified the séance-based ritual technology of Kardecian Spiritism (*espiritismo*) to communicate with the dead, and many houses crossed Spiritism with Ocha and Palo (González Wippler 1989:274–304, plates 61, 62; Brandon 1993:106–14; Castellanos and Castellanos 1992:192–202; Bermudez 1967, 1968). Thus, many practitioners access the spiritual energies of the *orichas*, *palos*, *muertos*, *eguns*, and Catholic saints through *espiritismo's* channels to the world of the dead. In a dramatic mid-nineteenth-century case, a Cuban *mulato* named Andrés Facundo de los Dolores Petít created a new syncretic *regla*, called La Regla Kimbisa del Santo Cristo del Buen Viaje (The Regla Kimbisa of the Holy Christ of the Good Voyage), incorporating elements of La Regla de Ocha, La Regla de Congo, and Catholicism, and then imported the principles of Kimbisa's Congo-based ritual medicines into the emerging branches of white Abakuá lodges (*juegos*) he sponsored in Havana as of 1857 (Cabrera 1986a, 1970:3; Ortiz 1952–54: vol. IV, 63ff.). It is said that Petít commissioned four thousand silver crucifixes from Milan, Italy, each adorned with a skull and crossbones at the feet of Christ. He embedded a special aperture in each crucifix with *nkisi* medicines for the *kimbiseros* to carry as protective charms.[6] The incorporation of *nkisi* medicines into the iconography of the white Abakuá branches supposedly protected the whites against attacks by orthodox black Abakuá who criticized Petít's "betrayal"— his "selling of the secret to the whites" (Ortiz 1952–54: vol. IV, 69). Petít's incorporation of crucifixes into the Abakuá, in general, endowed this underground mystical organization with a "licitness" that diffused the church's scrutiny and represented a "defensive process" against state persecution that Fernando Ortiz called "syncretic mimesis" (ibid., 79).

The condensation of cosmologies and the privatization of ritual practice radically miniaturized ritual space and rearticulated sacred festival cycles in Cuba as well as in Brazil. West African Yoruba kingdoms featured a spectrum of formal shrine spaces consistent with descending political units—public town shrines, multilineage quarter-shrines, and lineage or family compound shrines (see Apter 1992:35–69; 1995). Only the last, more private and individual unit remains in twentieth-century Afro-Cuban religion. The only New World practices on the magnitude of collective, town- and kingdom-based public worship are the feast days of Catholic saints, whose identities are doubly encoded as *orichas*.[7] And, in a "telescop[ing] of ecology," suggests Bastide, the Brazilian *candomblé* "temples, the [altars], the groves of sacred trees, the houses of the dead, [and] the spring of Oxalá (temple compounds)" were miniaturized as "reconstruction[s] of the sacred topography of the lost Africa." In short, the "spatial sectors of the Yoruba homeland [were] concentrated in the restricted space of the *candomblé*" (Bastide, 1978:247–48). While the large traditional Afro-Brazilian *candomblés* were able to establish their condensed pantheons on sizable tracts of owned land, the Afro-Cuban *oricha* pantheons were compressed more radically. Where the large *candomblés* could offer discrete little houses (*casas*) or rooms (*cuartos*) to each member of the *orixá* pantheon, in most cases, La Regla de Ocha installed all of the *orichas* in a single room, the *cuarto sagrado* or *igbodún* (sacred room or sacred grove), or even in a multishelved cabinet called the *canastillero*[8] (see figs. 4.1–.3).

Igbodún/Sala/Patio: The Classic Organization of Cuban Lucumí Space

Lydia González Huguet distinguishes three spaces characteristic of Cuban *ilé-ochas* or *casa-templos:* (1) the *igbodún* or *cuarto sagrado* (sacred room), in which *oricha* shrines are established and initiations are conducted; (2) the *sala*, a social space for the reception of clients, the gathering of ritual families, and the sequestering of non-initiates from the guarded *igbodún;* and (3) the *patio* or *solar*, a courtyard under the sky for drum dances (*tambores* or *bembés*), ritual meals, the cultivation of sacred plants, and a holding area for animals and fresh-cut plants to be used in initiations inside the *igbodún*. The *sala* might also serve as a ritual dining room in case of inclement weather (González Huguet 1968:44–46).

**4.1. Cuban *canastillero*, Havana (Marianao).
Domestic altar cabinet for ordering and protecting
oricha vessels. *Top of cabinet:* two Osun staffs, two
soperitas for the Twins (Ibeyi), *sopera* for Orunmila;
top shelf: Obatalá; *second shelf:* Yemayá; *third shelf:*
Ochún and Kofá de Orula; *bottom shelf:* miscellany;
floor to the right: Changó's vessel and pedestal;
floor front: two spray-painted Oyá vessels and one
shell-encrusted Olokun vessel; *foreground:* plate of
fruit offering.**

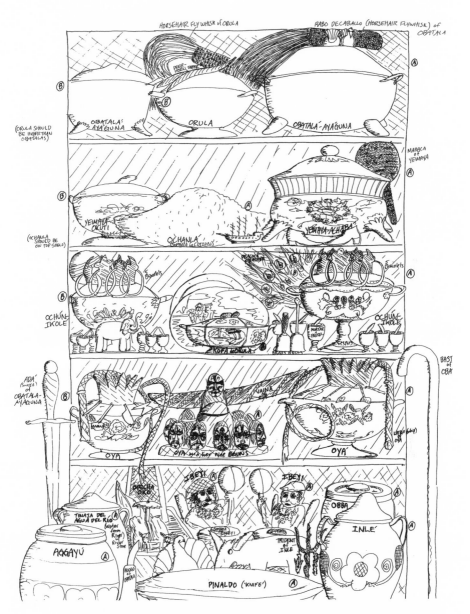

4.2. Collective *canastillero,* **Manhattan. A hall closet organizes the** *orichas* **of a woman and her son. Hers occupy the right side and his the left side, from top to bottom, with his Orula (he is a** *babalawo***) in the center, top. Collares de Mazo, which drape each vessel, are not shown. Corresponds to the floor plan depicted in figure 4.7 (hall closet).**

4.3. Small collective *canastillero* for Eleguás and Ogúns, Manhattan. *Canastillero* located adjacent to the front door of the house places Eleguá on top shelf and Ogún/Ochosi on bottom shelf.

Older Cuban houses of colonial Spanish conception became especially fitting for Afro-Cuban ritual and social use. They were "built around a courtyard [that] took the place of the gardens beloved by the Anglo-Saxons [but which] often had . . . fountains, orange, pomegranate, or mignonette trees" (Thomas 1971:143). While some ex-slaves built their rural *ilé-ochas* on the model of African compounds (Gómez Abreu 1982), Spanish-style houses were ideally suited for ritual conversion. The courtyard (*patio*) in Afro-Cuban hands became an ethnopharmacological garden and a preferred performance space for drumming, dancing, and spirit possession. In cramped urban settings, on the other hand, *igbodún* and *sala* collapse into available domestic spaces, such as bedrooms and living rooms. In the absence of courtyards, gatherings take place in interior rooms cleared of furniture. Basements, large living rooms, and rented halls have become the ritual spaces of choice in U.S. cities (see Alvarez 1997).

Igbodún, "Town," and "Bush": Sacred Groves and the Urban Landscape

The Lucumí *igbodún* contains the material embodiments of the *orichas'* power (*aché*), consisting of sets of consecrated stones enclosed in decorative ceramic, wood, and metal vessels. These stones, called *fundamentos,* are accompanied by artistic beaded attributes and sometimes chromolithographs and statues of the Catholic saints with which the *orichas* are associated (González Huguet 1968; D. Brown 1989:chap. 7; 1993; Thompson 1993:166–72). The *igbodún* is also the site of initiation, in which the room becomes a crucible of *aché. Aché* is "tapped" from nature in the form of fresh plants (*ewe*), cool water (*omi tutu*), and sacrificial blood (Mason and Edwards 1985a:3). Priests with the requisite deep knowledge channel *aché* in order to consecrate new *orichas' fundamentos* and initiate new priests. Through sacrifices, called *ebó,* prescribed through methods of divination, priests heal illnesses and solve problems. The room's powerful and secret proceedings are protected from the eyes of the uninitiated and the unwanted influences of disturbed spirits of the dead by entry prohibitions and ritual treatment of the threshold. The room is sealed with a symbolically purifying white sheet and mounted with a curtain of young palm fronds (*mariwó*) that acts as a spiritual cleansing brush. In significant ways, the *igbodún* is an excellent example of Eliade's paradigm of the sacred and profane, which Mary Douglas revises as "purity and danger":

> Sacred things and places are to be protected from defilement. . . . [S]ome . . . restrictions . . . are intended to protect divinity from profanation, and others [are] to protect the profane from the dangerous intrusion of divinity. Sacred rules are thus merely rules hedging divinity off, and uncleanliness is the two-way danger of contact with divinity. (Douglas 1978:7–8)

Important values are constituted by the opposition of "inside" and "outside" of the room. The room's threshold represents the fulcrum of neophytes' initiatory rites of passage and irrevocably divides their old lives from their new lives "in the *santo.*"

Still, the opposing field of values constructed by the threshold is more complex and subtle than the sacred–profane/purity–danger paradigms. The room is a controlled ritual space for the transformation of nature's raw and unpredictable *oricha* power (*aché*) into a usable healing force for the benefit of the human community. The *igbodún* represents just one ritual space on a continuum of sacralized sites on the larger natural and social landscape. The difference between the *igbodún* and the larger landscape outside is not the sacred versus the profane. It is more like the difference between the predictable and controlled space of the "town" —

whose activities are subordinated to sociopolitical hierarchies and kinship relations—and the dangerous, unpredictable space of the "bush" in Yoruba cosmology (Apter 1987:232–47; 1992:98–100).

The Afro-Cuban *igbodún* is a unique and creative urban adaptation, Joseph Murphy notes, wherein "the African grove of the *orishas* . . . [a] cleared area . . . between town and bush . . . [is] brought into the heart of the city. New York will not accommodate [the African] tradition of the *igbodún*, and so a somewhat cramped area of Padrino's basement must serve" (Murphy 1988:57). Although the interiorized *igbodún* reproduces some of the symbolic conditions of a bush grove, it still remains within the "town"—or more precisely, within the "house" (literally, the physical space of the *oricha* temple, and figuratively, the network of kinship relations of *santo*). A more explicit "bush" shrine is, in fact, constructed for the initiation of the fierce "warrior" *orichas* who live "outside" the house in the dangerous spaces of the street and the bush (*monte*). A three-sided "throne of the patio" (*trono del patio*), made of leaves, whose fourth wall is created by a white sheet, is erected outside the house for initiations into the priesthoods of Eleguá, Ogún, and Ochosi (see fig. 4.4). While initiates of these three *orichas* spend seven days and nights under a similar leafy throne in the *igbodún*, major portions of their consecration ceremonies are performed outside under the *patio* throne—a backyard symbolic representation of their bush habitat. Until these consecration ceremonies are performed, the *aché* of these *orichas* is too raw and unpredictable to be brought into the house. Yet, these consecration ceremonies proceed only after the initiate has been taken to an "actual" *monte*, ideally a densely wooded site. Of course, this *monte*, usually an untraveled clearing in a local park, is itself a representation of the "bush."

All initiates, prior to the major consecration ceremonies, are taken to "the river" (*el río*) for an initial purification. The river, owned by Ochún, the *oricha* of "sweet water," is typically a local brook or stream. Then, following seven days of seclusion in the room, initiates are taken to "the market" (*la plaza*), a space of community, social exchange, and transition owned by the *oricha* Oyá. These differentiated symbolic spaces and sequential ritual outings constitute the paradigmatic and syntagmatic axes, respectively, for initiatory transformation. "Religious meaning is mediated through the spaces ritual establishes for the body," Evan Zuesse observes (1979:142–44). In terms of the rites-of-passage model that Zuesse and scholars of Afro-Cuban religions have borrowed from Victor Turner, the Lucumí initiation's syntagmatic axis begins with an opening divination and sacrifice of "entry" (*ebó de entrada*) and a ritual outing to the *monte* and/or the river, which mark the neophyte's "separation"; the initiate's ritualized entrance into the room marks the beginning of seven days of

4.4. *Trono del Patio* (Throne of the Patio) for Eleguá, New Jersey. This throne of "leaves" is built outside the house to conduct portions of the initiation of priests of Eleguá, Ogún, and Ochosi—in this case Eleguá.

"liminality"; the initiate's exit from the room and trip to the market on the "Day of the *Plaza*" mark a "reincorporation" into the community (see Turner 1969; Castellanos 1977:85–99).

Priests of La Regla de Ocha remap the urban landscape according to the categories of Lucumí cosmology in order to perform ceremonies of initiation and sacrifice (fig. 4.5). For example, ritual work with the *oricha* of iron, Ogún, is carried out at a "live" railway line, including the subway tracks. Some initiates must be taken to make sacrifices and tributes at other sites on the landscape, such as a well, various species of trees, an old stone wall or ramparts, a house in ruins, a church, a hill, a market, a bar, a *bodega*, the sea, a crossroads, a police station, a prison, a bakery, a hospital, etc. The natural sites among these are sought in parks or small woods, or on the outskirts of suburban towns. Many of these sites are defined as the property and domain of a particular *oricha*, using the metaphor of "house" (*ilé*). The river is the *ilé-Ochún*, the house of Ochún. The sea is the *ilé*

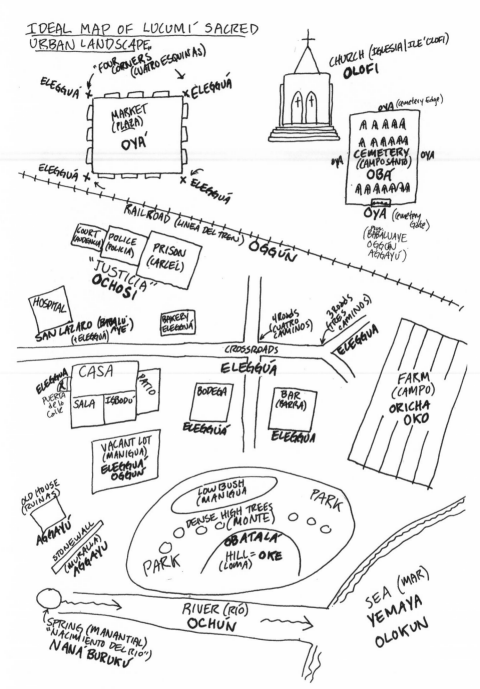

4.5. Rendering of "Ideal Map of Lucumí Sacred Urban Landscape." These are places that the orichas own, and where rituals are performed outside the house.

Yemayá. The cemetery (*campo santo*) is called the *ilé Yansan* (House of Oyá-Yansan). Its entrance and perimeter are owned by Oyá, the *oricha* who manages the transition between life and death. The marketplace (*plaza*) is also the house of Oyá (*ilé aboyá*), although the "four corners" (*cuatro esquinas*) that define its perimeter are owned by Eleguá—to whom the initiate, on the way to the market, must make tribute. The jail, police station, and courthouse combine as the *ilé Ochosi* (House of Ochosi), the "hunter *oricha*" who entraps and captures his prey. And the "Hospital" (*Ilé Aro,* House of Sicknesses) is the sphere of San Lázaro (Babalú Ayé), *oricha* of skin diseases, illnesses of certain internal organs, and the poor (see D. Brown 1989:chap. 6). The Lucumí "house-temple" (*casa-templo*) thus occupies part of a larger, spiritually imbued landscape of "houses" owned by the *orichas,* each sector of which embodies a portion of the *aché* God distributed to the *orichas* at the creation of the world.

The Lucumí spatial conception of the landscape is quintessentially urban. The principle of taking initiates of Eleguá to bars and bodegas and initiates of Oyá to "nine cemeteries" could have been conceived only in the context of urban sociality, density, and differentiation. In any given city, individual priests use their imagination and common sense to identify appropriate sites to perform their ritual work. The "crossroads" of Eleguá for one New York priestess is represented by the intersections that form her Manhattan block of 56th Street, between 11th and 12th Avenues. Natural formations of hills and mountains (*lomas* and *montañas*) are where

> you go and get the stuff to make Obatalá, because Obatalá lives there. You have to go to a mountain. Where will I find a mountain in New York City? You have to find a similarity, Riverside Drive, you stand at the base of it [the rocks] and to you that's a mountain. People I know go to the Cloisters, or have taken that ride out to Yonkers to 200th and Dyckman, which is the last exit before Yonkers.[9]

The landscapes of particular cities, such as Havana and New York, impress themselves boldly upon the religious imagination. In New York City, Ochún's house is found nowhere more impressively than in the East and Hudson Rivers. The house of Yemayá, goddess of the sea and "salt water," is New York Harbor in Manhattan and the Bay of Havana in Cuba. For years, one Brooklyn priest made an annual pilgrimage to the beloved aqua-tinted Statue of Liberty on December 31, the feast day of the master of the depths of the sea, Olokun, where he offered the *oricha's* favorite foods directly to the water. "The Statue of Liberty to other people represents freedom, but to me she represents Olokun, because she lives right on the Island, surrounded by the sea, and she blesses everybody" (Brown 1989:370).[10] Eighteenth- and nineteenth-century Lucumí practitioners transformed the Virgin of the Havana seaport town of Regla into Yemayá in their remapping of Havana's landscape. They redefined the Virgin's blue-and-white-painted shrine and nautical imagery, her mass-produced chromolithographs, and the church building itself, which stands as a sentinel over the bay, as attributes of Yemayá. This is precisely what Barbara Kirshenblatt-Gimblett meant when she wrote that a "sense of the city is something accomplished rather than discovered, something constituted rather than uncovered" through expressive behavior. In this case, a Lucumí sense of the city is accomplished through the ritual performance of sacrificial obligations.

What the Lease Doesn't Reveal (Part I): *Oricha-Owners of Afro-Cuban Urban Domestic Space*

Lydia González Huguet's research on Cuban *casa-templos* provides the founding principle of Afro-Cuban ritualized domestic space: "Each house where an initiate or *asentado* resides is converted, in fact, into a temple [*templo*]. . . . The *santos* [*orichas*] . . . come to be new members of the house, but in fact, become its owners, so that nothing can be done in the house without consulting them first" (González Huguet 1968:34). The *orichas* live in determinate spaces within the house, and rules of protocol and decorum govern their address and treatment. Their priestly custodians salute them with prayer, one by one, every morning, and attend to each of them more intensively with *obi* (coconut) divination and small sacrifices on particular days of the week. Eleguá, *oricha* of beginnings and openings, is "given *cocos*" on Mondays to commence the week, for example. Protocol demands that "all who enter [the house] should salute [the *orichas*] immediately after greeting the *santero* of the house" (González Huguet 1968:34). Priests and guests salute the *orichas'* shrine with a prone submission to the floor, a gesture called *moforibale* (see Mason 1994). Some *santeros* explicitly proscribe certain behavior in the vicinity of their *oricha* shrines, such as undressing and sex. Regular consultations with the *orichas* through methods of divination provide not only important advice about the priest's well-being and obligations, but also minute prescriptions and proscriptions about the organization and appearance of the house and its contents.

The *orichas*, enclosed in their lidded vessels, reside on shelves or in cabinets (*canastilleros*). Depending upon the means of the house, they may have their own separate room, called the *igbodún* or *cuarto sagrado* (sacred room), or share a corridor, living room, or bedroom with the dwelling's human occupants (see figs. 4.1 and 4.2). Consistent with their status as owners of the house, the *orichas* are arranged hierarchically on their shelves according to their cosmological rank, "parental" relationship to their priest(s), and other measures of seniority. Thus, Obatalá—sky-dweller, arch-*oricha* of the pantheon, and the "owner of all heads"—is normally placed on the highest shelf. The priest's tutelary or "guardian" *oricha*, considered the priest's principal "parent" (if it is not already Oba-talá), occupies the next-lowest shelf. This parent is followed by the priest's secondary parent, an *oricha* of the opposite gender from the first parent. A New York priestess and her son, for example, who shared a small Manhat-tan apartment during the 1980s, are the "children" of Obatalá. They place their "father" Obatalá in the highest position, followed by Yemayá, the *oricha* who is "mother" to both of them (see fig. 4.1). However, the son is also a *babalawo*, the high priest-diviner of the all-male Regla de Ifá, the governing deity of which is the diviner Orunmila. Because *babalawos* and their followers consider Orunmila to be "higher" in rank than the other *orichas*, he is often placed on the highest shelf, although in this case, because of spatial limitations, he shares a shelf with the Obatalás. Spatial protocols thus register the relative ranking of the two principal cult groups of the Regla Lucumí: the Regla de Ocha (*oricha* priests of the pantheon) and the Regla de Ifá (Orunmila's diviners of Ifá).

Finally, spatial protocols also register the mythico-historical rank of Changó as the archetypal royal *oricha*. Changó was the Fourth Alafin (king) of the Oyo Empire. Thus, Changó resides not in the *canastillero* with the other *orichas*, but in a prominent place in the house upon his own permanent "throne" throughout the year. Changó's powerful *fundamentos*, his polished "thunderstones," reside in a lathed wood receptacle (*batea*) atop his traditional inverted mortar (Lucumí *odó*; Sp. *pilón*), a multivocal symbol of the royal cults of the Oyo Empire, the sacred tree on the Cuban landscape dedicated to Changó (the royal palm), the castle tower icon borrowed from Changó's Catholic counterpart, Santa Barbara, and Chan-gó's phallic lightning rod (see figs. 4.6 and 4.6a). The New York priestess provided her Changó with a grander throne, a huge tree trunk that stands in a corner of her living room (fig. 4.7).

In contrast to the refined and elevated *orichas* of the *canastillero* and the royally enthroned Changó, the group of four "warrior" *orichas* (*guerr-eros*) resides elsewhere in the house. The warriors Eleguá, Ogún, and Ochosi, who embody characteristics of itinerants, soldiers, hunters, herbal-ists, and rough street types, reside behind or near the front door to the house (*puerta de la calle*), either on the floor or in a little cabinet. Along with their companion, the fourth *guerrero*, called Osun, they protect the head of the priest and the house, as well as maintain vigilance over all its comings and goings (see Cabrera 1983 [1954]:85; González Huguet 1968:34–35; see figs. 4.3, 4.9, and 4.11).

4.6. Living room of Union City apartment with *bóveda* for spirit mass, Changó on pedestal in corner, painting of José Lamece on wall. On the right is the long wall of the living room drawn in figures 4.11 and 4.12.

La Puerta de la Calle: The Guerreros and Ritual Protection of the Threshold

Eleguá is first in all things and quite particular about proper treatment. Guardian of "crossroads" and "doorways," he controls the influx and efflux of human and spiritual traffic. Through the *puerta de la calle* (door to the street) may pass fortune and health or tragedy and ills. Insidious influences in the form of disturbed spirits of the dead may "seep" in. "These are the dark ones [*oscuro*]," explains Miami priest Ernesto Pichardo, "who come in disguised, unseen, covered up, transfigured. Egun masquerades unseen. Eguns bring ills: sickness, tragedy, problems, death."[11] The *guerreros* protect against such unwanted intrusions, especially the silver staff of Osun, whose powerful herbal medicines, vigilant

4.6a. (*detail*) Changó on his pedestal in a corner of the living room.

rooster figure, and four little bells scare off disturbed spirits of the dead.[12] The *puerta de la calle* sees a felicitous house grow and prosper as clients and new godchildren enter, and sees a house plagued by gossip and arguments (*chismes* and *disgustos*) wither as godchildren and clients flee. "If you are curious about comings and goings, ask the doorsill," goes a West African aphorism (Gleason 1987:185). The *puerta de la calle* may also bring sudden violence and unwanted entanglements with *La Justicia* (The Law), phenomena controlled by Ogún and Ochosi, respectively. The warriors stand at the threshold between inside and outside because of their experience with parts unknown and dangerous: the street and the bush. As soldiers, travelers, hunters, and killers, they deal with protection, exchange, transition, and securing life's nourishment. The brainy and shrewd Ochosi hunts food, the powerful Ogún kills Ochosi's prey, and the universal

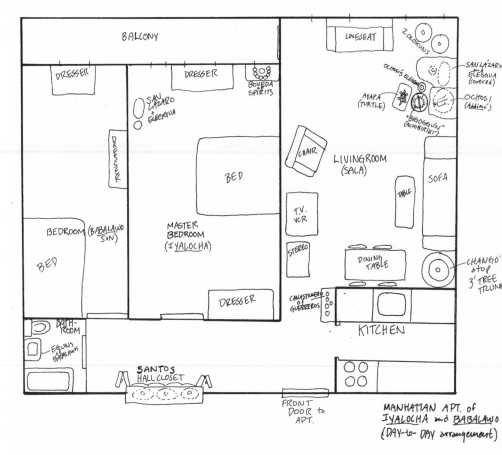

4.7. Floor plan of daily use of Manhattan apartment.

mediator Eleguá ferries messages and sacrifices between God, the *orichas*, the dead, and human beings (see Thompson 1983:18–61; Mason and Edwards 1985a). Together with Osun, who is placed on a high shelf like a sentinel, they offer a fierce phalanx against material and spiritual dangers.

The warriors protect the house from external intrusion and also are vigilant against disrespect within the house. They are sensitive to the way they are treated and can as easily bring trouble in as keep it out. In a cycle of legends (*patakí*), Eleguá punishes the other *orichas* for ignoring his basic needs of food and shelter. Their selfishness sets up roadblocks to their own advancement. They can "open the road"—or the "door," as the case may be—only by recognizing Eleguá through proper sacrifice. In one story, Orunmila slights and devalues Eleguá, and as a result, Eleguá refuses to refer clients, who stand at a moment of decision or crisis at Eleguá's "crossroads," to the diviner Orunmila's house for consultation. Orunmila becomes increasingly impoverished for lack of business. He realizes the cause of his problems but selfishly persists in his ways and attempts to sweet-talk Eleguá:

> "[Eleguá], I'm going to fix you up a room in the back so you'll be comfortable, where you'll live and eat well."
> "A room deep in the house? *Cosi!* [No way!] No Sir! Put me here at the entrance, in the doorway . . . there, to one side."
> "But you're going to eat all of that [food]—smoked fish, bushrat, palm oil, corn, rooster, rum—in the doorway?"
> "Yes, sir, right here. And if you don't feed me, I'm going to shut the door on you from the outside!" (Cabrera 1983 [1954]:84)

"This is why," Lydia Cabrera's elderly Cuban informants explain, "Eleguá lives in a *velador* [night table], a box, or little cabinet next to the [front] door . . . and if you don't take care of him, he'll go ahead and punish you" (Cabrera 1983 [1954]:85; see fig. 4.3). Even the "highest" *oricha*, Orunmila, can fall by neglecting first things first: Eleguá. Posted at the front door, Eleguá requires not sweet-talk but sweet sacrifices.

The front door itself is the object of constant ritual attention. It is a process-assemblage of protective technologies. Divination readings and spiritual inquiries counsel that certain kinds of objects and ingredients be hung on the back of the door or its frame. In her 1968 study of *ilé-ochas* in Cuba, Lydia González Huguet details the customary objects of protection, propitiation, and adornment clustered on and around the *puerta de la calle*. These include flags bearing the colors of the tutelary *orichas* of the house, Eleguá's red and black hooked staff (*garabato*), curtains of palm fronds (*mariwó*), small loaves of bread for the impoverished beggar Babalú Ayé, curtains of Oyá's nine-colored strips of cloth that symbolize the dead, and combined images of the *Ojo Divino* (Divine Eye) and a tongue cut by a dagger (*lengua atrevesada por un puñal*). Eleguá's hooked staff "is used symbolically to attract to the home and life of the *santero* all that is good and needed, or to keep away that which is bad." *Mariwó*, often hung over the doors and windows in houses ruled by Eleguá, Ogún, Ochosi, Changó, and Orula, screens out bad spiritual influences. The bread, González Huguet explains, "ensures that food is always present in the house." In other words, the gift of bread for Babalú Ayé—the mendicant (*mendigo*) who goes from house to house for alms—petitions for the countergift of well-being in the form of nourishment. The curtain of nine colors beseeches Oyá (Owner of the Cemetery) to keep Death (*Ikú*) at a distance. Like Eleguá, Ogún, and Ochosi, who are always present at the scene of bloodshed and violence, Babalú Ayé and Oyá both reside at the cutting edge of life and death. Babalú Ayé owns mortal plagues and delivers unfortunate victims by deathcart to Oyá, who stands at the cemetery's gate to receive them. The Divine Eye and dagger-pierced tongue "ward off the evil eye and gossipy enemies" (González Huguet 1968:38). The cowrie divination sign called Obara (six cowries) may advise that a priest hang a fresh beef tongue, pierced by knives and pins, from the ceiling of the house in order to stop an antagonist's gossip. The eye and tongue together can also prescribe respect in the house: "you may look, but don't wag your tongue."[13] Most of these objects are sacrifices (ebó) or "works" (trabajos) intended to solve problems raised in divination readings; oracular information includes precise instructions as to their composition and intended location.

Two classes of flags (banderas) are customarily mounted behind or above the front door. One identifies the permanent tutelary oricha "ruler" of the house (the guardian angel of the resident senior priest) by a set of colors associated with this oricha's traditional beadwork. Obatalá's colors are white, Eleguá's are red and black, Changó's are red and white, Yemayá's are blue and white, and so forth. A second flag, the bandera del año (flag of the year), represents a male and female pair of orichas determined through divination each January 1 to "govern the year." Intensive divination determines the design and iconography of the flag each year.[14] On this day, once the identity of the two ruling orichas is ascertained, possible color combinations for the field and the border, and likely iconographic symbols, are proposed one at a time to the oracle for confirmation or rejection. Those present disseminate the information to their godchildren and friends so that the same flag flies in all the oricha houses in the community.[15] The flag of the tutelary oricha and the flag of the year are signs of respect and spiritual identity. The tradition of banderas associated with Afro-Cuban institutions originated in the colonial cabildos of the African nations, whose carnival processions were led by flags bearing the colors and iconography of a cabildo's Catholic patron saint—a covert sign of the group's ruling Lucumí oricha (Ortiz 1960 [1920]; Ortiz 1921). When drummers are hired to provide the sacred music for ritual events, they define their authority over the sacred performance space by hanging their group's bandera on the wall behind them (see D. Brown 1989: figs. 1 and 2). The flag of the year also functions like an ebó. It not only announces the identity of the spiritual rulers of the year but also invokes their protective influence over the house.

Other ebó (sacrifices) or trabajos (spiritual "works")—tied or tacked to the door—are loci of ritual processes of shorter duration. They are taken down when a particular ritual task is accomplished. During 1986 and 1987 in the Union City apartment of Adólfo Fernández and Ramón Esquivél (hereafter the Union City apartment), a string of twelve dried okra (quim-

bombó) hung for a time above the door. Okra is one of Changó's favorite foods. Later, a chain of garlic bunches (*ajo*) was added to the center of the door (for Babalú Ayé). Garlic is a curative and a charm against witchcraft and the evil eye (Cabrera 1983 [1954]:295–96). Soon these were gone, and a small loaf of Italian bread was nailed to the upper right frame of the door (also for Babalú Ayé). For a month or two, a fierce *trabajo*—a hunting knife whose handle was stuck with feathers, draped with Eleguá's red and black beads, and tightly bound with purple thread—was driven into the upper left corner of the door frame. The knife was accompanied by a slender red and black cloth-wrapped *garabato* (staff of Eleguá) that hung above it from the curtain of Changó's protective *mariwó* (see fig. 4.8). An equally fierce set of protective objects hung across the back of a Brooklyn priest's door during 1987: an *achabá* (the chain of Ogún's iron tools) and the deer horn of the hunter Ochosi tied with a red ribbon (see fig. 4.9). A spirit of the dead (*muerto*) had instructed the priest during a *misa espiritual* (Kardecian spirit mass) to mount these objects on the door. Ernesto Pichardo observes, "when you have to put an *achabá* by the doorway, this guy's got himself a fight. It's a war flag, a protective flag. You also have to symbolize Ochosi by the horn . . . in the sense of 'capturing the enemy.'"[16]

The January 1, 1987, Ifá reading of the year in a New Jersey/New York community not only advised that objects of *ebó* against witchcraft and attacks be hung from the door, but also cautioned behavior in relation to this critical threshold of social interaction:

> Take care with the door to the house, much *brujería* [witchcraft] comes, dark *eguns*, and things sent: *polvos* [sorcerer's powders]. After you have gotten into bed, don't get up to open the door to anyone, or there will be assaults. Feed the door, put a prickly cactus [*tuna espinosa*] with a red string behind the door in order to curb this. Don't chat in the doorway of your house. Put an Ochosi [bow and arrow] behind the door, and refresh [appease] Ogún and Eleguá and feed them.[17]

These *ebó* suggest Ifá's insights into the social and spiritual phenomena of the threshold, the *puerta de la calle*. It is a potentially dangerous liminal space between the inside and outside, the known and the unknown, particularly at night. Lingering social intercourse in the threshold invites problems inside. The prescribed *ebó* are the weapons of this struggle at the threshold, of which the *guerreros*— Eleguá, Ogún, Ochosi, and Osun—are the main gatekeepers and protectors. When hung at the back of the door, the prickly cactus, a plant sacred to Obatalá, the owner of heads, "sends away enemies" (Cabrera 1983 [1954]:551), just as the warriors and the Osun staff, in particular, fight for and protect the spiritual head of the priestly owner of the house (see Thompson 1983).[18]

4.8. Front door (*puerta de la calle*) of Union City apartment bearing palm fronds, bread, hooked staff, flag of the year, embedded knife.

4.9. Front door of Brooklyn apartment with chain of Ogún (*achabá*) and deer horn.

What the Lease Doesn't Reveal (Part II): Orichas, Eguns, Palos, Muertos, and the Division of Domestic Space

The implications for the everyday life of a practitioner of multiple Afro-Cuban religions are considerable. The *orichas* and as many as three classes of spirits share domestic space with their priests. While only two names may appear on the lease, far more inhabitants occupy the home. The *orichas* and the spirits demand space, daily attention, and a household budget that recognizes their needs.

The distinction between Lucumí *orichas*, ritual and family ancestors (*egun*), other multifarious spirits of the dead (*muertos*), and the Kongo-Cuban *nkisi* spirits (*palos*) is realized and made concrete in fundamental divisions of domestic space, as well as in temporal cycles of ritual practice. All of these supernatural beings are "spirits" in the most general sense, but they are ontologically and experientially different. They occupy different cosmological levels or domains, which some practitioners and scholars represent as a hierarchical matter–spirit continuum (Drewal, Pemberton, and Abiodun 1989:14; Brandon 1993:110; Harwood 1977:40; Wafer 1991:85, 106). For example, New Jersey Obatalá priest, *palero*, and *espiritista* Ramón Esquivél explained to me that the fierce *palo* spirits, certain recently deceased spirits, and *oricha*-warriors such as Eleguá, Ogún, and Ochosi are "more material"—closer to the human lifeworld—while the Catholic saints, highly "evolved" remotely deceased spirits, and certain *orichas* close to the sky, are "more spiritual."[19]

Orichas. Orichas have their historical origins in the principal regional *òrìṣà* of Yorubaland. As direct participants in the Creation or as delegated distinct domains by God, the *orichas* control aspects of the natural and human social worlds and their various forces, workings, and transformations. They may represent principles of nature and also may be deified humans who were the kings and queens of Yoruba history and mythology. The *orichas* are ranked and differentiated by their particular characters and relative closeness to the human lifeworld.

Eguns. Though many practitioners use the term *egun* loosely to refer to all spirits of the dead, *egun* from an orthodox Lucumí perspective most properly refers to the ritual family ancestral line (*familia de santo*) and the deceased members of the blood family (*familia de sangre*) of the house.[20] When venerated ritually, the proper names, Lucumí praise names (of the priests), and personal Ifá divination signs (of the *babalawos*) of these deceased figures are invoked in prayers called *moyubas* ("I pay homage"; see Mason and Edwards 1985b:11; Ramos 1982).

Muertos. Spirits of the dead are classified according to character archetype and ranked according to whether they are "more material" or "more spiritual," that is, "less evolved" or "more evolved" on the matter–spirit continuum. According to Ernesto Pichardo, whereas the egun category is "more focused" on a particular level of deceased—recent and remote priestly and family ancestors—the category of muertos is like "the United Nations, in a spiritual sense."[21] Muertos may be Gypsies, Arabs, South American or North American Indians (chiefs or warriors), Congos and other Africans, Buddhas, Chinese, children, Catholic priests, monks (Franciscan, Dominican, etc.), nuns, paleros, oricha priests, followers of particular Catholic saints, Haitian or French "Madames," Argentine doctors, or deceased family members. Spirits may make themselves known to a person through dreams, visions, voices, mediumship, and various formal divination methods. The dead need human beings to do unfinished healing work in the world that also helps these spirits "evolve" and attain "light" on the spiritual plane. However, some spirits are jealous of the world and want only to use (and abuse) the human body to smoke, drink, carouse, and cause trouble. Such destructive or malignant spirits are "dark" (oscuro) and may intrude violently into daily life and dreams, bringing torment to the living. While some of these unevolved muertos oscuros need to be dispatched as soon as possible through spirit masses and cleansings, others can be "socialized" so that they can attain light and work for the good. Spirits of Indians, monks, Catholic priests, nuns, Arabs, and doctors "deal with celestial things and are 'light,'" explains Melba Carillo.[22] They are "spiritual, less material, more gentle and intelligent," Ramón Esquivél adds,[23] and work with prayers, flowers, perfumes, and candles. In contrast, the "Congos and Congas are more material and are more useful for brujería."[24] In other words, because they and other "more material" spirits struggled and "suffered in their lives," particularly under slavery, they are adept at solving difficult problems in the world. They work with strong herbs, cigars, fiery rum (aguardiente), and, sometimes, human relics. Where deceased Catholic priests may come into their mediums and reverently read from the Bible, the strong Congos gruffly demand rum and cigars in their "Congo" tongue, an archaic Afro-Cuban creole called bozal, which is heavily marked with Bakongo-derived lexicon and peppered with Cuban slang (see Cabrera 1984; Castellanos 1990; 1977:125–27). Wholly unlike the more evolved spirits that do not "eat," the Congos may also "draw blood" (sacar sangre) in the form of animal sacrifices.[25]

The muertos comprise a person's cuadro espiritual, one's corps of personal spirit guides and helpers. Some of these spirits may be familiares, such as one's deceased mother, father, or aunt, and, as such, blur the category of cuadro espiritual spirits with that of the priestly and family eguns. At the same time, some of the cuadro espiritual's Congos were, "in life," initiated priests of the Palo Monte religion. They "have *prenda*"; that is, they do their work in very "material" ways with Central African–derived *nkisi* medicines. They represent a critical bridge to the fourth class of spirits, those of the Palo Monte/Mayombe religion, which is also called La Regla de Conga (Cabrera 1986b).

Palo Monte/Mayombe spirits. Palo Monte practice revolves around vessels variously called *ngangas, nkisis* (alt. *nkisos*), and *prendas.* These powerful vessels (hereafter *nganga* for consistency) are "charged" with spirit-imbued earth, sticks, and animal and human bones (see Cabrera 1983 [1954]:118–48; Cabrera 1986b; Thompson 1983:117–25; Thompson 1993:47–108).[26] Each *nganga* contains not a single, unitary, anthropomorphized spirit, but rather a compound of various spirits from the natural world that maintain a contractual relationship with a principal spirit of the dead. This spirit of the dead (Congo *mfumbi*; Sp. *muerto*) is embodied in a set of human relics, for example a skull (*kiyumba*), and is the "slave" of the human priest who marshals and commands the other forces (Cabrera 1983 [1954]:131). Definitions of this complicated object's constituent elements and interpretations about its chain of spiritual command vary among practitioners.[27] These *ngangas* were established in Cuba as a pantheon of nine or more principal archetypes and were cross-indexed with (but remain ontologically distinct from) the principal Lucumí *orichas.* The pantheon includes Lucero Mundo (Eleguá), Zarabanda (Ogún), Nkuyo Watariamba (Ochosi), Tiembla Tierra (Obatalá), Nsasi/Siete Rayos (Changó), Kalunga/Madre de Agua (Yemayá), Mama Chola or Chola Wengue (Ochún), Centella Ndoki (Oyá), and Cobayende (Babalú Ayé) (see Castellanos and Castellanos 1992:138).

In short, there are four distinct "spirit" categories: *orichas, eguns, muertos,* and *palos,* linked to three distinct but related "religions" or religious "roads": La Regla de Ocha, La Regla de Congo, and Espiritismo. Catholicism represents a fourth, related religion, not least because many of the *muertos* of Espiritismo were intimately associated "in life" with the cults of the saints of the church and because the *orichas* and *palos* borrow iconography from the saints.

A corollary to the cosmological classification of spirits is their separation in space and time. Each category and several subcategories are provided with their own altar spaces and temporal periods for appropriate address. Each category is addressed in context-specific ways, marked particularly by distinctive codes of language, gesture, iconography, and regimens of ritual attention, such as care, feeding, and cleaning. Highly "crossed' (*cruzado*) Afro-Cuban spiritual practices blur many of the distinctions and separations more orthodox priests strive to maintain (see Stanford and Drufovka 1996).[28] Ernesto Pichardo, a rigorous and orthodox practitioner of La Regla de Ocha and Espiritismo in Miami, reflects on these complex arrangements:

> We worship them according to their level, and we are tapping into different orders. We are always concerned with certain unwanted intrusions, and thus do each ritual within its own order and space, so that all relevant beings are recognized and dealt with in their time, with no confusion. Each has different norms . . . rules, patterns . . . and behaviors. The sense of behavior and order are different for each. Will a rabbi conduct a service at a Catholic altar in a church?[29]

Creative and flexible spatial solutions are necessary to maintain such "order," especially in small apartments. As the practice of multiple religions emerged historically among predominantly poor Cuban populations residing in cramped inner-city tenements (*solares*) and tiny houses in the surrounding suburban *barrios*, models of compressed spatial economy have been passed down along with the religious traditions themselves. The *orichas* reside in closets, in cabinets, or on shelves in bedrooms, living rooms, and hallways—and sometimes (but more rarely) in their own rooms. The ritual and family ancestors (*eguns*) are most often enshrined on the floor of the bathroom under the sink. Aside from being a convenient, discrete room for separating *eguns* from the other classes of spirits, the bathroom is also the distinctive place in the house for bodily cleansing with flowing water—a principal medium for the spiritual cleansing of bad influences carried by "dark" dead spirits. To some priests, the bathroom's vertical pipes represent water-borne conduits between the spiritual and material worlds.[30] Ocha priests address these *eguns* in formal Lucumí *moyuba* chants. Through their bathroom altar, ritual and family ancestors receive table foods and luxuries consumed by the living, including plates of rice, beans, chicken, and fried plantains, cups of coffee, beer, fruit, and cigarettes. Their altar is lit by candles, marked with Lucumí ritual chalk (Lucumí *efún*; Sp. *cascarilla*), and presented with Lucumí sacrificial offerings of coconut shards (*obi*), palm oil (*epó*), and African pepper grains (*pimienta guinea*), arranged in sets of nine, the sacred oracular number of Oyá and the dead (see fig. 4.10, bottom center, and Mason and Edwards 1985b:4). In contrast to most of the deceased spirits of the *cuadro espiritual*, the priestly and family *eguns* receive blood sacrifices, either applied to their distinctive wood staff adorned with Oyá's nine colors (*bastón de egun*) or delivered directly into grave-like holes dug in the backyard (see Valdés Garríz 1991:64–65).

In marked contrast to the Lucumí *eguns* on the floor of the bathroom, a site that, to some priests, also registers the spirits' link to the ancestral earth of the Yoruba, the diverse *muertos* of the *cuadro espiritual*

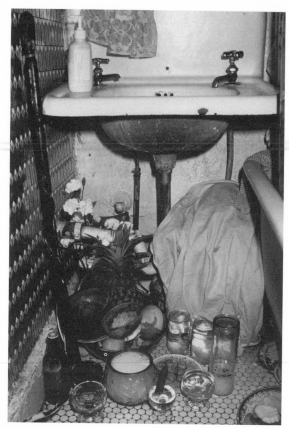

4.10. *Egun* shrine in bathroom of Union City apartment. The wood *egun* staff stands to the right.

are elevated in the manner of Allen Kardec's "white table" (*mesa blanca*). The white table, commonly called the *bóveda*, may stand in the bedroom, hallway, or living room (see figs. 4.6 and 4.14) The Spanish term *bóveda* literally means "vault" or "crypt." The white cloth-covered table supports a cluster of nine (or an odd number of) goblets or tumblers filled with water that may be perfumed with cologne or *Agua Florida*, vases of flowers, candles, rosary beads, Christian Bibles, and Allen Kardec's books of orations (see, e.g., Kardec n.d.), cigars, statues and chromolithographs of saints, and diverse figures, dolls, paintings, and photographs representing particular deceased spirits.

The *bóveda* taps into the spirit world through the water goblets and myriad visual representations. According to Ernesto Pichardo, each goblet of water is designated for a "line" or "commission" (*comisión*) of spirits. The commissions, archetypes of a sort, are identified with particular forces or kinds of spiritual work—for example, the work of "clarifying," "healing," strong "cleansing," and "removing malevolent intrusions." The spirits of one's *cuadro espiritual* work within, and draw on the power of, their *comisiones*. Some *comisiones* revolve around particular Catholic saints and *orichas*—for example, Santa Clara, San Lázaro (Babalú Ayé), the Virgin of Regla (Yemayá), and the Virgin of Cobre (Ochún).[31] "Santa Clara *aclara*" [Saint Clara clarifies], one Spiritist song refrain goes. Santa Clara, whose name literally means "light," is "traditionally invoked by Catholic petitioners with sore eyes" (Kelly and Rogers 1993:63). San Lázaro is associated with poverty, skin illnesses, and problems with certain internal organs. Strictly speaking, Spiritist work in the name of particular *orichas* does not tap directly the *aché* of the *fundamentos* of the *oricha* shrine, but the "spiritual side" of the *orichas*. It approaches the *orichas* indirectly, tapping their particular functional domains through the metacategory of the dead (*muerto/egun*), employing the spiritual work of deceased who "in life" were priests of those *orichas*. Other *comisiones* revolve around the aforementioned group types, such as Congos, Indians, Arabs, Chinese, and Gypsies, or are associated with professions or vocations, for example, the Catholic priests, the doctors, and the Haitian Madames.

Visual images, such as a saint statue of San Lázaro, are often placed next to a particular goblet to elaborate the general identity of the goblet's *comisión* or to identify the spiritual associations a specific deceased person maintains. A portrait on the *bóveda* of one's deceased mother indicates that she is working spiritually with the *bóveda*'s living owner. The mother may work in relation to the *comisión* of a particular saint with whom she "had a tendency" (*tendencia*) in life, such as the Virgin of Regla. Thus, the mother's picture, as well as a statuette of the Virgin of Regla, may appear near a goblet. The particular representations that cluster around, or near, the glass of water flesh out "what [the mother] was known for" in life, "what spirits she made use of, what was her strong side."[32] In short, the *bóveda* visually maps the *cuadro espiritual* of the priest of the house and invites the spirits to take up residence there.

The Congo spirits often appear on the *bóveda* in the form of statues or paintings, but their *nganga* cauldrons are ideally segregated in separate rooms, in closets, or even outside the house in a shed. If the term *bóveda* refers to the burial vault or crypt of the dead, its principal means and iconography (prayer, white cloth, water, candles, perfume, flowers) embody the "more spiritual" end of the matter–spirit continuum. The *nganga*, embedded with earth, sticks, and human relics, and fed sacrificial animal blood, is "material" in the extreme; indeed, it is a miniaturization of the cemetery and the "bush" (*manigua*) rolled into one. A "world in miniature," the Congo *nganga* embodies the "spirit of trees and plants; spirits that work in the cemeteries, on street corners, on hills, in rivers, in the

ocean, in the bush [*manigua*]—which is the home of all the spirits"
(Cabrera 1983 [1954]:130–31). The *nganga*'s metaphors of spiritual work
are not associated with the elevated human professions of the *bóveda*'s
doctors, nuns, or Buddhas. The *nganga*'s metaphors of work are the slave
gang, the military campaign, and the wage contract (Cabrera 1983
[1954]:130–31; Palmié n.d.), as well as the hunting, hard-laboring, or
predatory animal and insect avatars, such as dogs, buzzards, ants, and
spiders.

Case Study of Space and Spirits in a Union City, New Jersey, Apartment

Two Afro-Cuban men in their fifties live in a five-room flat in a five-
story walk-up at the corner of 14th Street and Palisade Avenue in Union
City, New Jersey. Adolfo Fernández and Ramón Esquivél moved into the
small apartment in 1983, having arrived in the United States in the 1980
Mariel Exodus from Havana.[33] Senior priests and masters of ceremony
(*oriaté*) in Ocha, both are also talented *paleros* and *espiritistas*. Adolfo,
who became a priest of Changó in 1959, is a *tata nganga* of Changó's
Congo counterpart, Siete Rayos (Seven Lightning Bolts), having been
initiated into Palo Monte as a child in Guanabacoa, one of the historic
Havana strongholds of Ocha and Palo. Ramón, born in Matanzas Province
and initiated in Guanabacoa in 1969 as a priest of Obatalá Yecú-Yecú, also
works with Obatalá's Congo counterpart, Tiembla Tierra (Earth Trembles).[34] Both "live in the religion"—Ocha, Palo, Espiritismo—and work it
"24–7," a godchild noted. They depend upon a sizable interlocking network of godchildren in Ocha and Palo, some of whom rejoined them in
New Jersey from Guanabacoa, for the extensive ritual work they perform
for the house and for their large private clientele.

A corridor leading from the front door to the living room passes a
long kitchen and long bathroom. The living room is connected to the
single bedroom by an archway. A small additional room extends from the
bedroom (see fig. 4.11). The corridor and every room are occupied by
altars and representations of spirits. Most of the time, the men's *orichas* live
in two ornate wood cabinets with glass doors (*canastilleros*) in the small
additional room at the *fondo de la casa* (back of the house). More than
twenty-five *orichas* live in this cramped shrine room, the permanent
igbodún or *cuarto de santo* of the house. It is divided from the rest of the
house by a curtain. This *cuarto de santo* becomes a consultation room
when the traditional reed mat (Lucumí *até*; Sp. *estera*) is spread upon the
floor just inside the curtained threshold. Barefoot, Adolfo and Ramón

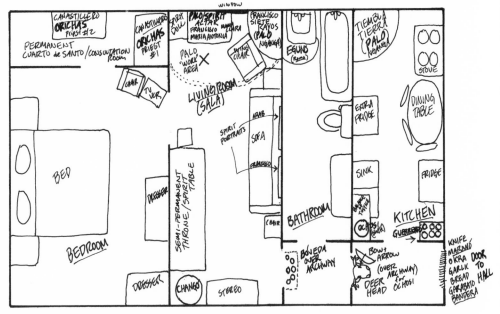

4.11. Floor plan of daily use of a Union City apartment, showing the distribution of spirits and *orichas: guerreros* at the front door and in adjacent kitchen; *palos* in the kitchen and one end of the living room; *eguns* in the bathroom; throne for spirits and saints in the living room; *orichas* in cabinets in room off bedroom.

chant their *mojuba* prayers and cast the cowrie shells (*dilogún*) upon the mat for clients, who are called one at a time from the *sala* (living room), which serves as a waiting room. The *cuarto de santo* also serves as a storehouse for a prodigious collection of religious adornments, including sacred garments, bolts of cloth, porcelain vessels, flower vases, and plaster statues.

The legions of other *orichas, palos,* and spirits have claimed their preferred places in the house. Adolfo's Changó, wearing the dazzling beaded and fringed crown of his *oricha*-sister Dadá, reigns proudly from his lathe-turned lightning mortar in a corner of the living room (figs. 4.6 and 4.6a).[35] Adolfo and Ramón's *guerreros* (Eleguá, Ogún, Ochosi, and Osun) are ensconced on shelves just inside the portal to the kitchen, adjacent to the *puerta de la calle* (see figs. 4.11 and 4.12). Reinforcing the spiritual protection of the front door by the *guerreros*, a full-sized stuffed deer head belonging to the hunter Ochosi, adorned with a real bow and arrow, is mounted near the ceiling of the corridor and stares down at the front door.

From time to time, a tiny *bóveda* of water glasses appears on a high shelf in the corridor over the portal to the living room (fig. 4.11). The Lucumí priestly and family *eguns* reside under the sink on the floor of the bathroom (see figs. 4.12 and 4.10). The two men's principal spirits, represented by goblets of water, lavishly dressed dolls, plaster statues, and oil paintings, grace virtually every spot in the living room. A semipermanent *bóveda* stands along the long wall of the living room. Its representations, goblets, and ingredients change daily with the state of spiritual work in the house (see figs. 4.11 and 4.6).

The living room's long wall serves as a rotating site for the altars of *orichas*, Catholic saints, and spirits. The Lucumí throne (*trono*), a special altar consisting of a proscenium-like canopy of expensive cloth to present the *orichas* for drummings and festivals, is also often used in this house to celebrate *palos* and Catholic saints. On Ramón's annual July 30 "birthday" (*cumpleaños*) celebration—the anniversary of his 1969 initiation as a priest of Obatalá Yecú-Yecú—a dazzling white satin throne is constructed for this

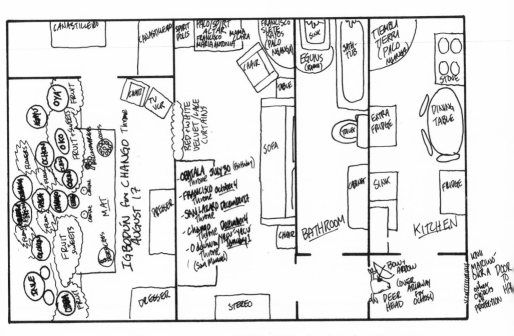

4.12. Floor plan of cyclical festival use of same Union City apartment. It shows the *orichas* arrayed on Changó's birthday throne in the rearranged bedroom, and indicates the series of thrones constructed against the long wall of the living room.

4.13. Birthday throne for Changó in Union City apartment bedroom (August 17, 1986). Corresponds to the floor plan shown in figure 4.12.

oricha of coolness and purity, who is associated with San Manuel. Elaborate thrones of satin, vases of flowers, and statues are erected for the house's annual October 4 *misa palera* (Palo mass) for Adolfo's Siete Rayos, the December 4 feast day of Santa Barbara/Changó, the December 17 feast day of San Lázaro/Babalú Ayé, and the January 1 feast day of San Manuel/Odúa/Obatalá Yecú-Yecú. The hybrid *bóveda*-throne in figure 4.6, which elevates an image of the Virgin of Regla over the table of water goblets and images, was erected in mid-June 1986 for a *misa* dedicated to the spirit of Ramón's deceased mother, who "had a tendency" toward this Virgin and her *oricha* counterpart, Yemayá.

These thrones orient ritual attention and performance in the living room space, converting it from a simple social gathering place or consultation waiting room (*sala*) into the *igbodún/cuarto de santo* itself. Prayers, tributes of gifts and money, and physical submissions to the floor (*moforibale*) are rendered to the room's enthroned *orichas*. Draped in purple or red cloth, the throne constructed for Siete Rayos doubles as a Spiritist "white table" for the dramatic *misa palera* held annually on the evening of October 4, in which the apartment is transformed into a Spiritist center filled with pungent cigar smoke and the aromas of *Agua Florida*, cologne, and *aguardiente* rum. The white table form and the ritual of the Spiritist mass not only shaped, but also flexibly accommodated, local spirit cosmologies wherever it was adopted in the Western Hemisphere, whether in Puerto Rico, Cuba, or Brazil (see R. Ortiz 1989; Bermudez 1967, 1968; Castellanos and Castellanos 1992:192–202). In Cuban practice, the *misa espiritual* becomes the *misa palera* when it is focused to attract and facilitate the work of *muertos* whose vocation in life was in service to the *nganga*. The *misa espiritual* and *misa palera* are typically conducted by two *espiritistas* — in this case, Adolfo and Ramón — seated at the table's two outer corners. Those attending sit in straight-backed chairs facing the table. Participants cleanse themselves before the *bóveda* with water containing *Agua Florida* and flower petals, and throughout the evening they "pass" spirits (become possessed and speak) and participate in detailed spiritual inquiries into the lives and problems of all those present. The evening reaches its climax as Adolfo is possessed by his principal *muerto* (Francisco), who works with the energies of Siete Rayos to clean spiritually and dispense advice to each participant (see below).

Adolfo's Spirits: A special small *bóveda* for a cluster of spirits associated with Adolfo's *cuadro espiritual* occupies the far left corner of the living room, adjacent to a large corner wing chair, behind which sits the huge *nganga* cauldron of Siete Rayos. This end of the living room has become a working area dedicated specifically to Palo Monte (see figs. 4.11 and 4.14). A closer look at this *bóveda's* representations illuminates the complex spiritual network present in the two priests' lives. Adolfo works most intensively with a core group of three spirits. Beautifully dressed, adorned, and carefully positioned, they are always present in the living room or bedroom—depending upon the preferences they regularly and vociferously express. They are formally presented on the adorned Spiritist *mesa* when Adolfo gives a *misa palera*. They are (1) Francisco Siete Rayos Brazo Fuerte (Francisco Seven Lightning Bolts Strong Arm), (2) María Antonia de Baró-Cuatro Vientos (Four Winds), and (3) José Lamece.

Francisco is an elderly stooped Congo rendered in a painted plaster statue (figs. 4.6 and 4.14). Adolfo dresses Francisco in white satin or burlap pants. Sometimes Francisco goes shirtless; sometimes he wears a natty red satin blouse. He carries the signature staff of Congo spirits, the hooked tree branch called *lungowa*. The *lungowa* staff, one of the key natural constitu-

4.14. Spirit *bóveda* in "Palo working space" in Union City apartment, with cauldron of Siete Rayos behind wing chair. Corresponds to the floor plans of figures 4.11 and 4.12 (end of living room).

ents of the *nganga* cauldron itself, is the veritable stick of the *monte*—the forest source of sacred leaves and medicines that gives Palo Monte its name (see Cabrera 1984:77; Thompson 1993:60–64). Francisco also sometimes carries strong cigars, two-dollar bills, crucifixes, and red flowers in his hand or in his shirt pocket. He often wears red satin headbands, necklaces associated with Siete Rayos (red and white), as well as the *banda de guerra*, the Palo Monte war sash of multicolored beads, chains, seeds, and animal teeth associated with fierce struggle and protection.

María Antonia de Baró-Cuatro Vientos (seated on a raised pedestal next to the *bóveda* in fig. 4.14) lived in the village of Perico in the province of Matanzas, Cuba. A priestess of both Ocha and Palo in her life, she served two parallel sets of tutelary spirits—her "fathers" and "mothers" in both religions. These were Eleguá and Yemayá in La Regla de Ocha and Lucero Mundo and Madre de Agua in Palo Monte. "Cuatro Vientos," meaning the four cardinal points of the world, is a praise name associated with the Palo mediator Lucero Mundo (Bright Star of the World). María is represented by a large plastic doll (*muñeca*) with black skin and realistic eyes, hair, and eyelashes. She possesses an extensive wardrobe of dresses and gowns that are handmade by local dressmakers commissioned by Adolfo and Ramón. Her lace-and-gingham everyday dresses and lace-and-satin festival gowns, complemented by masses of bead necklaces, range from red themes that mark her association with Eleguá and Lucero Mundo, to blue themes that mark her association with Yemayá and Madre de Agua. She wears silver and diamond brooches of sea snakes and carries beautiful decorative fans, attributes of the sea dwellers Yemayá and Madre de Agua. For special "works" and festive occasions, her cheeks are adorned with Yoruba-Lucumí facial markings (/// \\\) of the kind worn by initiates into La Regla de Ocha.

José Lamece is represented by a three-by-two-foot oil painting of a white-bearded elderly black man wearing a white shirt. He is seated and holds a crucifix in his clasped hands (see fig. 4.6). José Lamece is an *espiritú familiar*, a family spirit who in life became Adolfo's guardian after the death of Adolfo's father. José Lamece was a priest of Obatalá, whose Lucumí praise name was *Ocha Linú*, and who also was a priest of the Palo Monte spirit Tiembla Tierra (Earth Trembles). The painting is not a portrait of the actual José Lamece but registers his spiritual attributes. The figure's age, race, white hair, gentle countenance, and crucifix identify him as a respected traditional Afro-Cuban *religioso*, a priest of the old, patient, and pure Obatalá, whose archetypal "children" have white hair (*canoso*). However, as a cluster of attributes, the painting could also be used to represent other spirits. Indeed, over time, Adolfo apparently designated this painting as a representation of at least three different spiritual personages. First he told me it was an *abuelo* (grandfather), which apparently meant an old ancestor spirit. Later he specified that it was Casimiro Fernández, a deceased paternal uncle. In 1989 he told me it was José Lamece, but at other points he told me it was the Congo Francisco. Indeed, *abuelo*/Casimiro/José bears a great resemblance to the statue of the Congo Francisco.

Adolfo's spirits Francisco, María, and José are, in fact, specific local elaborations upon the meta-archetypal *comisiónes* of *africanos* and *congos* of the Afro-Cubanized Spiritist discourse. Female *africanas* or *congas* typically identify themselves at first, in dreams or masses, with names such as María, Francisca, Simona, or Tomasa, or just *abuela*. Males typically identify themselves as Francisco, José, Miguel, Tomás, or *abuelo*. Ramón's cherished female African spirit, who often shares the *bóveda* with Francisco, María, and José (figs. 4.6 and 4.14), combines African and Spiritist attributes. She is Mama Clara, an old *africana* who works not only with Obatalá and Tiembla Tierra, but also, presumably, with the spiritual force of "clarification" associated with the name Santa Clara. Over time, the identity of each archetypal spirit that approaches a person is deepened and individuated. During a Havana Palo initiation in the *barrio* of Pogolotti during the summer of 1994, for example, the spirit of a fierce old male Congo slave possessed his initiate for the first time, a five-foot nine-inch black fashion model wearing the sleek plaited hair extensions that came into vogue that year. In her body, the Congo dragged his chained or crippled right leg behind him, threw himself to the ground, and thrashed around on the dusty floor before he was persuaded by the officiating *tata nganga* to take a seat and reveal his name. After considerable chest pounding and gruff resistance to the interrogation, he uttered his name, "Tomás." Smiling excitedly, those present talked among themselves about this *tremendo muerto* (a tremendous and frightful dead spirit), who had just begun his socialization as the young woman's powerful Palo Monte protector.

Adolfo's principal *muerto*, Francisco, is not only a spirit of the *bóveda* who is "tapped into" through a glass of water and a statue; he also "has *prenda*"—that is, he works with the cauldron of Palo Monte (*prenda*, *nganga*). In many cases, Adolfo works *palo* through the *muerto* Francisco—that is, Francisco possesses Adolfo—in order to mobilize the forces of the *prenda/nganga* on behalf of clients. Francisco's name and identity are elaborated metonymically through his intimate association with the *nganga* Siete Rayos: "Francisco Siete Rayos Brazo Fuerte." The plaster representation does not anthropomorphize the *nganga* Siete Rayos, but figures the *muerto* Francisco, who is "the jockey of the *nganga*."[36]

The *muertos* Francisco Siete Rayos, María Antonia de Baró, José Lamece, and Mama Clara; the deceased mothers of Adolfo and Ramón;

an Arab who works with Ramón; and two other deceased Lucumí priests who work with Adolfo (an herbalist [*osainista*] who lives in a medicine gourd, and a beautiful priestess of the *oricha* Oyá, named Beneranda Gutierrez) are integral to the spiritual work performed in the house. They are vigilant and vocal presences. María Antonia, for example, demands that she be included in all of the Ocha and Palo ceremonies Adolfo conducts, so he carries her along when he travels to officiate as *oriaté* at Ocha initiations. Dressed in Yemayá's blue satin best, she is posted in or near the Ocha initiation room and warns the officiants about gossip and bad influences in the vicinity.[37] Not only does Mama Clara claim a place on the *bóveda*, but as a priestess of Obatalá in life, she also likes to be included on the *oricha* throne for Obatalá during Ramón's birthday celebrations.[38] The combining of spirits from the two men's *cuadros espiritual* on the same *bóveda* registers the bonds of important relationships that are social as well as spiritual. All of these cherished spirits are well known by the godchildren who pass time and contribute assistance in the house. These spirits, as well as those of the godchildren, are integral members of an expansive community that includes humans and spirits.

"The Country and the City": Ocha, Palo, and the Differentiation of Urban Spaces

The powerful *nganga* cauldrons of the Palo Monte religion are ideally kept at a significant distance from the *orichas* and, if possible, from day-to-day domestic life. The spirits of the *nganga* are considered to be fierce, unruly, and unpredictable denizens of the forest and the cemetery.[39] While most of the *orichas* are represented as refined "kings" and "queens" of the palace, the Congo spirits who work with *ngangas* are typically represented in slave dress. *Bóveda* representations of the Congo recall nineteenth-century engravings by Landaluze and Miahle of rural plantation slaves recently arrived from Africa (*bozales*) and the legions of shirtless, barefoot, machete- or rifle-wielding *cimarrónes* who broke their chains, fled the plantations, and established their proud fortified outposts (*palenques*) in the mountains and forests (see Marrero 1988, vol. 14:205–34; 1986:299; Landaluze 1881; Miahle 1838).[40] The fierce iconography of the Congo also recalls the attributes of the Afro-Cuban fighters of Antonio Maceo's columns during the nineteenth-century Cuban Wars of Independence. These guerrillas lived off the land, knew the intimacies of the forest, fought with machetes, and concocted herbal poisons (see Thomas 1971:255, 323–24; also Barnet 1980 [1966]:50–56, 130). The Congos share these hunter, warrior, pathfinder, and herbalist vocations with the hardy *oricha guerreros*, Eleguá, Ogún, and Ochosi, and Osun, whose attributes contrast sharply with those of the other *orichas* of the Lucumí pantheon. "The Congos have much more strength than the Lucumís," declared ex-slave Esteban Montejo. "They are more hardheaded [*cabeza mas dura*]. They work very *material!* Everything is based on sticks, bones, blood, and trees from the forest" (Barnet 1980 [1966]:130). A Palo priest interviewed by Lydia Cabrera "had his *inkiso* [*nganga*] carefully separated from his Lucumí *Santos*—theoretically irreconcilable with the powers of *mayombe* [Palo]" (Cabrera 1983 [1954]:122).

Ocha and Palo may be "theoretically irreconcilable" and have very different West African cultural origins. Nevertheless, as the Yoruba and Kongo religious systems were selectively distilled and condensed into the Afro-Cuban *reglas*, Ocha and Palo became mutually defining semantic and practical fields, serving complementary ritual purposes (see D. Brown 1989:300–301). The versatile *orichas* are appealed to in all areas of endeavor, particularly in their expansive and elaborate systems of divination (*Ifá* and *dilogún*). Yet, because the *palos* are "more hardheaded and material," they are called on to perform the most difficult and "dirty jobs" shunned by the *orichas*, including intense spiritual guerrilla warfare and, sometimes, works of revenge.[41] "The difference between the Congo and the Lucumí," Esteban Montejo explained, "is that the Congo resolves problems but the Lucumí divines the future" (Barnet 1980 [1966]:34). While the Lucumí *orichas* clearly solve problems with their *ebós* and *trabajos*, they are like nobles who grant largesse, resist pressure, expect obedience, and shun quid pro quo exchanges. In contrast, the *palos*, who make "pacts" or "contracts" with their human priests, are believed to work quickly and effectively upon payment like wage laborers or upon command like soldiers or slaves (see Cabrera 1983 [1954]:118; González Wippler 1989:239–40; Palmié n.d.). Nevertheless, if the spirits of the *nganga* are like "gangs of slaves," they are far from slavish and, according to Lydia Cabrera's informants, they "sometimes rebel" (1983 [1954]:131).

Priests practice Ocha and Palo together in tiny urban apartments in Cuba and the United States. Where the daily ritual routine involves both *orichas* and *palos*, the problem of separation is one of context or framing, not always of great physical distance or material barriers. The ritual work performed can shift from one frame and its cast of spiritual characters to another, with shifts in ritual intentionality, style of language and iconography, kinds of bodily gesture, and classes of ritual ingredients, as well as with spatial and temporal shifts (see Bauman 1975; Marks 1974; Glazier 1985). In the small Union City apartment of Adolfo Fernández and Ramón Esquivél, the objects of Francisco Siete Rayos Brazo Fuerte and Tiembla Tierra reside in the far corners of the living room and kitchen respectively (see figs. 4.11 and 4.12). Rooms and walls separate them from the majority of the *orichas*, who live in their *canastilleros* (cabinets) in the tiny room off the bedroom. During festival periods when *oricha* thrones are mounted in the living room, however, the *orichas* must live side by side with the *palos* for the week. Changó, enthroned on his mortar in the living room, lives within earshot of *bóveda* spirits most of the year (fig. 4.6). If the Congo ritual language is intoned within earshot of the Lucumí *orichas*, presumably they say to themselves, "They're not talking to me."

Urban priests of Ocha and Palo fortunate enough to own a home with a backyard, such as one Bronx priest of Changó and Siete Rayos, often keep their *ngangas* outdoors, on or beyond the *patio* in enclosed sheds (see Castellanos 1977:114–24). This house and yard setting reproduces the symbolic sectors of "town" and "bush," and provides the *palos* with their own urban *palenque*. A creative Bronx priest—a Puerto Rican Palo godchild of Adolfo Fernández, named Juan—built a seven-by-seven-foot shed of green boards and standard roofing in one corner of his row house lot, a grassy area dotted with saint statues and medicinal plants (see figs. 4.15 and 4.16). The small shed contains two *nganga* cauldrons jammed with sticks and *lungowas*. Each cauldron is embedded in the earth through an opening cut into the shed's floorboards.[42] Juan keeps his shed securely locked at all times, opening it only to work with the *ngangas*. During a break in a Spiritist mass held in his Bronx row house on a hot early September night in 1984, Juan opened the door to the shed and flicked on the lights. Red bulbs illuminated the tight space with a diffuse warm glow. In this electric simulacrum of an eternal dusk in the *monte*, the two *ngangas* reposed beneath metallic cutouts of stars and the moon adorning the walls near the ceiling. Densely packed with tall sticks, the *ngangas* scraped the heavens like thick trees. As I peered into the shed, Juan's wife called out from the sliding doors on the patio a few yards away, warning me to be careful because the *palos* are so *fuerte* (strong). "If a Congo saw you sticking your nose where it didn't belong," ex-slave Esteban Montejo remembered, "watch out! you could be hurt" (Barnet 1980 [1966]:130).

Apartment dwellers who lack private outdoor space are forced to rely on a time-honored urban solution: the rigorous division of indoor space. A Brooklyn priest of the Lucumí *oricha* Agayú and the *nganga* Siete Rayos—a Palo godchild of Adolfo Fernández named Idalberto—kept his *orichas* in their own airy, sunlit room adjacent to his bedroom and his *palos* in a small, dark, locked walk-in closet at the other end of the apartment. The two rooms were entirely different sensory worlds. Idalberto explained that when he visited the Palo room housing Siete Rayos and two smaller Lucero Mundos, their fierceness was so palpable that he would stiffen up. In expressing this to me, he made his body erect and taut, planked his arms

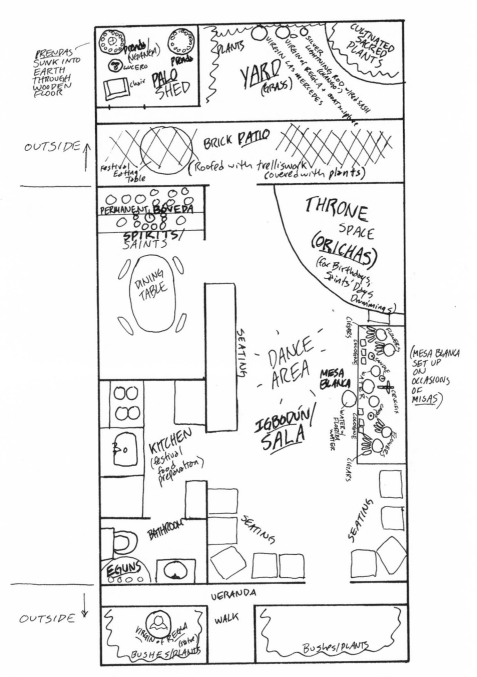

4.15. Floor plan of ground floor of Bronx row house showing interior areas for altars/festival for spirits and *orichas* and exterior patio and backyard area— with shed for *palos*.

4.16. Palo Monte shed in backyard of Bronx row house. Corresponds to floor plan depicted in figure 4.15.

at his sides, held his breath, narrowed his eyes, and peered about with caution. In contrast, he explained, when he visited his *oricha* room, "it was so calm and peaceful." He let his body relax now, elevated his head slightly, and softened his voice. "I go in there and lie on the floor, and give them fruit, and I eat some, and I talk to them. Sometimes I stay there for hours. It is so peaceful." Eventually he became so unnerved by the presence of the Siete Rayos cauldron in the apartment that he buried it beneath a tree in the *campo* (countryside), an untraveled region of a park in the Bronx. He rides from Brooklyn to the *campo* by subway train when he needs to feed his Siete Rayos.

> I got my *prenda* [*nganga*]. I made my own *prenda* [Lucero] a long time ago, and then I received one from Adolfo about five years ago, or six years ago [Siete Rayos]. I don't like the *prenda* in the house. You hear things all the time. You hear things. Sometimes you hear the dishes in the kitchen: BLAH-BLAH-BLAH [loud rattling], and you go there and the dishes are completely normal, nothing broken, it's funny. I don't have [Siete Rayos] in that room [anymore], I have it someplace in the countryside, in the *campo*. My house

has a Lucero, two Luceros. That's the only thing I have in the house. But the *prenda's* supposed to be buried someplace. . . . If you have a backyard it's perfect, a garden, but most people do it far away, in the *monte*.[43]

The terms "country" and "city," Raymond Williams argues, do not signify essential, mutually exclusive geographic areas. The contrasting and complementary values of "country" and "city" are portable and can constitute meaning at a number of levels and in many contexts (Williams 1973:chap. 25). Not least, they can constitute meaning in the condensed micro-ecologies of row house lots or within differentiated inner-city terrains. Lydia Cabrera's experience with Ocha and Palo priests in the bustling, densely inhabited Havana of the 1940s and 1950s taught her that

one should not think that only a "stretch of uncultivated land filled with trees" is meant by the word *Monte* or *manigua* [brushland]. . . . In Havana, any vacant lot [*terreno baldío*] filled with bushes is considered a *"monte"*—or savanna! (as an avocado or laurel tree may be called a *mata* ["grove"]!). The weeds that grow in the smallest, most barren *"solar"* [courtyard] will simply be called a *"monte"* or a *"manigua."* Every space in which grass can grow and thicken is an appropriate place to deposit a "request" or an *ebbó* [sacrifice], the common offering that in *La Regla de Ocha* goes to a Santo that "is not of the water." (To those that personify the river or the sea, like Oshún or Yemayá, generally offerings are taken to the river and to the edge of the sea.) In this way Havana Blacks need not go far to find a *"monte."* (Cabrera 1983 [1954]:67–68)

In short, for most twentieth-century urban practitioners of Afro-Cuban religions, the experience of *la naturaleza* is encapsulated within built-up urban areas. As Juan Manuel García Passalacqua might have said, the traditional Lucumí herbalist is a Bronx herbalist these days (see n. 3).

Domestic Space and Ritual Performance: A Palo and Ocha Cleansing in Union City, New Jersey

On August 3, 1987, Adolfo Fernández performed a spiritual cleansing for a client, drawing upon the resources of the Congo Francisco Siete Rayos and two Lucumí *orichas*. He conducted the major work of this *despojo*, a "stripping" of bad influences, in the far end of the living room before the special *bóveda* of the Congo spirits—something of a *palo* shed without walls within the small Union City apartment (see figs. 4.11, 4.12, and 4.14). Once a year, between July 30 and August 5, the living room is host to the expansive white satin birthday throne of Ramón Esquivél's guardian *oricha*, Obatalá Yecú-Yecú. During this period, the spatial proximity of the *orichas* and *palos* is greatly heightened. Adolfo strategically incorporated Obatalá and his throne into the cleansing process.

On that hot August afternoon, the client drove two hours to reach Union City. After stops at two *botánicas* in Spanish Harlem and a *florería*, *licoría*, and *supermercado* in Union City, he arrived at the apartment carrying a brown shopping bag brimming with seven types of fresh plants, a tube of cocoa butter (*manteca de cacao*), a small glass jar of viscous, amber-colored balsam of Peru (*balsamo de Perú*), a bottle of Perla brand *aguardiente* (strong cane rum), a bouquet of white carnations, a box of Johnson and Johnson thick cotton roll, and a clean white change of clothes. In a preliminary informal consultation two months earlier, Adolfo had constructively framed the client's problem—friction with an antagonist—as one of *la envidia* (jealousy), and had written out a prescription for the ingredients. Now he asked the client to take a seat on the long sofa while he prepared the ingredients and organized them in front of the small *bóveda*. Sitting on the green sofa, the client faced the expansive, brilliant white satin and silver lamé throne of Obatalá.

The cleansing would be a two-step process, a *trabajo* ("work") handled by the Lucumí *orichas*, and a *despojo* with strong herbs and other ingredients performed by the Congo Francisco Siete Rayos. First, with the aid of the messenger and mediator *oricha* Elegúa, Obatalá, father of calmness and purity, would "pacify" (*apaciguar*) the client's antagonist. Then the *brujo* Francisco Siete Rayos Brazo Fuerte would use the plants and other ingredients to strip (*despojar*) the client of the spiritually toxic *envidia* clinging to his "back." Four of the plants, including Rompe Zaragüey (*rompe* = "break"), are commonly used to strip *brujería* (witchcraft) in strong *despojos*, and one is used to drive away bad spirits of the dead. The names of the two others, Siempre Viva (Always Alive) and Abre Camino (Open the Road), poetically advertise their virtues.[44]

Adolfo asked the client to write the name of the *enemigo* (enemy) on a scrap of brown paper torn from the shopping bag. He then placed the name in a small cylindrical glass jar half-filled with the thick *balsamo de Perú*. After screwing the lid down firmly, Adolfo wrapped the jar in the cotton, daubed this compact white package with Obatalá's cooling *manteca de cacao*, and placed the jar on a side table. Symbolically, the jar of the thick amber would capture and still the enemy, and the cotton and cocoa butter would cool and neutralize the enemy's jealous intentions.

When Adolfo had set out the other ingredients on the *bóveda* (the flowers) and on the floor before it (the *aguardiente*, plants, cologne, and an enamel bowl of water perfumed with refreshing *Agua Florida*), he closed the window curtains and summoned the client to sit on a low stool (*taburete*) facing the statue of the Congo Francisco on the *bóveda*. Francisco, dressed in white satin pants and a red sash, held a cigar in his right hand. Accompanying him on the *bóveda* was the immaculately dressed Mama Clara. María Antonia, who wore a blue satin and lace gown, sat to the right side (see fig. 4.14).

Removing his shoes and shirt and rolling up his white trousers to the knees, Adolfo pulled the bright purple satin sash covering Siete Rayos's *nganga* cauldron behind the wing chair and tied it around his waist. Adolfo was now the mirror image of the Congo Francisco. Adolfo cleaned himself with the perfumed water and the cologne by rubbing the liquids over his arms, chest, and head, and then vigorously snapped his hands away from himself toward the *bóveda* in efficient Cuban *espiritista* fashion. He lit a fat, pungent cigar, as well as a tall white seven-day candle. To complete the preliminaries, he purified the client with the same liquids and shotgunned cigar smoke over the client's body in a spiritual fumigation. He rubbed the bouquet of flowers briskly over the client's head, neck, and shoulders, the petals crumbling to the floor, while intoning an inspired Spiritist sequence of Kardecian songs to God, the spirits, and the Catholic saints, especially San Salvador (see Kardec n.d.; Castellanos and Castellanos 1992:192–99). Sitting at the edge of the wing chair, with Siete Rayos's *nganga* at his back, Adolfo continued singing, now more softly and with deep concentration. His hand rested upon his brow, and he moved his thumb and forefinger gently back and forth. Francisco quickly and suddenly possessed Adolfo. Using Adolfo's body, Francisco would now carry out the most subtle and difficult work of the cleansing.

In a manner characteristic of the old African spirits, Francisco clucked his tongue, effected some facial tics, and began to speak in the clipped Afro-Cuban *bozal* language spoken by the Congos: "*Dici carao dici.* . . ."[45] Eyes alert and visionary, he conducted a detailed, remarkably accurate spiritual inquiry with the client, pinpointing the exact physical whereabouts of the *enemigo* and confirming that the client often felt the *enemigo*'s dark presence "behind him" (*detrás*), a baneful influence that prevented the client from "advancing" (*avanzando*). Francisco delineated the *enemigo*'s height, hair color, and skin complexion, and he revealed that the *enemigo* "didn't believe in the Religion but had some things of the Santo," that the *enemigo* "walked with" a co-conspirator, and that these two were currently "out of the country." He accurately summed up the nature of the *envidia* and offered some additional information about the client's personal *cuadro espiritual* and ritual needs. The client "had an Indian guide that accompanied him" and also needed a "protective charm [*resguardo*] to carry in his pocket." Francisco concluded the inquiry by saying that the client would later have to "give two *palomas* [doves] to Obatalá and a *gallo* [rooster] to Eleguá" in gratitude for the work they were now performing.

Francisco prompted the client to stand and then doused the bunch of plants with cologne and *aguardiente*. From behind, wielding the bunch of plants by the stems, Francisco began gently beating the client's head, neck, back, arms, and legs, finally brushing downward vigorously from neck to heels to strip the enemy's influence from his back. All the while he sang to San Salvador and San Miguel. Lively Latin salsa music wafted through the window from an apartment across the airshaft. Francisco now made a round of the entire apartment with the bunch of plants, purifying every corner, nook, and threshold to eliminate any remaining negative influence, which could take the form of an intrusive dark *muerto*. He returned to the client's back and placed the bunch of plants, now much-shredded, upon the nape of the client's neck, telling him to grasp and break it in half while saying, "*Dios, quiero que me quites lo malo*" (God, I want you to take this evil from me). The salsa music took a marvelous turn just at this moment, reinforcing the client's petition as an otherworldly echo. The vocal *montuno* chorus, as if accompanying the client rather than the band's own soloist, broke into an uncanny refrain just as the petition rolled off the client's lips: "*Quítate lo malo, quítate lo malo.*"[46] Francisco instructed the client to cast the now-broken bunch of plants to the floor and stand on it. With an eight-inch kitchen knife, Francisco proceeded to cut through the client's clothes at the back of the legs and small of the back, motioning for the client to tear the tainted cloth from his body. Francisco then directed the client, bare to the briefs, to swill down his body thoroughly with the liquid in the bowl and to put on the spotless white clothes he had brought. Francisco departed as suddenly as he had come. Adolfo, now out of his trance, quietly rolled down his pants and replaced his shirt and shoes. With a broom, Adolfo swept the plant and flower remains into a black garbage bag and whisked it out of the room. His apartment-mate, Ramón, came in to help and remarked to the client, who now wore white from head to toe, "You look so *clean*." A priest of Obatalá and Spiritist himself, Ramón knew what he was talking about.

Adolfo returned and immediately directed the client away from the site of the cleansing to the throne of Obatalá, about five feet away (see figs. 4.11, 4.12). Adolfo would now assume his alternate role as a *babaloricha*, a senior priest of La Regla de Ocha, before the throne of Obatalá. He instructed the client to kneel in supplication on the mat (*estera*) before the throne while saluting Obatalá with this *oricha's* conical silver *agogó* bell. In mixed Lucumí and Spanish, Adolfo beseeched Obatalá to pacify the enemy so as to give the client *la tranquilidad* (tranquility). The *babaloricha* then picked up the *trabajo*—the cotton-swaddled, amber-filled jar in which the enemy had been set like a scarab—and placed it atop the throne's elevated white pedestal behind the lidded porcelain *sopera* containing Obatalá's *fundamentos*. The *enemigo*, though miles away, would remain in Obatalá's grasp until the work was completed—at which time Eleguá would dispatch the *trabajo* to a location on the landscape determined through divination.[47]

Adolfo told the client to make himself comfortable on the sofa once again, and Ramón served sweet refreshments: a piece of Obatalá's white birthday cake from Ramón's *cumpleaños* and soda pop. Having come with a bitter problem, the client would depart with a clean constitution and a sweet taste in his mouth.

Before the client departed, he asked Adolfo what the Congo Francisco wanted in return for the cleansing. "Just bring him some *aguardiente* and roses sometimes," Adolfo replied. The roses and rum would satisfy the humble Francisco, but Obatalá and Eleguá would require blood sacrifices of the fowl eaten by them, *paloma* (dove) and *gallo* (rooster), respectively. Adolfo later explained that although "Francisco is a *brujo* [sorcerer] of Palo Monte and Obatalá is a Lucumí *santo*, they work together for good." If the two religions are at all "theoretically irreconcilable," their pantheons nevertheless live and work together in complementary ways through the medium of their multitalented priest with whom they share the small Union City apartment.

The Festival Cycle:
Lessons in Afro-Cuban Interior Design

If time-lapse photography could record the changing interior decor of the ritually active Union City apartment over the course of a year, the film would reveal a whirlwind of furniture, dolls and dresses, paintings, porcelain vessels, Chinese vases, beads, flowers, mountains of fruit, carpeting, linoleum, wallpaper, drapes, bedspreads, wall hangings, and gimcrackery. An establishing shot of the circulation of these objects between the commercial marketplace and the sacred economy of the apartment's religious practice would reveal the vastness of this whirlwind's path. Any consideration of Afro-Cuban space should take into account the aesthetically rich system of *oricha* iconography, which manifests itself not only in consecrated ritual objects but also in personal preferences for room decor that gild inner-city priestly dominions.

Changes in interior decor reflect a cycle of calendrical and periodic festivals, daily ritual work, and priests' concerted efforts to keep the house beautiful for all of its inhabitants and regular visitors. *Oricha* birthdays mean elaborate preparations, including dazzling thrones of cloth and mountains of food and fruit. The most important calendrical events require a reallocation of space, the movement of furniture, and enhanced interior redecoration. The small Union City apartment is, like every Ocha and Palo house, always a more collective than private space given the constant presence of ritual family; for festival days the apartment is prepared to accommodate an even greater number of guests. An extra refrigerator in the kitchen holds gallons of soda pop. Chairs for the *sala* are borrowed from neighbors and godchildren. The kitchen is set up cafeteria-style, and food is served across a table spanning its threshold to guests who line up in the corridor.

On August 17, the anniversary of Adolfo's initiation, Changó's "birthday" throne *(trono de cumpleaños)* is always constructed in the bedroom, the largest room in the apartment, for Changó is the guardian angel of the house's senior priest, Adolfo Fernández. Changó is, in truth, the head of the house. Thrones for other *orichas*, saints, and spirits, in contrast, are constructed against the long wall of the living room facing the sofa (see fig. 4.12). With the bedroom set stored in the building's hallway, borrowed seating arranged in the living room, and a curtain draped over the archway to the bedroom, the adjoining bedroom and living room spaces are transformed into the classic Lucumí *igbodún-sala* configuration. Changó is moved from his year-round mortar throne in the living room to a huge, lavish, canopied throne for the seven-day period of the *cumpleaños*, during which he is the center of attention (compare figs. 4.11 and 4.12 and see fig. 4.13).

Adolfo and Ramón like to hang curtains on the windows and bedroom archway that match or complement the colors associated with the spirit or *oricha* being celebrated. The aesthetic effect is a total environment bathed in color and reflected light. They choose from their storehouse of many and varied curtain colors and materials: satin, velvet, and lace in greens, blues, reds, and white. During Changó's birthday week of August 17–23, 1987, Changó's red and white motif dominated the two rooms. The throne's red and white canopy spanned the length of the room, and multiple vases of red and white gladiolas rose among the mounds of fruit distributed upon the straw mats. Curtains of red velvet and white lace divided the temporary bedroom *igbodún* from the *sala*, whose single window was similarly curtained.

Three months later, in December 1987, the entire apartment was transformed by new paint and floor tile in honor of San Lázaro (Babalú Ayé) and San Manuel (Odúa/Obatalá Yecú-Yecú), whose feast days are December 17 and January 1, respectively. Adolfo had made a *promesa* (promise) to San Lázaro for the healing of a severe spleen puncture he had received while working construction in the early 1980s. In return for his health, Adolfo agreed to host a *velada* celebration (vigil) "to wait for" San Lázaro every December 16–17.[48] He also agreed to collect alms (*limosnas*) door to door for the eventual purchase of an expensive, realistic, life-sized statue of the saint. Each *velada* begins at a few minutes to midnight on the sixteenth. Adolfo faces the throne, raises his shirt, points to his abdomen, and thanks San Lázaro for his help. In early December 1987, Ramón and Adolfo laid decorative blue and white linoleum, the colors of segments of San Lázaro's Lucumí beadwork, and they painted the walls and ceilings a brilliant white, the color of Odúa. The particular manifestation (*road*) of Ramón's Obatalá, called Yecú-Yecú, is identified by a pure white and is also associated, in this house, with San Manuel. Adolfo and Ramón painted the bathroom walls and ceiling a shiny royal blue and installed a new blue shower curtain with swan motifs.

A creative Bronx priestess of Ochún, Josie García, who is related ritually to Adolfo, Ramón, and the Manhattan priestess, has conceived a total approach to interior and exterior decor. Elaborating on the theme of water as a spiritual conduit, she painted her parlor floor, corridor, and bathroom in the very same shiny royal blue. She maintains her priestly and family *eguns* in this bathroom and her *bóveda* for the spirits nearby in the corridor. Inspired by the iconography of her *oricha* mother and father, Ochún and Obatalá, respectively, she wallpapered and painted her kitchen and dining room in yellow (Ochún) and white (Obatalá). The song of parakeets, a yellow one for Ochún and a blue one for Yemayá, filled these two rooms (see also Ramón and Adolfo's living room, fig. 4.6). Finally, she painted the entire building white with yellow trim on the windows, doors, corners, rain gutters, and foundation. There could be no more exuberant and proud a *bandera* for these two *orichas* to whom she has devoted her life than the façade of her three-story row house.

Duties and Dilemmas:
Private Rituals and Public Urban Spaces

Priests of the Afro-Cuban religions depend upon the privacy and security of their homes to carry out their sacred work, particularly a fundamental practice that has become highly controversial in the United States: blood sacrifice (*eyé ebó*; see Mason and Edwards 1985b; Brandon 1990). In order to carry out ritual events that require blood sacrifice, such as initiations and strong cleansings, priests must convert their homes into ritual abattoirs. Garages, patios, and bathrooms become holding pens for live animals. Kitchens, living rooms, and bedrooms become killing floors. Priests can purchase fowl at live poultry dealers, but four-legged animals must be bought at livestock farms beyond the city limits. Priests in Union City and West New York, New Jersey, for example, can purchase fowl (e.g., roosters, chickens, and hens) at live poultry stores on Bergenline Avenue, but must drive to western New Jersey or into Pennsylvania for four-legged farm animals (e.g., sheep and goats). Priests in Washington, D.C., drive to farms in Maryland or Pennsylvania for their fowl and four-legged animals.[49] Upon their arrival to the bustling streets of the District, the animals, often concealed in black garbage bags, are whisked up into tiny apartments, where they may await their fate standing in empty bathtubs.

Afro-Cuban Religions and State Authorities, 1792–1959

Afro-Cuban priests have always practiced their religion underground. Between 1792 and 1884, the clubs and brotherhoods (*cabildos*) of the African nations that supported religious practice were spatially marginalized, legally regulated, and eventually suppressed by the Cuban government. Between 1902 and the early 1920s, the houses of Lucumí and Palo Monte priests were the special targets of ferocious police raids intended to stamp out *brujería* (witchcraft), perceived to be responsible for social "delinquency" in general and the ritual murder of white children in particular (see Helg 1995:107–16; Ortiz 1973 [1906]:181–219; Castellanos 1916; Roche y Monteagudo 1925 [1908]:166–249). Drawing on Italian sociologist Cesare Lombroso's medico-criminological model of social hygiene, as well as the analogy of the Yellow Fever epidemic—which plagued Cuba at the turn of the century—Fernando Ortiz regarded the houses of Afro-Cuban practitioners as "sores" and "centers of infection" that needed to be wiped out (Ortiz 1973 [1906]:20, 223, 230; Mullen 1987; Castellanos 1916; Helg 1995:96ff.).[50]

The *afrocubanismo* (Afro-Cubanist) literary, cultural, and artistic movement of the 1920s, 1930s, and 1940s positively reevaluated African-derived "folkloric" practices in an efflorescence of poetry, ethnography, painting, and even public Lucumí and Abakuá musical performances—sponsored by Fernando Ortiz himself (see Blanc, Herzberg, and Sims 1992; Kutzinski 1993:137ff.; J. Martínez 1994:74–92; Ortiz 1937; Moore 1994). The period culminated in the historiography's most important ethnographic and folkloristic accounts of Afro-Cuban sacred ritual, music, and dance (Ortiz 1952–54, 1950, 1985 [1951]; Cabrera 1983 [1954]). However, the legacy of social stigma and racism from before the 1959 Revolution, combined with revolutionary suspicion of religious institutions after 1959, kept Afro-Cuban houses mostly underground on the island. Since the early 1960s, the Afro-Cuban religions, subject to co-optation as "national folklore," have been the focus of intensive scholarly research, ethnographic museum exhibition, and theatrical display, especially within the tourist sector (see Moore 1986; Balea 1984; León 1964; Hagedorn 1995). Nevertheless, Havana priests remember police raids on ceremonies as recently as the 1970s. Police permits must be obtained for ritual gatherings, and the police always post themselves in force outside the gates of Abakuá festivals in the Havana town of Regla.[51]

Afro-Cuban Ritual Practice and U.S. Law

Cuban priests who came to the United States after 1959 did not realize that they would encounter vigorous opponents in the form of animal-rights advocates, city governments enforcing cruelty and health statutes, fundamentalist Christians, and, in one major case, other Cuban Americans defending their own particular notion of Cubanness (Palmié 1988, 1990). Cuban American Ocha and Palo priests have come to realize that the sacred necessity of sacrifice has become the most controversial aspect of their religion as practiced in the United States. For priests and their clients, these sacrifices help to transform lives, solve problems, and heal illnesses. For animal-rights activists and the American Society for the Prevention of Cruelty to Animals (ASPCA), the sacrifices torture, mutilate, and needlessly kill helpless animals; for city governments, they violate agricultural zoning laws, endanger public health, and can soil a town's wholesome public image; for Christian fundamentalists, they serve Satan's demonic purposes (see Ellenberg 1987; Sunday 1987).

Newspaper readers since the 1970s in the New York metropolitan area and in south Florida have been fed a steady diet of sensational reports about the Afro-Cuban religions under the catch-all rubric of Santería. Santería has been represented mostly as a malign growth infecting assimilated middle-class urban cultural space. In south Florida, readers have been informed that "ancient Cuban voodoo flowers in Miami soil" (Dahlburg 1983), and that this "animal sacrifice cult attracts U.S. following" (Langer 1984). Miami's perceived malaise and decay in the early 1980s were symbolized by drug running, illegal aliens (particularly Mariel Cubans), ecological pollution, and headless animal carcasses floating in the Miami River (Nordheimer 1983). During this period, the turn-of-the-century Cuban hysteria over *brujería* and child murder was replaced by the belief that human skulls and cherished pets were being stolen everywhere for gruesome cult rituals (Spring 1983; Buchanan 1983). Fortunately for mainstream Miami "neighbors living in fear of cultists" (Bearak and Jones 1987), the incessant "drums, shrieks in [the] night," and reports of "chants and disappearing pets" were "tip[ping the] cops" to the

Santería "sacrifice cult" (Hampton 1979; Jones 1978). Called in to identify a series of human skulls found among ritual-looking objects, Dr. Charles Wetli, the deputy chief Miami medical examiner, and his Cuban American law enforcement colleague, Rafael Martínez, unwittingly revived and revalidated the antiquated criminological nexus of Afro-Cuban religion, malign witchcraft (*brujería*), and delinquency (see Wetli and Martínez 1981, 1983; Martínez and Wetli 1982). Their collaborative articles on Santería and Palo Monte from a forensic science and social psychology perspective cited the early criminological-ethnographic writings of Fernando Ortiz (1973 [1906]), and the well-intentioned and soft-spoken Dr. Wetli was quoted widely in national supermarket tabloid and news magazine articles on rising cult activity (e.g., Spinks 1979; Reese and Coppola 1981).[52] Miami newspapers regularly ran sensational stories linking Santería with drug dealers and mysterious deaths (Morgan 1983; Buchanan 1973). Articles informing readers that "voodoo" (Santería) was a part of "our rich ethnic culture" and laudatory biographies of priests as bearers of sacred Afro-Cuban traditions were greatly in the minority (Cicero 1980; Duarte 1986). Once again, Santería and its allegedly even more sinister cousin, Palo Monte, had become "centers of infection," but this time on our shores. Cesare Lombroso, Fernando Ortiz (Ortiz 1973 [1906]), and Havana's famous forensic pathologist, Israel Castellanos, rose from the dead just around the time 125,000 unwanted Cubans provoked a social and political crisis by arriving in Miami between April and October 1980 in the Mariel Boatlift (see Dixon 1982, 1983; Clarke 1981).

In 1983, Miami animal protectors were especially emboldened by the December decision by then Dade County State Attorney Janet Reno that "her office would vigorously prosecute all animal-cruelty cases" (Spring 1983). The consequences for Afro-Cuban ritual practice and the privacy and security of priests' homes were grave. The National Wildlife Rescue Team and the Humane Society of Greater Miami offered a $2,000 reward "for information leading to the arrest and conviction of persons who kill animals in the practice of *santería*, an Afro-Cuban religion that involves the sacrifice of birds, lambs, goats, and deer" (Spring 1983). In the New York metropolitan area, enforcement chiefs for local Societies for the Prevention of Cruelty to Animals (SPCA) stated their intention to "stake out" and "raid" the homes of priests.[53] Jack Kassewitz, Jr., head of the National Wildlife Rescue Team, declared, "Our goal is to catch them in the act. All we need is information about where a ritual is going to happen and we'll infiltrate with our people and the police" (Spring 1983).

As early as 1978, the *Humane Activist News* had "applauded the work of the Hoboken police" in pursuing animal sacrificers "and hope[d] that raids and investigations [would] continue." A *Humane Activist News* hand-bill urged the public to boycott live poultry shops and "keep their pets under supervision," pledging to help stop this "cult" from "torturing its victims."[54] Throughout the mid-1980s, successful raids were regularly reported by newspapers. In New York City in 1983, acting under health and agricultural marketing laws, police (with the help of a convoy of ASPCA trucks) raided a Manhattan apartment and saved fifty-two farm animals from the sacrificial knife (*Miami Herald* 1983). In a dramatic arrest worthy of today's popular *Cops*-type programs, two men were appre-hended near a stream at the Dyckman Approach to the Palisades Parkway in Englewood Cliffs, New Jersey, on July 20, 1985. They were charged with "mutilating and killing [two white chickens] by cutting off their heads." The Bergen County SPCA sergeant proudly announced, "This is our first major breakthrough and there will be a major investigation into a very large-scale voodoo cult operation. . . . Because of the intelligence information found, we have issued notification to all police departments saying this cult is dangerous both to animals as well as to humans" (Dribben 1985; Meyer 1985). While the two headless chickens "were [being] tagged and bagged and marked as evidence," along with a knife and a white candle, one of the two men arrested, a Santería priest, revealed his intentions under police questioning. The police report read: "[my] partner . . . is very ill and . . . he made a sacrifice of two chickens . . . so as to ride [*sic*] him of all evil spirets [*sic*] as to gain the devinity [*sic*] of power to nurse [him] back to spirtual [*sic*] health."[55] Apparently, the two men had gone to the stream to cleanse away the illness with the flowing cool waters of Ochún, owner of the river. The names and addresses of the men were published in at least three newspaper articles, one of which was headlined "pair charged with cruelty in gruesome animal ritual" (Meyer 1985).

Such public humiliation has given pause to many priests who regu-larly suffer the dilemma of how to fulfill private ritual obligations in urban public space. American cities offer a margin of liberty for such activities in their tolerance of low-level eccentric public behavior (see Kirshenblatt-Gimblett 1983:197). Nevertheless, priests fear embarrassment and arrest. "Sometimes when you've gotta make an *ebó* [sacrifice] and you have to throw something out, you always find somebody there. It's amazing, you always find somebody. You look around and there's nobody, and the moment you go to do it there they are," one New York priestess reported. Directed by divination to dispose of a red snapper (*pargo*, a common ingredient in Ocha and Ifá cleansing rituals) in a "river," she pretended to make a phone call in a booth near the Circle Line wharf on the Hudson River in midtown until a police officer passed on his beat.[56] One person's ritual obligation is the city's definition of littering, a misdemeanor. "When [the policeman] turned his back, I went, *voom!* [threw it]. I just had to get rid of it because they'll take, hey, you'll go to jail if you throw something out," she explained. Her performance was, in Michel de Certeau's sense, a "tactic" of the oppressed. A tactic is a "guileful ruse" that takes advantage of fleeting "opportunities" and "cracks" in social surveillance as it "maneuvers" and "play[s] on and with a terrain imposed on it and organized by the law of a foreign power" (de Certeau 1984:37). Such "maneuvers" take their toll, however, and an aging Brooklyn priest is no longer up to such risk taking. He no longer asks the *orichas* where they want him to dispose of sacrifices, because they might tell him to go to the deities' public dwelling places, such as "the river" or "the crossroads." Thus he "put[s] everything in the garbage because it gets to them eventually."[57]

The stakes are highest and priests' fears are the greatest when private homes are filled with crowing and bleating farm animals. Dread is never far behind the spiritual "elation" one priestess experiences in the successful initiation of a new priest. She desperately looks forward to the termination of the major sacrifice [*matanza*] at the end of the first day of initiation. The animals are taken out of the room and are cleaned and cooked. "I say, 'Man! It's finished and everything went well.' Because the police can come while you're killing the animals. That is one of our biggest fears, now even more [1987]. Lately we have that fear until after the animals are taken away, even though it's been two years since [the police] came to the house." On that occasion, according to this priestess, the director of the initiation furtively blew a magical powder (*afoché*) concealed in his hand in the direction of the officers to throw them off the trail. Just as the police were about to open the door to the room that held scores of live animals, they were distracted momentarily by the "ugliness" (the policemen's word) of the house's large cement Eleguá figure, which sat in a nearby corner. In effect, the trickster Eleguá, guardian of doorways and crossroads, saved the day by turning the police away from the closed room. In not a few cases, including this one, rival groups aware of the grave consequences "drop a dime" to tip off the police to the presence of live animals. Such fears have led to a strategy of calculated unpredictability.

> One woman planned a *santo* [initiation] for Saturday, but at the last minute she began it on Thursday instead of Friday night. She called me and said, "Come on Friday" [to work the *santo*]. She had a [divination] reading telling her that the police would come on Saturday, so she did the *matanza* the day before, on Friday, rather than on Saturday, and sure enough, on the "Middle Day," Saturday, the police came. Only pots of meat were cooking on the stove.[58]

Newspaper accounts of the responses of prosecutors, elected political officials, concerned citizens, and animal rights protectors suggest that animal sacrifice not only has fallen on the wrong side of the law, but also threatens a spectrum of American middle-class values and economic interests. In Atlantic City, New Jersey, in 1985, the police and SPCA officers burst in on an initiation ceremony, arrested nineteen priests, and confiscated the *orichas'* sacred *fundamentos* and attributes—which ended up in a Heineken box that was later hauled out as evidence in court. The "crime scene"—as described by the president of the Atlantic County SPCA who presided over the raid—was "sick," "vile," and "smelled so bad I wanted to throw up." As Freud once said, "dirt is matter in the wrong place" (Freud 1908:172–73). Indeed, the most sensational aspect of the scene was the specter of a sleeping baby's bedroom invaded by "animal torture," "mutilation," and "dissection." The newspapers reported that "a four-year-old child slept on a bed covered by a clean, white sheet. When the officers raised the end of the sheet from the floor, the mutilated bodies of dead lambs were lying under it" (Proctor 1985:68).

Moreover, sacred objects, such as the *oricha* Ogún's iron railroad spikes, were said in court to be the brutal instruments of animal torture. As a result of their arrests and the negative publicity, the two priestesses lost their apartments and Atlantic City casino jobs (Proctor 1985:70, 93; see also Zatwaska 1985; Checchio 1985). The Atlantic City prosecutor, Steven Smoger, summed up the case in this way: " 'Nine of the 19 people arrested live outside the jurisdiction of Atlantic City. . . . Now why would they select an apartment on North Texas Avenue to conduct a ritual mutilation? Is Atlantic City seen as conducive to that type of behavior? . . . I just don't want this city to be perceived this way. . . . [T]heir belief must give way to the law of the land. Here we have defenseless animals, and as human beings we are here to protect them" (Proctor 1985:70, 69). A protracted religious freedom case in the city of Hialeah, Florida, beginning in 1987, would test these kinds of claims made by public officials on the part of local and state governments.

The protection of defenseless animals and the "emotional injury to children who witness the sacrifice of animals" were chief among the official concerns of the city of Hialeah and the United States District Court in a now-famous Miami sacrifice case (Supreme Court of the United States 1997:8 [508 U.S. 520, 113 S.Ct. 2217]). However, despite a host of official reasons—among them, child protection, public health, and animal safety—the authors and supporters of anti–ritual sacrifice ordinances in Hialeah were, according to Supreme Court documents, engaged in a kind of social and religious cleansing of their municipal space.

In June 1987, the City Council of Hialeah, supported by Florida's attorney general, enacted three anti–ritual sacrifice ordinances that specifically "targeted" and sought to "suppress" the newly opened Church of the Lukumí, Babalú Ayé (Supreme Court 1997:11, 4). The church was founded by the Pichardo family in 1973, and opened its first public facility on the site of a former used-car business in Hialeah in the spring of 1987. From the beginning, the Pichardo family's intention was to legitimize the Lucumí religion and to educate the public about its practices. Immediately, the Pichardos and their church were attacked by the combined forces of animal rights organizations, Hialeah's Cuban mayor and City Council members, groups of fundamentalist Protestants, and a number of resentful Anglos apparently looking for a scapegoat. While the fundamentalist Protestants sought to defend the "supreme reign of Jesus Christ in Hialeah" and the Anglos sought to defend the "American way of life" (see Ellenberg 1987; Sunday 1987; Gentile 1987b), Cuban American members of the Hialeah City Council sought to defend their notion of what it was to be a Cuban American (Palmié 1988, 1990). City Council members explicitly invoked the righteous precedent of the Cuban nation's early twentieth-century *brujería* prosecutions. For example, "Councilman Martínez, a supporter of the ordinances, stated in a packed Hialeah City Council meeting of June 9, 1987, that in prerevolution[ary] Cuba 'people were put in jail for practicing this religion,' [and] the audience applauded. . . . '[I]f we would not practice this [religion] in our homeland [Cuba], why bring it to this country?'" (Supreme Court of the United States 1997:14). During the meeting, *santeros* were accused of everything from spreading AIDS to cannibalism and human sacrifice. In tune with the sentiments of the Anglo constituency, "Councilman Cardoso said that Santeria devotees at the church 'are in violation of everything this country stands for'" (Supreme Court of the United States 1997:14; and see Hialeah City Clerk 1987). Jane Gentile, an Anglo columnist for Dade County's *Home News*, read by 90,000 people each week (according to the paper's masthead), reinforced Cardoso's patriotic claims when she wrote two days later,

> How dare, in this, the greatest country on earth, a slime bag so called leader [Pichardo] (who professed to be Cuban but has never lived in Cuba) have the unmitigated gall to defend sadistic barbarism and disguise it as a "religion." We are One Nation under God—not one nation under goats, chickens, pigs, ducks or any other animal sacrifice and if these satanic blood drinkers do not like the American Way of Life they are welcome to leave THIS country. (Gentile 1987b)

The Pichardos, with the support of the American Civil Liberties Union, fought the three Hialeah anti–ritual sacrifice ordinances. Losing in both the federal and appeals courts, they succeeded in overturning the three ordinances before the U.S. Supreme Court in 1993. The narrow ruling did not explicitly affirm the legality of animal sacrifice, but it declared the three ordinances non-neutral and discriminatory. Hialeah had trampled on the Santería practitioners' constitutional free exercise of religion when the municipality could have, in fact, more reasonably enacted ordinances of general applicability to regulate the zoning of livestock and abattoirs, the treatment and health conditions of animals, the method of killing, and the sanitary disposal of animal remains (Supreme Court of the United States 1997:5, 13–17).

The Pichardos' stated intention was to transform the Lucumí religion's underground relationship to Miami's public sphere, "to bring the practice of the Santeria faith, including its ritual of animal sacrifice, into the open" (Supreme Court of the United States 1997:7). With its growing economic and political clout, the church's constituency would one day, Pichardo hoped, be able to conduct their sacrifices in legally zoned and regulated ritual abattoirs and gain official exemption from cruelty statutes — as had earlier been granted to Jewish kosher practices (Supreme Court 1997:12–13; DeQuine 1985; Ellenberg 1987).[59] Despite the absence of an explicit legalization of animal sacrifice, for Pichardo, the Supreme Court victory nevertheless put Santería on the legal map as a legitimate religion and affirmed its practitioners' protection by the Free Exercise Clause of the Constitution of the United States.

Conclusion

Priests of the Afro-Cuban Lucumí, Palo Monte, and Spiritist religions reconceptualize and transform their environments to realize their religious obligations. With the immigration and exile of Cubans and other Latinos since the mid-1940s, the Afro-Cuban religions have grown up almost entirely inside preexisting urban infrastructures from New York to California. Space, architecture, and mass-produced and modified goods are the media of an urban art of transformation wrought through aesthetic elaboration of shrine spaces and public and private ritual performances. Urban "spaces" and the built environment are transformed into "places" not only through the daily material struggle of immigrant families, but also through the annual and periodic rituals of initiation, divination, sacrifice, spirit possession, and collective ritual work. The community of creative agents includes not only human priests but also the pantheon of Lucumí deities and numerous spirits of the dead, who make their wishes known through spirit possession and formal divination methods. The Afro-Cuban drawing board of interior design and its map of the urban landscape are informed by the identities and preferences of the *orichas* and spirits, the symbolic requirements of Lucumí rites of initiation, and certain events and types from Cuban cultural history.

The Afro-Cuban map of the urban landscape exists in the mind as well as on the ground. Cities are lived spaces, and are re-created each day in practical ways. "Pedestrian movements," de Certeau suggests, "form one of these 'real systems whose existence in fact makes up the city.'" The "intertwined paths [of myriad footsteps] give their shape to spaces. They weave places together" (de Certeau 1984:97). Similarly, for Kirshenblatt-Gimblett, ordinary and extraordinary expressive behaviors "constitute . . . a sense of the city" for individuals and groups. Yet, a particular group's sense of the city persists not only in the "traces" of footsteps left behind (de Certeau 1984:97). It is also registered in shared bodily experiences, cognitive orientations, and discursive conventions. A sense of the city includes local systems of place names (toponyms) and geographic orientations, for example, the particular ways people note landmarks, give directions, and learn to navigate features of the urban environment with their bodies (Kirshenblatt-Gimblett 1983:191). New expressive behaviors that emerge in response to the peculiar features of urban landscapes are less static "traditions" than the emergent and "traditionalized" practices of particular groups (Kirshenblatt-Gimblett 1983:185, 208ff.).

Afro-Cuban religious practitioners remap local urban landscapes as their ritual intentions and footsteps take them beyond their apartments to deposit or gather materials for sacrificial *ebó*. Practitioners respond to the natural and human-made features of particular cities, such as Havana and New York. Individual priests work out their own solutions to ritual problems—where can I find the *loma* of Obatalá in New York City? (in the mountainous terrain of Fort Tryon Park)—and pass along the information to other practitioners. In this way, particularly good and accessible sites are traditionalized within the networks of *oricha* houses. Priests also pass along directions, which narratively weave the natural domains of the *orichas* within the commercialized fabric of the landscape of the New York metropolitan area. One New York priestess knows how to find the "sea," the place where she works with Yemayá, because the turnoff is near a particular fast-food restaurant in Elizabeth, New Jersey. A friend picks her up by car on the West Side of Manhattan. They take the Lincoln Tunnel to the New Jersey Turnpike and follow the landmarks. Exiting at Port Elizabeth, they "follow Jersey Avenue, near where the Kentucky Fried Chicken is— and Jersey Avenue ends up at the sea."[60] The practitioners of these religious systems do not live in miniature urban folk societies—i.e., ethnic "enclaves." They interact with and transform their environments, as well as actively challenge the perceptions of other groups.

The case studies I have presented illustrate the creativity of priests' religious work within the constraints of often cramped urban conditions. Small apartments, especially where multiple religious practices are found, demand spatial compromises, while larger row houses with backyards provide the luxury of more comfortably differentiated spaces. A cleansing that utilized the resources of the Ocha, Palo, and Spiritist systems illustrates the strategic shifting between three distinct but complementary cosmologies and ritual modes of spiritual work. In a highly compressed proxemic setting, the living room of a small Union City, New Jersey, apartment, the complementary practices of Ocha, Palo, and Espiritismo were contextually marked by aesthetic adornment and spatial organization, ritual intention, and particular ingredients, speech codes, and bodily gestures. In the homes of priests in Brooklyn and the Bronx, spaces dedicated to different, even "theoretically irreconcilable," pantheons of spirits represented qualitatively different sensory worlds—in effect, different kinds of ritual *habitus* (Bourdieu 1977: chap. 2, 89; Jackson 1989:128–31)—existing but a few steps from one another.

Michel de Certeau delegates furtive "tactics" to the oppressed and developed public "strategies" to the powerful in the social competition for resources. The agents of tactics lack their "own" places, while the agents of strategies—governments, businesses, armies, and research institutions—have the privilege of organizations and bases of operation established on their own spaces, which are protected with panoptic technologies of surveillance (de Certeau 1984:35–36; see also Foucault 1979). Nevertheless, since the 1940s and 1950s in New York and New Jersey and the 1960s and 1970s in south Florida, practitioners of Afro-Cuban religions have developed material infrastructures to facilitate their ritual practices, i.e., their own spaces and organizations. Religious families, connected by ritual kinship and mutual aid, have pooled their resources, bought property, and established "temples." Many of these are legally organized, not-for-profit corporations with constitutions, rosters of officers, and bylaws. The exotic ingredients of ritual practice are available and plentiful because enterprising retailers and wholesalers have emerged to serve local communities of priests. The specialty store called the *botánica* and many cottage industries that produce artful ritual attributes (e.g., *oricha* iron-, bead-, and clothwork) serve tens of thousands of priests in New York, New Jersey, south Florida, Chicago, and California. *Botánicas* specializing in fresh medicinal plants, such as Manhattan's Botánica El Congo Real, import these essential ritual ingredients daily from Florida, Puerto Rico, and the Dominican Republic. Individual priests regularly send fresh plants around the country via Federal Express; for faster service, they go directly to the cargo desks at local airports. New Jersey priest Adolfo Fernández could write his client a prescription for specialized ingredients, including seven fresh subtropical plants, with the expectation that the client would meet with complete success in obtaining all of them.

As shown, the practices of priests—"choosing the ways they want to live"—have not gone unconstrained and unchallenged in cities in the United States. As social, cultural, and political systems, cities are arenas of intense contestation. Instances of arrests in cases of animal sacrifice demonstrated the determination of state and city agencies in south Florida and the northeast to enact and enforce health, zoning, and anti-cruelty laws, as well as to protect dominant cultural mores and city self-image. The prolonged and intense six-year drama (1987–1993) of the Church of the Lukumí, Babalú Ayé versus the city of Hialeah galvanized groups of sacrifice opponents and supporters in highly visible ways. All forms of rhetorical persuasion, media events, and political intimidation were mobilized by all participants. In print, on radio call-in shows, and eventually in court, the antagonists skirmished over such issues as how the neck of an animal is severed, city property values, the direction of political careers, the contents of Cubanness and Americanness, the cosmic struggle of good and evil, and the free exercise of religion under the United States Constitution. Still, while animals, children, and God emerged as significant concerns, economics and machine politics were crucial factors in the contest over the Church of the Lukumí's occupation of the 43,000-square-foot space on Okeechobee Road between North Fifth and Sixth Streets in Hialeah. Journalist Todd Ellenberg reported that "[t]he church is located on a prime piece of commercially zoned real estate that was the target of an FBI probe involving a former Hialeah councilman and a personnel board member." Hialeah councilman Sebastian Dorrego was eventually convicted of attempting to extort $15,000 from Hialeah developer Julio Navarro, who owned the land rented by the Church of the Lukumí, Babalú Ayé. The mayor of Hialeah himself, Raul Martínez, had earlier attempted unsuccessfully to develop the same piece of property (Ellenberg 1987:9).

The church left the Okeechobee Road property in January 1988 and reopened in April in a former hardware store at 700 Palm Avenue in Hialeah. If the Okeechobee Road property was a thorn in the side of the city's powerful interests, the new location was a symbol of the Pichardos' staying power and in-your-face approach to local politics. The building's entrance and its painted banner bearing the church's name were visible from the mayor's fourth-floor City Hall office window several blocks away at Palm Avenue and Fifth Street. Still, Hialeah remained too "hot," Pichardo explained, and at the beginning of 1990, the Church of the Lukumí, Babalú Ayé made its exit to another, more discreet location in Miami. Despite their bruises, the Pichardos understood this transition in terms of a spatialized religious mythology and as the fulfillment of a prophecy. The Church of the Lukumí, Babalú Ayé had to leave Hialeah just as the *oricha* Babalú Ayé, the mendicant who walked on crutches, left ancient Yorubaland. With the aid of the great warrior-king Changó, Babalú Ayé crossed into neighboring Dahomean territory, where he was crowned king.[61] In leaving Hialeah, the Church of the Lukumí, Babalú Ayé was out of the heat, but Hialeah was not. Changó saw that Babalú Ayé's Hialeah antagonists remained "in the fire." In 1990, for example, a number of Hialeah political officials were brought down in a huge federal corruption scandal (Ramos 1990; Ramos and Rogers 1990; Rogers 1990; Harrison 1990a, 1990b).[62] Other officials reportedly suffered a variety of physical ailments. On June 11, 1993, the date of the Supreme Court's decision in favor of the church, a redeemed Babalú Ayé was indeed crowned king. Though the decision did not legalize animal sacrifice, municipalities will likely hesitate to enact ordinances that could cost them the hundreds of thousands of dollars in legal expenses paid by the city of Hialeah (Associated Press 1989). The Church of the Lukumí, Babalú Ayé reopened on April 4, 1997, with the support and blessing of local politicians and business people, at the corner of Palm Avenue and Fourth Street in Hialeah, exactly one block from the Hialeah City Hall. As of 1997, if the newspaper of record is any indication, Santería is indeed becoming a part of the American way of life as this "once-hidden faith leaps out into the open . . . suddenly growing very popular, and public" (Alvarez 1997).

Notes

Parts of this essay were researched during the tenure of my 1987 Wenner Gren Foundation for Anthropological Research predoctoral fellowship, which enabled me to conduct fieldwork in New York and New Jersey. Early versions of this narrative appeared in chapters 5 and 6 of my doctoral dissertation (1989), written with the kind support of a Charlotte Newcombe Pre-doctoral Fellowship. I want to acknowledge the kind support of Melba Carillo, Luís Castillo, Idalberto Cárdenas, Josefina García, Adolfo Fernández (*ibae*), Ramón Esquivél (*ibae*), Luís Bauzo, Ernesto Pichardo, Nydia Pichardo, Fernando Pichardo, Carmen Plá, Miguel Willie Ramos, Nena, Dr. Charles V. Wetli, Rafael Martínez, Karl Eder, Hermes Valera Ramírez, Zenaida Villanueva Justíz, Natacha López, Robert Orsi, Barbara Kirshenblatt-Gimblett, Michael Atwood Mason, Andrew Apter, Stephan Palmié, Joseph Sciorra, Brenda Seiton, Morris Brown, Sylvia Brown, and Alan Brown. Katherine Hagedorn meticulously edited the essay, and Mark Bauerlein read and critiqued the final draft.
1. Kirshenblatt-Gimblett (1983:181–82), drawing on such writers as Hannerz (1980), critiques Wirth's (1964) ideal type of the city, which has as its chief negative characteristics segmentation, depersonalization, exploitation, and anomie. However, for Wirth, the city's positive characteristics consist of sophistication, cosmopolitanism, rationality, relativistic perspectives, and greater tolerance for differences (181). Wirth's ideal type of the city is the diametric opposite of Robert Redfield's ideal type of the

"folk society" (1947). Kirshenblatt-Gimblett also critiques Herbert Gans's work, which reacted to Wirth and the ecological emphasis on social pathology of the Chicago School of Sociology. Gans's "enclave" idea essentially transplants the "folk society" into the city. See Wirth 1964 and Gans 1968a and 1968b.

2. The *orichas* are the Yoruba-derived (Lucumí) Cuban deities; *eguns* are deceased members of a Lucumí practitioner's ritual line of descent and family by blood (the original Yoruba *égún* or *egúngún* is not pluralized, but the Cuban Lucumí can be: *eguns*); *palos* are the Kongo-derived spirits of the Palo Monte/Mayombe religion (I use Kongo with a "K" when I refer objectively to the regional source cultures of Central West Africa from which Palo Monte derived [i.e., "Kongo-Angola"] [see Thompson 1983 [1954]:103] and use Congo with a "C" when I refer to Cuban usage [see Cabrera 1986b]); *muerto* (dead spirit) refers to diverse deceased spirits that guide—and sometimes torment—individuals.

3. As Juan Manuel García Passalacqua notes ironically, "the traditional [Puerto Rican] *jíbaro* is a Bronx *jíbaro* these days" (García Passalacqua 1985). *Jíbaro* means "peasant," "farmer," or "rustic person."

4. This religion is also called *Palo Mayombe* or *Mayombe*, probably derived from the name of the ethnic group Mayombe (Bakongo), a people of Central West Africa (Congo-Brazzaville, Lower Zaire, Northern Angola).

5. The Dahomean-derived Regla Arará is mostly confined to the province of Matanzas; however, the famous Arará priest Pilar Fresneda brought the Arará cults to Havana early in this century. Also, Regla Lucumí practitioners worship roads of Babalú Ayé connected to the Arará. The Abakuá is confined to the three major port cities of western Cuba: Havana (Havana, Marianao, Regla, Guanabacoa), Matanzas, and Cardenas (the last two are in Matanzas Province).

6. Personal communications with Regla de Ocha, Regla de Ifá, Regla Kimbisa, and Abakuá practitioner Jesus Varona, January 1, 1996, Havana.

7. In what Bastide described as "pouring African material into a Western mould," calendrical Saints' Days became the annual slots for huge public celebrations honoring a local saint and its *oricha* counterpart (Bastide 1971 [1967]:155; Cabrera 1980: chaps. 1 and 2; Ortiz 1921; Tesser 1988).

8. A *mae de Santo* at the Bahian *Candomblé terreiro* Axé Opô Afonjá told me that when the members visit the huge white house of Oxala—each *orixá* possesses a charming, color-coded residence complete with verandah and tile roof on the premises—they say they are "going to Ifé." When they are to visit Xango's house, they are "going to Oyo." When they are to visit Oxossi's house, they are "going to Kêtu." Each "town" represents the site in Yorubaland where one of those Afro-Brazilian *orixás* originates. However, James Wafer reports that in Bahia, "[I]n smaller [poorer] *terreiros* all the *orixás* may be seated together in a single house, or in a room, called the 'room of the saints'" (Wafer 1991:16).

9. Interview with Melba Carillo, March 20, 1987, Manhattan.

10. Interview with Idalberto Cárdenas, July 25, 1987, Brooklyn, New York.

11. Interview with Ernesto Pichardo, February 6, 1991, Miami.

12. Osun, the protector of the priest's *orí* (spiritual head), may reside on a high perch near the roof/ceiling or with the *guerreros* on the floor, depending on the house. Constructed of a silver stemmed cup or chalice topped with the figure of a rooster and hung with four little bells, Osun is a twenty-four-hour sentry who scares away negative influences from the priest's *orí*. Union City priest Adolfo Fernández used to refer to the bells as *espanta muerto* (literally, "scarer of the dead").

13. In a house I visited in the *barrio* of La Correa in the town of Guanabacoa,

Havana, an eye and tongue-pierced dagger image bears the inscription *ojo sí, lengua no* ("eye yes, tongue no" — in other words, "be respectful: look but don't talk").

14. Some houses use the Ifá divination system of La Regla de Ifá, exclusive to *babalawo* and his tutelary *oricha*, Orunmila, and others use the cowrie shell system (*dilogún*), which all initiated priests of the *orichas* are authorized to use.

15. In the Union City, New Jersey, apartment of two Cuban priests, Adolfo Fernández and Ramón Esquivél, an eight-by-eight-inch square flag was tacked to the back of the door from January 1, 1987, until December 31, 1987. Ifá divination determined that Ogún and Ochún ruled the year 1987 for the particular New York/New Jersey *oricha* community to which Fernández and Esquivél belonged. The flag consisted of a yellow background, Ochún's color, with a small appliqued black machete, the weapon of the *oricha* of iron, Ogún (see fig. 4.7). On January 1, 1988, Ifá divination determined that the governing *orichas* of the year were to be Ochosi and Ochún. The *bandera del año* was to be pink with a yellow border, and was to contain an image of Ochosi's bow and arrow in the center. (Pink is a color often specifically associated with Ochún's sister, Obba. However, it is appropriate to Ochún.)

During the 1980s, Fernández and Esquivél were members of New Jersey's Templo Bonifacio Valdéz, an organization modeled after the Afro-Cuban *cabildos*, whose aim is to support religious education and practice. Founded in the 1970s by Cuban American *babalawos*, Templo Bonifacio Valdéz sponsors the annual Ifá Reading of the Opening of the Year (*Registro de la Apertura del Año*), in which the *babalawos* divine the religious predictions, prescriptions, and proscriptions for the new year. They implemented the reading's instructions for the new year's flag, in other words.

16. Interview with Ernesto Pichardo, February 6, 1991, Miami.

17. Text from the official transcription of the January 1, 1987, Ifá Reading of the Opening of the Year, Templo Bonifacio Valdéz.

18. *Historias* (stories) from the cowrie divination sign called Osá, a sign heavily connected to witchcraft, reveal that through proper sacrifice, the "children of the cotton ball [*aú*]" (an apparent metaphor of the pure white spiritual head [*orí*]) were protected by sharp spines against the vicious attacks of pecking birds, the classic Yoruba trans-Atlantic avatars of insidious and desiccating witchcraft (see Elizondo n.d.:46; Thompson 1983:47–51). Indeed, this is very much how the head of the priest is protected symbolically by Osun, whose Brazilian iconographic counterpart is, in fact, a bird-topped staff surrounded by sharp spikes (Thompson 1983:51).

19. Interview with Ramón Esquivél, May 7, 1990, Union City, New Jersey.

20. Julio Sanchez (1978:29) defines *eguns* as those deceased members of the priestly ritual family (*familia de santo*) and the natural family (*familia de sangre*), but also uses the term *egun* to refer to those spirits in the *cuadro de protecciones* of a person — a group of spiritual guides. Miami priest Miguel Willie Ramos insists that the term *egun* is improperly used when applied to the group of spiritual guides. Personal communication with Miguel Ramos, August 7, 1992.

21. Telephone interview with Ernesto Pichardo, August 17, 1992.

22. Interview with Melba Carillo, March 14, 1987, Manhattan.

23. Interview with Ramón Esquivél, May 7, 1990, Union City, New Jersey.

24. Interview with Melba Carillo, March 14, 1987, Manhattan.

25. Interview with Ramón Esquivél, May 7, 1990, Union City, New Jersey.

26. *Nganga*, a Bakongo and Central African term for "priest," was applied to the cauldron/pot itself in Cuba. The priest of the cauldron may be called *tata nganga*, *ngangulero*, *palero*, *vrillumbero*, or *mayombero*. *Nkiso* is a variation on *nkisi*. *Prenda* is the Spanish term for "valuable thing" (see Cabrera 1984:38).

27. Lydia Cabrera determined that the charged vessel is variously called *nganga*, *nkiso*, and *prenda* "by association." Strictly speaking, however, *nganga*, *nkiso*, and *prenda* refer to the spiritualized group (*conjunto*) of diverse elements contained in the vessel—a pot (*cazuela*) or cauldron (*caldero*)—including the *muerto* who directs a hierarchy of subordinate spirits (1983 [1954]:131). Tata Nganga Jesus Varona of Havana revises and nuances Cabrera's definitions (interview of July 25, 1997). For Varona, *nganga* and *nkis[i]* are synonymous with another Congo term that Cabrera's sources also used, *mpungu* (Cabrera 1983 [1954]:134). *Mpungu* refers to the archetypal spiritual force (what Wyatt MacGaffey and Robert Farris Thompson would define as a Kongo "medicine" type [MacGaffey 1986; Thompson 1983]) that gives the *conjunto* of elements its particular identity and function, such as Zarabanda, Siete Rayos, or Madre de Agua. *Prenda* ("valuable thing") refers generally to the *conjunto* of elements—including the *mfumbi/muerto*, the *mpungu*, and all of the sticks, earths. Varona insists that the *mpungu* (*nganga*) is the essential commander of all the spiritual forces within the cauldron and, at the behest of the *tata nganga* (the priest), gets the *mfumbi/muerto/*"slave" to perform the required spiritual work of the whole *prenda*. As the priest of the *prenda*, he works directly with the *mpungu* and does not believe it is necessary to work through a Congo spirit mediator like Adolfo's "Francisco" (see below), who lives on the *bóveda* table.

28. For example, although one New Jersey priest, Juan Eduardo Núñez, is possessed by Changó and his *muerto*, Miguel, in a consecutive sequence representing a clear temporal separation, both of these spiritual beings perform within a single healing context that blurs the rituals and resources of Santería, Palo, and Espiritismo far more than Adolfo Fernández does in the Union City cleansing (see Stanford and Drufovka 1996).

29. Telephone interview with Ernesto Pichardo, August 17, 1992.

30. Rural priests in Cuba have enshrined the *eguns* on the *patio* near drain openings, a practice that may register the Yoruba tradition of feeding the ancestors through holes in the ground in sacred groves near wells of water (see Apter 1992:100). González Huguet (1968:46) found cases in semirural Cuba in which the *eguns* were enshrined and propitiated at the drainpipe at the edge of the *patio* or in the outhouse, while in urban Cuba the bathroom served just as well. Gleason's character Raymond, in her novel *Santería, Bronx* (1975:94), is told that to "speak to the dead" he should begin "concentrating at the source, where the running water is, for . . . [u]p the drain, up the peeling lead pipes we had bandaged with rags so they'd leak less, from subterranean springs beneath our industrial-gray painted basement, the dead would come—were I to call them correctly—into the sink, or the bathtub, or even into the antiquated wooden tank above the toilet."

31. This explanation of the goblets on the *bóveda* and the concept of *comisión* comes from a phone interview with Ernesto Pichardo, August 17, 1992.

32. Phone interview with Ernesto Pichardo, August 17, 1992.

33. Fernández and Esquivél lived in this Union City apartment until 1989. Adolfo died in 1991, and Ramón in 1993. I use the present tense for ease of exposition. Union City and its neighboring towns in Bergen County have become vital northeastern Cuban enclaves as a result of the several waves of Cuban migration since the 1950s. These towns, along with New York's boroughs, are meccas particularly for Afro-Cubans who found the "almost lily white," Cuban-dominated Miami less hospitable (Dixon 1983:6–9, 14–15). For more detailed information on Cuban migration, the Mariel Exodus, geography, and race, see Clarke 1981 and Dixon 1982 and 1983.

34. Given the protocols that govern the initiation of an individual into multiple religions, a person who is initiated into Ocha first cannot then be initiated into Palo.

The ontological category of the dead is anterior to the ontological category of *oricha*. Therefore, Palo cannot be "put on top of" Ocha. However, one can, as Ramón did, receive a surrogate ritual called *la jubilación*, literally "retirement." This enabled him to receive the Palo objects of the *nganga* Tiembla Tierra, which cross-indexed with the Lucumí Obatalá.

35. Dadá, Changó's "sister," is known for her red and white beaded and fringed crown. In Yoruba mythology, Changó (Sòngó), Dadá (Dàda [Yoruba orthography]), and Babalú Ayé (Sònpòn:non) were the three children of the original royal house of the Oyo Kingdom (Abraham 1946:680). A cowrie-encrusted crown (baàyónnì) belonging to Sòngó's sibling, Dadà, was worn by Sòngó's priests when they ritually excavated their deity's thunderbolts from houses struck by lightning (Abraham 1946:622). The Cuban Lucumí Dadá came to be known as the "crown of the saints." The receiving of this auxiliary *adimú-orisha*, called Dadá Bañañí, culminates and crowns a priestly career in the Cuban Lucumí religion, Adolfo Fernández and Melba Carillo explained to me on a number of occasions (see also Angarica n.d.:45).

36. Personal communication with Patti Yaques, November 12, 1992, Miami. This working configuration is evidently quite common in Cuba and the United States but is not universal and not without its critics. Jesus Varona maintains that he works directly with the *mpungu* of his *prenda* and does not need a Congo spirit of the *bóveda* to mediate this relationship.

37. On a Sunday afternoon in 1987, I asked one of Adolfo's godchildren why Maria Antonia—a *muerto*—was present in the *igbodún* during the "Middle Day" celebration (the formal presentation of the *oricha* initiate). She explained that Maria Antonia had insisted on being present. The day before, Maria Antonia had alerted the group that two people were engaged in vicious gossip just outside the window to the house.

38. Some orthodox Ocha priests criticize the practice of incorporating these *muertos* (*eguns*) into Ocha ceremonies. It is, they say, dangerous and confusing to "cross" the category of *oricha* with the category of *egun*. Even though these spirits "had Ocha" in life, the "crown of Ocha" is removed at one's death, and they are not authorized to enter the room of initiation or the domain of Ocha proper. Personal communication with Ysamur Flores-Peña, October 15, 1992, Jacksonville, Florida.

39. There are said to be two main classes of *ngangas: cristianos* and *judíos*. The latter are "unbaptized" (*judío*) and thus unpredictable and unrestrained. The former are "baptized" and carry crucifixes as part of their iconography. They can be controlled more easily. See Cabrera 1983 [1954]:123.

40. The Spaniard Victor Patricio de Landaluze lived in Cuba from 1851 to 1889 and produced *Típos y costumbres de la isla de Cuba* (1881). The Frenchman Pierre Toussaint Fédéric Miahle, who taught painting in Havana, produced *Album Pintoresco de la isla de Cuba* in 1838. Both documented popular rural and urban Cuban life (see Kutzinski 1993:45–46, 60–61; Blanc, Herzberg, and Sims 1992:53–56; and Bettelheim, ed. 1993).

41. Interview with Idalberto Cárdenas, July 25, 1987, Brooklyn.

42. Upon their original fabrication, Lydia Cabrera's informants told her, *ngangas* are buried for twenty-one days in the cemetery and twenty-one days under a *ceiba* or *jagüey* tree in the *monte*, in order to fully "ground" or "charge" them (Cabrera 1983 [1954]:123–24). Under the sky the *nganga* gathers and concentrates the forces of all the elements of nature (*la naturaleza*). An old Cuban Palo priest who could no longer walk "sent away his *nganga*" (*le dió camino*) by burying it under a *jagüey* tree. He no longer worried about it, and anyway, the "*nganga* could not live in a room with a mosaic tile floor" (Cabrera 1983 [1954]:132).

43. Interview with Idalberto Cárdenas, July 25, 1987, Brooklyn.

44. Adolfo Fernández had written out the Spanish common names, like a prescription, two months before. The fresh plants were (1) Zabadera (alt. Salvadera, *Hura crepitans*); (2) Rompe Zaragüey (*Eupatorium odoratum*, owned by Changó); (3) Abre Camino (*Eupatorium villosum*, owned by Ochún); (4) Alamo (*Ficus religiosa*, owned by Changó); (5) Siempre Viva; (6) Altemisa (*Ambrosia artemisifolia*, owned by Osain, Obatalá, and San Lázaro); (7) Almasico (*Elaphrium simaruba*, owned by Eleguá and Changó). The Latin plant names of nos. 2, 4, 6, and 7 come from the alphabetical catalog in Cabrera 1983 [1954]; the Latin name of no. 3 comes from Díaz Fabelo (1960:110). Nos. 2, 4, 6, and 7 are used in cleansing *brujería* in *despojos*, and no. 1 cleans away spirits of dead, according to Cabrera 1983 [1954].

45. The expression *dici carao dici* typically opens the old Congo's discourse. *Dici* is the standardized unconjugated verb form for "to say" (I say). *Carao (carajo)* is a popular expletive that marks the Congo's gruffness and fierceness. This phrase keys the performative frame of the Congo's oracular possession speech and marks his agency as distinct from that of the priest, whose body he is using.

46. *Quítate lo malo* means "take that which is bad off from yourself," that is, "purify yourself." A recent version of this refrain, in the song *Santa Palabra* (ARTEX S.A. 1992) by the famous Cuban band N. G. La Banda, goes *despójate, quítate lo malo, échalo pa' atrás, quítate mi hermano* ("clean yourself, take the bad from you, cast it behind you, take the bad off, my brother").

47. Typically, Obatalá would be asked through coconut divination (*obí*) whether the work was completed, and then where the *ebó* should be deposited: to the "hill," the "river," the "crossroads," the "bush," and so on.

48. All feast day celebrations for saints and *orichas* begin the evening before. Priests say they gather "to wait for" the arrival of the saint/*oricha*. *Velada* refers to a festive event held at night, which employs votive candles (*velas*). The *velada* for San Lázaro, which I attended in 1985 and 1986, entailed the building of a throne with San Lázaro's saint elevated image, a prayer of gratitude by Adolfo to San Lázaro, and the lighting of a votive candle by each of the participants. (See my photograph in Thompson 1993:221, plate 236.)

49. The distance has posed a serious crisis in the practitioner community in Washington, D.C., because most of the priests do not have cars.

50. Ortiz studied criminology under Cesare Lombroso and Enrico Ferri in Italy during 1902–1905 and Lombroso wrote the *carta-prólogo* to Ortiz's 1906 work, *Los negros brujos* (see Ortiz 1973 [1906]:xx–1).

51. *Babalawo* Hermes Valera Ramírez recounts a police raid in the 1970s in which the priests had to flee out the back door and climb several fences to escape their pursuers. Priests planning drummings and the annual divination reading of the year must get a permit from the police (I accompanied the organizer of one such divination to the police department in El Cerro, a suburb of Havana). I have noted the police presence outside the gates of the Abakuá lodges.

52. Dr. Wetli was also, according to Martínez (1982), assistant professor of clinical pathology at the University of Miami School of Medicine. Martínez was, in 1982, research assistant to the chief assistant state attorney of Dade County.

53. The enforcement officer of the Hudson County SPCA told me that he had every intention of "staking out" and "raiding" houses where sacrifices are being conducted and would do so if he had information or could plant an informer. Telephone interview with Hudson County enforcement chief, January 5, 1987, and interview with Bergen County enforcement chief, November 20, 1985.

With the aid of police, local SPCAs enforce cruelty statutes and make arrests and seizures where persons "unnecessarily or cruelly . . . or needlessly mutilate or kill a living animal or creature" (see NJASPCA 1985:13; and ASPCA 1984).

54. *Humane Activist News* photocopy handbill from June–July 1978.

55. From photocopies of SPCA documents generously given to me by Chief Karl Eder of the Bergen County, New Jersey, SPCA.

56. Interview with a Manhattan Ocha priestess, August 7, 1987.

57. Interview with Idalberto Cárdenas, July 25, 1987.

58. Interview with a Manhattan Ocha priestess, 1987.

59. Pichardo's intention to develop legally zoned and regulated ritual abattoirs for Santería as part of his program to legitimize the religion legally and culturally was conveyed to me in various personal communications from 1987 to 1993.

60. Interview with Melba Carillo, March 20, 1987.

61. According to Ernesto Pichardo, the Church's January 1, 1988, divination reading of the year informed the family that they had to "make a change" and "not stay here." Hialeah was too "hot" because this and other readings indicated a campaign of "witchcraft" leveled against the church. After the January 1, 1989, reading of the year, the church moved again, to southwest Miami. This information from phone interview with Ernesto Pichardo, September 26, 1990. Since then, the church has moved several times, including into a huge fence-enclosed property in a Miami neighborhood. The new Palm Avenue space is the most prestigious public location it has occupied.

62. Telephone interview with Ernesto Pichardo, September 26, 1990. Pichardo invokes the Lucumí myth-legend (*pataki*) of Changó's aid to Babalú Ayé as the foundational destiny narrative of the Church of the Lukumí, Babalú Ayé (see Ecún 1986:88–90; Cros Sandoval 1975:228). Ernesto Pichardo, his brother Fernando, and his wife Nydia are all priests of Changó.

Bibliography

Abraham, R. C. *Dictionary of Modern Yoruba.* London, Sydney, Auckland, and Toronto: Hodder and Stoughton, 1946.

Alvarez, Lizette. 1996. "A Neighborhood of Homesteaders: Hispanic Settlers Turn Bronx Shacks into an American Dream." *New York Times*, December 31, A14.

———. 1997. "A Once-Hidden Faith Leaps Out into the Open: After Years of Secrecy, Santería Is Suddenly Growing Very Popular, and Public." *New York Times*, January 27, B1, B3.

Angarica, Nicolas Valentin. N.d. [1955]. *Manual de Orihate: Religión Lucumí.* Havana: N.p.

Apter, Andrew. 1987. "Rituals of Power: The Politics of Orisha Worship in Yoruba Society." Ph.D. dissertation, Yale University.

———. 1992. *Black Critics and Kings: The Hermeneutics of Power in Yoruba Society.* Chicago: University of Chicago Press.

———. 1995. "Notes on Orisha Cults in the Ekiti Yoruba Highlands: A Tribute to Pierre Verger." *Cahiers d'Etudes Africaines* 138–39, XXXV–2–3: 369–401.

ASPCA. 1984. *Laws Protecting Animals in New York State and New York City.* New York: ASPCA, Humane Enforcement Division.

Associated Press (AP). 1989. "Priest, Hialeah Wage Animal Sacrifice War." *Florida Today*, March 28.

Balea, Mirta. 1984. "Guanabacoa Museum, Black Roots: African Slaves Had a Powerful Influence on Cuban Culture." *Prisma* 2 (July): 24–26.

Barnet, Miguel. 1980 [1966]. *Biografía de un cimarrón*. Narr. Esteban Montejo. Havana: Editorial Letras Cubanas.

Bastide, Roger. 1971 [1967]. *African Civilizations in the New World*. Trans. Peter Green. London: Hurst.

———. 1978 [1960]. *The African Religions of Brazil: Toward a Sociology of the Interpenetration of Civilizations*. Trans. Helen Sebba. Johns Hopkins Studies in Atlantic History and Culture. Baltimore: Johns Hopkins University Press.

Bauman, Richard. 1975. "Verbal Art as Performance." *American Anthropologist* 77 (June): 290–311.

Bearak, Barry, and Brian Jones. 1987. "Neighbors Living in Fear of Cultists." *Miami Herald*, April 9, 1D, 3D.

Bermudez, Armando Andres. 1967. "Notas para la historia del espiritismo en Cuba." *Etnología y Folklore* 4: 5–22.

———. 1968. "La expansion del 'Espiritismo del Cordón.'" *Etnología y Folklore* 5: 5–32.

Bettelheim, Judith, ed. 1993. *Cuban Festivals: An Illustrated Anthology*. New York and London: Garland.

Blanc, Giulio V.; Julia P. Herzberg; and Lowery S. Sims. 1992. *Wifredo Lam and His Contemporaries*. Exhibition catalog. New York: Studio Museum in Harlem.

Bourdieu, Pierre. 1977. *Outline of a Theory of Practice*. Trans. Richard Nice. Cambridge Studies in Social Anthropology, vol. 16. Cambridge: Cambridge University Press.

Brandon, George E. 1983. "'The Dead Sell Memories': An Anthropological Study of Santería in New York City." Ph.D. dissertation, Rutgers University.

———. 1990. "Sacrificial Practices in Santería, an Afro-Cuban Religion in the United States." In *Africanisms in American Culture*, ed. Joseph E. Holloway, 119–47. Blacks in the Diaspora. Bloomington: Indiana University Press.

———. 1993. *Santería from Africa to the New World: The Dead Sell Memories*. Blacks in the Diaspora. Bloomington: Indiana University Press.

Brown, David H. 1989. "Garden in the Machine: Afro-Cuban Sacred Art and Performance in Urban New Jersey and New York." Ph.D. dissertation, Yale University. University Microfilms International, 1990.

———. 1993. "Thrones of the Orichas: Afro-Cuban Altars." *African Arts* 26, no. 4: 44–59, 85–87.

———. 1996. "Toward an Ethnoaesthetics of Santería Ritual Arts: The Practice of Altar-Making and Gift-Exchange." In *Santería Aesthetics in Contemporary Latin American Art*, ed. Arturo Lindsay, 77–148. Washington, D.C.: Smithsonian Institution Press.

Brown, Karen McCarthy. 1991. *Mama Lola: A Vodou Priestess in Brooklyn*. Berkeley and Los Angeles: University of California Press.

Buchanan, Edna. 1973. "'Voodoo Rite' Ends in Death." *Miami Herald*, October 15.

———. 1983. "Robbers Break into Coffin, Remove Head; Investigators Suspect Santería Cultists of Theft." *Miami Herald*, May 3, 1C, 4C.

Cabrera, Lydia. 1970. *La Sociedad Secreta Abakua: Narrada Por Viejos Adeptos*. Miami: Ediciones C.R.

———. 1980. *Yemayá y Ochún*. New York: C.R. Publishers.

———. 1983 [1954]. *El monte: Igbo-finda, ewe orisha-vititi nfinda; notas sobre las religiones, la magia, las superstitiones, y el folklore de los Negros criollos y el pueblo de Cuba.* Miami: Colección del Chicherekú en el Exilo.

——. 1984. *Vocabulario Congo (el Bantu que se habla en Cuba).* Miami: Ediciones C.R., Colección del Chicherekú en el Exilo.

——. 1986a. *La regla Kimbisa del Santo Cristo del Buen Viaje.* Miami: Ediciones Universal.

——. 1986b. *Reglas de Congo, Palo Monte, Mayombe.* Miami: Colección del Chicherekú.

Castellanos, Isabel Mercedes. 1977. "The Use of Language in Afro-Cuban Religion." Ph.D. dissertation, Georgetown University.

——. 1990. "Grammatical Structure, Historical Development, and Religious Usage of Afro-Cuban Bozal Speech." *Folklore Forum* 23, nos. 1/2: 57–84.

Castellanos, Israel. 1916. *La brujería y el ñañiguismo en Cuba desde el punto de vista médico-legal.* Havana: Lloredo y Compania.

Castellanos, Jorge, and Isabel Castellanos. 1992. *Cultura Afrocubana 3: Las religiones y las lenguas.* Miami: Ediciones Universal.

Checchio, Michael. 1985. "Two Women Admit Ritual Slaughter." *Atlantic City Press,* September 11, 1, 16.

Cicero, Linda. 1980. "In Our Rich Ethnic Culture, Voodoo Is a 'Matter of Faith.'" *Miami Herald,* March 6, 1C.

Clarke, Juan M. 1981. *The 1980 Mariel Exodus: An Assessment and Prospect—A Special Report.* Washington, D.C.: Council for Interamerican Security.

Cros Sandoval, Mercedes. 1975. *La religion Afrocubana.* Madrid: Colleción Plaza Mayor Libre.

Dahlburg, John-Thor. 1983. "Ancient Cuban Voodoo Flowers in Miami Soil." *Asbury Park Press,* May 1.

De Certeau, Michel. 1984. *The Practice of Everyday Life.* Trans. Steven Rendall. Berkeley and Los Angeles: University of California Press.

DeQuine, Jeanne. 1985. "Fostering a New Image for Santería." *Miami News,* September 21, 1–2C.

Deschamps Chapeaux, Pedro. 1964. "Margarito Blanco: Ocongo Ultán." *Boletín del Instituto de Historia del Archivo Nacional* 65 (July–December): 97.

——. 1968. "Cabildos: Solo para esclavos." *Cuba: Revista Mensual,* January, 50–51.

Díaz Fabelo, Teodoro. 1960. *Olórun.* Havana: Ediciones del Departamento de Folklore de Teatro Nacional de Cuba.

Dixon, Heriberto. 1982. "Who Ever Heard of a Black Cuban?" *Afro-Hispanic Review* 1 (September): 10–12.

——. 1983. "An Overview of the Black Cubans among the Mariel Entrants." ERIC Documents (ED 233104).

Douglas, Mary. 1978 [1969]. *Purity and Danger: An Analysis of Concepts of Pollution and Taboo.* London: Routledge and Kegan Paul.

Drewal, Henry John; John Pemberton III; and Rowland Abiodun. 1989. *Yoruba: Nine Centuries of African Art and Thought.* Exhibition catalog, ed. Allen Wardwell. New York: Center for African Art in association with Harry N. Abrams.

Dribben, Melissa. 1985. "Pair Charged." *Bergen Record,* July 21, A53.

Duarte, Patricia. 1986. "Introducing . . . Juan Raymat, Santería Musician." *Miami Herald,* December 12, 2E.

Ecún, Obá (Cecilio Pérez). 1986. *Itá: Mitilogía de la religión "Yoruba."* Gráficas Maravillas.

Eliade, Mircea. 1959 [1957]. *The Sacred and the Profane: The Nature of Religion.* Trans. Willard R. Trask. New York: Harcourt Brace.

Elizondo, Carlos. N.d. [1934]. *Manual de la religión Lucumi.* New Jersey: n.p.

Ellenberg, Todd. 1987. "Santería Showdown: Authentic Religion or Satanic Cult?" *The Wave: Miami's Alternative Newspaper,* October 8–21, 7–9, 17.

Fernández Carillo, Enrique. 1881. "El Ñáñigo: Carta cerrada y abierta." In *Tipos y costumbres de la isla de Cuba.* Artist, Victor Patricio de Landaluze. Introduction by Antonio Bachiller y Morales. Havana: Miguel de Villa.

Foucault, Michel. 1979. *Discipline and Punishment: The Birth of the Prison.* Trans. Alan Sheridan. New York: Random House, Vintage.

Franco, José Luciano. 1963. *La conspiración de Aponte.* Havana: n.p.

Freud, Sigmund. 1908. "Character and Anal Eroticism." In *The Standard Edition of the Complete Psychological Works of Sigmund Freud,* vol. 9 (1906–1908), trans. James Strachey, 168–75. London: Hogarth Press and Institute of Psycho-Analysis.

Galzagorry Madan, Juventino. 1983. "Desarollo del rito Arará en Jovellanos." Unpublished paper. Primer simposio de la cultura Matancera.

Gans, Herbert J. 1968a. "Urbanism and Suburbanism as Ways of Life: A Re-evaluation of Definitions." In *People and Plans: Essays on Urban Problems and Solutions,* 34–35. New York: Basic.

———. 1968b. "Urban Vitality and the Fallacy of Physical Determinism." In *People and Plans: Essays on Urban Problems and Solutions,* 25–33. New York: Basic.

Gentile, Jane. 1987a. "The Way I See It." Editorial. *Home News,* May 21, 5.

———. 1987b. "The Way I See It." *Home News,* June 11.

Glassie, Henry. 1975. *Folk Housing in Middle Virginia: A Structural Analysis of Historic Artifacts.* Knoxville: University of Tennessee Press.

Glazier, Stephen D. 1985. "Syncretism and Separation: Ritual Change in an Afro-Caribbean Faith." *Journal of American Folklore* 98, no. 387: 49–62.

Gleason, Judith. 1975. *Santería, Bronx.* New York: Atheneum.

———. 1987. *Oya: In Praise of the Goddess.* Boston: Shambhala.

Gómez Abreu, Nerys. 1982. "Estudio de una Casa Templo de Cultura Yoruba: El Ile-Ocha Tula." *Islas* 71: 113–38.

González Huguet, Lydia. 1968. "La casa-templo en la Regla de Ocha." *Etnología y Folklore* 5 (January–June): 33–57.

González Wippler, Migene. 1989. *Santería: The Religion—A Legacy of Faith, Rites and Magic.* New York: Harmony Books.

Greenberg, David, and Hilda Diaz. 1987. "Santería Sect Bids for Hialeah Backing: Group Complains City Keeps It Out of New Church." *Miami News,* June 5.

Hagedorn, Katherine J. 1995. "Anatomía del proceso folklórico: The 'Folkloricization' of African Based Religious Traditions in Cuba." Ph.D. dissertation, Brown University.

Hall, Edward. 1966. *The Hidden Dimension.* Garden City, N.Y.: Doubleday.

Hampton, Ellen. 1979. "Drums, Shrieks in the Night Upset SW Dade Residents." *Miami Herald,* November 25, 19B.

Hannerz, Ulf. 1980. *Exploring the City: Inquiries toward an Urban Anthropology.* New York: Columbia University Press.

Harrison, Carlos. 1987a. "Santería Church Planning Service Tonight." *Miami Herald,* June 4.

———. 1987b. "Santería Service Held in Parking Lot." *Miami Herald,* June 5.

———. 1990a. "Allegations of Bribery, Conspiracy Color Hialeah's Past." *Miami Herald,* April 4, 13A.

———. 1990b. "Federal Corruption Probe Has Long, Tangled History." *Miami Herald*, April 4, 1A, 13A.

Harwood, Alan. 1977. *RX: Spiritist as Needed: A Study of a Puerto Rican Community Mental Health Resource*. New York: John Wiley.

Helg, Aline. 1995. *Our Rightful Share: The Afro-Cuban Struggle for Equality, 1886–1912*. Chapel Hill: University of North Carolina Press.

Hialeah City Clerk. 1987. *Official Recorded Minutes of the City of Hialeah City Council Meeting, June 9, 1987*.

Jackson, Michael. 1989. *Paths toward a Clearing: Radical Empiricism and Ethnographic Inquiry*. Bloomington: Indiana University Press.

Jones, Brian. 1978. "Chants, Disappearing Pets, Tip Cops to Sacrifice Cult." *Miami Herald*.

Kardec, Allan. N.d. *Nuevo devocionario Espiritista: Colección de oraciones escogidas*. N.p.

Kelly, Sean, and Rosemary Rogers. 1993. *Saints Preserve Us! Everything You Need to Know about Every Saint You'll Ever Need*. New York: Random House.

Kirshenblatt-Gimblett, Barbara. 1983. "The Future of Folklore Studies in America: The Urban Frontier." *Folklore Forum* 16 (Winter): 185–234.

———. 1988. "Ordinary People/Everyday Life: Folk Culture in New York City." In *Urban Life: Readings in Urban Anthropology*, ed. George Gmelch and Walter P. Zenner, 3rd ed., 549–62. Prospect Heights, Ill.: Waveland.

Kutzinski, Vera M. 1993. *Sugar's Secrets: Race and the Erotics of Caribbean Nationalism*. Charlottesville: University Press of Virginia.

Lachatañeré, Romulo. 1961. "Tipos etnicos africanos que concurrieron en la amalgama Cubana." *Actas del Folklore* 1 (March): 3–12.

Landaluze, Victor Patricio de. 1881. *Tipos y costumbres de la isla de Cuba*. Havana: Miguel de Villa.

Langer, Gary. 1984. "Animal Sacrifice Cult Attracts U.S. Following." *Sunday News (Miami)*, May 6, A6.

León, Argelier. 1964. "Concierto de música Abakuá." Playbill. Havana.

López Valdés, Rafael L. 1985. "La sociedad secreta Abakuá en un grupo de trabajadores portuarios." In *Componentes Africanos en el etnos Cubano*, 151–85. Havana: Editorial de Ciencias Sociales.

MacGaffey, Wyatt. 1986. *Religion and Society in Central Africa: The Bakongo of Lower Zaire*. Chicago: University of Chicago Press.

Marks, Morton. 1974. "Uncovering Ritual Structures in Afro-American Music." In *Religious Movements in Contemporary America*, ed. Irving I. Zaretsky and Mark P. Leone, 60–134. Princeton: Princeton University Press.

———. 1982. "'You Can't Sing Unless You're Saved': Reliving the Call in Gospel Music." In *African Religious Groups and Beliefs: Papers in Honor of William R. Bascom*, ed. Simon Ottenberg, 305–31. Delhi: Folklore Institute.

Martínez, Juan. 1994. "Cuban Art and National Identity: The Vanguardia Painters, 1920s–1940s." Dissertation, Florida State University.

Martínez, Rafael, and Charles V. Wetli, M.D. 1982. "Santería: A Magico-Religious System of Afro-Cuban Origin." *American Journal of Social Psychiatry* 2 (Summer): 32–38.

Mason, John, and Gary Edwards. 1985a. *Black Gods: Orisa Studies in the New World*. Brooklyn: Yoruba Theological Archministry.

———. 1985b. *Four New World Yoruba Rituals*. Brooklyn: Yoruba Theological Archministry.

Mason, Michael Atwood. 1994. "'I Bow My Head to the Ground': The Creation of Bodily Experience in a Cuban-American *Santería* Initiation." *Journal of American Folklore* 106 (423–24): 1–17.

Meyer, Josh. 1985. "Police Get New Lead in Animal Cruelty." *Bergen Record,* July 26.

Miahle, Pierre Toussaint Frédéric. 1838. *Album pintorésco de la isla de Cuba.* Berlin: Storch and Kramer.

Miami Herald. 1983. "New York: 52 'Sacrifice Animals' Are Seized by Police." September 18, 12A.

Moore, Carlos. 1986. "Congo or Carabalí: Race Relations in Socialist Cuba." *Caribbean Review* 15 (Spring): 12–15, 43.

Moore, Robin. 1994. "Representations of Afrocuban Expressive Culture in the Writings of Fernando Ortiz." *Latin American Music Review* 15 (Spring–Summer): 32–54.

Morgan, Elizabeth. 1983. "Drug Gangs Use Skull, Symbols to 'Hex' Police: Traces of Santería Found Often among Drug Dealers, Police Say." *Miami Herald,* October 29, 1B, 2B.

Mullen, Edward J. 1987. *Los negros brujos:* A Reexamination of the Text." *Cuban Studies* 17: 111–32.

Murphy, Joseph. 1988. *Santería: An African Religion in America.* Boston: Beacon.

N. G. La Banda. 1992. *Echale limón.* Havana: Artex. Compact disc.

NJASPCA. 1985. *Laws of the State of New Jersey for the Prevention of Cruelty to Animals.* North Brunswick, N.J.: NJASPCA.

Nordheimer, Jon. 1983. "Miami's 6-Mile River: Pollution, Aliens and Drugs." *New York Times,* August 1, 8.

Orsi, Robert. 1985. *The Madonna of 115th Street: Faith and Community in Italian Harlem, 1880–1950.* New Haven: Yale University Press.

Ortiz, Fernando. 1921. "Los cabildos Afrocubanos." *Revista Bimestre Cubana* 16 (January–February): 5–39.

———. 1937. "La música sagrada de los negros yorubas en Cuba." *Ultra* 3, no. 13: 77–86.

———. 1950. *La africanía de la música folklórica de Cuba.* Havana: Ministerio de Educación, Dirección de Cultura.

———. 1952–54. *Los instrumentos de la música Afrocubana.* 4 vols. Havana: Publicaciones de la Dirección de la Cultura del Ministerio de Educación.

———. 1960 [1920. *Revista Bimestre Cubana* 15, no. 1: 5–26]. *La antigua fiesta afrocubana del "día de reyes."* Havana: Ministerio de Relaciones Exteriores, Departamento de Asuntos Culturales, Division de Publicaciones.

———. 1973 [1906]. *Los negros brujos: Apuntes para un estudio de etnologia criminal.* Miami: Ediciones Universal.

———. 1985 [1951]. *Los bailes y el teatro de los Negros en el folklore de Cuba.* Havana: Editorial Letras Cubanas.

———. 1988 [1916]. *Los negros esclavos.* Havana: Editorial de Ciencias Sociales.

Ortiz, Renato. 1989. "Ogun and the Umbandista Religion." In *Africa's Ogun: Old World and New,* 90–102. African Systems of Thought. Bloomington: Indiana University Press.

Palmié, Stephan. 1988. "Santería and the Contest of Cultures in South Florida." Paper presented at the American Studies Association Conference, Miami.

———. 1989. "Ethnogenetic Processes and Cultural Transfer in Afro-American Slave Populations." Unpublished conference paper.

———. 1990. "'Kulturkampf' in South Florida: The Case of the Church of the Lukumi Babalu Ayé." Paper presented at the meeting of the Gesellschaft für Karibiksforschung, Vienna.

———. 1993. "Ethnogenetic Processes and Cultural Transfer in Afro-American Slave Populations." In *Slavery in the Americas*, ed. Wolfgang Binder, 337–63. Würtzburg: Königshausen und Neumann.

———. N.d. "Objects of Power: Violence and Depersonalization in the Making of an Afro-Cuban Religious Formation." Unpublished paper.

Proctor, Patricia. 1985. "The Last Rite." *Atlantic City Magazine*, December.

Ramos, Miguel "Willie." 1982. *Dida obi: Adivinación atraves del coco*. Carolina, P.R. n.p.

Ramos, Ronnie. 1990. "Charges Threaten Career of Hard-Fighting Politician." *Miami Herald*, April 4, 12A.

Ramos, Ronnie, and Peggy Rogers. 1990. "Martinez Denies All Allegations." *Miami Herald*, April 4, 1A, 12A.

Redfield, Robert. 1947. "The Folk Society." *American Journal of Sociology* 52: 293–308.

Reese, Michael, and Vincent Coppola. 1981. "A Cuban Ritual Disturbs Miami." *Newsweek*, June 22, 44.

Roche y Monteagudo, Rafael. 1925 [1908]. *La policía y sus mistérios*. Havana: n.p.

Rogers, Peggy. 1990. "New Mayor; Councilmen Sworn In: Under Charter Rules, Council President Julio Martinez Takes Top Post." *Miami Herald*, April 4, 13A.

Sanchez, Julio. *La Religión de Las Orichas: Creencias y Ceremonias de Un Culto Afro-Caribeño*. Puerto Rico: n.p., 1978.

Sciorra, Joseph. 1990. "'I Feel Like I'm in My Country': Puerto Rican *Casitas* in New York City." *Drama Review* 34 (Winter): 156–68.

Shammas, Anton. 1996a. "Autocartography: The Case of Palestine, Michigan." In *The Geography of Identity*, ed. Patricia Yeager. Ann Arbor: University of Michigan Press.

———. 1996b. "Finding Palestine" [published excerpt]. *Harper's*, June, 24–28.

Shore, Eric. 1987. "Santerians Claim City Officials Are Members." *Home News*, August 20, 1, 9.

Sosa Rodríguez, Enrique. 1982. *Los Ñáñigos*. Havana: Ediciones Casa de Las Americas.

Spinks, Mandy. 1979. "Voodoo in America." *National Examiner*, May 22, 18.

Spring, Suzanne. 1983. "Reward Offered for Information on Pet Sacrifices." *Miami Herald*, February 17, 9C.

Stanford, Ron [director], and Iván Drufovka [producer]. 1996. *Yo soy hechicero/I Am a Sorcerer*. Videotape.

Sunday, Dan. 1987. "Jesus Christ Reigns Supreme in Hialeah." *Home News*, June 11, 1, 9.

Supreme Court of the United States. 1997 [1993]. *Church of the Lukumi Babalu Aye, Inc. and Ernesto Pichardo, Petitioners v. City of Hialeah*. Opinion. 508 U.S. 520, 113 S.Ct. 2217.

Tesser, Elisa. 1988. *Mother of Waters*. Independent documentary video. Distributed by Naomi Katz, Oakland, California.

Thomas, Hugh. 1971. *Cuba: The Pursuit of Freedom*. New York: Harper and Row.

Thompson, Robert Farris. 1983. *Flash of the Spirit: African and Afro-American Art and Philosophy*. New York: Random House.

———. 1993. *Face of the Gods: Art and Altars of Africa and the African-Americas*. Exhibition catalog. New York: Museum of African Art.

Tuan, Yi-Fu. 1977. *Space and Place: The Perspective of Experience*. Minneapolis: University of Minnesota Press.

Turner, Victor W. 1969. *The Ritual Process: Structure and Anti-Structure*. Symbol, Myth, and Ritual Series. Ithaca: Cornell University Press.

Urrutía y Blanco, Carlos. 1882. *Las criminales en Cuba y el inspector Trujillo: Narración de los servicios, prestados en el cuerpo de polica de La Habana*. Barcelona: F. Giró.

Valdés Garríz, Yrmino. 1991. *Ceremonias fúnebres de la Santería Afrocubana: Ituto y honras de egun*. Puerto Rico: Sociedad de Autores Libres.

Vlach, John Michael. 1978. *The Afro-American Tradition in Decorative Arts*. Exhibition catalog. Cleveland: Cleveland Museum of Art.

Wafer, James W. 1991. *The Taste of Blood: Spirit Possession in the Brazilian Candomblé*. Philadelphia: University of Pennsylvania Press.

Wetli, Charles V., M.D., and Rafael Martínez. 1981. "Forensic Sciences Aspects of Santería, a Religious Cult of African Origin." *Journal of Forensic Science*, July, 506–14.

———. 1983. "Brujería: Manifestations of Palo Mayombe in South Florida." *Journal of the Florida Medical Association* 70 (August): 629–34.

Williams, Raymond. 1973. *The Country and the City*. New York: Oxford University Press.

Wirth, Louis. 1964. "Urbanism as a Way of Life." In *On Cities and Social Life: Selected Essays*, ed. Albert J. Reiss, Jr. Chicago: University of Chicago Press.

Zatwaska, Stephanie. 1985. "Alleged Mutilation during Ceremony—19 Plead Innocent to Animal Cruelty in Resort." *Atlantic City Press*, August 7, 45, 46.

Zuesse, Evan. 1979. *Ritual Cosmos: The Sanctification of Life in African Religions*. Athens: Ohio University Press.

Moses of the South Bronx

Aging and Dying in the Old Neighborhood

Jack Kugelmass

From 1980 to 1985, I conducted ethnographic fieldwork at the Intervale Jewish Center, the only synagogue still in regular use at that time in New York's South Bronx. Location alone—in the 1970s the local precinct was nicknamed "Fort Apache"—would have made the study of any institution in the area interesting. Many New Yorkers who lived outside the Bronx were afraid to set foot in the borough (hence the critical scene in Tom Wolfe's *Bonfire of the Vanities* in which a panicked stockbroker lost in the South Bronx commits a murderous act in his desperation to get out of the area), and news accounts a few years earlier had underlined the vulnerability of residents, particularly elderly people, to arson and muggers. It was widely believed, therefore, that those who stayed in the area did so because they had no alternative. But this was hardly the case for many of the people I got to know. There has been a certain bravado to living in the South Bronx over the past two decades—a bravado shared by its elderly Jewish residents, too. And though the South Bronx has been called "Hell on earth,"[1] there was nothing hellish about the quotidian or the weekend religious life of the Intervale Jewish Center. Quite the contrary.

But there were factors beyond locale that drew me to this religious community. The congregation had been dwindling for decades, and at least since the 1970s it had felt itself to be on the threshold of closing. The causes were clear enough, making this story hardly unique in the annals of contemporary American Jewish history: a general decay of the area's aging housing stock brought on by rising costs and frozen rents; the immigration of large numbers of minority populations occupying overcrowded and increasingly underserviced apartments; the attendant social problems of unemployment and low-wage jobs, the result of a decline in New York's light industrial economy, once the foundation of the city's working and middle class; and the earlier loss of a younger generation of middle-class Jews because of a shortage of available housing immediately after World War II, and to subsequent social and geographic mobility. All of this gave rise to an increasingly aging and frail congregation with very limited prospects for replacement. That latter fact alone lent a certain drama to the Intervale Jewish Center's existence: How long could this synagogue survive? And there were other elements that made this community interesting. Many congregants were the sole survivors of synagogues now closed. Others had very limited religious experience: they were lonely, for the most part elderly people who were concerned about their mortality and were therefore attending services now for the first time in their lives. Some had almost no interest at all in the religious dimension of the synagogue. They came mostly for the weekly food, holiday "CARE" packages, and frequent outings provided by Hatzilu, a Jewish charitable organization. Only advanced age and survivorhood induced the most irreligious of them to participate in the memorial rites that form a regular part of Jewish services.

But the most compelling aspect of this community was the imaginative and charismatic nature of its leader, Moishe Sacks. Russian-born, Sacks immigrated to America as a teenager to join his father in New York. Lured to the Bronx more than sixty years ago by work, Sacks began attending Intervale only after a shul closer to his apartment closed; for at least two decades, until his death in 1996, he was the congregation's designated leader, rabbi, Torah reader, fundraiser, and caterer. Sacks was extremely articulate, in a peculiarly poetic way—and with a surplus of wisdom to dispense, he enjoyed the role of leadership the congregation bestowed on him. Indeed, years of directing fellow workers and a string of bosses at Moshman's Hunts Point bakery groomed him for this position. Accustomed to having things and people bend to his will and supporting family and friends through a voracious appetite for work (when I first met him he was in semi-retirement and therefore worked *only* sixteen hours a day), Sacks continually shaped the Intervale congregation, challenged rather than put off by its many idiosyncrasies.

Sacks was as knowledgeable in rabbinics as in worldly matters, and he used that knowledge to counsel congregants as well as instruct and reassure them about proper ritual practice. For years each Sunday morning, he supplied the congregation with a brunch of juice, coffee, and fresh rolls, either from his bakery or, after its closing, through the goodwill of Hatzilu. After the weekly repast, he proceeded with a review and explication of the Torah reading. The technique he used to engage his audience was to relate the world of the Bible to the familiar landscape of the Bronx. The story of Jacob's struggle with the angel, for example, was retold by Sacks as a mugging.

But Sacks's storytelling was not based solely on biblical narrative. He also constructed a myth about the Bronx congregation itself that identified it as the "miracle shul." According to Sacks, despite the ever-present threat that a dwindling Jewish population would force the closure of the synagogue, whenever a congregant died or moved away (usually to enter an old-age home), God made sure that someone new would take his or her place. In this way the *minyan* or ritual quorum of ten adult Jewish men (the minimum necessary by Jewish law to maintain a Jewish community) continued, guaranteeing a certain immortality to the community as a whole. During the course of my study, I found Sacks's assertion to be true: new members inevitably appeared as older ones retired. And when I stopped attending, another young man came along to fill the void.

After the publication of my book *The Miracle of Intervale Avenue* in 1986, and particularly after leaving New York City some years later, I visited the synagogue with decreasing frequency. I moved on to other research projects, and there seemed little more that I could or even wanted to say about this community. But a decade after completing my study, and given the increasing advancement in age of Intervale's leading character (Sacks at the time was approaching ninety—or so he had us all believe), I decided to return in the early 1990s to update things, realizing that this would be the last time such revisiting would be possible.

There were questions that those who know my work frequently asked and for which I had no answer. The minyan, after all, remained the miracle of Intervale Avenue. Had it continued? If not, what impact had the apparent mortality of congregants and congregation had on Intervale's master storyteller? In resuming my fieldwork for this essay, it quickly became apparent that changes in the congregation and community were significant, but rather than abandoning his assertion that God had a pact with the community through the minyan much the way that the existence of ten righteous men would have saved Sodom from God's wrath, Sacks had come to accept death as the only permanent link to God. Sacks had changed from exhibiting complete defiance of death to an accommodation with it, but an accommodation that continued to be infused by a staunchly redemptive vision. As I shall argue, that underlying and redemptive vision was not only Sacks's strength but his appeal for us as well. Indeed, it is the religious sensibility in all of us, albeit frequently in secular garb, that relishes Sacks's God-filled re-envisioning of a landscape too often deemed apocalyptic by outsiders.

Certainly the greatest irony here is that the end of the minyan occurred in the face of a rejuvenated South Bronx.[2] Physically, Fort Apache is no more; even the precinct house is closed, awaiting official designation as a historical landmark. An ill-conceived plan to demolish the elevated train station at 163rd Street following a botched robbery attempt that ended in the would-be robbers' setting fire to the eighty-year-old wooden structure[3] was abandoned after strong protest on the part of the community and local merchants. And the physical signs of that resurgent community are apparent everywhere. Prefabricated townhouses and flats are sprouting, while once-abandoned apartment buildings are undergoing total renovation, the result of some $5 billion of state and federal money earmarked largely for the Bronx and intended "to create 252,000 units of affordable housing and reclaim some of the worst neighborhoods in the nation."[4] So extensive is this project that New York City's housing commissioner at the time, referring to the initial phase getting under way in 1989, could claim, "After two decades of decline in the Bronx, we're seeing the rebirth of entire neighborhoods." Ed Koch, who was still mayor when the project began, called the work "the greatest construction program since the Pharaohs built the pyramids." Ever given to hyperbole, Koch boasted further that the Bronx project is of greater import than the Pharaohs' edifices, because "then there was just one person per pyramid. These 15,000 apartments will be homes for close to 60,000 people."[5]

The contemporary Bronx seemed to inspire such biblical metaphors, just as a decade or two earlier it had summoned forth metaphors associated with the Wild West—Fort Apache and Little House on the Prairie (the latter in the 1980s, when crime subsided and many of the abandoned buildings had been dismantled, leaving behind an oddly renaturalized landscape). There is in part a historical evolution of tropes here, and in part a struggle by those who encounter the Bronx to impose upon it a narrative consonant with their own national, religious, or personal mythology. I shall comment later on this use of biblical imagery. For now let it suffice that Koch has not been the only one to make use of it to describe the resurgent Bronx. Without resorting to grandiose imagery, it is fair to say that although the area may not be getting gentrified, it is gradually recovering at least a part of the population displaced through the abandonment, burning, looting, and dismantling of buildings during the 1970s and 1980s. Given the high cost of housing elsewhere in the city and the availability of city and state subsidies for working families who buy homes in the Bronx, the new construction is attracting a significant number of middle-income occupants.[6]

The shul, too, had had some repairs made to its exterior, including a new sign and fresh paint; inside a new alarm had been installed, and work had been done on some of the structure's mechanicals. These upgrades notwithstanding, the building appeared to me on my return very much the same as it had when I first saw it in January 1979; then and later it looked decrepit, almost forlorn. Time was always the master here, and after seven decades of existence, the Intervale Jewish Center looked its age.

Despite the physical upgrading of the area, the economic condition

5.1. Moishe Sacks unlocking Intervale Jewish Center.

of many of the area's long-term residents remained unchanged. Indeed, older residents sometimes imagined that their new neighbors were rich, so they knocked on their doors to ask for money.[7]

Violence remained a problem in the area in the early 1990s, but whereas in an earlier era crime there was largely related to thefts, muggings, or the arson of buildings (after the inhabitants were alerted to the danger), much of the violence was drug-related, involving big money and often resulting in deadly shoot-outs.[8] A *New York Times* article on the killing of a crack dealer by rivals in an area undergoing rehabilitation described the nearby 40th Precinct as "among the most violent in the city." A friend of the victim philosophically insisted, "You can't be afraid of death. If you're going to die, you are going to die," adding by way of advice, "but you try to avoid it."[9] Much of this is known to readers of the national press or media consumers, although they might not have been as aware of

5.2. Moishe Sacks climbing stairs inside Intervale
Jewish Center.

the concurrent rehabilitation of the South Bronx. These two simultaneous
realities—positive change and persistent drug-related violence—gave an
air of urban schizophrenia to the South Bronx of the early 1990s.

But to me, on my return to the Bronx, the most significant change
had less to do with the surrounding neighborhood than with the physical
condition of the elderly congregants themselves. Many of the people I had
known and cared for were no longer present; they had entered nursing
homes, and most had eventually died. Mr. Abraham, Sam and Lucy, Mr.
Flisser, Rose Cutler, and many others were gone. And yet, very much like
the building itself, even with the departure of so many friends, the congregation retained its distinct, even eccentric, quality. Much of this was due to
the extreme individuation of elderly people, what Barbara Myerhoff referred to as their combination of "toughness, fearlessness, idiosyncrasy, and
creativity" resulting from social irrelevance, personal autonomy, long ex-

5.3. Moishe Sacks with local Jewish store owner and sales staff.

perience, and the urgency of a shortened future.[10] Although the net population at Intervale was dwindling, the group continued to draw some new members from among the area's elderly Jewish and sometimes non-Jewish residents.

Not all of the new congregants were elderly, furthermore. Shoshana, for example, was the progeny of a black non-Jewish father and a Jewish mother. Several years earlier, her parents had moved to the area in search of inexpensive loft space from which to run their business silk-screening children's t-shirts. The couple eventually separated, and mother and daughter became regular congregants. Shoshana was in grade school at the time. The youngest member of the congregation (her mother, Gail, held the distinction of second youngest), she was given the honor of opening and closing the ark, with Mordechai, the congregation's cantor, picking her up so that she could reach its decrepit velvet cover. Another new member, Benjamin, was, in a sense, my replacement. His parents were from Puerto Rico. Benjamin had begun attending services at Intervale after coming across the synagogue quite by accident one day as he rode his bicycle through the area. He claimed to be of *marrano* background, and his interest in the synagogue was an attempt to recapture his family's Spanish Jewish heritage.

Other new congregants included Bessie, who had worked in Sacks's bakery until it closed. For years she attended services only during the High Holidays, but then she too became a regular Saturday congregant. After Mrs. Miroff's departure for a nursing home, either Dolly or Bessie set out the food for the Saturday *kiddush* (benediction over wine accompanied by a light repast). One long-standing "new" member was Mr. Sorkin, a retired man who several years earlier had moved to the Bronx from Manhattan. Amiable and jocular, he filled Mr. Abraham's place, a possibility enhanced in Sacks's view by the newcomer's first name, Abraham.

The most ominous change in the congregation, and the most difficult for me to witness, was that Sacks had grown older, noticeably so since a mugging had left him with a concussion that interfered with his balance and deprived him of the ability to walk without a cane or to get around the area unescorted by taxi. Despite this grievous setback, Sacks continued to have the strength and moral stamina to minister to the needs of a demanding congregation. And in part because of its contentiousness and in part because of its polyethnic composition, he increasingly referred to it as "the mixed multitude," an allusion to the rabble that Moses led out of Egypt. The reference clearly connected his own task to the labors of his biblical namesake and suggested a continuing link between the world of the Bible and the landscape of the South Bronx, long after the security of a continuing minyan had ceased to provide Sacks with similar assurance of God's immanence.

Although the move in the late 1980s and early 1990s from "miracle shul" to "mixed multitude" might suggest a degree of spiritual devolution on the part of the congregation and a sense of despair on Sacks's part, nothing could have been further from the truth. Likewise one might have thought that the end of the minyan meant for Sacks that there was nothing eternally sacred about this particular shul. But in fact Sacks interpreted these new realities as evidence that God's covenant went well beyond a particular time and space, ultimately guaranteeing to all a permanent future with Him.

In our conversations a decade or so earlier, Sacks had often said that the bricks of the shul reminded him of the Temple in Jerusalem. But in our later conversations he seemed reluctant to make this analogy, insisting instead that the shul had no *essential* quality to it. It simply was what it was in the eyes of the beholder and believer. His new reluctance to associate the shul with anything more than itself was less a retrenchment in the face of apparent defeat than an expansion of his redemptive vision to all of the surrounding landscape. And Sacks accomplished this by switching tropes, moving from the chronotope[11] or space/time of the *axis mundi*[12] —the shul as a timeless point of mediation between heaven and earth—to the space/time trope of motion and becoming within mytho-historical time—the biblical story of the rabble or mixed multitude that Moses led from Egypt. This shift in redemptive vision expressed as well Sacks's *imitatio dei*, or in this case an imitation of someone very close to God—Sacks's namesake, Moses. And beneath it lay a profound transformation in Sacks's thinking, which had moved from the purely cyclical temporality of existence at the sacred center—the shul with its miracle minyan eternally renewed even as its individual members died—to the more linear time of Exodus. In the time frame of the Exodus, a people's covenant with its God was renewed while they in turn were transformed from a mixed multitude into a people en route to the Promised Land.

The transformation in Sacks's thinking also suggested a move away from a sacred immortalizing vision to a sacred mortalizing one, from a vision that all but denied death and finitude to one that made peace with these realities. Now, as Sacks, too, acknowledged his own mortality, that sense of journey, of becoming, had considerable poignancy. I use the term "*sacred* mortalizing" vision to distinguish Sacks's narrative work from a "*secular* mortalizing" one. The former is redemptive and makes its peace with death by incorporating mortality into a grander vision of renewal and salvation; the latter typically connects death, destruction, and decay to the banality of evil, if to anything at all. But without an overarching sense of redemption, the connection becomes pornographic, as exemplified by much of the writing, popular and journalistic, about the devastation of the South Bronx, and of American cities generally.

Sacks's imagination roved restlessly over the South Bronx at the end of his life, using its ruins to uncover an image of the city as a space where God was immanent. The proximity of death was a key contributor to his mortalizing vision. If there was any single way to summarize the changes at Intervale between my first fieldwork there and my later return, it was this. Death had lurked in the background in the earlier period, showing its face now and then, but it was always dispelled through sheer determination and good-humored narrative. This was part of the miracle of Intervale Avenue. But death no longer lurked on my return; it paraded itself and taunted the congregation, like the rat that since Dave's death had roamed unmolested through the building. But death had hardly become master in the shul (as it had failed to do in the South Bronx), in part because the community's memory—largely at Sacks's instigation—continually integrated the dead into the everyday world of the living. I found Sacks steadying himself with Sam Davis's cane much the way in earlier times he had used his dead friend Brodsky's cane to pull pans out of the oven. And death was not regnant also because Sacks had found a way to engage death philosophically.

To illustrate how all this figured in Sacks's thinking, let me turn to my field notes. I have added explanatory material wherever necessary.

Saturday, November 9, 1991

I arrive at the Intervale Jewish Center at 10:30. There are only five men present—not enough for the ritual quorum of ten. The service is an abbreviated one, and just before the reading of the Torah, Malachi Parkes, Intervale's Ethiopian-born and staunchly orthodox cantor, complains about the congregation: "This is the strangest shul that I've ever been at. People sometimes show and sometimes don't show. You can't rely on them. Then all at once five people show up." Malachi is agitated. Losing his place while Sacks reads the Torah, Malachi corrects him but is himself corrected by Kaplan. Mordechai, Malachi's son, sits near the ark at the front of the synagogue. Intervale's King Canute, he tries vainly through the use of an aerosol deodorizer to hold back malodorous waves of musty air wafting from the damp and rotted wooden floor.

No other men arrive, but a few additional women do. Betty hobbles in, cane in hand, complaining: "I'm in such pain. I decided I had to take a cane, although I didn't want to because it's a sign of old age. I took some painkillers, but it doesn't do much good."

I ask about various people who are not present today. Sacks reveals that Dave, Intervale's resident trickster, sign painter, and kaddish sayer, died this past spring. Having lost his vision over a period of years, he had entered a home after becoming entirely blind. "We went to the funeral. There were only nine present, and the young rabbi didn't think you could say the kaddish [prayer for the dead]. So I explained how we count here at Intervale, the minyan with nine [with God standing in for the tenth]. I also explained that the kaddish is not so much a way to say goodbye to the dead as to say hello to the living—Dave's nephew and sister were there [people whom Sacks had never met before]. The rabbi liked that and said that he would remember it."

"How is Mrs. Miroff?" I ask.

"Mrs. Miroff is in the hospital with pneumonia. She's in a nursing home now permanently, and I don't think she'll be coming to shul anymore."

"Pneumonia!" Betty interjects. "That's it. If you get pneumonia, you're finished!"

"Betty," Sacks retorts, "she's in the hospital. With God's help she'll recover."

"Oh, in the hospital," she responded, obviously reassured by Sacks's comment. "That's better. They take better care there than at a home."

Saturday, August 15, 1992

After the others have left, Sacks and Bessie linger. She complains about the ignorant character of the other congregants and their constant bickering. Sacks responds by talking about the Ten Commandments and the need to respect one's elders: "When most people are presented with the Ten Commandments and they hear the first four, they're not interested, because they have to do with respect for God. But when they hear about respect for elders, they are interested because they know that ultimately it will come back to them."

"It's like the hiltsener shisl," Bessie comments. "You know, the story about the boy who watches the father serving the grandfather on a wooden plate. The father sees the son playing with wood and asks why. The son answers that he's preparing for when he'll serve him in the same way that he now serves the grandfather."

"So, you see," Sacks says, "you really should respect God. If people respect God and the first four commandments, then they will naturally obey the Fifth Commandment to respect one's elders." Bessie and Sacks seem intent on lingering, and after a little more conversation I decide to head out. Sacks asks whether I will join them tomorrow for the Hatzilu outing. I decline the invitation.

Monday, August 17, 1992

I call Sacks in the morning and tell him that I will be at his apartment in about an hour. The front door buzzer doesn't work, so when I arrive, I find him standing half inside the building, his head jutting out to scan the street. Just before Sacks spots me, a young boy talks to him for a moment, then runs outside. Sacks's odd triangular-shaped building looks a little more dilapidated than Mrs. Miroff's just across the street. But it, too, is fully inhabited. Mrs. Miroff recently passed away, and her tiny tailor shop—once a haven for homeless men—has been transformed into a women's beauty parlor (an appropriate metamorphosis considering her meticulous attention to dress and grooming). The abandoned apartment next to hers, like so many other buildings in the area, is undergoing a total renovation. Having seen the ruined interior firsthand escorted by the building's squatters, I find the contrast startling. According to Sacks, the people who lived there (Mrs. Miroff referred to them affectionately as "mine bums") and who frequented Mrs. Miroff's shop are all dead. Only Betty, the retarded black woman who *for years was Mrs. Miroff's constant companion, is still alive. She resides in the area with her mother. There are other street types who stand propped against a wall, drinking beer from a brown paper bag.*

Sacks gets into the car and immediately compliments me on my choice of vehicle. I respond by suggesting that he compliment the bank. Bantering in our familiar style, we become like friends of old. Once inside the shul, I begin to unpack my tape recorder, microphone, and cameras. Sacks remarks on the amount of equipment that I now have. "Even with all the equipment, a good photograph still depends on the competence of the photographer. It's like the story you were telling the other day about baking," I comment.

"You mean that hand-baked bread tastes better than machine-baked because of the human touch and the bacteria inserted by the baker through his hands."

"Yeah. Do you miss baking?" I ask.

"I miss it to an extent mentally. I don't miss it physically because I don't think I'm up to it. I confess I dream a lot about baking. And in those half-dreams that you have sometimes between waking and sleeping, [I] actually visualize the process of baking, and the arguments that we would have. It's a continuous process of living the baking life. But at the same time now I have an added process of visualizing the present life, the life of conducting services, the extra study that I give to it which I didn't give at that time, [like] looking for little points in the Talmud or little points in the droshe *(homily) of the week, which, unlike those days, now I [have to] find it more by looking [for it]."*

"You used to tell me that one reason you remained in the area was the bakery. Now that [the bakery is] gone, I wonder whether you stay because you find something special about the Bronx itself."

"Anything special about a place? I don't know. What can I put to you that is special about the Bronx?"

"Do you think there's anything special about . . . " I try to ask, but Sacks interrupts me before I can finish.

"New York City?" Sacks asks.

"No. About this synagogue here in the Bronx?" Sacks seems unresponsive to the drift of my question, so I try a more direct approach. "You used to talk about seeing the bricks of the shul and their reminding you of the stones of the Temple of Jerusalem. Is there something unique about this place?" I had been trying to get Sacks to elaborate on this theme. Impatient with his slow response, I throw him an entirely new question without realizing its lack of connection to the previous one. "Does God love the Bronx?" I ask.

My impetuousness is my good fortune. Sacks takes it as a mental challenge and begins to assemble a line of reasoning that I have not previously heard. "That's a very, very hard question. A very hard question.

Tell me, I'll ask you one question. If it came to loving a place, why would God pick the Bronx against any other place? There are places like Jerusalem, places like Meah Shearim *He would love, places like in Brooklyn where there are Hasidim, or places that are more Orthodox than we are. It's not the place that He loves. He doesn't hate any place. My answer to you is this: God does not hate any place that He created. That's the answer. I'm not going to tell you He loves the Bronx or He hates the Bronx. He doesn't. In God's estimation He created the world. The world includes Jerusalem, Sefad, Bronx, everything else. It's all together. I don't think He would pick one place over another."*

"But you picked one place in which to live."

"There were practical reasons for it at that time that made me pick. Practical reasons. Plus the fact, I can still call them practical, that it gives me something to do, and my physical abilities are not as good as they used to be, so I still remain here in the Bronx."

An astounding comment! Yet I remember going with the congregation on a Hatzilu outing to a congregation in Long Island. The bus driver couldn't find the way, and surrounded by trees on a beautiful country lane, congregants voiced concern about life in the suburbs: "I'd hate to live here," one announced. "I'd never find my way around." But Sacks's idea of the practical goes well beyond the actual meaning of the word. Sacks's decision to remain in the Bronx is coupled to an unsuccessful attempt years ago to move to Israel (well past retirement age, he was unable to find work)—while here in the Bronx he, like so many of the other congregants, is needed. These "practical" reasons are not in conflict with more elevated concerns.

"I don't know," Sacks continues. "We seem to forget a good lesson that we learned in the Bible that two and a half tribes decided to stay on the other side of the Jordan. And the important ruling that sometimes people don't bring out is that they [the tribes] came to the conclusion that the same God that gave them the Torah on Mount Sinai would also be on the other side of the Jordan. You understand? They were influenced by the fact that there were more practical things for them there. But the original idea of the First Commandment is this, that God said God is there. God is beyond the other side of the Jordan, too. He won't, as soon as the nine and a half tribes cross the other side, go with them, and leave the other two and a half alone. He wouldn't do that. He'd remain there. He'd remain with the other ones [too]. So, does that answer your question somehow or doesn't it?"

It does. But I'm still trying to get some image of the city from Sacks. For a man who has lived in one location for sixty years, and for a man as poetic as Sacks is, how does he envision the surrounding landscape? So I ask point-blank, "When you look at the Bronx today, what do you see?"

"When I look at the Bronx today? [laughs] I am in the position of a worm or something or other who has only looked at a certain thing, and even after an earthquake or a deluge or whatever, he looks around and his environment looks the same. It's not that you can see anything different. It's not this catastrophical event that happened that they say how the dinosaur was wiped out or this or that was wiped out. The Bronx is here [pounds table]. The air is here. God is here. And that's all there is to it. Human beings have changed a little bit, but not too much fundamentally. They have changed a little bit. The characteristics of human beings . . . the way God created them, that's the way they are."

Sacks's assertions are more than passing observations. They are deeply polemical, intended to refute commonly held associations of a devastated landscape with evil inhabitants. In Sacks's worldview, God is king. Evil lifts its head now and then but is pretty much held in check by divinity. That worldview not only keeps a tight rein on evil, but it also ensures a critical sense of human continuity. No matter what the changes are to the Bronx, no matter who comes and goes, Sacks sees the world as fundamentally unchanged. The same holds for the Intervale Jewish Center.

As Sacks speaks, I mention that I intend to take some shots, and that he should just keep on talking since the tape recorder is running. "So it shouldn't be a total loss," I say. Sacks chuckles at my use of one of the late Mr. Abraham's phrasings. "A total loss," Sacks repeats, then comments, "Mr. Abraham is a very nice gentleman, too. The new one. By the way, we call him Mr. Abraham, which is sort of a throwback to ourselves. We are trying to think of the first Mr. Abraham. His name—the new one—is actually Mr. Sorkin. Abraham Sorkin. But when we say 'Mr. Abraham,' we sort of remember the original Mr. Abraham, and as usual we don't want to forsake our past so we say 'Mr. Abraham.'"

"And he doesn't object?"

"No. As a matter of fact, we have called him so much Mr. Abraham that when he signs his name in Hebrew—I taught him in Hebrew how to write his first name, Avrom—he forgets to use the name Sorkin. He signs Avrom. He's satisfied that he is Avrom, and we're satisfied that we sort of have remembered Mr. Abraham. That's how the human mind works."

"Does he know the association?"

"He does not. Whether he has an inkling or not, I don't know. I don't know whether he would object or not. You see, the idea is this—that we know the association and we do it. Mr. Abraham is dead, but he's not gone." This reference to a dead friend makes me wonder about ways of commemorating other deceased congregants.

"Tell me," I ask, "do you miss Dave and Mrs. Miroff?"

"We miss them in the fact that they were present. We miss Mrs. Miroff. We miss the constant . . . "

"Quarrels?"

"Quarrels. We miss the same thing with Dave. He was here, and of course the idea of the value of what he did [Sacks is probably referring to his hand-painted signs and off-color remarks] was his idea, but at the same time he never subtracted from the value of this place. So to say we don't miss him, that's ridiculous. To say we don't miss Sam, we don't miss Brodsky, we don't miss Abraham, we don't miss Katz, we don't miss any one of the people that were here before, it's ridiculous. You miss every person. At the same time we recognize all the idiosyncrasies of every person who was here."

Sacks is apparently not feeling all that nostalgic. Since he seems determined to speak in generalities, I decide to probe by widening the scope of my questions. "Speaking of idiosyncrasies, do you think the shul has lost any of its character?"

"The shul hasn't lost any of its character. The fact is, it's . . . "—for a moment, Sacks seems to stumble mentally, trying to grasp the thrust of my question—" . . . I honestly don't know what you mean by "the character." The character of a shul is not the shul, it's the character of the person who comes in and looks at the shul. You understand what I mean or you don't?"

"I'm not sure," I reply. I am a little confused. Although I thought that I was heading toward familiar turf, Sacks has something else that he wants to tell me, some new idea.

"You're not sure? All right. You take a man that comes in here off the street who fixes the boiler. He comes in, he looks at the sanctuary, he says, 'The lights are burning; everything is OK in here. It looks all right.' To him this is not a place like a synagogue. It's not a church. To him it's just a panoramic presentation of something where everything is working. You take another person who is disturbed for a moment. And he comes in, and somehow or other, by coming down the steps, looking there, and sitting down and listening to a couple of the prayers which he does not even understand, it quiets him a little bit. So the shul gets a different character presented to him. So that's not the shul that presented itself; it's how he looks at the shul that makes the character of the shul. Now you understand what I'm talking about? It's the person who looks at the shul that gives the character to the shul. The shul does not give the character to the person; it's the person who looks that gives the character to the shul."

I'm still not entirely certain where Sacks's thoughts are heading, so I try to bring them back to my own work. "So you think, then, that the book that I wrote is the character that I saw?"

"Definitely. The character that you saw and the character that was exemplified to you by the others that you tried to depict there that they saw. That's what you saw and that's what you put down on paper."

"Is it an accurate picture?"

"It's as accurate as a description of what they saw and what you saw. Character is a thing that you can't depend upon as being accurate or inaccurate. It's not like a molecule of H$_2$0. Hydrogen plus oxygen makes water. Or you can say in mathematics, 'Definitely, this is it!' Character is subjective. It's something that has no definite boundaries. No determination. You depicted it as they saw it, and as they saw it, it was accurate to them, and it was accurate to you."

"But is it accurate to you?" I am still floundering, groping for a line of inquiry that will at least let us review some old material. Sacks has other intentions.

"I depict it as I told you just lately that I'm trying to look to see . . . I had a definite character opinion of the shul. Now I'm getting to the point that the shul is depicting its character to me, too. Or I am getting a different character opinion."

"Than the one you had ten years ago."

"Yes, ten years ago."

"And that difference is?"

"The difference, it's how I look at the present time. And how I looked ten years ago. It's like what I was telling you about Mr. Abraham. We have that rare human ability not to let go. We just don't want to let go. And I don't know. Is it good? Is that ability good not to let go? That's also one of the topics I was questioning myself about. They ask me here, 'The future, future, future. What is the future of this place?' And when they say, 'What is the future?' I'm trying to tell them what we're trying to do is to get a permanent future here. A future that is not terminated by time. A future, naturally, that is connected to God. And that is the future, you understand? That future is more of a future than the future that is a practical future that the people want. Now, which is really the future that you would be more satisfied with? Would you be satisfied with a practical future, or would you be satisfied with a future that is permanent but not practical? I think people would be better off if they really believed that they're trying to build themselves up for a permanent future. That's pretty tough to do. Even Moses, as much as he believed, he still didn't like the death part, the death sentence on him, in one respect. The respect is that he figured that his past wasn't fulfilled. So he still wanted the fulfillment, the practical fulfillment. Our liturgy says the same thing. 'Lo hamesysim yahalluyo, velo kol yordey dumo'—dead people don't praise God. And we in our life, when we could reach to the point where we would acknowledge death being a beautiful future, a permanent good future, then we'll be happy. That's the point that we have to reach. And it's a hard lesson, a hard one to reach. Because you have to be so nonsubjective that it's almost impossible. Because whatever you do, you're still subjective. Can you just take yourself out of the picture? I honestly don't know. But with the mere thought of recognizing that, believe it or not, just the mere thought—I lay in bed and I recognized that—I said to myself, 'Well, even in practical terms I have a future. That's the future of not having a practical future.'"

"But you envision some other future?"

"I envision a future. Not a practical one. A future of being near to God. By envisioning the possibility of there being a future. That mere thought of there being a future is enough to sustain this presence. Am I being too philosophical for you?"

"No. When I first came here, I was a young man. And now twelve, thirteen years later I'm not old, but I'm not so young, either. And it struck me when I came in on Saturday that when you made the misheberakh [a prayer wishing good health typically recited for those who are called to the Torah or who request it because of illness] for me, it felt not just like a thing to do but actually like something that I needed. My body feels different. It doesn't feel as youthful as it did twelve, thirteen years ago. It feels more vulnerable. [Sacks smiles.] Just the knowledge that things are wearing out for me and you can't replace them . . . so it resonates well what you're saying with my own . . ."

"It does? Now imagine how it does for the other people. Take Mrs. Flisser, who has terminal cancer. She is terminal to the respect that, as much as I hate to say it, within six months or a year or so, she'll be. . . . But still in all, the idea of her getting used to having a future more than a practical future, she's getting used to it, believe it or not. And I see that she's getting used to it through the possibility of the suffering. She's getting used to the idea that her practical future is limited. Her real future will remain. So, I don't know. As you said with the misheberakh, and I just said the same thing . . . the mere thinking of this thing that you're dealing towards, you're dealing with something that once upon a time it used to be you were afraid. I mean not once upon a time. During the time of a man's life, he doesn't think of death. But then it comes to a time when he's afraid. But if he gets to the period when he accepts death as a beautiful permanent future, then he has it made. He can get over the fear and accept it as a permanent future for himself."

"That may be true for the older people who come here, but it seems to me that the younger ones have a very different agenda. The older people are looking for a way to prepare for death . . ."

"You don't have to prepare for death. You don't prepare for death. What you do is you have to acknowledge the fact that in the last analysis that's the permanent future."

"OK. But the younger people who come here it seems to me are looking for some kind of Jewish connection that's more meaningful to them than other . . . " My question, of course, assumes a very significant divide between the two groups. Sacks's answer suggests something else—that in his mind, at least, the commonality between them has much to do with the trope of "the mixed multitude."

"Which is in reference to Murray Elman, who called me up. . . ." Murray used to work at the 41st Precinct, the "fort" of Fort Apache. He has since transferred to other precincts, and as an active member of the Shomrim, the benevolent organization of Jewish police, he maintains close ties to a congregation the organization has long had a soft spot for. "He asked my permission for a few of his secretaries or treasurer or workers or whatever to come in here on Rosh Hashanah. I says, 'You know it's very foolish for you to ask. Certainly they can come in. As far as I'm concerned, whether his name is Angelo or what is her name, it makes no difference to me. If she's looking for something which will alleviate her feelings, I don't care; she can come here. Rosh Hashanah she is invited.' He says, 'You have a seat for her?' [obviously joking, since the large room is nearly empty even during the High Holidays]. I says, 'Any seat that she wants. She can sit on the men's side, on the women's side. The seat will be here.'"

I asked Sacks about the other younger people who Gail had told me have now become regular congregants. Sacks believes that their coming to Intervale frequently connects to the fact that they are married or considering marriage to non-Jewish spouses. "So quite a few young people come here. It seems to me that the average age has gotten younger," I comment.

"Yes. Much younger. The average age not only is getting younger, but younger Jews have bought houses not far from here. Every time they come by, they say hello to me. They help me with this and that. I ask them to come into the synagogue. They say, 'Don't start like they do at synagogues in Queens, in Kew Gardens!' I say, 'I'm not asking you. When you're ready, come in. You'll look in, you'll see the shul. You'll sit wherever you want. You don't have to come in, but you have to know, as I told the people yesterday at the Hatzilu outing, that the shul does not need people; it's the people that need the shul.'

"The people in this neighborhood, no matter how they are connected, they've got to have a shul. They still have to have a beacon in here in this neighborhood. This shul, if it will stay for 150, 160 years, it will always have people to come in. They may be Catholics, they may be like the other shuls [that are now churches]. But it will always have people. But the Jewish people here need a shul. There are a lot of Jewish shuls that have been turned into churches. The Jewish churches here, the churches that have been [turned into churches], they don't need people. They get people. You go there, you see ten times the attendance that I have here, fifty times the attendance. But the Jewish people that are outside, they need a place that is still Jewish. And *that's what the shul needs. That's what the people from the Jewish multitude or the Jewish mixture, whatever you want to call it, from this neighborhood need to know. There is a shul. Maybe that will keep it up."*

"So the future of the shul looks very good, then?" I ask, more as a pause for me to consider what to ask next than as a real question. But Sacks takes the question seriously, and his reply admits, if not a small degree of doubt, then at least a large amount of tiredness, certainly a recognition that his time is limited, and that at some point in the future, if the Intervale Jewish Center is to have a future, it will be a future without Moishe Sacks.

"I don't know. You call it good? It all depends. It's like in every other thing, you have to have one or two key people who are willing or able to take over a little bit of the burden. We'll see what's what. I don't know."

While Sacks speaks, I hear a rustling noise coming from the nearby cabinet upon which the telephone sits. Suddenly a dark furry creature appears and darts down the aisle. "There's a rat over there!" I shout.

"Yeah? So what. What can I do? They're also . . . they're residents." Sacks's response is an obvious reference to Dave, the former caretaker of the shul whose job it was to dispose of dead rodents. As he carried them out, Dave often joked about whether the rats should be included in the minyan or whether he should recite the kaddish for them. But Sacks's response probably also stems from a sense of realism—given his own physical condition, there's little that he can do about the intruder.

"You look very tired," I comment.

"I am tired."

"Would you like me to take you home?"

"Yeah." I pack up my equipment and we head to the car. Sacks points the way as we drive, telling me to stop at a red light and wait for it to turn green. The moment he says the word "green," the light changes, and I compliment Sacks on his abilities. "Vayehi or" [There was light], Sacks announces, pronouncing the biblical phrase describing the creation.

Approaching Faile Street, I cannot help but think of Mrs. Miroff. We talk about the role she played as mother to the congregation, procuring and serving the food for the shabbes kiddush. "Things are different now, especially when Dolly handles the food," I comment.

"You see," Sacks replies, "it's like in the Bible. First there's the seven fat years, then there's the seven lean years. When Mrs. Miroff was in charge, there was always plenty of food. Now when Dolly serves the food, I have to argue with her to put enough on the table. We're serving tea, so I tell her to put sugar on the table. So she counts the number of people present, and she puts one packet of sugar for each person. I tell her, 'What if someone wants two packets of sugar?' She says, 'Too much sugar isn't good for their health!'"

Despite such criticism, I am struck by Sacks's deference to Dolly: He avoids yelling at her the way he did at Mrs. Miroff. Perhaps it's because Dolly could give back twice the earful. I had noticed, however, that Sacks seemed to yell at Bessie much the way he used to scream at Mrs. Miroff: "Is Bessie a replacement for Mrs. Miroff?"

"No. I yell at everybody."

"So you're an equal opportunity yeller." Sacks chuckles. He gets out of the car while insisting futilely that I remain inside. We shake hands, and he asks when I'll be back. I tell him, "Soon, I hope." Then Sacks disappears into a corner bodega.

In the course of our long relationship, I came to know and admire four aspects of Moishe Sacks: the craftsman/baker; the psychologist; the social worker; and the theologian. When I first met him, these four sides were in a precarious balance, although the craftsman/baker and the psychologist were predominant. It was through the bakery that Sacks acted as social worker, keeping an eye out for all the congregants in the neighborhood, providing them with food and intervening on their behalf with the police or welfare agencies who also frequented his establishment. And it was also through the bakery that Sacks demonstrated a peculiar *imitatio dei*, creating through the sweat of his brow and the skill of his hands South Bronx's manna, a seemingly endless supply of baked goods.

Sacks the psychologist revealed a certain delight in controlling others without having actual power. Sacks ran the bakery he worked in, a supervisory role claimed on the basis of his own personal authority, even to the point of intimidating the shop's various owners whenever a foul mood or workplace irritation got the better of him. He used the same skills at Intervale over the years, hoodwinking feisty congregants into more generous behavior than they otherwise felt inclined to exhibit.

After he retired, Sacks the theologian increasingly gained the upper hand. Although he was by no means passive and was still adept at finagling money from relief agencies or private donors on behalf of a client congregation, his concerns had shifted to the central dilemma of human existence—not only the purpose of life in the face of death, but the very imminence of death for himself and his aging congregation. The shift was from a struggle to control his surroundings to a struggle to gain inner mastery when the steady deterioration of his body had become increasingly evident. If the story of the miracle shul was a story about defiance and resistance to the ravages brought on by age—whether to the body itself or to the city more generally—Sacks's late theological musings indicated less the desire to do battle with God's will than a need to resign himself to it, to take comfort from the belief that death is indeed an integral part of God's plan and would bring him closer to God physically in a way that a continuing minyan can do only symbolically.

In his study of the life cycle, the psychoanalyst Erik Erikson argued that in old age there exists a struggle between integrity and despair, the outcome of which is very much determined by the successful meeting of similar types of challenges earlier in life. Moreover, the sense of integrity confirms critical decisions in one's life—in Sacks's life, the commitment to living out his years in the Bronx's forbidding landscape with its risk of physical harm. According to Erikson,

> Although aware of the relativity of all the various life styles which have given meaning to human striving, the possessor of integrity is ready to defend the dignity of his own life style against all physical and economic threats. For he knows that an individual life is the accidental coincidence of but one life cycle with but one segment of history and that for him all human integrity stands and falls with the one style of integrity of which it partakes. . . . The lack or loss of this accrued ego integration is signified by despair and an often unconscious fear of death: the one and only life cycle is not accepted as the ultimate of life. Despair expresses the feeling that the time is short, too short for the attempt to start another life and to try out alternate roads to integrity.[13]

It is precisely this integrity that continued to fortify Sacks even as he faced the end of the miracle and the final days of his own life.

But Erikson's model, like much of psychoanalytic literature, frames the individual as an absolutely autonomous agent unaided by the resources of culture. The great texts of all traditions, for those who value them, not only give comfort in distress but also act as scripts or charters for future action. Throughout his life in the Bronx, Sacks combed the texts of his tradition for patterns of the self through which his identity could be shaped in its journey. Earlier in his life, *imitatio dei* took place through work; at the end it was not God he emulated, but Moses—an indication, I think, of how much advanced age had made even Sacks a little humble.

Still, that *imitatio*, whether of God or of Moses, generated Sacks's deeply religious need to redeem all he came into contact with, including the Bronx itself. (Sacks always knew that it would be rebuilt!) Realizing this, I decided at the end to ask Sacks about redemption and why it figured so prominently in his thoughts. "Why?" he responded. "Well, maybe it's a selfish reason. The selfish reason is this: Redemption means the continuation of life. I have reached the end of my life . . . [*then quickly corrects himself*] towards the end of my life. When you get to the end, you hope for something in the future so there'll be a continuation of an existence."

I have no doubt that Sacks's anticipation of death was a contributing factor to his thoughts at our meetings in 1991 and 1992. But his redemptive vision long predated his frame of mind at that time. His was not an entirely unique sensibility, moreover. There was something deeper in Sacks's soul that made him see the world as he did—something that clearly had its roots in earlier life experiences and in earlier choices he had made. In *The Protean Self*, psychoanalyst Robert Jay Lifton argues that social dislocation and the "death imprint" caused by witnessing actual or impending disaster such as the Holocaust or nuclear annihilation has rendered the survivor experience universal at the end of the twentieth century, and these exigencies in turn are challenging traditional configurations of selfhood. The "struggle for meaning" can head in two directions: toward fundamentalism or a shutting down of the self, or toward proteanism, an opening outward.[14] This latter direction permits the self to assume a multiplicity of forms, which Lifton terms "protean" after the multiformed Greek sea god. According to Lifton,

> Greatly contributing to the odd combinations and transformations of the protean self are certain vicissitudes having to do with loss or absence, as well as with perceived threat. The first category includes feelings of fatherlessness, homelessness, and the absence of clear mentorship—feelings that can be painful but are at the same time necessary to the protean self. These vicissitudes can lead to confusion, and certainly to restlessness and flux. Yet they also provide strong motivation, and a certain content, for the self's quest for form.[15]

Lifton goes on to argue that the feeling of fatherlessness and homelessness gives one both freedom from the weight of the past and the freedom to create oneself anew.

Sacks's life history, particularly his childhood, was marked by his father's emigration to escape conscription during the Russo-Japanese war and Sacks's own wanderings through a collapsing state in search of sustenance during the Russian civil war, first with his mother, then later with a group of young people all trying to emigrate. These experiences fostered early on a need to fend for himself and to create order out of chaos. It left him, too, with a profound sense of the ironic nature of human existence, and with the recognition that momentary instability and disappointment might often be the key to future survival and happiness. (Sacks's career as a baker was sealed when his father's remarriage left him unable to lend his son the money he needed for medical school.) That ironic sensibility permitted the very fluid sense of community that shaped the persistence of the minyan at the Intervale Jewish Center. According to Lifton,

> For the protean self, communities are partial, fluctuating; come in odd places and combinations; are often at a distance; and vary greatly in their intensity and capacity to satisfy the needs of members. Community may well be the most grave problem facing the protean self; yet here, too, the

improvisations convey the sense that something new is always on the verge of being created.[16]

In Lifton's view, we are all now driven by factors similar to those that affected Sacks's early development. Dislocations are as much the result of the electronic media as they were earlier in the century the consequence of mass migration and revolution. And the fear of extinction has been given special urgency by the experience of genocide, famine, and ethnic warfare in the middle and latter part of the twentieth century. These, together with much earlier challenges to traditional ways of ordering the world brought on by the Enlightenment, make the quest for meaning urgent and its location problematic.

So the appeal of Sacks's musings is not just the result of his peculiarly persuasive and charismatic personality. It has also to do with the contemporary search for order in the face of critical skepticism and for the possibility of redemption in the face of disbelief.

The timing and the ways in which we seek redemption vary in each of us. It may be instigated by a sudden and intense awareness of death or despair coupled with the strength and determination to master them in particularly positive ways that are appropriate to the possibilities available at that time. And it may result in finding, as I did, a community of hope and affirmation in one of the most notorious of America's calamitous urban landscapes in the post-industrial United States. Death is conquerable (only totalitarians worship it), and that lesson is as real to me now as it was in 1979. When Sacks was most anxious about the possibility of redemption as he grew older, he turned to his biblical namesake, from timelessness to time, and to a new hopefulness grounded in the recognition of the possibilities of multiplicity. If the miracle minyan was in jeopardy because of the diminishing numbers of its Jewish congregants, Sacks was determined to foresee new members, and thus to assure himself that the Intervale Jewish Center did indeed have a future. He did so by recognizing the potential within the non-Jewish population of the revitalizing South Bronx—those from mixed marriages or who otherwise exhibit or claim some Jewish ancestry to seek solace within his sanctuary, Jewish newcomers to the neighborhoods—"the mixed multitude." To him in the last years of his life, they were much like the rabble that his namesake Moses led out of Egypt on their journey to the Promised Land. And if they were good enough for the Moses of the Bible, they are certainly good enough for this Moses of the Bronx.

August 13, 1993

I arrange to pick Sacks up at his apartment in the late morning, and we drive to a coffee shop on Southern Boulevard. Sacks is a regular at the *place, and as soon as we enter, he shouts at the short-order cook not to prepare the usual scrambled eggs. I am not sure why—perhaps there is something he does not want me to know, like the time years ago that we sat in the former bakery, now turned into a pizza parlor, and he objected to my photographing him eating a slice of pizza. He may not be an ordained rabbi, but he ministers to a congregation and is reluctant to flagrantly violate religious proscriptions concerning comestibility. Over coffee, Sacks tells me about overcoming the latest disaster at the shul—the giving out of the seventy-year-old water main and the $4,000 bill for the repairs. The net cost to the synagogue was zero because merchants in the area chipped in to cover the amount, including the Greek Orthodox owners of the coffee shop. Sacks believes that the generosity was prompted by both spiritual and practical considerations: on the one hand, a desire to see that all religious people in the area have a place of worship; on the other, a concern that if the synagogue were to close, the building might serve as a hangout for drug dealers.*

Our conversation drifts along, a chance for me to catch up on what has happened to the congregation over the past few months. Sacks seems much more energetic than at our last meeting. The repaired water main has fanned the flame of victory. It seems appropriate, then, to mention my ideas about redemption and his association with Moses. I explain the direction my writing is taking, and Sacks listens attentively. When I finish, I ask him point-blank, "Do you identify with Moses?"

"I don't!" Sacks responds emphatically.

"But he also dealt with a mixed multitude," I counter. Sacks's initial denial soon gives way to what I take to be tactful ambiguity.

"I don't identify," Sacks replies. "In my own opinion I don't identify. You see, Moses always believed in the fundamental goodness of the Jewish people. The fundamental goodness. He said that no matter what they do, no matter how much God will punish them, He will always remember that. In the end He will think of them. He will always remember that even though He is mad at them, they still did what no other people did. Came out with Him to the midbar, the desert. They did His observance. He said, 'Never will I ever forget what you did for me, no matter how bad you were.' This is the same thing at Intervale. No matter what the people there, the quasi-Jewish people, the half Jewish people, the ones we term completely Jewish because their mother is Jewish [but] their fathers are not Jewish, the persons who come there because they don't know what their [background is], we provide them with a place the same way as Moses said, 'He'll provide you. God will provide you no matter what you do. In the end He'll always take you back.' So I believe the same thing for Intervale. No matter what they'll do, no matter who will be there, in the end there will always be a core of people there

who will take care of the place. And they will think of that as their synagogue. I'm not a Moses."

"But the mixed multitude here is like the mixed multitude that Moses led out of Egypt," I counter.

"As a matter of fact it is." This is as far as I can take things. The association is obvious, but Sacks was being modest. And how could he not be? So was Moses.

Epilogue

In the summer of 1995 I was getting ready to head to New York, and I was looking forward to talking once again to Moishe Sacks. Shortly before I left Madison, I opened the *New York Times* and learned through an obituary that on Monday, June 12, 1995, Moishe Sacks had died.

He had been ill for months, had reluctantly entered the hospital to treat a condition brought on by diabetes, suffered the amputation of a leg, never quite lost the will to live—he anticipated moving into a newly constructed building opposed the shul so he could attend services in a wheelchair—but never left the hospital. The obituary had at least two errors: it located him in Longwood rather than Hunts Point and, best of all, conferred upon him the title of rabbi. Had he been alive to read it, he would have had a good laugh. And he would have had another laugh on almost all who knew him: it accurately pegged his age as eighty-two. According to a sister, Sacks purposely conveyed the impression of being a good ten years older. He figured that doctors would consider his advanced age before completing a diagnosis and report that for a man of his years he's in pretty good health.

Notes

I would like to thank Robert Orsi for inviting me to write this essay long after I thought the subject forever in my past. I am particularly grateful for his insights on this project, many of which I incorporated into the essay. As always, I am deeply and forever indebted to Moishe Sacks for his patience in responding to my endless questions.

1. Herbert Meyer, *Fortune*, November 1975.

2. The filming of *Bonfire of the Vanities* in 1990 was somewhat anachronistic given the changes to the borough already under way. For an article about local responses to the filming, see Tim Golden, "Filming Puts Bronx Vanities out of Joint," *New York Times*, April 24, 1990, B1–2.

3. William G. Blair, "Intervale Pleads for Reopening of El Station," *New York Times*, December 26, 1989, B1, B4.

4. John J. Goldman, "Bronx Reborn: Housing Emerges from the Ashes," *Los Angeles Times*, March 27, 1989, 1.

5. James Barron, "$5 Billion Plan for Apartments Pushed in Bronx," *New York Times*, February 28, 1989, B4.

6. Matthew Purdy, "Left to Die, the South Bronx Rises from Decades of Decay," *New York Times*, November 13, 1994, 1, 20. See also David Gonzalez, "Seeking to Break Grip of Violence in the South Bronx," *New York Times*, February 21, 1993, B31.

7. Purdy, "Left to Die," 20.

8. Any perusal through the *New York Times* Metro section provides ample testimony to this fact. See, for example, Dennis Hevesi, "Gang Leader Tells of Terror by Bronx Drug Ring," *New York Times*, March 1, 1995, B12.

9. Ian Fisher, "One Killed and 4 Hurt in Shooting," *New York Times*, July 14, 1993, B2.

10. Barbara Myerhoff, "Rites and Signs of Ripening: The Intertwining of Ritual, Time, and Growing Older," in *Age and Anthropological Theory*, ed. David Kertzer and Jennie Keith (Ithaca: Cornell University Press, 1984), 311.

11. According to Bakhtin, through the chronotope "spatial and temporal indicators are fused into one carefully thought-out, concrete whole. Time, as it were, thickens, takes on flesh, becomes artistically visible, likewise, space becomes charged and responsive to the movements of time, plot, and history." M. M. Bakhtin, *The Dialogical Imagination: Four Essays* (Austin: University of Texas Press, 1981), 84.

12. Mircea Eliade, *The Myth of the Eternal Return: or, Cosmos and History* (Princeton: Princeton University Press, Bollingen Series, 1974), 12–13.

13. Erik Erikson, *Identity and the Life Cycle* (New York: Norton, 1980), 104–105.

14. Robert J. Lifton, *The Protean Self: Human Resilience in an Age of Fragmentation* (New York: Basic, 1993), 82.

15. Ibid., 74.

16. Ibid., 103.

The Religious Boundaries of an In-between People

Street *Feste* and the Problem of the Dark-Skinned Other in Italian Harlem, 1920–1990

Robert A. Orsi

The Myth of the Greenhorn and the Black Man

The children and grandchildren of Italian immigrants to the United States all seem to know a story, which they insist is true, about a greenhorn just off the banana boat who is walking one day down a street in New York (or Boston or Chicago or St. Louis) when he sees a black man. The poor greenhorn is mesmerized. He has never seen a black person before. What is this? Stumbling to keep up, he trots alongside the black man, staring in consternation and incredulity at the strange sight. But what can this be? the greenhorn asks himself. Finally, he can't take it anymore. He runs up to the stranger, grabs the startled man by the arm, and starts rubbing his skin furiously to see if the black color comes off.[1]

A Dangerous In-betweenness: An Interpretation of Italian American History

"Swarthy," "kinky-haired" immigrants from southern Italy (as they were almost always described by the press in the United States during the late nineteenth and early twentieth centuries) were as fascinating to white Americans as the black man in this story was to the greenhorn, and for similar reasons: they could not figure out what they were looking at. Were the olive-skinned newcomers white or black, the only two possibilities in the domestic racial taxonomy? In the American South, where the arrival of this new brown population coincided with the tightening of Jim Crow legislation, the immigrants' "in-betweenness," in John Higham's word, was especially evident—and dangerous.[2] While southern legislators fretted that the influx of Italians meant another unassimilable race in their midst, and nativists in Mississippi campaigned to keep Italian children out of white schools, the citizens of Tallulah, Louisiana, took matters into their own hands. In 1899, five Sicilian men were lynched, ostensibly in a dispute over a goat, but really because they had violated the protocols of racial interaction. Genetically ambiguous themselves, they had made the further mistake of associating on apparently equal terms with the local blacks among whom they lived and worked.[3]

But the issue of racial in-betweenness existed in the urban, industrial North as well, where most of the immigrants from southern Italy settled. The clarity of the dilemma of the immigrants' anomaly in the South serves to focus attention on the fact, largely ignored by historians, that Italian American history began in racially inflected circumstances everywhere in the United States. The issue of the immigrants' place on the American landscape vis-à-vis other dark-skinned peoples fundamentally shaped not only the contours of their everyday lives at work and on the streets but also the "Italian American" identity they crafted for themselves in this environment. And the engagement of "Italian Americans" with dark-skinned people in the difficult years after World War II to the present cannot be understood apart from these earlier circumstances.

Four factors, rooted in specific social conditions in Italy and the United States during the early days of southern Italian immigration to this country, converged to constitute the dilemma of in-betweenness for the immigrants and their children in northern and midwestern cities: the use of racist categories by northern Italians to distinguish themselves from and to exclude southern Italians, the assumption of this same discourse by American commentators on southern Italian immigration, the coincidence of this migration with the movement of other darker-skinned peoples into North American cities, and the determination of southern Italians to make dignified lives for themselves in the terms of the new environment.

The people who lived south of Rome had little identification with the newly formed Italian nation-state, to which they were most closely bound by oppressive taxation policies, not patriotic ties. Their primary loyalties were to their villages and families. Northern Italian politicians dismissed southern Italians as dark-skinned outsiders; the ancient term of abuse for them was "Turks." While the slur obviously draws on religious hostilities, it was glossed again by the racist discourse that developed in Europe after the sixteenth century; in the early days of immigration to the United States, it was explicitly colorized.[4] Openly racist language has long been used to describe and ridicule the people south of Rome by Italians north of it: southern Italians, who come from the region of Italy that is both closest to Africa and most burnt by the hot sun (hence its designation as the *mezzogiorno*, or midday), are derided as "Africans," and their family patterns, dialects, dark skin, and kinky hair have been (and still are) exaggerated and lampooned in Italy's popular media.[5] The immigrants brought the memories of this stigmatization with them to America.

Here too they found themselves cast in the familiar idioms of racist exclusion by American journalists, politicians, and social workers. Lest they forget the mark of the Turk in the new setting, the immigrants were reminded of it by the prominent progressive and Social Gospeler Edward A. Ross, who wrote in 1914, "After allowing for every disturbing [environmental] factor, it appears that these children, with the dusk of Saracenic or Berber ancestors showing in their cheeks, are twice as apt to drop behind other pupils of their age as are the children of the non-English-speaking immigrants from northern Europe."[6] An invidious comparison was always made between the fair-skinned and allegedly more industrious and law-abiding northern Italians, called "Teutonic Italians" by Henry Cabot Lodge, who were said to be welcome in this country, and the dark-skinned southerners, who were described as lazy, criminal, sexually irresponsible, and emotionally volatile.[7] Home visitors (and social workers after them) brought these attitudes with them into Italian neighborhoods; the well-intentioned but prejudiced do-gooder is a standard (and fiercely drawn) figure in immigrant autobiographies.[8] The Dillingham Commission did not include southern Italians in the white race.[9] Italians were "one of the most despised" immigrant groups, Leonard Dinnerstein and David Reimers write in *Ethnic Americans*, and the language of contempt used against them was racist.[10]

The immigrants heard the same racially charged language in their churches. In many places, southern (not northern) Italians were made to sit in the back rows of Catholic churches with black congregants; sometimes they heard themselves denounced as "dagos" from the pulpit.[11] In a special publication prepared in 1921 to introduce Italian Americans to other Catholics, John Howard Mariano acknowledged that the racial ancestry of the lowest sort of southern Italian immigrant, whom he identified as the "ideo-emotional" or "tenement type," was uncertain, and suggested that this and not "environment" accounted for their questionable social characteristics.[12] A prominent Italian American Catholic writer, Aurelio Palmieri, complained in 1923 that the Irish considered Italians to be of another "racial origin."[13]

The image of African Americans and southern Italian immigrants sharing the back pews of a city church points to the third factor making for the latter's in-betweenness. The skin color of emigrants to the United States has been darkening over the last two centuries as points of departure have shifted from northern Europe, where the nation's first immigrants originated, to southern and eastern Europe, the Caribbean, East Asia, and Mexico, and then again most recently to South Asia and South and Central America.[14] The immigration from southern Italy coincided with the great migration of southern African Americans, African Caribbeans, and (a little later) Puerto Ricans and Mexicans northward. Viewed from this perspective, Italians belonged to the first wave of dark-skinned immigrants, and they inevitably found themselves living next to and working alongside other dark-skinned peoples in northern and midwestern industrial cities.

The history of this intersection has not been written yet, but at least a rough chronology is possible and necessary here. In a review of African American journalism about Italian immigrants, Arnold Shankman identifies three initial periods of interaction between the two populations: 1880–1900, when competition for jobs was fiercest and black fear of and resentment at being replaced by immigrant laborers was most intense; 1900–1929, years of relative peace, when the two peoples[15] accommodated themselves to each other's presence; and 1929–1936, a time of renewed and intensifying hostility, as blacks and Italians once again battled over scarce work during the Depression.[16] The years after World War II, to extend Shankman's periodization, were marked by a further deterioration of relations between the two populations. A revolution in agricultural technology brought a new wave of black migrants northward into crumbling neighborhoods that Italian Americans now considered theirs, even as they were leaving them for better housing in outlying city areas and suburbs. Those Italians who were determined (or compelled) to stay on longer became nervous guardians of the insecure borders first of the old neighborhoods and later of the areas of second settlement. Social pressures of various sorts combined to make this latter period a bitter one.[17]

This has been the trajectory of interaction between African Americans and Italian Americans over the last century.[18] Throughout the Northeast and Midwest, the immigrants and migrants, equally ill-prepared for industrial work, competed with each other for jobs, housing, and neighborhood power and presence. Italians moved into established black neighborhoods at the turn of the century in Philadelphia, St. Louis, Cleveland, and Greenwich Village, among other places; fifty years later, African Americans were displacing Italians in these same locations.[19] Italians broke into occupations that had long been primarily black domains, such as barbering, restaurant service, brickworking, and garbage collecting, in most cases coming to dominate the industry and excluding African Americans. Later in the century, the Italian monopoly of these industries would be challenged by newly arriving dark-skinned migrants from Mexico, the Hispanic Caribbean, and Asia. At times, competition yielded to cooperation, at least before the hard years of the 1930s, and sidewalk coexistence and even cordiality were possible, even amid the deteriorating circumstances after World War II. But whatever form the interaction took, Italian Americans have been closely connected with other dark-skinned people for the length of their history in this country.

The men and women of the *mezzogiorno* came into this setting determined to become *cristiani*, their word for "human beings" (and obviously the opposite of "Turks"). They were going to shed the mark of the "Turk" at last. This is the final factor shaping the interaction of dark-skinned peoples with Italian Americans, because in the United States the mark of the Turk was color, and so the immigrants, and even more their children and grandchildren, learned that achievement in their new environment meant successfully differentiating themselves from the dark-skinned other.

George Cunningham writes that Italian immigrants in the South discovered that in order to survive, they had to "look with loathing upon everything the native whites loathed," including, or especially, African Americans.[20] Gerald Suttles observed a "universal fear of stigma" among Chicago Italians in being associated with blacks arriving in the city in the 1960s. Even in California, where the presence of despised Asians, according to Micaela di Leonardo, deflected racial animosity against southern Italians, the immigrants' children confided to her that they were terrified of being associated with blacks.[21]

But the racial boundary was obviously not going to be an easy one for the "olive-tinted guineas" (a slang term for Italian Americans derived from the name given black slaves from West Africa)[22] to establish. Furthermore, the immigrants had the additional misfortune of entering the United States at a time of "reborn nativism," as Alexander DeConde has pointed out.[23] American anxieties about dangerous immigrants, whom they saw as physically decrepit, politically dangerous, and genetically inferior, were intensified to the point of hysteria amid the uprootings, dislocations, and moral uncertainties of the brutal heyday of industrial capitalism. There was a new concern in this period for drawing and defending boundaries—between us and them, white and black, Protestant and Catholic, American and foreign—and the idiom most often used to build the reassuring partitions was the specious science of race.

Southern Italians found themselves caught up in this desperate racial mapping of American identities, and they became "Italian American" on this turbulent and shifting terrain. Neither term in the designation had (or has) any intrinsic meaning. The immigrants were transformed first into "Italians" in this country, initially in the perceptions of others who were hostile to them and their dark skins; then they had to become "Americans" at a time when this identity itself had become the site of bitter, often racially charged conflict. The meaning of "Italian American" emerged along a series of contested borders in the neighborhoods, churches, and workplaces, and in the imaginations of *americani*. The immigrants' in-betweenness and the consequent effort to establish the border against the dark-skinned other required an intimate struggle, a contest against the initial uncertainty over which side of the racial dichotomy the swarthy immigrants were on, and against the facts of history and geography that inscribed this ambiguity on the urban landscape. Proximity—actual and imagined—to the dark-skinned other was pivotal to the emergence of the identity "Italian American."

This is evident in the folklore of Italian American communities. Suttles, for example, understands the belief, widely shared among the immigrants' children, that Italian American families never accepted public assistance (which is not true, of course) as an effort to draw a clear border against blacks.[24] It is also apparent in the diligence with which Italian Americans have studied African American ways, carefully marking the distance (as they noted the similarities) between these and their own customs.[25] During the ethnic revival of the 1970s, finally, the old tensions of this long campaign to establish place by differentiation from the proximate other exploded in the angry rhetoric of the revivalists.

Micaela di Leonardo says that it is one of the ironies of American history that an ethnic group that itself had been depicted as having "distinctly improper families" should turn around and mount savage attacks on the family lives of people poorer (and darker) than they. Jonathan Rieder, in his study of Brooklyn's Italians, calls it a "minor irony" of this community's history that "their Saracen blood gave the Southern Italians a dark complexion that sometimes resembles African more than Caucasian hues."[26] But these ironies are neither surprising nor minor. Irony is the dominant register of Italian American history, a reflection of the in-betweenness that constituted these people as they struggled to escape it.

Harlem East and West

One of the largest Italian communities in the United States began taking shape in the northeast corner of Manhattan in the late 1870s.[27] Drawn by construction jobs in central Harlem, where a boom in luxury housing was under way, and on the city's expanding network of subways and elevated trains, southern Italians moved up to the relatively cleaner air and more open spaces of northern Manhattan from the squalid blocks of the downtown Little Italy, then sent for relatives and *compari* in the old *paese*. By the mid-1920s, East Harlem had become Italian Harlem—just at the time that central Harlem, in the wake of the collapse of the real estate market there, had emerged as "Harlem," the nation's premier black metropolis and the city of dreams for black men and women in small towns around the country.[28]

Historians have usually treated the stories of Black (West) Harlem and Italian and then Spanish (East) Harlem as distinct, but the people who lived in these worlds understood that they were bound together by all sorts of connections. It is true that the borders of the various territories in Harlem, east and west, were marked by the people who lived there. Italian Americans recognized that west of Lexington Avenue was no longer their world, and young blacks and Puerto Ricans believed they had to keep away from the Italian sections on the east side—if they could—because they knew "that sometimes you don't fit in," as Puerto Rican writer Piri Thomas recalled of his East Harlem youth, "like if you're a Puerto Rican on an Italian block."[29]

But just as often the boundaries were crossed; Thomas, after all, was remembering here the time in the 1940s when his family had moved to an "Italian" block. Every day the people of the various neighborhoods of Harlem—African Americans, African Caribbean Americans, Italians, Puerto Ricans, and other Hispanic Caribbeans—were brought together and forced to confront each other by the logic of shared social, economic, and geographical circumstances. Their children went to the same public schools, and when they were a little older, they danced in the same ballrooms and battled each other in gang fights on the converging streets of their neighborhoods.

But human beings always live in places that are also ideas of places— their own ideas about their places and the way others think of them—and Harlem's Italian Americans and, later, Puerto Ricans (especially those with lighter skin) gradually realized that they were living in the wrong idea.[30] By the 1920s, "Harlem," in the imagination of white people downtown in New York City and elsewhere in the country, signified both a squalid, dangerous slum and a mythic kingdom of illicit erotic delight, but from either perspective it was thought to be a black community, on the margins of New York's life and culture.[31] This had consequences for the way the Italians of Harlem were perceived, too. A priest who has spent his whole life in the community told me that the Irish American clergy in the archdiocesan offices downtown "thought we were Africans." They believed "that there was something weird [about us]. . . . We were always looked upon as though we were doing something wrong . . . and I knew from my experience . . . [that] they looked down on us." As late as 1946, the writers at *Time* attacked the area's progressive congressman, Vito Marcantonio, by describing his constituents as "hordes of Italians, Puerto Ricans, Jews and Negroes" living in a "verminous, crime-ridden slum." Marcantonio was caricatured as "the Hon. Fritto Misto" (Mixed Fry), ostensibly a reference to his complex political base, but also a titillating symbol of the sort of racial and cultural mixing outsiders feared about Harlem, which was itself a *fritto misto* too.[32]

Throughout the 1930s, as economic conflict between Italians and blacks intensified and as the immigrants' children and grandchildren began to define themselves in more explicitly American idioms, the borders between the two communities came to be better guarded. Young Italian Americans lied about where they came from when they went out looking for work, as lighter-skinned Puerto Ricans would later. Italians took over particular industries across northern Manhattan and excluded blacks, who in turn fought to expel Italian merchants from their blocks. Italy's invasion of Ethiopia gave an international cast to deepening local animosities.

But this necessity of lying to outsiders and forcibly excluding the other was only the most obvious and exigent expression of a deeper and more pervasive Harlem strategy. Each of northern Manhattan's peoples defined themselves against a racial other who they declared themselves not to be. Living within the tight parameters of a common everyday life on the streets, northern blacks set themselves off from southern blacks,[33] lighter-skinned blacks and Puerto Ricans from darker ones, African Caribbeans from African Americans, other Spanish-speaking peoples from Puerto Ricans, and Italian Americans from blacks and Puerto Ricans. Motivating all these efforts at self-constitution through the strategy of alterity, within the broader context of American racial semiotics, was the zealous attempt to distinguish oneself from the others with darker skin. The strategy never worked completely, however, because outsiders did not always share the local precision in marking out the cultural and racial hierarchies, and because the actual borders among the communities were never absolute. Geographical avoidance and denial were not proof enough against the ironies of in-betweenness.

"It really bugged me," Thomas confesses in his autobiography, "when the paddies [white ethnics] called us Puerto Ricans the same names they called our colored aces." When his closest friend, a young black man named Brew, calls him a Negro, Thomas insists, to his friend's sorrow, that "I'm a stone Porty Rican," a statement he immediately regrets. "Was I trying to tell Brew that I'm better than he is cause he's only black and I'm a Puerto Rican dark skin?" His friend warns him, "So you're gonna put the Negro down jus' cause the paddy's puttin' yuh down. . . . Ain't gonna bring nothin' from us exceptin' us puttin' yuh down too." But Thomas never gets it right, remaining instead "hung up between two sticks, " as he names his own in-betweenness.[34]

Thomas eventually undergoes a religious conversion that frees him from the burden of trying to define himself through the strategy of alterity. "We're all the same when it comes to our souls and spirits," he discovers in a visionary experience in prison.[35] Conversion represented for Thomas a liberation from Harlem's racial hall of mirrors, but street religion in New York has not always served this purpose.

The Madonna of 115th Street and the Meanings of "Italian American"

The devotion to Our Lady of Mount Carmel was brought to East Harlem in 1881 by immigrants from the town of Polla in the province of Salerno near Naples.[36] The first celebration of the Madonna's feast day in New York, on July 16, 1881, was a simple affair limited to immigrants from Polla, but over the next several years the devotion developed into the central communal event of Italian Harlem, drawing immigrants from all over southern Italy, not just from Polla or Salerno, and from all the neighborhoods of East Harlem to a huge annual midsummer street celebration. The *festa* took place in the blocks around the Church of Our Lady of Mount Carmel, which was built in 1884 at the northern edge of the Italian section by the Pallotine Fathers, an order of men dedicated to work among Italian immigrants. The priests purchased the statue of Mount Carmel, which had been acquired by the members of the mutual aid society for Pollese immigrants, and eventually enthroned her over the main altar of the church, from where the Madonna was believed to preside over the lives of her people in Harlem.

The annual celebration of the feast of Mount Carmel was Italian Harlem's central public event and the site for the construction, elaboration, and performance of the various emergent meanings of "Italian American" by the immigrants and their children in the changing circumstances of their American lives. In the rituals and practices associated with the celebration, in the stories that were remembered and told over and over about past *feste* both by the people who stayed in Harlem and by those who left it after World War II, and in the immigrants' insistence that their children make public demonstrations of submission to the norms of the family during the annual celebrations, Harlem's Italians gave meaning and resonance to their new identities as "Italian Americans."

This ongoing process of ethnic self-constitution must be understood diachronically as well as synchronically, because the "Italian American" subjectivity that took shape in the celebrations was always changing. Like neighborhood boundaries, ethnic identities are labile and porous, despite the solidity they come to acquire in the stories people tell about themselves.[37] In the earliest years of the settlement, when Italian Harlem was largely a colony of men who had preceded their families in search of work, what seemed most important about the *festa* was that it allowed these first immigrants to articulate and practice in their devotion to the Madonna a faithfulness to the women they had left behind. Later, in the 1920s and 1930s, as a bitter generational conflict erupted in the community, the annual *festa* both declared "Italian Americans" to be a family-centered people and imposed these values on the adolescents constrained to attend the street celebrations against their wills.

The *festa* also took its place, however, and acquired its meanings, in the competitive and volatile world of Harlem's ethnic complexity, amid the contests of racial and ethnic identities sketched out above. Each July 15th and 16th, a replica of the statue over the main altar (or on special occasions the Madonna herself) was (as it still is) taken out of the church and placed on a flatbed truck, where it was surrounded by flowers and neighborhood girls in white First Communion outfits. Then the Madonna and her attendants were (and are) drawn up and down the streets of the Italian neighborhoods by young men in tuxedos. In this way, as the Madonna made her way through East Harlem, Italians marked out certain sections of the neighborhood as their own, and at least on these days, with the Madonna in the streets underneath the arches strung by her faithful people, East Harlem was "Italian Harlem."

But the streets of Harlem did not belong exclusively to the Italians. Even in the days when Italian concentration was at its greatest, there were close to fifty other ethnic groups living in the community, according to Leonard Covello, the principal of Benjamin Franklin High School and a prominent observer of the community.[38] The assertion that this part of Harlem was "Italian Harlem"—*bella Harlem, nostra Harlem*—represented not a demographic fact, but a victory over the street life of the community achieved through the exclusion of the others.[39]

Faces that were not Italian could always be seen in the crowds at the annual *festa*—Irish policemen in the early days, Jewish and German immigrants still living in what had been their old neighborhood, and prosperous tourists from the West Side. But the world around the Madonna began to change most dramatically in the years after World War I, when migrants from Puerto Rico took over the places gradually vacated in the neighborhood by Italian Americans prosperous enough now to move out of its decayed tenements and filthy streets. Throughout the 1940s and 1950s, the Italian population of East Harlem slowly decreased while the number of Puerto Rican inhabitants grew. This change was evident in the streets and markets, and it could be seen most vividly in the new faces looking down from once-familiar windows and fire escapes on the Madonna as she made her way through the old neighborhood.

But if Italian American identity in the United States meant denying the proximity of the too proximate racial other, how would the immigrants and their children deal with the arrival of this dark-skinned other now right in their midst?

Fieldwork in the Fissure of Past and Present: A Comment on Method

Before I turn to this question, I must say something about my own relationship to the neighborhood and its memories and about my research there. I began studying Italian Harlem's history and present circumstances in 1978. For my historical research I relied on a number of archives (especially the Covello Papers at the Balch Institute in Philadelphia), and at first I thought that this would be mainly how I learned about Italian Harlem. But it quickly became clear to me that although it was not the thriving community it once had been, *cara* Harlem continued to exist in a number of ways: as a remnant of old-timers in its northernmost sections, in the memories of men and women who left it only two decades or so ago, and, most importantly, during the annual *festa*, when in an uncanny way memory took shape in the streets so that the past became present again for a short while. During the annual celebrations, the neighborhood was (and still is) crowded with Italians again; old neighbors met in the streets as if they still lived in the surrounding tenements; and familiar faces fussed around the Madonna's float and prepared the statue for the procession.

So I also did a kind of layered fieldwork. Over a two-year period I traveled around the outer boroughs and New Jersey, talking with people who had once lived in East Harlem, and I spent many months in the old neighborhoods, in various venues, meeting older and more recent residents and community leaders. Italian Harlem is caught between memory and the present, not completely gone yet but not still there, either, and this accounts for the dual research orientation I have followed in exploring the community.

Since this initial work, which began in 1978, I have attended the annual *festa* of Our Lady of Mount Carmel regularly, actually never missing one, and now I am a recognized fixture at the event. People seek me out to add to stories they have already told me. I have been invited to participate in various aspects of the *festa* over the years, and like returning Harlemites—which I am not—I visit with old acquaintances during the days before and after the celebration. I have made some very good friends in the community, but everyone understands that my interests in and connections to Harlem are different from theirs: I "study" Harlem, and my acquaintances there know that when I talk with them, I am trying to better understand the life of the place. Some are enthusiastic about this, others neutral; some do not much care.

The conversations about Puerto Ricans and Haitians recounted here took place mostly during the weeks of the *feste* between 1988 and 1991. Some occurred on the streets, but most were in prearranged sit-down meetings at the church. Everyone understood that at the time I was working explicitly on relations between Italian Americans and the other two communities. All conversations, with the exception of one with a priest I met in 1991, were with men and women I have known since the start of my work in Harlem. The talks were frank. I took notes, as I always do in East Harlem, but I did not tape the conversations. All quotations are from my notes, and I have changed any features that might identify my sources. Relevant information about particular sources, such as age and residence, is included in the narrative.

I am an Italian American myself, from the Bronx (where many Harlemites came in the 1940s and 1950s), and this certainly plays a role in my work on 115th Street. Sometimes it gives me access to material that others could not get and to communications they might miss, like ironic tones, secret allusions, and the subtle commentary of bodily gestures. Just as often, I am sure, this closeness inhibits me. My written work is well known among people who come to the *festa* and former residents of Italian Harlem, but with the exception of one close friend from the community (who has taught me much), I have not made a special point of showing my writings to my sources. But when we talk, I always tell them what I am thinking about what they are saying, and I have tried to be sensitive to their commentary on what I say about them. I have incorporated this into my interpretations to the extent I think appropriate.

I am using ethnographic work to help me uncover some of the themes of the Italian American encounter with Puerto Ricans and Haitians in the years after World War II. All my sources, even the younger ones (meaning those in their thirties), were a part of this story. I have set their remarks in a broader historical context that is crafted from other kinds of sources, but since much of what I am concerned with here is the way events are construed and "remembered," and especially with the imaginative role of the Madonna as a pivot of this construal and remembering, the use of this kind of data to make both a historical and an anthropological argument about inner-city ethnicities was necessary. Because memory and the present converge during the annual celebration in honor of the Madonna of 115th Street, it serves as a rich site for this work.

"The So-Called Puerto Ricans"

The Puerto Ricans who began migrating to East Harlem in increasing numbers just before World War II were coming into an ironic local situation.[40] Although Italian control of the area was never complete, it was as complete in these years as it would ever get. Local political life was presided over by a powerful machine, and East Harlem was securely connected to city government by LaGuardia, who had been the community's congressman, and to national politics by his protégé and successor, Marcantonio. But just when this moment of power was finally attained, younger Italian Americans began to leave the community—and their older kin—for better housing in the outer boroughs, a trend that would increase dramatically after the war. As a result, in this brief season of local hegemony, Italian Harlem's people felt most vulnerable and threatened. Furthermore, for all its political clout, the community was not able to stop the onslaught of various urban renewal programs. Between 1945 and 1963, eleven public housing projects were built in the neighborhoods, displacing the local (Italian) population with more than twelve thousand low-income black and Hispanic families. By the latter date, an East Harlem social worker could recall "nostalgically" the old "Italian band concerts [and] colorful street fairs" that were no more.[41] In slightly more than a decade, *cara Harlem* had become *el barrio.*

So Puerto Ricans were moving into an Italian Harlem that was not as secure as it appeared; its public strength and presence, which included the annual festivities in honor of the Madonna of 115th Street, masked a more intimate enervation. Italian Harlem knew that its children were leaving: the dark-skinned strangers, after all, were moving into apartments vacated by them. It was a painful time for a community that defined moral worth as familial loyalty, by which it meant the proximity of all generations. The dilemma of in-betweenness that erupted in East Harlem between Italians and Puerto Ricans in the 1950s and 1960s, and the stories Italians told to restore the border against the dark-skinned other, must be understood against this background of Italian American loss and moral distress.[42]

In his efforts to convince himself that he was not a "Negro," Piri Thomas clung to the fact that his native tongue was Spanish: language would separate him from the other dark-skinned peoples around him. But when Thomas turned the other way, toward his Italian neighbors, he looked to language as the basis for connection and acceptance. Just before he was beaten up by a gang of Italian American boys, Thomas heard some older people speaking Italian. "I couldn't help thinking," he says, "how much like Spanish it sounded. Shit, that should make us something like relatives."[43] But as far as Italians in the neighborhoods were concerned, the trouble started with the fact that a black man could speak a language that sounded like theirs.

Puerto Ricans were a Latin people who spoke a Latin language and shared many of the same values as Italians, and many of them were Catholics, at least initially. But they were also poor—and dark-skinned. Puerto Ricans had been racially discriminated against in the U.S. Army during the war; on the home front, white Harlem identified the newcomers as "niggers."[44] They lived among American blacks in the neighborhoods' housing projects and in the less desirable blocks at the southern fringe of the area. Darker-skinned migrants may in fact have been in the majority, since dark skin correlates with poverty in Puerto Rico. Lighter-skinned Puerto Ricans urged their children to advance the race [adelantar la raza] by marrying white, and they ridiculed "bad" or crespo hair; their darker-skinned relatives used powders to lighten their skin.[45] Sociologist Maxine Gordon claimed that the effort among Puerto Ricans to draw a sharp line between themselves and African Americans was particularly intense in Spanish Harlem, because everyone else seemed determined to blur it there.[46] By the 1950s, the rest of the city was telling the sorts of stories about East Harlem that they told about black Harlem. So the other had come close again.

The inner complexities of the encounter between Italian Americans and Puerto Ricans in Harlem was reenacted for me one afternoon in 1979 by a fifty-year-old Italian American man who had been born and raised in the neighborhood and still worked there, although he had moved away some years before.[47] We were in the middle of a conversation on the corner of Third Avenue and 115th Street when my acquaintance suddenly interrupted us to comment on the Puerto Rican dialect we could hear around us on the crowded street. He began (just as his parents' generation had done in the 1930s and 1940s) by noting the similarities between Italian and Puerto Rican cultures—both peoples are Catholic, he reminded me; both loved the Mother of God; both were especially anxious to protect their women's honor. He added that the two peoples spoke a similar language.

But these observations brought Puerto Ricans too close, and as the anxiety of ambivalence overcame him, he hastily reworked similarity into difference. Although he could recognize some of the words his neighbors spoke, he said, "Puerto Rican" was really a corrupted barbaric form of Italian, nothing like his mother's and grandmothers' language. Having in this way safely reestablished the linguistic barrier separating him from Puerto Ricans, he went on to say that his Hispanic neighbors were dirty, thieving, and lazy. He concluded by circling back to language and ridiculing the velocity and staccato qualities of his neighbors' speech. He was such a skilled mimic and had such a practiced tongue that it was clear he had been listening attentively, at least, if not anxiously, to the sounds of his neighbors' voices for a long time.

"Italian Americans" are not "Puerto Ricans." Harlem's Italians, both as part of the process of fending off the threat of ambiguity posed by the proximate other and as a way of narrating (and understanding) their loss of East Harlem, tell a story about how the Puerto Ricans came to be among them. They say that Congressman Vito Marcantonio brought the migrants to New York City as a way of defending himself against the attempts by other New York politicians to gerrymander him out of office.[48] Although Marcantonio is otherwise fondly remembered by his old constituents, in this one instance they insist that he betrayed them.

The arrival of the Puerto Ricans was woven in this way into the familiar southern Italian epic of political treachery and malfeasance, and even though in this case it was not true, the tale of Marcantonio's betrayal and the coming of the Puerto Ricans allowed Italians to deny what was really happening in their community—Italian Americans were finally well-off enough to get out. But leaving behind old parents and grandparents in order to improve one's own circumstances was a violation of the fundamental norms of family sacrifice and submission that occupied the central place in the Italian American moral economy.[49] Seen in this context, Puerto Ricans served as substitute villains in a drama of betrayal that was actually a kind of communal screen memory to occlude this other, much more distressing treachery. "We were literally forced out," a forty-year-old Italian American woman told me about the departure of her family in the 1950s, in the same language that every Italian I have spoken to uses to describe these years, even though, like other Harlem Italians, her parents chose to move away to better schools, cleaner air, and safer streets for their children. (It is significant that in the screen myth, ultimate responsibility for the demise of the neighborhood rests with an Italian American; this much made it past the community's censors.)

But Marcantonio's betrayal is only one of the themes of the story of the arrival of the Puerto Ricans; a second concerns the identity of these dark-skinned people. A priest prominent in the Italian community during the peak years of Puerto Rican migration told me recently that the first arrivals from the island "looked like TB. They were sickly people. They were all sick—no one had any food." Other people's memories echo his remarks: Puerto Ricans were wastrels, underfed and poorly clothed. Although the earliest migrants (like the Italians before them) were indeed poor, the Puerto Ricans' distress is alluded to more often in scorn than in commiseration, and in a community that articulated love and power in the idioms of food, as Italian Americans have done, the empty stomachs of the new arrivals were taken to mean that this was not a real people with a moral culture of its own. Again the message was that Puerto Ricans are not like us. Expressing his wish that these bad non-people would simply disappear, this priest would refer to Puerto Ricans only with third-person pronouns — "they," "them" — or as "the so-called Puerto Ricans," a final denial of their subjectivity.

According to Harlem's Italian chroniclers, these sickly "so-called Puerto Ricans" who were "pouring into" the neighborhood destroyed *cara* Harlem and laid siege to the Church of Our Lady of Mount Carmel. "Our Puerto Ricans from 115th Street steal everything," another priest, seventy years old, born and raised in Harlem, told me. "We have more trouble with them" than with anyone else in the neighborhood.

There was clearly going to be no place for the Puerto Ricans at the annual *festa* of Our Lady of Mount Carmel. Puerto Ricans in *el barrio* have told me that they always understood that the celebration belonged to the Italians, even though everyone could see that there were fewer and fewer of them (and more and more Puerto Ricans) in the neighborhoods. On the days of the *festa*, despite all its colorful enticements, Puerto Ricans knew to stay away, because on these days and nights Italian Americans were in the grip of a profound experience of their own power and identity (conflicted and polysemous as this was) and would not tolerate the appearance of "outsiders" among them, especially those "outsiders" who lived inside the neighborhood. This sense of exclusion was so forceful that Puerto Ricans came to hate the celebration. One young man remembers that his father, a Pentecostal minister in *el barrio*, forbade his children from crossing the route of the Madonna's procession during the period of the *festa*, dragging them far out of their way to avoid stepping on the same ground that the Madonna had touched.[50]

The final move in the narrative construal of Puerto Ricans was then to account for their absence from the *festa*. If they are so much like us (as we fear), then why don't they come to show respect for the Madonna as we do? The answer is that "they have no devotion to Mount Carmel," according to a former pastor of Mount Carmel, who well knows how dangerous it would have been for a Puerto Rican to attend the celebration. Puerto Ricans, he said, "were for some unknown reason scared of the Italians at Mount Carmel" and kept away, but this was just "excuses." The real reason is that Puerto Ricans are not good people, even though they have their own devotions, although this man would not admit to knowing what they were.

The Italian American expulsion of Puerto Ricans was most vividly performed at the Mount Carmel feast. This was the site where the exclusion of the too proximate other was most publicly articulated and enacted in Harlem. From the vantage point of the procession, grouped among their own kind (including many who no longer lived in Harlem), safe in the space of the Madonna's train, Italian Americans walked through the old blocks staring out at the changed faces and declaring them unwelcome. It is not surprising that today during the celebrations, the local Puerto Rican population go about their business along the route of the Madonna's passing as if she were not there. Boys wash their cars at fire hydrants, forcing the devout to march past them on wet and soapy streets; children play across the line of pilgrims; and Puerto Rican women leaning out of windows call to each other over the Madonna's head. Now that Italian Harlem has become *el barrio*, it is the Puerto Ricans' turn to use the other community's sacred occasion to deny its existence. The *festa* of *la Madonna del Carmine* remains for both peoples the most public expression of what they think about each other.

So the *festa* stayed "an Italian feast," as I was told by a participant recently, even in the years of the transition to Spanish Harlem. But then in the early 1980s, a new group of dark-skinned people began appearing for the July celebration, and again Harlem's Italians (and the Italian Americans who had moved away from the neighborhood but came back to honor *la Madonna* each year) were faced with the problem of what to do with the other in their midst.

Was the *festa* inevitably or inexorably the site of exclusion?

"The Haitians Are Not Considered Black"

There is a church dedicated to Our Lady of Mount Carmel in Greenpoint-Williamsburg (founded as an offshoot of the church on 115th Street) and another one in the Belmont section of the North Bronx, and at first Haitian pilgrims traveled around the city visiting each representation of the Madonna of Mount Carmel, who is also the patroness of Haiti. But the migrants came to prefer Harlem's Madonna, perhaps because she most closely resembles the figure of the Virgin who is said to have appeared over a palm tree on the island as she is depicted in island iconography.[51] The Haitians, who did not live in Harlem, came to the *festa* in long pilgrimages from Brooklyn by car, chartered bus, and subway.

There are some important differences between the Haitians and the Puerto Ricans in the Italian American experience. Because they did not live in the neighborhood, the Haitians never posed a direct threat to the Italian sense of place (which has remained strong in the area just around the church). The Haitians also came to the *festa* in great numbers, generally equal to, although at times surpassing, the number of Italian American participants, which had been declining steadily by the early 1980s. The powerful and evident piety of the Haitian pilgrims, furthermore, which was there for everyone to see in the aisles of the church and the streets of the neighborhoods, deeply impressed and moved the Italian Americans, who openly express respect for Haitian spirituality during the annual event.

Most important, by the time the Haitians got to East Harlem, the Italians had conceded that most of the neighborhood was no longer theirs. The local battle was over. So the Haitians were not coming into *Italian Harlem*, but to a special place of cherished memory, a place constructed a certain way in the practices of remembering, to which most of the Italian Americans at the *festa* themselves were returning in order to express their respect for their ancestors' struggles and achievements. The Haitians were not seen as taking anything away, and so the newcomers then were not assimilated to a narrative of loss and betrayal. Indeed, in the context of the memorializing of East Harlem that takes place at the *festa* these days, just the opposite was the case, as we will see.

The Haitians are treated very differently than the Puerto Ricans were. The priests at Mount Carmel open the church to Haitian groups by special request and allow them to spend the night there in vigils at any time during the year. Haitian pilgrims move through the inner passageways of the church and rectory with easy familiarity during the *festa*. Haitian altar boys participate in the official ceremonies of the *festa*; the Haitian national anthem is played (along with the Italian and American) at the start of the processions of the Madonna, and the Haitian flag is carried in the streets.

But how is it that Italian Americans could make room for the Haitians in the same event that had played such an important role in excluding another dark-skinned people in the neighborhood? Although there were some initial anxieties among the organizers of the *festa* about racial tensions, these never developed, at least as far as the Italians are concerned. "The mosaic Dinkins talks about?" I was told during the celebration in 1990 by a sixty-five-year-old Italian American who still lives and works in East Harlem. "It's here. For some unknown reason, it's here."

Again the response to the other was organized into a narrative that is both framed with reference to the Haitians' relation to the Madonna and confirmed by it. The foci of this narrative parallel those of the story of the Puerto Ricans, but in each case—arrival, the identification of the new people, and the presentation of their religious culture—the narrative tropes are inverted. Mount Carmel's chroniclers treat the appearance of the Haitian pilgrims from Brooklyn as something of a mystery and a miracle, an uncanny event. Suddenly one year, as Italian Americans at the church say, completely unexpectedly, crowds of Haitians began coming to the annual celebration of the feast (from Brooklyn, no less, which in Harlem can seem as far away as Haiti itself). When they talk about this,

Italian Americans use phrases such as "as far as I can determine" to mark the strangeness of this turn in the history of Mount Carmel.

The uncanniness of this moment is then used as a way of absorbing the disconcerting appearance of the Haitian pilgrims into another, older narrative, this time about Italian Harlem itself. The arrival of the Haitians, one church worker told me, is not really that surprising, since "this site has always been favored" by heaven, and she went on to allude to some of the miracles worked at the church by Harlem's Madonna, a number of which had happened for Haitians. In this way the Haitians are called on as witnesses to the power of the Italian Madonna in what used to be Italian Harlem. Their presence confirmed the enduring power of a place that had once been powerful because it was Italian.

But who were these people who had so miraculously appeared? Were they like the black people of Harlem? Language again served as the pivot on which this story of interaction turned. Haitians speak French, I was reminded by one of Mount Carmel's priests, and sing and pray "so beautifully" in Latin. He added that many of the Haitian pilgrims to East Harlem had even asked for the words to Italian hymns so they could learn these too. The Haitians' command of Latin is particularly important to the Italian Americans marching beside them in the procession: this identifies the strangers as "traditional Catholics," and in recognition of this, Mount Carmel hosts a Latin mass on the first Saturday of every month especially for Haitians devoted to Our Lady of Fatima.

This linguistic move opened the way for the central claim made by Harlem's Italians about the Haitians: they are not black people. I was told many times by Italian Americans in Harlem, during the *festa* and in conversations afterward, that, as the priest previously quoted and as other Italian Americans I have spoken to put it, "Haitians are not considered black people." In support of this assertion, Italians turn to the Haitians themselves, who are said to despise African Americans and to want to have "nothing to do with them." In this way, one community's strategy of alterity (the Haitians' differentiation of themselves from African Americans) is called upon by another community in its own reworking of local boundaries, and Italians could feel secure that the men and women praying in their church and walking beside them in the streets were not "them."

With this denial, however, came another. Italian Americans at Mount Carmel do not really see what the Haitians are doing around them. Priests at the church and volunteer custodial workers (some of whom are former residents of the neighborhood who come back to help) are uneasy with some Haitian practices, particularly those which they suspect are connected with "that Vodou stuff," as the current pastor puts it. The suspicion is accurate: Our Lady of Mount Carmel appears in Haiti's Vodou pantheon as the powerful figure Ezili Danto, and the pilgrims from Brooklyn leave burnt food as offerings in the plaster folds of the traditional Italian saints whom they see in two idioms, Catholic and Vodou. Church workers also know that Haitians "spread around perfume," as one woman told me, during Vodou rituals at the church.

But Italian Americans flatly deny that any of these practices are significant or meaningful. They say that Vodou practices represent the handiwork of only "a few crazy ones." I was told by an Italian American custodian that the writings on the statues are just expressions of teenage love (even though she could see as clearly as I could that they were entreaties for assistance from the spirits). Just as Italians assert that Haitians are not black, so they say, despite all the evidence they know so well, that "Haitians are not involved in Vodou."

Such tolerance is not extended to Puerto Rican Santería, however, even though much less of this is seen in the church than Vodou. The real religious problem at Mount Carmel today, I was told (in 1990), comes not from Haitian teenagers writing innocent love messages on the old Italian statues but from Puerto Rican *santeros* who come into the church all dressed in white and surrounded by their followers. Italian American church workers believe (and fear) that these *santeros* come to "steal power" from the statue of the Madonna, and although the pastor of the church shrugged at this interpretation as if he were refusing to take it seriously, he went on to say that this was another example of the widespread problem of "satanism" in New York City, which had recently prompted the Cardinal to appoint a diocesan team of exorcists.

The story of the vampire *santeros* come to drain power from *la Madonna del Carmine* recalls the major theme in the account Harlem's Italians gave of the arrival of the Puerto Ricans in the community. Like the *santeros*, the Puerto Ricans came to steal the power and presence of the Italian community in Harlem. The explicit fantasy of exorcism here suggests that at least in this domain, in the idioms of spiritual conflict, the Puerto Ricans were not going to get away with it. Vodou, on the other hand, practiced by people who did not pose so immediate a neighborhood threat, was an aberration in an otherwise admirable culture.

Conclusions: Exorcism, Ethnicity, and Theodicy in the City

The historical circumstances of Italian American history—the four converging factors constituting "in-betweenness"—have given a special urgency to African American–Italian American engagement that has gone largely unnoticed by historians. From 1900 to 1930, a period Shankman identifies as "bittersweet," Italians were constrained—but also willing—to associate relatively freely and closely with blacks; occasionally, there was even intermarriage between the two communities.[52] Traces of this attitude may still be seen today in the peculiarly intense and unique "love/hate" relationship, as di Leonardo calls it, that exists between Italian and African Americans.[53] Even the expressions of rage that have been evoked recently by a series of tragic events in northeastern cities disclose undercurrents of attraction, disappointment, and mutual implication. These two peoples have had to deal with each other for a century, sometimes for better, sometimes for worse.

But Italian immigrants and their children and grandchildren learned that to be "American" meant to divide the races a certain way. I have suggested here a rereading of Italian American history that puts the issues and contests of racial identity and difference at its center. The meaning of "Italian American," as both a community designation and a personally appropriated and assigned identity, took shape for the "in-between" people on the contingent and unstable borders between racial and ethnic communities and identities. Paul Ricoeur has written that the self achieves identity and meaning through the detour to the other, a process of meaning-making that is dialectical and works through negotiation and relationship.[54] Borrowing this language for the purposes of the study of urban cultures, ethnic groups in American cities defined themselves through a detour to the neighborhood of the dark-skinned other (which was often as close as the next block).[55] As Italian immigrants began the process of telling a story about themselves in their new environment in relation to the people around them, they drew on local idioms inflected by racial preoccupations and fears. So they learned to talk about themselves as Americans, because on a fundamental level, "Italian American" means "not them." This attitude hardened over time in Harlem, one expression of the wider strategy of self-constitution through the exclusion of the dark-skinned other in which all the peoples of Harlem participated.

In their studies of Italian American enclaves in transitional years, both Suttles and Rieder have noted the importance of a certain kind of shared storytelling in urban ethnic communities. Because of the flux and heterogeneity of their worlds, city folk create a sense of moral order for themselves by anchoring the flow of their everyday lives in an ongoing, mutually constructed narrative. Urban folk become, in Rieder's words, "archeologists of the moral life," scanning their streets for "signs of vice and virtue,"[56] which are incorporated into the story they tell about themselves. This narrative is then mapped onto the landscape: it is safe here, our kind of people live there, we understand the codes in force here but not there. Conversation becomes cartography.

Community-constituting moral talk, furthermore, moves back and forth from the communal to the personal. The urban self is closely tied to the urban landscape. People in East Harlem (and other immigrant and migrant communities) identified themselves (and were identified by others) with their blocks, neighborhoods, and stoops. In the rounds of stories that city people tell about themselves, individual subjectivity is defined with reference to space, its qualities disclosed in the public theater of the neighborhoods and pressed into the landscape. During the days of Italian Harlem, to say of someone "He's from 106th Street" was to have said something substantive about the kind of person he was. A group of retired men, all from the same block in East Harlem, gather in the Bronx for periodic reunions today, calling themselves "the 106th Street Gang."

This means that the boundary-marking and meaning-making work of street religion is always both an inner process and a street performance, a psychological struggle as well as a neighborhood contest, because the boundaries of urban communities and urban selves are both so porous and so interconnected. The cartographical practices of street religion and sidewalk moral discourse in East Harlem always included two overlapping domains: first of all, the immigrants and their children had to map the meaning of their own identities and places in American society, and this mapping most often took place in relation to the proximate dark-skinned other.

This is what accounts for the terror and rage with which the arrival of the "so-called Puerto Ricans" was greeted in Harlem in the traumatic and contradictory years after World War II. Older Italians, many of them immigrants, watching their children betray the local codes of domestic fidelity by moving away, were brought face to face with the intimate costs of success in America. The neighborhoods were breaking up. The old maps were becoming irrelevant. The result was a local sense of crisis. As Rieder says of the similar situation that Brooklyn's Italians went through some years later, Italian Americans viewed the passing of their old neighborhoods as "the epic event in the history of recent time and space."[57] In Harlem, as in other Italian American communities around the country after the war, the first appearance of the dark-skinned other was taken as a sign of cultural doom. The struggle took on cosmic resonance against enemies threatening the world, even though these were not the real enemies.[58]

Harlem's Italians responded by securing their boundaries against the dark-skinned newcomers, who were too much like them for comfort, while incorporating them into an overarching narrative that held them responsible for the demise of the community. There were two distinctly religious purposes or dimensions to this story. First, it was, a scapegoating exorcism:

by personalizing the social forces converging to bring about Italian Harlem's end, blaming the "so-called Puerto Ricans," Harlem's Italians were denying the real causes of the community's end and their own, perhaps inevitable, complicity in it. Puerto Ricans did not ruin *cara* Harlem; they were assigned the bitter task of being responsible for it.[59] Second, the narrative was a theodicy, a story that endeavored to make sense of the great change, to account for the decisions to leave, to respond to the genuine sorrow people felt at the passing of a once-thriving Italian world, and to repair the fragmenting moral order. The denial of Puerto Rican subjectivity may be read as a way of reestablishing Italian American meaning in a transitional time. By means of a narrative inversion of what was actually happening on the streets, Puerto Rican subjectivity was diminished in the hope of reconstituting the Italian American neighborhood. The strategy of alterity became in this way Italian Harlem's last stand.

The feast and figure of Our Lady of Mount Carmel had always been the pivot of Italian Harlem's most important stories about itself, and it was around them now that difference and exclusion were narrated and performed and a story about the meaning of the passing of the old world communally spoken. This was not the only site of such discursive practice, of course, which also proceeded in social clubs, taverns, and living rooms in Harlem and outside. But it was through these tales of the Puerto Rican absence from the *festa*, their disrespect for the Madonna and her house, their vampirish impulses and sacred looting, that the cosmic dimension of loss and threat was expressed. And it was through the denial of Puerto Rican subjectivity that some transitional meaning was found for "Italian American," even if this meant only a people set upon by dark-skinned outsiders.[60]

Richard Alba points out in *Ethnic Identity*, his study of contemporary white ethnics in the United States, that for the grandchildren (and great-grandchildren) of immigrants, ethnic identity remains "frequently in the background and [emerges] most forcefully under special circumstances, such as the challenge of competition over residential turf and jobs with nonwhites, Hispanics, and recent immigrants."[61] But the history of Italian Harlem suggests that this has always been the case, and the Italian Americans' engagement there with Puerto Ricans teaches that this contemporary practice of ethnic self-constitution is situated in a larger narrative collectively crafted in response to the breakup of the old enclaves. Ethnic claims in the years after the war bear within them this mythology of loss and exile, as well as the memory of a fight to the death with the dark-skinned other. Understanding this history may shed some additional light on the situation and motivations of contemporary white ethnics struggling with further changes and transitions.

Urban narratives are not purely functional, as Suttles suggests; nor are they primarily elaborations of popular morality, as Rieder treats them. Instead, this kind of creative activity has both conscious and unconscious dimensions. The engagement of different races on city streets is as much a matter of fantasy as fact.[62] The "facts" that street lore organizes into a moral narrative are worked out of fear, desire, guilt, and hope: the narrative built with them is susceptible not only to ideologically motivated distortion but also to repression, denial, displacement. Among Italian Americans, the struggle against in-betweenness has generated costly narrative strategies of denial (of particular aspects of Italian American history, for example, as well as of the proximity of the dark-skinned other in that history), projection (holding the dark-skinned other responsible for social forces that threatened the community), and disassociation.

But it is not simply that street religion *excludes* the other, as the example of the Haitians at the *festa* shows. Rather, urban street religion is one of the privileged sites at which different peoples with a variety of complexions encounter each other and enact their understandings of themselves in relation to the other, in ritual and story, for themselves and others to see and hear, over the changing moments of their histories. This is why violence is so often dreaded at such events, even though it erupts less frequently than it is feared. People understand that these public religious occasions are times of conflict and contestation, when the world and one's place in it are played out in the streets.

The Greenhorn and the Black Man Again

What was the greenhorn doing, then, rubbing a black man's skin, and why is this story so often told by the greenhorn's American relatives?

The story functions on several levels. It records a community memory of uncertainty, and perhaps unease, with the newly encountered other within the standard tropes of the tales of the maladroit greenhorn. The black man seems to represent all that is strange and unnerving about the new world. But at the same time, there is no fear or hostility in the story. The immigrant, with the greenhorn's typical naïve insouciance, can go over and actually touch the stranger in the street, the way a child reaches out to feel something interesting. This is the innocence of greenhorn time, a transitional moment when the immigrants suddenly found themselves between cultures, with the old codes irrelevant, the new ones as yet unlearned.[63]

But the discursive power of the myth arises in the disjuncture between the innocence of the moment it records and the time of its narration, and here the main register is ironic. The poor fool in the story believed that underneath the startling exterior, the black man will be the same as everyone else—the gesture of rubbing, which only a greenhorn would attempt on a city street, assumes or expects an identity beneath the difference. The narrator, however, and his or her listeners know better: the irony of the tale marks the distance Italian Americans have traveled since greenhorn time. The speaker and his or her hearers know the score. They know that black skin is not white skin, and they know this because they are not greenhorns anymore, but "Italian Americans."

The sorrow of the story, of course, is that it also discloses a peculiarly American loss of innocence. When I first began studying the devotion to *la Madonna del Carmine* in East Harlem, I was eager to find out if the *festa* had ever served as a meeting ground for the two Latin peoples who shared the same neighborhood. This was a greenhorn's question. I wanted to think that a popular religious celebration in a troubled, ethnically hetero-geneous, economically marginal, inner-city neighborhood could be a site of solidarity and unity for the various peoples in the neighborhood, per-haps even the focal point for popular local political initiatives. This was a greenhorn's hope.

Nevertheless, others have shared the same sorrow and the same hope. In 1938, at a time of some tension in Harlem between Italian Americans and Puerto Ricans, a Puerto Rican boy was run down by a truck in the neighborhood. Leonard Covello used the occasion to try to ease some of the local hostilities. In an open letter to his students, Covello described the great sorrow of the young man's mother and grandmother. Then he moved from this evocation of the *pietà*, which he knew would resonate with some of the Italian American community's deepest feelings, to a plea for neighborhood harmony. "Let us strive," Covello wrote his students and their parents, "to live on a family basis with all our neigh-bors—remembering that the gesture of sympathy is more noble than the gesture of hate."[64] Covello was using here a language rooted in the popular religious traditions of southern Italy—which included a high valuation of the place of the family in human experience—in an effort to build some ties between Italians and their new Puerto Rican neighbors.

Covello knew from his own experience at Benjamin Franklin that urban boundaries are porous and that the people of these neighborhoods do interact and encounter each other, as urban sociologists have been insisting for years.[65] In the intersection of different cultures on the urban landscape, new and interesting cultural forms have taken shape. "Goatee Rock," for example, represented the fusion of black rock-and-roll and blues idioms with the romantic melodies of southern Italy.[66] In contemporary Brooklyn Italian neighborhoods, groups of young men known as "B-boys," for "black boys," imitate the styles and mannerisms of their African American neighbors. African American clothing fashions in this century have drawn on elegant Italian couture, and there are now Italian American rappers.

During the July celebrations in Harlem, Haitian and Italian women wash each other's faces with wet cloths; an Italian band plays the Haitian national song; Haitian pilgrims sing Italian hymns that the grandchildren of the immigrants never learned; and Italians say they are moved by Haitian piety, while Puerto Ricans who live in the Madonna's neighborhood but were kept out of her home ignore her as she passes. Urban street religion generally, and the *festa* of the Madonna of 115th Street in particular, cannot be simply cast as the site either of racist exclusion or of solidarity and community in the inner city. It was, rather, the place where the dilemmas and dangers of in-betweenness in the complex circumstances of American city life were encountered, explored, enacted, and narrated.

Notes

Reprinted, with revisions, from *American Quarterly* 44, no. 3 (September 1992). Copyright 1992 American Studies Association.

1. I have been told this story, always with the same details, by many different people in Italian American communities around the country, and I am confident in identifying it as one of this culture's fundamental moral tales. Following Bruce Lincoln's typology, I call it a "myth," which is identified by Lincoln as a story that possesses both "credibility and authority" and has the status of "paradigmatic truth." Bruce Lincoln, *Discourse and the Construction of Society: Comparative Studies of Myth, Ritual, and Classification* (New York and Oxford: Oxford University Press, 1989), 24–25.

2. John Higham, *Strangers in the Land: Patterns of American Nativism, 1860–1925* (New York: Atheneum, 1977), 169. On the subject of Italian American "in-betweenness" in the southern and central United States, see Ernesto Milani, "Marchigiani and Veneti on Sunny Side Plantation," *Italian Immigrants in Rural and Small Town America,* ed. Rudolph Vecoli (Staten Island: American Italian Historical Association, 1987), 18–30. For more general comments on the subject, see Alexander DeConde, *Half Bitter, Half Sweet: An Excursion into Italian-American History* (New York: Scribner, 1971), 102–103. Richard Alba refers to this as the "problematic racial position" of southern Italian immigrants in *Italian Americans: Into the Twilight of Ethnicity* (Englewood Cliffs, N.J.: Prentice-Hall, 1985), 68. Many black southerners shared these anxieties and prejudices, but for slightly different reasons. Booker T. Washington, for example, warned that the immigrants posed "a racial problem . . . more difficult and dangerous than the one which is caused by the presence of the Negro." Quoted in Higham, *Strangers in the Land,* 169. Washington's anti-Italian sentiments were motivated in part by the fear, not completely mistaken, that whites were attempting to replace black agricultural laborers with immigrants. See Arnold Shankman, "The Image of the Italian in the Afro-American Press," *Italian Americana* 4 (Fall/Winter 1978): 30–49; Patrick Gallo, *Old Bread, New Wine: A Portrait of the*

Italian-Americans (Chicago: Nelson-Hall, 1981), 113, 116. Shankman notes that it was not clear until around 1900 that Italian immigrants would not displace blacks in southern agriculture (34).

3. Higham discuses the incident at Tallulah in *Strangers in the Land*, 169–71. See also Paul Giordano, "The Italians of Louisiana: Their Cultural Background and Their Many Contributions in the Fields of Literature, the Arts, Education, Politics, and Business and Labor" (Ph.D. dissertation, Indiana University, 1978), 70–71. Commenting on relations between the first Sicilian immigrants in Louisiana and local African Americans, Richard Gambino notes, "Coming from a land which had absorbed wave after wave of alien cultures and peoples over three thousand years, including two centuries of Arab rule, and where statues of black skinned Madonnas were found in old churches, the Sicilians were tolerant" of and "even friendly" with blacks. Gambino, *Vendetta: A True Story of the Worst Lynching in America, the Mass Murder of Italian-Americans in New Orleans in 1891, the Vicious Motivations behind It, and the Tragic Repercussions That Linger to This Day* (Garden City, N.Y.: Doubleday, 1977), 56–57. Called "black dagoes" in Louisiana, the immigrants were listed on separate payroll lists, "neither white nor black." On the Mississippi campaigns, see DeConde, *Half Bitter, Half Sweet*, 125.

4. See Jack D. Forbes, "The Manipulation of Race, Caste, and Identity: Classifying Afroamericans, Native Americans, and Red-Black People," *Journal of Ethnic Studies* 17 (Winter 1990): 1–51.

5. I have discussed some dimensions of popular racist discourse in contemporary Italy in "Forte, nera, e potente: il discorso razzista nella cultura di massa italiana," *I giorni cantati: culture popolari e culture di massa* 1 (January–March 1987): 27–30.

6. Edward A. Ross, "Italians in America," *Century Magazine* 87 (July 1914): 443–45. For the broader context of thought, see R. Jackson Wilson, *In Quest of Community: Social Philosophy in the United States, 1860–1920* (New York: Wiley, 1968).

7. Leonard Covello notes in his study of Harlem's Italians that initial American commentary on the new immigration maintained that southern Italians were biologically different from northern Italians, almost a different species. Covello, *The Social Background of the Italo-American School Child: A Study of the Southern Italian Family Mores and Their Effect on the School Situation in Italy and America* (Leiden: E. J. Brill, 1967), 19–22. See also Salvatore LaGumina, comp., ed., *Wop: A Documentary History of Anti-Italian Discrimination in the United States* (San Francisco: Straight Arrow, 1973), 52–71, 137–38, 148–53; Gallo, *Old Bread, New Wine*, 107–49; DeConde, *Half Bitter, Half Sweet*, 99f.; and John Andreozzi, "Italian Farmers in Cumberland," in Vecoli, *Italian Immigrants in Rural and Small Town America*, 110–25. On the severity of American prejudice against southern Italians, see Virginia Yans-McLaughlin, *Family and Community: Italian Immigrants in Buffalo, 1880–1930* (Ithaca: Cornell University Press, 1971), 112–17, and Richard Gambino, *Blood of My Blood: The Dilemma of the Italian-Americans* (Garden City, N.Y.: Doubleday, 1974), 103–12. For Henry Cabot Lodge's distinction, see Gallo, *Old Bread, New Wine*, 121.

8. See, for example, Leonard Covello, *The Heart Is the Teacher* (New York: McGraw-Hill, 1958); Constantine M. Panunzio, *The Soul of an Immigrant* (New York: Macmillan, 1921); and Garibaldi M. Lapolla, *The Fire in the Flesh: A Novel* (New York: Vanguard Press, 1931) and *The Grand Gennaro* (New York: Vanguard Press, 1935). The latter two are autobiographical novels.

9. This is discussed in William M. DeMarco, *Ethnics and Enclaves: Boston's Italian North End* (Ann Arbor: UMI Research Press, 1981), 35–36.

10. Leonard Dinnerstein and David M. Reimers, *Ethnic Americans: A History of*

Immigration and Assimilation (New York: Harper and Row, 1982), 36. See also Micaela di Leonardo, *The Varieties of Ethnic Experience: Kinship, Class, and Gender among California Italian-Americans* (Ithaca: Cornell University Press, 1984), 24, n.16. Di Leonardo refers to the "racist oppression" of Italian immigrants in the late nineteenth and early twentieth centuries. Yans-McLaughlin notes that disturbances among "swarthy" Italians in Buffalo in 1907 were classified by local authorities as racial trouble; *Family and Community*, 113–14.

11. Rudolph Vecoli, "Prelates and Peasants: Italian Immigration and the Catholic Church," *Journal of Social History* 2 (Spring 1969): 217–68.

12. John Horace Mariano, *The Second Generation of Italians in New York City* (Boston: Christopher, 1921), 88, 105–10.

13. Rev. Aurelio Palmieri, "The Contribution of the Italian Catholic Clergy to the United States," in *Catholic Builders of the Nation: A Symposium on the Catholic Contribution to the Civilization of the United States* (Boston: Continental, 1923), vol. 2, 145. See also John V. Tolino, "Solving the Italian Problem," *Ecclesiastical Review* 99 (September 1938): 246–56; Albert R. Bandini, "Concerning the Italian Problem," *Ecclesiastical Review* 62 (March 1920): 278–85; John Zarrilli, "Some More Light on the Italian Problem," *Ecclesiastical Review* 79 (September 1928): 256–68; Gabriel A. Zema, "The Italian Immigrant Problem," *America* 55 (May 16, 1936): 129–30; John V. Tolino, "The Priest in the Italian Problem," *Ecclesiastical Review* 109 (November 1943): 321–30.

14. This trajectory is analyzed in a number of recent publications on the "new immigration," including Alejandro Portes and Rubén G. Rumbaut, *Immigrant America: A Portrait* (Berkeley and Los Angeles: University of California Press, 1990); Lawrence H. Fuchs, *The American Kaleidoscope: Race, Ethnicity, and the Civic Culture* (Hanover, N.H.: Wesleyan University Press, 1990), and Mary C. Waters, *Ethnic Options: Choosing Identities in America* (Berkeley and Los Angeles: University of California Press, 1990). It is also helpfully discussed by di Leonardo in *Varieties of Ethnic Experience*, 24. Eric Wolf sets immigration to the United States at the turn of the century in the context of a worldwide movement of peoples from agricultural areas to industrial centers, in Eric Robert Wolf, *Europe and the People without History* (Berkeley and Los Angeles: University of California Press, 1982), 354–83. On early Italian American work patterns in this global perspective, see Alba, *Italian Americans*, 51–55.

15. The use of "peoples" here should not obscure the fact that both "communities" were internally complex and heterogeneous, divided along fissures of class, regions of origin, generations, and color.

16. Shankman, "Image of the Italian in the Afro-American Press," 30–31.

17. My understanding of postwar relations between African and Italian Americans has been shaped by Jonathan Rieder, *Canarsie: The Jews and Italians of Brooklyn against Liberalism* (Cambridge, Mass.: Harvard University Press, 1985); Gerald D. Suttles, *The Social Order of the Slum: Ethnicity and Territory in the Inner City* (Chicago: University of Chicago Press, 1968); and Jim Sleeper, *The Closest of Strangers: Liberalism and the Politics of Race in New York* (New York: W. W. Norton, 1990). See also Robert C. Freeman, "The Maintenance of New York City's Italian-American Neighborhoods," in *The Melting Pot and Beyond: Italian Americans in the Year 2000*, ed. Jerome Krase and William Egelman (Staten Island: American Italian Historical Association, 1987), 223–37, and the papers in Pat Gallo, ed., *The Urban Experience of Italian-Americans* (Staten Island: American Italian Historical Association, 1977). On the postwar migration from the South, see Nicholas Lemann, *The Promised Land: The*

Great Black Migration and How It Changed America (New York: A. A. Knopf, 1991). Specific local studies of black and Italian engagement are cited below.

18. The one area of the country for which this general history is not relevant is California. See di Leonardo, *Varieties of Ethnic Experience.*

19. Gary Ross Mormino, *Immigrants on the Hill: Italian-Americans in Saint Louis, 1882–1982* (Urbana: University of Illinois Press, 1986); Donald Tricarico, *The Italians of Greenwich Village: The Social Structure and Transformation of an Ethnic Community* (Staten Island: Center for Migration Studies of New York, 1984); Adria Bernardi, *Houses with Names: The Italian Immigrants of Highwood, Illinois* (Urbana: University of Illinois Press, 1990); and Shankman, "Image of the Italian in the Afro-American Press."

20. George E. Cunningham, "The Italian: A Hindrance to White Solidarity in Louisiana, 1890–1898," *Journal of Negro History* 50 (January 1965): 23–35.

21. Suttles, *Social Order,* 34; di Leonardo, *Varieties of Ethnic Experience,* 100–101; see also Susan Olzack, "Causes of Ethnic Conflict and Protest in Urban America, 1877–1889," *Social Science Research* 16 (1987): 185–210.

22. Alba, *Italian Americans,* 68.

23. DeConde, *Half Bitter, Half Sweet,* 98.

24. Suttles, *Social Order,* 37.

25. This is an explicit theme in Suttles, *Social Order.* Rieder also refers to the care with which urban residents scan the "visual landscape" for clues to the meaning of other communities; *Canarsie,* 60ff.

26. Di Leonardo, *Varieties of Ethnic Experience,* 177; Rieder, *Canarsie,* 32.

27. For a fuller history of this community, see Robert A. Orsi, *The Madonna of 115th Street: Faith and Community in Italian Harlem, 1880–1950* (New Haven: Yale University Press, 1985), 14–49.

28. On the early history of Harlem, see Gilbert Osofsky, *Harlem: The Making of a Ghetto—Negro New York, 1890–1930* (New York: Harper and Row, 1971); James Weldon Johnson, *Black Manhattan* (1930; reprint, New York: Arno, 1977); David Levering Lewis, *When Harlem Was in Vogue* (New York: Vintage, 1982); Jervis Anderson, *This Was Harlem: A Cultural Portrait, 1900–1950* (New York: Farrar Straus Giroux, 1982).

29. Piri Thomas, *Down These Mean Streets* (1967; reprint, New York: Vintage, 1974), 26.

30. On the ideational dimension of geography, see Yi-Fu Tuan, *Topophilia: A Study of Environmental Perception, Attitudes, and Values* (New York: Columbia University Press, 1990), 173ff.

31. On Harlem as the playground of the white id in the 1920s, the creation of white need and fantasy, see Nathan Irvin Huggins, *Harlem Renaissance* (New York: Oxford University Press, 1971), 11, 84ff., and Malcolm Cowley, *Exile's Return: A Literary Odyssey of the 1920s* (New York: Viking, 1951), 237.

32. *Time,* November 4, 1946.

33. The clearest expression of this conflict can be found in Claude Brown, *Manchild in the Promised Land* (New York: New American Library, 1965), 167, 291.

34. Thomas, *Mean Streets,* 127–37.

35. Ibid., 319.

36. See Orsi, *The Madonna of 115th Street,* 50–74.

37. My thinking on the way ethnicity takes shape along the borders between groups and in specific situations of conflict has been influenced by Frederick Barth, ed., *Ethnic Groups and Boundaries: The Social Organization of Cultural Difference* (Bos-

ton: Little, Brown, 1969); Michael Moerman, "Ethnic Identification in a Complex Civilization: Who Are the Lue?" *American Anthropologist* 67 (1964); Anya Peterson Royce, *Ethnic Identity: Strategies of Diversity* (Bloomington: Indiana University Press, 1982); Werner Sollors, ed., *The Invention of Ethnicity* (New York: Oxford University Press, 1989); and Manning Nash, *The Cauldron of Ethnicity in the Modern World* (Chicago: University of Chicago Press, 1989). This understanding of ethnicity is now widely accepted. Recently, in the study specifically of American ethnic groups, there has been an emphasis on the "symbolic" and voluntary character of ethnic identity and self-ascription. See, for example, Peter K. Eisinger, "Ethnicity as a Strategic Option: An Emerging View," *Public Administration Review* (January/February 1978); William Yancey, Eugene Eriksen, and Richard Juliani, "Emergent Ethnicity: A Review and Reformulation," *American Sociological Review* 41 (June 1976); Don Handelman, "The Organization of Ethnicity," *Ethnic Groups* 1 (February 1977); and Herbert J. Gans, "Symbolic Ethnicity: The Future of Ethnic Groups and Cultures in America," *Ethnic and Racial Studies* 2 (January 1979).

38. See Orsi, *The Madonna of 115th Street*, 43, 182.

39. On the heterogeneity of Italian enclaves in the United States, see Humbert S. Nelli, *From Immigrants to Ethnics: The Italian Americans* (New York: Oxford University Press, 1983), 61, and John W. Briggs, *An Italian Passage: Immigrants to Three American Cities, 1890–1930* (New Haven: Yale University Press, 1978), 118–19.

40. There is, unfortunately, no comprehensive social or cultural history of Spanish Harlem (and no history of the transitional period when Italian Harlem was giving way to el barrio). I have learned from Patricia Cayo Sexton, *Spanish Harlem: An Anatomy of Poverty* (New York: Harper and Row, 1966); Dan Wakefield, *Island in the City: The World of Spanish Harlem* (Boston: Houghton Mifflin, 1959); Edward Rivera, *Family Installments: Memories of Growing Up Hispanic* (New York: Morrow, 1982); and Joseph Fitzpatrick. S.J., *Puerto Rican Americans: The Meaning of Migration to the Homeland* (Englewood Cliffs, N.J.: Prentice-Hall, 1971). Italian Americans undertook a similar process of differentiation from Mexican Americans. See Valentine J. Belfiglio, "Italians in Small Town and Rural Texas," in Vecoli, *Italian Immigrants in Rural and Small Town America*, 31–49.

41. Ellen Lurie, "Community Action in East Harlem," in *The Urban Condition: People and Policy in the Metropolis*, ed. Leonard J. Duhl (New York: Simon and Schuster, 1963), 246–58.

42. For this moment in the history of Italian Harlem, see Robert A. Orsi, "'Southern Italy' in the Memories of the Immigrants and the Lives of Their Children in Italian Harlem," *Journal of Family History* 15 (April 1990): 133–48.

43. Thomas, *Mean Streets*, 27.

44. My discussion here of discrimination against Puerto Ricans and of Puerto Rican racial attitudes relies on Nancy A. Denton and Douglas S. Massey, "Racial Identity among Caribbean Hispanics: The Effect of Double Minority Status on Residential Segregation," *American Sociological Review* 54 (October 1989): 790–808; Angela Jorge, "The Black Puerto Rican Woman in Contemporary American Society," in *The Puerto Rican Woman: Perspectives on Culture, History, and Society*, ed. Edna Acosta-Belen (New York: Praeger, 1986), 180–87; Maxine W. Gordon, "Race Patterns and Prejudice in Puerto Rico," *American Sociological Review* 14 (April 1949): 294–301. The information about racist denigration of the newcomers is from Nicholasa Mohr's autobiographical novel, *Nilda* (New York: Harper and Row, 1973), 89–90.

45. Denton and Massey, "Racial Identity among Caribbean Hispanics," 792–94. The information about skin whiteners comes from Mohr, *Nilda*, 99.

46. Gordon, "Race Patterns and Prejudice in Puerto Rico," 296.

47. A word about my relation to this man: By the time we had this conversation, he and I had spent many hours at his workplace talking about his family's history and his own coming of age on the streets of Harlem. I had been introduced to him by mutual friends, and we were able to establish a nice rapport. It was after several visits to his workplace over a number of weeks that the reported conversation occurred; by this time I had also read and studied his autobiography.

48. On Vito Marcantonio's political career in the wider context of the culture of Italian Harlem, see Gerald Meyer, *Vito Marcantonio: Radical Politician, 1902–1954* (Albany: SUNY Press, 1989).

49. See Orsi, *The Madonna of 115th Street*, 75–106.

50. This story was told to Karen McCarthy Brown at Drew University by a Puerto Rican graduate student from East Harlem.

51. On the Haitian community, see Karen McCarthy Brown, *Mama Lola: A Vodou Priestess in Brooklyn* (Berkeley and Los Angeles: University of California Press, 1991); for an excellent study of Haitian participation in the devotion, see Elizabeth McAlister, "The Madonna of 115th Street Revisited: Vodou and Haitian Catholicism in the Age of Transnationalism," in R. Stephen Warner and Judith G. Wittner, *Gatherings in Diaspora: Religious Communities and the New Immigration* (Philadelphia: Temple University Press, 1998), 123–60.

52. Shankman, "Image of the Italian in the Afro-American Press," 40.

53. Di Leonardo uses this phrase to describe the "self-contradictory" understandings of African Americans she found among the Italian Americans she spoke to on the West Coast; *Varieties of Ethnic Experience*, 175.

54. Paul Ricoeur, "What Is a Text?" in Ricoeur, *Hermeneutics and the Human Sciences: Essays on Language, Action, and Interpretation*, ed., trans., and with an introduction by John B. Thompson (New York: Cambridge University Press, 1981), 158.

55. Monsignor Gino Baroni, who founded Catholic University's Center for Urban Ethnic Affairs in 1971, once observed that a fundamental characteristic of "white ethnics" was that of all white Americans, they lived closest to blacks and Hispanics in the old industrial belt. Quoted in Perry L. Weed, *The White Ethnic Movement and Ethnic Politics* (New York: Praeger, 1973), 18.

56. Rieder, *Canarsie*, 61.

57. Ibid., 92.

58. See Tricarico, *The Italians of Greenwich Village*, 160; Mormino, *Immigrants on the Hill*, 239; Peter A. Peroni, *The Burg: An Italian-American Community at Bay in Trenton* (Washington, D.C.: University Press of America, 1979), 113ff. Salvatore J. LaGumina, on the other hand, focuses more on the way blacks and Italians on Long Island in the 1960s and 1970s negotiated some local peace; *From Steerage to Suburb: Long Island Italians* (New York: Center for Migration Studies, 1988), 203ff.

59. Rieder uses the word "exorcism" to describe the stories Brooklyn's Italians tell, too; *Canarsie*, 58.

60. Rieder makes a similar point about Brooklyn's Italians later in the century. He says that in response to the perceived threat of the encroachment of blacks and Hispanics in their neighborhoods, Italian Americans adopt the "identity of the injured," presenting themselves as victims; *Canarsie*, 96.

61. Richard D. Alba, *Ethnic Identity: The Transformation of White America* (New Haven: Yale University Press, 1990), 313–14. For a similar argument, see Waters, *Ethnic Options*, 156. Waters writes, "The implicit and sometimes explicit comparison

for [the construction of] this symbolic ethnicity has been the social reality of racial and ethnic identities of America's minority groups."

62. See, for example, Louis Harris and Bert E. Swanson, *Black-Jewish Relations in New York City* (New York: Praeger, 1970); Paul B. Sheatsley, "White Attitudes towards the Negro," in *The Negro American*, ed. Talcott Parsons and Kenneth B. Clark (Boston: Houghton Mifflin, 1966); Reynolds Farley, Howard Schuman, Suzanne Bianchi, Diane Colasanto, and Shirley Hatchett, " 'Chocolate City, Vanilla Suburbs': Will the Trend toward Racially Separate Communities Continue?" *Social Science Research* 7 (December 1978): 319–44.

63. We can also see now that the myth of the greenhorn and the black man inscribes memories of a time of real solidarity and cooperation between the immigrants and African Americans. A variant of the myth describes how in the early days in factories or mines, only blacks came to the assistance of disoriented and harassed immigrant laborers, showing them the ropes and helping them complete the impossible tasks assigned them by cruel bosses. See di Leonardo, *Varieties of Ethnic Experience*, 76.

64. Cited in Orsi, *The Madonna of 115th Street*, 88–89.

65. Sociologists have long debated whether interracial contact in the urban setting results in greater tolerance and integration. The literature on this question is huge, but see McKee J. McClendon, "Interracial Contact and the Reduction of Prejudice," *Sociological Forces* 7 (Fall 1974): 47–64; Claude S. Fischer, "Toward a Subcultural Theory of Urbanism," *American Journal of Sociology* 80 (1974): 1319–41; Thomas C. Wilson, "Urbanism and Racial Attitudes: A Test of Some Urban Theories," *Urban Affairs Quarterly* 20 (December 1984): 201–209; Steven A. Tuch, "Urbanism, Region, and Tolerance Revisited: The Case of Racial Prejudice," *American Sociological Review* 52 (August 1987): 504–10; Thomas C. Wilson, "Urbanism, Migration, and Tolerance: A Reassessment," *American Sociological Review* 56 (February 1991): 117–23. The debate was initiated by Louis Wirth's claim that city life did make for tolerance and mutual acceptance, but at the cost of personal anomie, in "Urbanism as a Way of Life," *American Journal of Sociology* 44 (July 1938): 1–24; it was stimulated anew by Herbert Gans's argument that urban ecology by itself could not account for attitudinal differences; see "Urbanism and Suburbanism as Ways of Life: A Reevaluation of Definitions," in *Human Behavior and Social Processes: An Interactionist Approach*, ed. Arnold M. Rose (Boston: Houghton Mifflin, 1962), 625–48. Widespread dissatisfaction among researchers on this question has lately provoked a reexamination of method. Farley et al., in " 'Chocolate City, Vanilla Suburbs,' " admit to frustration with the survey as a research tool; Olzack, in "Causes of Ethnic Conflict," calls for a historical approach to the question. What I have argued here is that "contact" is always mediated by narrative; there is no interracial engagement apart from the rounds of storytelling through which city folk constitute the meaning of their experience, or innocent of the needs and motivations that occasion such practices. The plot of these narratives obviously varies at different times in a community's history, and, a further complexity, the conscious narrative — what people say about the other — is crosscut by unconscious issues. I think attention to these inner-city narrative practices would help break the impasse that now grips the debate over "urbanism" and tolerance.

66. The term "goatee rock" is from "Heroes of Goatee Rock," *Musician* (December 1990): 114. My interest in Italo-American rock-and-roll as one of the points of intersection of black American and Italian American cultures originated in conversations with Beth Harrington and Joe Sciorra, two sympathetic and knowledgeable students of the music.

Heritage, Ritual, and Translation

Seattle's Japanese Presbyterian Church

Madeline Duntley

City skyscrapers and interstate highways loom behind the façade of Seattle's Japanese Presbyterian Church. Thirty years ago, the old church building was demolished to make room for a freeway, and the new Japanese-style sanctuary was erected near Rainier Avenue, where dilapidated storefront businesses, ugly telephone poles and wires, and garish, ill-repaired neon signs contrast sharply with the church's prim and balanced Asian architecture. Yet the design of Japanese Presbyterian Church [hereafter JPC] is appropriate to its location in Rainier Valley, an inner-city neighborhood known for its high density of ethnic Asians. In Seattle, "Asian" includes Chinese, Filipino, Hawaiian, Japanese, Asian Indian, Korean, Samoan, Vietnamese, Cambodian, Hmong, Laotian, Mien, and Thai ancestry—all contributing to the dazzling cultural milieu of a city where seventy-five different languages are spoken.[1] A mile from the church is the International District—Seattle's one-time "Japantown" and "Chinatown," now the cultural center of the city's Asian-Pacific American community. Because JPC's congregation embodies considerable generational, ethnic, and theological diversity, typical social science categories of race, ethnicity, and generation do not describe or define this church's communal identity. It is not simply an ethnic "voluntary association" in which members seek culturally uniform social networks. Instead, JPC has forged a sense of corporate identity through rituals such as commemorative worship gatherings.[2] These events celebrate JPC's diversity and translate its history as a Japanese American mission church in a way that is meaningful to its multicultural, multilingual congregation. The creative use of heritage, ritual, and translation allows JPC to define its communal boundaries and bonds in terms of Christian faith, not ethnic ties.[3]

Author's Note: The Japanese Presbyterian Church has experienced a number of changes over the past few years. This chapter was written in 1994; thus it reflects the staff and situation of the church at that time.

JPC defies categorization in many ways. It is inappropriate to classify it as an "immigrant" church, for the congregation was founded in 1907, and its membership ranges from first- to fifth-generation Americans. Neither should it be studied as a "neighborhood" church. Even though JPC is in a vicinity which is 36 percent Asian American,[4] nearly two-thirds of its members commute from suburbs and other neighborhoods in the city. So while it is an "urban" church, it has a largely "suburban" membership. Yet JPC takes its role and identity as an inner-city church quite seriously. This congregation was founded to serve the practical and spiritual needs of inner-city Seattle's Japanese immigrants and their families. This mission heritage is evident in JPC activities today. A high proportion of the members serve the church's local urban neighborhood through mission outreach to Southeast Asian Mien immigrants, the children of the surrounding communities, the homeless, and the elderly. Even though it retains the name "Japanese Presbyterian," the church sees itself as multicultural, multigenerational, and multilingual. To visit JPC is to know that there are many members who are not Nikkei (people of Japanese ancestry).[5] About 10 percent of the membership are Chinese American, 2 percent are Korean American, and about 8 percent are either Caucasian, interracial families, or people from other ethnic or Asian groups.[6]

Despite JPC's increasing ethnic diversity, its identity as a historically Japanese American church remains important to this religious community. Even young children are familiar with the story of the church's origins, and each year in June, Founders' Day is celebrated to honor the two men who established JPC. The church marks every five-year anniversary with a series of commemorative events, including a memorial service at the founders' gravesites, an all-church retreat, a catered afternoon dinner program, and a special worship service. These celebrations all serve to "translate" the past into the living memory of the present congregation.

The history of JPC begins in the 1880s, when Seattle was little more than a lumber settlement with a small clustering of hotels, bars, and shops. When the first handful of Japanese immigrants arrived in 1883, the total population of the frontier town was about 3,000. Immigration from Japan increased steadily, from 125 in 1890 to 3,000 at the turn of the century.[7] Although the first settlers were working-class men planning to make their fortunes in America and then return to Japan, by 1907 the so-called Gentlemen's Agreement, intended to halt the influx of Japanese immigrant laborers to the West Coast, changed the nature and focus of Japanese immigration. After this date, the Japanese government agreed to issue passports only to nonlaborers seeking "to resume a formerly acquired domicile, to join a parent, wife, or children residing there, or to assume active control of an already possessed interest in a farming enterprise."[8] As women, children, and parents emigrated, Seattle's Japanese community became more family-centered, and its population grew to approximately 6,000 in 1910.[9]

Churches near the International District saw new opportunities for Christian mission work in the Japanese community. It is no coincidence that JPC was founded in 1907—the same year the Gentlemen's Agreement took effect. Two years earlier, Dr. Mark A. Matthews, pastor of Seattle's First Presbyterian Church, had met the Reverend Orio Inouye, a Japanese Christian minister visiting the United States on a pledge drive for a church in Japan. The two began planning a Presbyterian mission program for Japanese immigrants and soon started mission Bible classes. This "Bible study" doubled as English-language instruction. The very origins of this church are thus rooted in the dual task of evangelization and "translation." As students learned how to translate from one language to another, the missionaries hoped that the curriculum would also "translate" or convey Christian culture and faith into the students' lives. The class eventually became so popular that the church published the lesson materials under the title A *Bible Primer for Foreigners*.[10] The Reverend Inouye decided to remain in the United States to work in this new mission and was installed by the Presbytery of Seattle as an assistant pastor of the First Presbyterian Church. JPC was organized as a mission branch of the First Presbyterian Church on June 1, 1907.

The JPC met on Sunday evenings in a rented Mission House for the first decade of its existence. It had an active Sunday school, a weeknight prayer meeting, and an operating budget of $1,700. All Japanese were welcome to join in the activities of the Mission House, even non-Christians. New converts joined the First Presbyterian Church in this early period, and by 1917 there were about eighty members. Plans were made to build a separate church for the congregation. JPC's first facility opened in 1920 at 9th and Weller, in the heart of Seattle's International District.[11]

To trace the several residences and building campaigns of the JPC is, in a sense, to trace the history of the church itself. Before the building was constructed at 9th and Weller, JPC was indeed a "mission church," housed in temporary quarters and largely under the control of First Presbyterian Church. But after the permanent building was opened in 1920, JPC entered an initial phase of growth and identity as a Japanese ethnic church. For the next twenty years, Japanese speakers dominated the leadership; the English-language members were primarily the children and grandchildren of immigrants. In 1942, JPC was forced to relocate when all Seattle residents of Japanese descent were sent to the Minidoka internment camp in Hunt, Idaho. After the war, the Seattle Presbytery stalled the reopening of JPC, hoping that its members would "integrate" into other, largely white, congregations in the city.[12] This misguided policy caused the congregation considerable alarm and dismay, especially the Japanese speakers. JPC eventually won its fight to exist as a separate ethnic church, and in 1947 the members resumed worship at 9th and Weller. By this time the balance of power had shifted from the first-generation immigrants to their American-born adult children. JPC had to move once more in 1963, because the building was in the path of the proposed route for Seattle's new Interstate 5 freeway. The church left the International District but settled nearby in its present location, at 1801 24th Avenue South. As the old building was being demolished, JPC was laying the foundations for a new phase in its history.

The new church building had a far different character than its ivy-covered, brick-and-stained-glass predecessor. Parishioners wanted the architectural style not only to display the church's Japanese heritage but to reflect JPC's regional and Christian roots as well. The architect so successfully rendered the community's history and identity in stone and wood that he won a coveted national architectural award for the design.[13] JPC's exterior design is Pacific Northwest–style cedar shake architecture, with a Japanese-inspired flared roof and a prominent wooden cross. The interior of the sanctuary is windowless, simple, and meditative, paneled with *shoji*, white translucent paper screens reinforced with wooden latticework and rafters, reminiscent of *Shoin*-style Japanese architecture. Windows in the narthex look onto a center courtyard and a small Japanese garden, which also merges both Christian and Japanese heritages in a gentle invitation to meditate and "cultivate the beauty of one's inner being and soul." The building is, in the words of the Reverend Richard Nishioka (one of JPC's two pastors), "an American space with a Japanese flair."[14]

It would be misleading to draw too many inferences about this church's ethnicity from an analysis of its Japanese-inspired architecture, however. There are proportionately few parishioners in the church today who date their membership from the time of the original planning of the 1963 building; for most people currently worshiping at JPC, the space is "inherited." The aesthetics of the worship space is a legacy of congregational history, not a contemporary ethnic or political statement about Japanese American religious culture. The space itself, furthermore, is not static and unchanging. Each new decade of worshipers since 1963 has been able to contribute some significant addition or renovation to the church structure, refitting this architectural inheritance to better meet the changing congregation's current needs. Twelve years ago, for example, the church added a new Christian Education wing to accommodate its growing number of families. A decade later, on Pentecost Sunday, May 22, 1994, the church dedicated an extension which enlarged the sanctuary

7.1. Japanese Presbyterian Church in 1992, with downtown Seattle skyscrapers visible in the background. Photograph by Mark A. Duntley.

and also added a new kitchen, a social hall, office space, classrooms, a soundproof viewing room for parents with small children, and several more bathrooms.[15] The aesthetics of the space is not sacrosanct—in other words, not a cultural relic. The space is made and remade, over and over, in response to the changing experience and self-understanding of the community.

Since both the architecture and the name of the church reflect its Japanese ethnic origins, one might presume that JPC has existed over the years as one of a number of ethnic "voluntary associations" dedicated to maintaining and sustaining Japanese culture. Most anthropological and sociological texts indeed see Japanese American religious institutions as performing this function.[16] Kaoru Oguri Kendis, for example, in a study of Sansei (third-generation) Japanese Americans, found that Los Angeles Japanese Americans tend to return to their "old neighborhood" for worship even after moving to the suburbs. She concludes that both urban and

7.2. Japanese Presbyterian Church in 1995, showing the new building addition. Windows in the northern section of the social hall provide a panoramic view of the city. Photograph by Mark A. Duntley.

suburban Japanese American Christian churches continue to exist because the members feel "comfort" in the ethnic networks sustained and forged there.[17]

The "comfort thesis" may seem plausible at first. Even though Seattle's Asian-Pacific American community is growing rapidly—from 1980 to 1990, the Asian population increased 56 percent, from 38,000 to 60,000[18]—Asians still represent only 11.8 percent of the total population. But because the general population is growing at the same time, the potential for growth in ethnic communities and churches continues to exist. Asian Americans now constitute the largest minority group in Seattle; the city's public schools are 24.6 percent Asian American.[19] Furthermore, while in earlier periods most Asian Americans lived near one another in distinct communities, this residence pattern has changed drastically over the past few decades. Census figures for 1990 reflect that "half of King County's Asian population live in the suburbs."[20] Most JPC members travel great distances to attend worship. Only one-third come from the zip codes in the surrounding neighborhood; another third travel from other parts of the city proper, and the rest commute from suburbs outside the Seattle city limits, some traveling thirty to forty-five minutes to attend this church.

So perhaps JPC's attraction is that it is one of the few ethnic Christian enclaves available in a white Protestant world. That is not the situation in this corner of urban Seattle, however.[21] Within a two-mile radius of JPC there are no fewer than four other mainline Protestant Japanese American churches: Methodist, Episcopal, Congregational, and Baptist; within three miles are a Pentecostal Japanese church, two Chinese American Protestant churches (Missionary Alliance Church and Baptist), and a Korean American Presbyterian church. This means that there are many options for both Japanese Americans and other Asians seeking an "ethnic" church. Thus an ethnic "comfort thesis" does not explain why parishioners choose one church over another; nor does it explain why non-Japanese are attracted to JPC. Even cursory interviews with JPC parishioners reveal that most of them spent time in one or more other churches before finding their way to JPC. One Chinese American member told me that after becoming a Christian in ninth grade, she spent several years attending in turn two Chinese American ethnic churches in the area before joining JPC's College Fellowship group. She eventually became one of the church's most active members. Her reasons for joining JPC included its "laid-back" informal worship style and the Bible study groups, which she said "sustained her spiritual life."[22] This woman's experience suggests that the "comfort thesis" must at the very least be opened out to a consideration of religious practice and preference, aesthetics, and the desire for a community that will encourage and support one's distinct spiritual orientation as significant factors in forging social ties in a church.

Despite their close proximity and similar theological orientations, there is no evidence of rivalry or competition between the Japanese Christian churches in this neighborhood. In fact, the five Japanese American churches have a long history of cooperation and association, dating from ecumenical involvement during the Japanese American internment at Minidoka. It was here that these Japanese American churches first formed an ecumenical confederation called the Domei, which they have maintained since.[23] The Domei churches hold a joint evening "Praise Nite" service once a month, advertise their weekly services together in Asian American newspapers, and cooperate in hosting visiting evangelists and supporting other mission projects throughout the city.

The Japanese-speaking congregations were at one time the largest and most powerful of these Domei churches, but in the past two decades the balance of power and numbers has shifted to the English-speaking churches. Traditionally, Japanese churches employed two pastors: one Japanese-speaking (typically a native of Japan or a Caucasian minister who had been a missionary in Japan), and an American-born English-speaking pastor to serve the children and grandchildren of the first-generation immigrants. It was also common to hold separate worship services for each language group. Today in Seattle, only two of these churches continue to employ full-time pastors for their Nichigo or Japanese-speaking congregations, and three hold separate Japanese- and English-language worship services. English speakers are now the dominant group in all the Domei churches.

Because JPC is one of the few Domei churches to hold worship services in two different languages, the "language barrier" remains a crucial dimension of its ethnic and interethnic diversity. It is language, not ethnic or age divisions, that separates the Japanese speakers, many of whom are older adults living near the church, from the younger, suburban English-speaking Japanese and non-Japanese members. In fact, the two groups find it necessary to meet for worship at different times: the 11:00 worship is a Japanese-language service, while the largest service, at 9:30, is reserved for English speakers. Although it is not uncommon for mainline Protestant churches to hold two Sunday morning worship services for members' convenience, in JPC's case the language barrier effectively creates two separate congregations. The two groups meet together in worship only on special ritual commemorative occasions four times a year: Founder's Day/Pentecost, Christmas, Easter, and World Communion Sunday. The English-speaking congregation numbers more than two hundred members, while the Nichigo congregation has less than fifty. Yet in terms of polity, the JPC is officially considered to be one church. The church is governed by one ruling Session and operates under one financial budget, and the two pastors are considered co-pastors of one congregation.

Not only are there two languages of worship at JPC, but there are two radically different styles of worship as well. The Japanese-language congregation utilizes a conventional, Reformed worship format, with a standard Presbyterian (Japanese-language) hymnal. Their dress is formal and their manner reserved. The English-speaking congregation is evangelical in theology and much more informal in dress and demeanor. Their worship opens with singing not from a denominational hymnal but from the "JPC" songbook, a collection of guitar-accompanied "praise" songs assembled for use by this congregation alone. The laity take an active role in the leadership of the service, providing an opening time for "testimonials" when members convey to each other how their Christianity relates to their everyday lives. When the two congregations meet together, elements from each group's program are incorporated into the one service, and every effort is made to blend these two distinctly different worship styles.

Even though the majority of JPC's members are of Japanese ancestry, similar ethnic background does not automatically denote cultural, generational, or even theological commonality in the congregation. JPC's own pastoral leadership is a good indicator of the linguistic and cultural diversity among its Japanese membership. The church has two full-time co-pastors. The Reverend Richard T. Nishioka is a third-generation Japanese American who has led the English-speaking congregation for the past twenty-seven years. He was born in Los Angeles and formerly held a pastoral position in Hawaii. The Reverend Umeko K. Momii serves the Nichigo congregation. She came to JPC several years ago from a Japanese American Church in Salinas, California. Pastor Momii is a native of Japan but has spent many years in the United States and is married to a Nisei Japanese American. Her church roots go deep: her father is the late Toyohiko Kagawa, a famous Tokyo theologian. As is typical of third-generation Japanese Americans, Pastor Nishioka is not fluent in Japanese; Pastor Momii is bilingual.

The church's Japanese American members confound the static categories of "generations" currently popular in anthropological and sociological texts on Japanese Americans. Scholars continue to rely heavily on "generational" status as a crucial focus of the cultural identity of this population. Nisei are "second-generation" Americans, born here to Issei, or immigrant, parents; Kibei are born in America but educated in Japan; Sansei are third-generation, born here to native-born parents; and Yonsei are fourth-generation Japanese Americans. While most of the members of JPC's English-speaking congregation are Sansei and Yonsei, there is considerable intermarriage between these two Japanese American "generations" as well as outside the Japanese community altogether, making it extremely difficult to label family units as reflecting the cultural characteristics of any one particular generation. The social-scientific generational paradigm also fails to note the significance of the new Issei—recent immigrant or visiting Japanese nationals.[24] For example, in JPC's Japanese-speaking congregation, there are only twelve surviving original immigrant Issei, eight of whom reside in the nearby Keiro Rest Home, which was endowed for Japanese Americans. Some Nisei, particularly Kibei Nisei, attend the Japanese-language services, but many others attend the English-language worship. As this contingent of Issei and Nisei Japanese speakers age, vitality and church growth within the Nichigo congregations are found in the new Issei. Most of Seattle's new Issei are visiting or immigrating college students and business people and their spouses.[25] Seattle's position as a port city on the Pacific Rim guarantees the arrival of many such new Issei.

While it is common knowledge among scholars that the congregations of Japanese American churches are composed of many different English-speaking "generations"—Nisei, Yonsei, Sansei—the Reverend Momii notes that her Nichigo congregation also has several different Japanese-speaking "generations" worshiping together on any given Sunday. Pastor Momii's laypeople are largely transient, though, unlike the English-speaking members. Some of the new Issei are now naturalized business people, but many are here on temporary three- to five-year business visas, and students remain only for the duration of their schooling. Like the founders of JPC more than eighty-five years ago, the Reverend Momii and her congregation are meeting the needs of new Japanese immigrants both practically, through English-language classes and social networks, and spiritually, through Bible study and evangelical outreach. Every two weeks Pastor Momii travels by bridge across Lake Washington to Bellevue, a suburban city where many new Issei settle, to hold a Bible study class for eleven new Issei living there.

With all these "generations" mingling together at JPC, strict generational and cultural categories seem clearly inadequate to describe the identity and focus of this community. Nowhere is this more apparent than in the study of members' spiritual experiences. One's generational category or immigrant status has little to do with one's Christian status. Not everyone who attends JPC on Sunday is necessarily an official member of the congregation or even a professed Christian. Many Sansei and Yonsei (third- and fourth-generation Japanese Americans) consider themselves to be "new" Christians: one young man used this designation for himself even though his grandmother was a pillar of this JPC years ago. Other

Japanese American members come from a long line of Christians and can trace their parents' and grandparents' involvement in the JPC; indeed, their ancestral American genesis in Seattle coincides with their families' Christian genesis. Being Japanese American for these members is inseparable from being Christian Japanese American. A significant number of Sansei and Yonsei come from families who attend the Seattle Buddhist temple about a mile away; they too are new Christians, the first in their families to convert. New Issei who are practicing Buddhists usually do not find their way to JPC but instead attend one of a number of Buddhist services in Seattle. Although a few of the new Issei and international students from Japan among the Nichigo congregation were Christians before they immigrated, most have very little religious background at all and initially attended the Sunday morning Japanese-speaking service for social benefit and contacts. Many Chinese American members' parents and grandparents emigrated from Communist China with no religious affiliation or experience whatsoever. This means that Chinese American members are often new Christians without being technically converts from one faith to another. It is no wonder that the most popular Christian education class at JPC is "Basic Christianity" for new or "inquiring" Christians.

As JPC continues to attract non-Japanese members, the issue of ethnic categorization becomes more problematic. "Japanese" seems appropriate for the Nichigo congregation but not for the English-speaking group. Since JPC is 92 percent Asian American, it might seem that the label "Asian American" would be a more accurate locus for ethnic identity among those parishioners. Indeed, some scholars see in Pan-Asianism the roots of a new ethnic identity. "Pan-Asian American ethnicity," Yen Le Espiritu writes, "is the development of bridging organizations and solidarities among several ethnic and immigrant groups of Asian ancestry."[26] Although she excludes religious groups from her analysis, Espiritu's description of a Pan-Asian institution could partially describe the JPC: "Pan-Asian institutions . . . provide a setting for persons of diverse Asian backgrounds to establish social ties and to discuss their common problems and experiences. As Asian Americans come together to coordinate, plan, and participate in the activities of these organizations, they become tied together in a cohesive interpersonal network."[27] Yet to relegate JPC to the vague status of an "Asian American ethnic church" would discount and ignore the different cultural exchanges occurring there: Chinese, Korean, Japanese, and Caucasian Americans all interacting in one community while at the same time struggling to communicate with recent Southeast Asian Mien immigrant Christians. Sharon M. Lee in a study of racial classifications in the U.S. census warns against "transforming diverse ethnic groups into pan-ethnic races." One must take care, she writes, not to "lump all Asian Americans together and treat them as if they were the same."[28] Glenn Omatsu observes how quickly the term "Asian American" becomes "unwieldy" and oblique."[29] "Asian American" is more appropriately used as a political category or a focus for civil rights political lobbying, these scholars agree, than as a denotation of cultural identity.[30]

Church members do not see themselves as participants in a Pan-Asian coalition. The Reverend Nishioka prefers to describe the church's interracial cooperation as a "synergism," meaning "the simultaneous action of separate agencies which, together, have a greater total effect than the sum of their individual effects." The word comes from the Greek word *synergos*, which literally means "working together."[31] While in a very real sense JPC self-consciously forges Pan-Asian ties, a substantial minority of the members are persons outside ethnic Asian groups. It is crucial to realize as well that JPC's multicultural ties are formed not in the interest of political activism but as a mandate of its evangelical Christianity.

JPC's main involvement in Pan-Asian activity is its connection with the Japanese Presbyterian Conference, an informal organization of the eighteen existing Japanese American Presbyterian churches. Founded in 1905, the Japanese Presbyterian Conference has a long history of engaging in activities such as lobbying the denomination's governing General Assembly, supporting social justice campaigns and education, sponsoring cultural seminars, fostering the spiritual renewal of local church members and pastors, and financially supporting young people in full-time Christian work and lay leadership. The conference also works collaboratively with churches and denominational agencies to develop specialized curriculum, liturgy, and commemoration of church anniversaries and other special occasions for the Japanese American community. Although these types of curricular and liturgical materials are inclusive of other Asian groups, they focus on the task of translating and reclaiming traditional Japanese cultural elements in a modern Christian context. Both Pastor Momii and the JPC's director of Christian education agree that the impetus and emphasis for learning how to introduce and integrate Japanese cultural practices and symbols into Presbyterian worship comes largely from conference members in California, whose churches on the whole tend to be less integrated than their Seattle counterpart. Yet JPC's connection with the Japanese Presbyterian Conference no doubt serves to strengthen and maintain its denominational identity as Presbyterian (the affectionate nickname for JPC continues to be "Presby") in the face of limited local denominational support.[32]

JPC occasionally uses church school curricula published by the Japanese Presbyterian Conference, such as Ellen Tanouye's "Learning

Parenting Skills Together in an Asian American Context," which was the focus of a congregational class several years ago. This ten-week church school course met on Sunday mornings after worship and was quite popular with young parents in the congregation. It featured exercises for learning and transmitting "family histories," as well as practical material on identifying "parenting styles," understanding family strengths, weaknesses, and dynamics, and learning how to communicate, encourage, and discipline one's children. The last two sessions, "Seeing Our Church as Family" and "Celebrating Our Family Histories," illustrate how churches such as Seattle's JPC work to integrate Christian history and ethnic identification. While conference publications are designed to promote Japanese and Asian ethnicities and "translate" them into present-day experiences, these materials emphatically teach church members to privilege Christian ties over any other type of ethnic or familial connection.

"Seeing Our Church as Family" opens with a class recitation of a poem that tells how "generations" are joined literally "in the flesh" through the bonds of Christian faith:

> These people who live six generations back and I
> We are linked forever throughout history.
> I am flesh of their flesh, but even more.
> I am the heart of their hearts, for who they are
> They gave away to those of us who followed
> And the children of Israel (back generation after generation)
> And I are linked together throughout eternity.

Class members discuss the poem and share ideas about what it means to "belong to a church family," according to the curriculum agenda, and questions for discussion include "How do people at church become your relatives and aunties and uncles for your children?" The lesson goes on to invite parents to reflect on specific ideas for sharing their "Christian history" with their children. They are asked, "Do you have stories about your family that have to do with becoming Christian?" Parents are challenged to ask other church members to share personal Christian experiences with the children. Finally, the lesson closes with a statement outlining the priorities of one's "family" allegiances:

> We are a part of a Christian family which gives our lives a meaning, a hope for the future, and a purpose in our daily lives. We are not like a JACL [Japanese American Citizens' League] or some ethnic club—we do bring to our families a sense of our culture, as Asians, as Americans . . . but we also bring to our families a sense of being Christian. We relate to one another by caring, giving, and suffering with one another. We develop loyalty and trust; we form mutual support systems. . . . We reach out to those in need, the unloved, the poor, the rejected.

Ironically, the one thing churches such as JPC claim *not* to be is the one thing most commonly ascribed to them in academic literature: the status of being an "ethnic club." Too often ethnicity is presumed to be the most important factor guiding immigrants' religious choices. A study of this church suggests otherwise. As Lesson 10 succinctly puts it, "We need to be careful about putting our families in too high a position and not putting our trust in God."[33] Within the context of one's Christian identity and practice, ethnicity is not prioritized over spiritual or "faith roots" and family. The author of this curriculum is well aware of the differences between voluntary ethnic and political associations such as the JACL and voluntary Christian associations such as the Japanese Presbyterian Church.

Since it appears that neither cultural similarities, ethnic categories, nor traditional forms of social analysis adequately describe or define the source of JPC's corporate identity, one must turn elsewhere to find the key to its solidarity. A close study and observation of this church's gatherings, in contexts such as joint worship services and church school sessions, can show how this church uses ritual creatively to translate its ethnic history in a way that is meaningful to its multicultural present. Robert Orsi has argued that ritual is one way a community "reveals itself to itself."[34] But for JPC, ritual represents both epiphany and cultural disclosure. Group values and cultural meanings are most clearly and poignantly communicated, articulated, upheld, and enforced through ritual action. Yet the "heritage" that serves to bind this church is not one of common ethnic ties but the experience of making, sharing, and translating a common "Christian" and congregational history. Anthony Buckley has noted how history can work both as "a 'charter' for action; and as a focus for allegiance." As charter, history provides "rules or guidelines for acting in the present." History also engenders allegiance through ceremonies and commemorations. Rituals, in turn, form community boundaries based on religious connections that will supersede and transcend ethnic or biological kinship ties.[35] This is how JPC understands its past, and why it repeatedly enacts or performs it: as a blueprint for guiding its current mission outreach priorities and as a way of promoting community while preserving the generational, spiritual, ethnic, and linguistic diversity within its ranks.

Commemorative worship ritual is one way in which JPC can both display and forge its unique corporate identity. These services are carefully designed to create a shared congregational history by linking the Christian heritage with JPC's historic roots as a mission church in inner-city Seattle. All major joint Japanese–English-speaking gatherings intertwine the congregation's past with the "founding" and unifying events of Christianity itself. All events referring to the Japanese heritage of the church are ritually commemorated and thereby integrated into a larger "Christian" story. The church thus celebrates its historical connection, involvement, and participation in the distinctive pattern and history of Seattle's Japanese American immigration, settlement, and acculturation without being ethnically exclusive. Even events that affected only the Japanese American members can be interpreted in relation to salvation history. When publicly remembering the experiences of many of JPC's elderly and deceased members in World War II internment camps, for example, this community liturgically affirms a collective spiritual journey of "exile and exodus," which they see as a link between themselves and fellow sufferers in the Old Testament scriptures. The creative merging of its Japanese American past with a biblical Christian heritage allows JPC to celebrate the ethnic and cultural diversity of its membership in a recognizably Christian idiom, and in this way JPC can successfully "assume an identity that is pluralist, multidimensional,"[36] while remaining rooted in its Japanese American historical identification.

This creative use of ritual was clearly evident as JPC publicly celebrated its eighty-fifth anniversary. Sunday morning worship on June 7, 1992, opened with an invocation that called the congregation to "speak in every language" for the Lord. Church members from various ethnic backgrounds translated the biblical story of Pentecost into different languages: Greek, German, Chinese, Mien, Korean, Japanese, Spanish. Translation was central to this commemoration. The anniversary celebration marked one of the few times each year that JPC's Japanese-speaking congregation joined with the English-speaking congregation for bilingual worship, making it a service of "translation" in terms of the pragmatic process of rendering or turning from "one language into another." This eighty-fifth anniversary celebration was also a translation in the meaning of "to bear, convey or remove from one person, place, or condition to another." It was carefully constructed to commemorate or remember the congregation's founders and to translate the meaning of the church's Japanese American heritage in a way that would be inclusive of its present multicultural congregation. JPC did this by linking the congregation's historic, regional foundations with nothing less than the "founding" of the worldwide Christian Church. Just as in 1907 JPC was commissioned to translate the Gospel to inner-city Seattle's immigrant and resident Japanese-speaking community, so were the Christian missionaries at Pentecost given the command to "translate" the Gospel to the world, in the gift of power to "speak in every language" for the Lord.

The story of JPC's founding was retold in many ways at several crucial moments in this commemorative service. As the children came forward for the "children's sermon," a layperson prepared packets of seeds and small containers of potting soil. The children were each given two seeds to plant, and as they did so they were told that the seeds represented the two founders of the JPC, Dr. Mark A. Matthews and the Reverend Orio Inouye. While they listened to the tale of the church's founding in 1907, the children busied themselves with tamping their seeds into the dirt, symbolically enacting what their leader called their potential to "plant things" for the Lord—seeds that might grow into something as big and fruitful as their own church.

The kids scampered away with their pots and seeds, and the adults were then treated to a "mission minute" presentation, which emphasized JPC's ongoing connection with its origins as a mission-oriented church. The speaker described how that heritage was being maintained through the church's current mission outreach programs. She talked about the "mission sandwiches" made by members in the social hour after Sunday worship, which JPC's young professionals employed in downtown office buildings distributed on their lunch hour to Seattle's homeless. She thanked the congregation members who tirelessly volunteered to staff a senior citizen daycare for elderly Japanese Americans offered weekdays in the church building. Not only was a large percentage of the church's annual budget devoted to overseas mission programs, but the church was sponsoring college-aged members who travel abroad for mission experiences. The speaker closed by reminding members that JPC also staffed its own large adult/child church school with more than forty volunteer teachers a year, and that every summer, JPC hosted and helped staff a six-week "Summer Academy" tutoring program for inner-city children.

Most of the congregation was well aware that JPC's most ambitious mission project to date was the "nesting" of a Southeast Asian Mien congregation.[37] The Mien are an agricultural people of Laos and northern Thailand who began entering the United States by way of refugee camps in Chiang Kham, Thailand, in the late 1970s. There was no written Mien language until the 1950s. A small percentage of refugee Mien became both literate and Christian through the work of missionaries in the Thai camps. Since 1980, Seattle's Mien Christian church has met at JPC on Sunday afternoons at one P.M., and it now has nearly a hundred members and affiliates. This group constituted the first organized Mien Christian church in the United States; today there are three thousand Mien Christians in churches up and down the West Coast, with thirteen different Christian denominations involved in Mien mission work. Besides providing facilities for worship, JPC also appoints a church officer to supervise the Mien church, helps support a pastor or missionary to lead them, and provides a dedicated group of more than thirty people to work with the Mien in a whole range of church school programs. Some JPC members have been working with the Mien for as long as eight years. As John and

Jeni Goddard, pastors of the Mien group at the church from 1990 to 1992, like to say, "JPC is extremely committed to ministry to another ethnic group. God is doing something here."[38]

Following the "mission minute," some young adults led the singing of a guitar praise song entitled "Spirit of the Living God." Then Pastor Umeko Momii mounted the pulpit for her sermon. She preached first in Japanese, instructing those who did not know the language to read their Bibles or songbooks for the duration of the sermon. The older adults from the Nichigo congregation listened intently. Small children quietly drew pictures with crayons as their parents silently tended to them; other members prayed, read the bulletin, or listened, uncomprehending, to the singsong rise and fall of the Japanese language, amusing themselves by recognizing biblical names and by mentally translating a few well-known Japanese phrases. Once the sermon began in English, the rest of the congregation became attentive, and many eagerly listened to her animated retelling of the "founding." She traced JPC's ancestry to the year 1889, when another "Pentecost experience" occurred in a charismatic revival in San Francisco, California—an event that ushered in the American Japanese Christian mission movement and helped to found ethnic churches up and down the West Coast. Today, the pastor noted, was a day of two "birthdays"—of JPC in 1907 and of the Christian Church in Pentecost nearly two thousand years ago.

After a short prayer, the Reverend Momii moved to the center of the chancel to join the Reverend Nishioka at the Communion table set with the elements of the sacrament. The "commemoration" of both Founder's Day and Pentecost was at this point ritually linked to the commemoration of Jesus' sacrifice in the Lord's Supper. "Translation" again played an essential role in forging group identity and solidarity for a congregation that reflected considerable ethnic, theological, and linguistic diversity. As the two pastors jointly led the Communion rite, the sound, the cadence, and the rhythm of the "words of institution" drew the worshipers together in the space they had made. Even though the congregation undoubtedly knew the content of the communion service, the precise sound of the words had to be heard and thus translated, while the silent gestures did not. The Christian meanings of the gestures transcended translation. Ruel Tyson has argued that "gestures are not instruments that translate into a language understood elsewhere."[39] Tyson claims that to closely study a group's ritual gestures is "to get closer to its genius than [by] using an abstract of its official beliefs," for gestures "are at once public and personal . . . with meanings unique to the person overlapping meanings commonly shared by the group." Pastor Nishioka led the sacrament of Communion: he recited the words of institution, took into his own hands the small loaf of bread, broke it, and poured the dark red wine into the gleaming chalice. Only one set of Communion gestures was necessary, one symbolic structure into which were silently inlaid two languages and many experiences.

The two languages converged after Communion as a hymn was sung in English and Japanese. Here "translation" operated on a different level. While the JPC has a "language barrier" which needed to be surmounted through the process of translation, this hymn sing showed that the congregation shared another Christian language in common, demonstrating that the text, or literal sense of the words, is secondary to the ritual experience of community and shared meanings. Congregants wanted to "hear" it in English and to "hear" it in Japanese—or as cultural theorist Trinh T. Minh-ha puts it, "Each language has its own music and its practice need not be reduced to the mere function of communicating meaning."[40] When sounds are similar, literal sense becomes less important. So when the two sang a hymn in their own languages, to the same tune, the jumble of languages together made no "literal" sense, but the hymn "sounded" the same. The sound overrode the sense. The act of singing *together* took precedence over singing the identical words. Indeed, only in singing different words could this complex congregation sing together as one. Clearly at JPC, words, much like traditions, languages, histories, ethnicities, and theologies, need not be identical in order to be fused and shared and sounded as one.

Critic George Steiner has observed that translation arises in an act of joining, "when two languages meet." The true language of community, I realized during my fieldwork at JPC, is not one of conformity but one of diversity. Even in the midst of community, every person maintains a "personal lexicon" of meaning. Thus, as Steiner writes, "The language of a community, however uniform its social contour, is an inexhaustibly multiple aggregate . . . of finally irreducible personal meanings."[41] The work of "translation" that goes on in JPC is done to maintain community in the midst of diversity, not to force congregants into one ethnic mold or into a position of theological conformity. Sherry Ortner has noted that "anthropological studies of the United States have had the chronic tendency to 'ethnicize' the groups (classes and even institutions) under study, to treat them as so many isolated and exotic tribes."[42] When we resist the temptation to merely "ethnicize" the JPC, we see revealed a remarkably complex community that uses ritual commemoration as a structure in which to celebrate diversity and as a way to forge and convey an identity that is at once historically Japanese American and today multicultural and multigenerational. Ironically, it is in a study of its most ordinary actions of community worship that JPC appears most "exotic"—for it is here that it expresses and enacts its creative, corporate, and individual translations of the sacred.

Notes

1. The statistic is based on the number of languages spoken by children in the public schools. See Sally McDonald, "Teaching Draws Those Who Love Job, Despite Pay—Few Minorities Enter Profession," *Seattle Times*, November 25, 1990, B11.

2. While the JPC members would prefer the word "worship" to "ritual" (they tend to associate "ritual" with the rites of Buddhists or Catholics), I will be using the term "ritual" because it is now a common category for scholarly analysis. In this chapter "ritual" will be used in the traditional, narrow sense of "the observance of formal religious rites and ceremonial or customary acts."

3. This chapter is based on participant-observation fieldwork conducted at the church and while I lived this Seattle community from May to August 1992.

4. In the Beacon–Rainier Valley community, the 1990 census lists 48,831 persons, of whom 32 percent or 15,754 are Asian/Pacific Islanders. See the Community Areas section of *Census 90, Population Changes in Seattle 1980–1990* (Seattle: Office for Long Range Planning, 1991), 24.

5. All statistical data on Japanese Presbyterian Church membership are derived from a surname analysis of 253 names and are based upon the JPC directory, 1992. (Excluded from the sample were names of members living outside the King County area.)

6. Again, these numbers are derived from the 1992 JPC directory. While the Nisei or Japanese-speaking congregation is almost entirely Nikkei, the larger English-speaking congregation is much more diverse. These statistics include both congregations in one sample, for the directory makes no distinction between them. The church operates with one budget and as one corporation. This means that if it were possible to statistically isolate the English-speaking group from the Nichigo group, the former might include even fewer Japanese American members.

7. For the statistics on settlement, see S. Frank Miyamoto, "An Immigrant Community in America," in *East across the Pacific*, ed. Hilary Conroy and T. Scott Miyakawa (Santa Barbara, Calif.: American Bibliographical Center/Clio Press, 1972), 219–20.

8. Masako Herman, ed., *The Japanese in America, 1843–1973: A Chronology and Fact Book* (Dobbs Ferry, N.Y.: Oceana, 1974), 53.

9. It is difficult to determine with accuracy the population of Japanese in Seattle in these early years, as records from this period are imperfect. Miyamoto ("An Immigrant Community") estimates 6,000 by 1910, but a document in the University of Washington's Pacific Northwest archives entitled "Report of the Committee on Orientals," dating from 1917 and issued by the Seattle Ministerial Federation, includes rather precise numbers on the Japanese American community, both Christian and Buddhist. This document numbers the Seattle Japanese community at 5,800 in 1917.

10. See Frances B. Loveless, *A Bible Primer for Foreigners* (Philadelphia: Westminster Press, 1922). In the introduction, on p. 3, Loveless notes that students attending these combination English and Bible classes are given a Bible, and "each session of the class work is closed by the singing of gospel hymns" and the repetition and memorization of selected Bible verses. Loveless states, "The real work of Christians is not Americanization alone, but also the Christianizing of those who enter our gates."

11. *We Are the Body of Christ: A Memory Book of the 75th Anniversary Celebration of the Japanese Presbyterian Church of Seattle* (Seattle: Japanese Presbyterian Church, 1987), 4–6.

12. This impulse toward promoting "integration" after the war was not unique to

the Seattle Presbytery—other Protestant judicatories also had ambivalent feelings about the continued need for "ethnic" churches. Richard Nishioka, interview with author, Seattle, May 28, 1992.

13. The architect, David McKinley, won the AIA National Award.

14. Richard T. Nishioka, telephone interview with author, April 15, 1992, and interview with author, Seattle, May 28, 1992; Jim Mayeno, telephone interview with author, August 12, 1992. Mayeno, a JPC member, is an architect who served on the building committee in the early 1960s.

15. The addition was built in keeping with the architectural style and did not significantly alter the appearance of the original 1963 building.

16. Two currently standard works on Japanese American ethnicity by David J. O'Brien and Stephen S. Fugita include very little information on religion; when the subject is mentioned at all it is only in terms of "voluntary associations." See *The Japanese American Experience* (Bloomington: Indiana University Press, 1991) and *Japanese American Ethnicity: The Persistence of Community* (Seattle: University of Washington Press, 1991), respectively.

17. Kaoru Oguri Kendis, *A Matter of Comfort: Ethnic Maintenance and Ethnic Style among Third-Generation Japanese Americans* (New York: AMS Press, 1989), 129ff. Kendis's fieldwork was done in the late 1970s.

18. *Census 90*, 1.

19. See *Seattle Post-Intelligencer*, October 21, 1993, A9.

20. Quote from *Puget Sound: The Region in Detail—An Environmental Assessment Published by the United Ways of King, Kitsap, Pierce and Snohomish Counties* (September 1991), I–11. This document utilizes 1990 census data.

21. Most studies of Japanese Americans have been done on California populations, and many of their findings about California residents' cultural life and ethnic identity may not be applicable to Seattle residents. See Shotaro Frank Miyamoto, *Social Solidarity among the Japanese in Seattle* (Seattle: University of Washington Press, [1939] 1981), for information on Seattle's pre–World War II community and religious life.

22. Debbie Eng, interview with author, Seattle, June 18, 1992.

23. *Domei* is a Japanese word meaning "federation." Today Domei stands for the Japanese Christian Church Federation of Seattle, Washington. For information on the practice of Christianity in the internment camps, see Lester E. Suzuki, *Ministry in the Assembly and Relocation Centers of World War II* (Berkeley, Calif.: Yardbird, 1979), and Toru Matsumoto, *Beyond Prejudice: A Story of the Church and Japanese Americans* (New York: Friendship Press, 1946).

24. Standard works on Japanese American Issei refer to the immigrant generation that arrived here in the early part of this century, not to recent immigrants or visiting nationals.

25. Other new Issei are the so-called war brides or Japanese-born spouses of American servicemen. While JPC's Nichigo congregation includes a few women who fit this description, this situation became the focus of a particular ministry of Whitney Memorial United Methodist Japanese American church in Tacoma, Washington, which is located near the U.S. military base at Fort Lewis.

26. Yen Le Espiritu, *Asian American Panethnicity* (Philadelphia: Temple University Press, 1992), 14, 162.

27. Ibid., 162.

28. Ibid.

29. Glenn Omatsu, "Asian Pacific Americans: In 'Motion' and 'Transition,'" *Amer-*

asia Journal 18, no. 3 (1992): 81, 84, 85. Omatsu also calls for new Asian Studies scholarship that will transcend the assimilation/acculturation model.

30. Sharon M. Lee, "Racial Classifications in the U.S. Census: 1890–1990," *Ethnic and Racial Studies* 16, no. 1 (January 1993): 84–85. For a history of Asian American activism, see William Wei, *The Asian American Movement* (Philadelphia: Temple University Press, 1993).

31. Richard T. Nishioka, phone interview with author, April 15, 1992.

32. Umeko Momii, interview with author, Seattle, August 20, 1992; Amy Sato, telephone interview with author, August 13, 1992.

33. Ellen Tanouye, "Learning Parenting Skills Together in an Asian American Context," 25–28. The poem quoted is by Ann Weems. These conference sources are small-scale publications, computer-generated or typed, then photocopied, bound, and informally distributed to Japanese Presbyterian Conference churches.

34. Robert Orsi, *The Madonna of 115th Street* (New Haven: Yale University Press, 1985), 187.

35. Anthony Buckley, "'We're Trying to Find Our Identity': Uses of History among Ulster Protestants," in *History and Ethnicity*, ed. Elizabeth Tonkin, Maryon McDonald, and Malcolm Chapman (New York: Routledge, 1989), 184.

36. The quote is from Michael M. J. Fischer, "Ethnicity and the Post-Modern Arts of Memory," in *Writing Culture*, ed. James Clifford and William Marcus (Berkeley and Los Angeles: University of California Press, 1988), 196.

37. "Nesting" is a term used for churches that allow a smaller, usually "immigrant" or ethnic, church to use their church building either gratis or for nominal rent. The churches need not be of the same denomination.

38. John Goddard, telephone interview with author, August 18, 1992. See also Donald W. Haines, ed., *Refugees and Immigrants: Cambodians, Laotians and Vietnamese in America* (Totowa, N.J.: Littlefield, 1989).

39. Ruel Tyson and James Peacock, eds., *Diversities of Gifts: Field Studies in Southern Religion* (Urbana: University of Illinois Press, 1988), 5.

40. Trinh T. Minh-ha, "Film as Translation," in *Framer Framed* (New York: Routledge, 1992), 128.

41. George Steiner, *After Babel: Aspects of Language and Translation* (Oxford: Oxford University Press, 1992), xii and 47. I am indebted to Ruel Tyson for recommending Steiner's work.

42. Sherry Ortner, "Reading America: Preliminary Notes on Class and Culture," in *Recapturing Anthropology: Working in the Present*, ed. Richard G. Fox (Seattle: School of American Research Press, 1991), 186.

"We Go Where the Italians Live"

Religious Processions as Ethnic and Territorial Markers in a Multi-ethnic Brooklyn Neighborhood

Joseph Sciorra

The intersection of Graham Avenue and Grand Street in the Williamsburg section of Brooklyn is a locally recognized boundary running between two existing ethnic communities. This dividing line has been officially recognized and reinforced by municipal legislation changing the name of one of the streets: lampposts on Graham Avenue's two southern corners sport city street signs that read "Avenue of Puerto Rico," while on the northern side, Graham Avenue is suddenly transformed into "Via Vespucci." This marked crossroads is a constant reminder to neighborhood residents and strangers alike that divisions exist in this multi-ethnic community. What the signage fails to convey is that this urban border is highly permeable; people pass effortlessly on their way to work, shop, play, and worship in complete disregard of the markers' ethnic and territorial implications. This interplay between boundary marking and border crossings is most profoundly articulated in the local production of religious processions and secular parades.

Such perambulatory events in northern Brooklyn, while temporally fleeting, are emotionally powerful and durable demonstrations of affiliation and diversity in this highly concentrated and heterogeneous urban area. Parades, processions, and festivals turn public thoroughfares into arenas of shared interests through convivial and/or religious display. The mundane and everyday spaces of bus stops and front stoops are transformed into extraordinary carnivalized and consecrated sites in dramatic and emotionally charged ways through the display of privileged objects and behaviors. In addition to using the cityscape as setting for these urban performances, perambulations also transform space into place, creating a sense of local identity.

For Williamsburg's Italian American residents, religious processional display articulates both intra- and intergroup dynamics. The procession and related street feast are sites where divergent groups within the larger ethnic and religious Italian American Catholic "community" express historical internal differentiation and emerging tensions. Attempts to influence and ultimately control the public religious displays are bids for authority over religious symbols and "community" representation. These annually staged public events are also territorial markers that map out geographic boundaries vis-à-vis the larger multi-ethnic neighborhood. Processional routes, in concert with religious and festive objects, are lines of affiliation woven across the urban grid that engender and reaffirm a sense of belonging. Religious movement through space illustrates a topography of activities and influence that situates Italian Americans in relationship to their non-Italian neighbors. For Italian Americans, the symbolic control of the streets through religious festive display contributes to the ongoing endeavor to define what constitutes the "neighborhood" and its inhabitants.

The local production of large-scale public display events is not confined to ethnic religious processions and the performance of difference. Parades and other public gatherings are also created in a conscious attempt to bridge deep-seated divisiveness in the service of larger area interests. These secular and multi-ethnic religious ceremonies grow out of a strong desire for a collective politics needed to address the myriad problems converging on this predominantly working-class community.

Religion and Ethnicity on the Urban Landscape

Williamsburg lies in the northeastern section of the borough of Brooklyn; with its northern neighbor, Greenpoint, it forms part of the larger municipal district Community Board Number One. District boundaries are the East River to the west, Newtown Creek to the north, the Queens border on the east, and Flushing Avenue to the south. Community activists and government officials often link the two neighborhoods into a single entity with a hyphen or solidus (i.e., Greenpoint/Williamsburg) when discussing problems of housing, crime, jobs, and environment common to both. As in many urban neighborhoods, there is no clear and mutually agreeable boundary that neatly divides Williamsburg from Greenpoint (Tuan 1981:169). The two areas merge into one another.

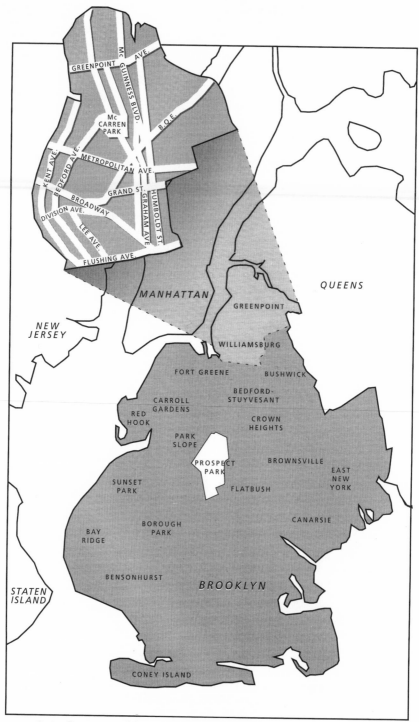

8.1. Greenpoint and Williamsburg, Community Board Number One, Brooklyn. Map by Michelle A. Sciorra.

The area has historically been home to working-class immigrants and their descendants, who have labored in local shipyards, factories, and warehouses. The continued migration of working people to this section of Brooklyn has not abated despite the deindustrialization and capital disinvestment of northeastern cities, which has all but decimated this former industrial mecca. Artists and white-collar professionals moved into Greenpoint and Williamsburg during the 1980s and 1990s, attracted by the area's proximity to Manhattan, its relatively inexpensive rents, and its ethnic diversity. However, the area has not experienced the large-scale gentrification undergone by other parts of the city despite this influx of college-educated and middle-class professionals.

Historical shifts in local ethnic and religious populations are evident in the modification of religious buildings for use by successive new communities (Miska and Posen 1983:14–15; Winkleman 1986:1–2). The building at 410 Graham Avenue, for example, was originally constructed as a Lutheran church; it was remodeled and used as a synagogue until 1950, when it was converted into the current headquarters of the Society of St. Mary of the Snow, an Italian American Catholic lay association. The First Italian Baptist Church, established in 1911, was renamed the Devoe Street Baptist Church in 1977 to accommodate the majority of African American worshipers, who reside in the nearby Cooper Park Housing Project. The church's one o'clock Sunday service is given in Korean. One need only attend a Spanish-language mass at St. Mary's Roman Catholic Church and read the German, Irish, and Italian names listed on the memorial plaques beneath stained-glass windows and posted on pews to get a sense of the impact of the global migration of labor and its religious consequences on this urban neighborhood.

A diversity of ethnic and religious communities exists within the district borders of Community Board Number One. In addition to its Irish and Latino residents, Greenpoint, located north of McCarren Park, is home to approximately fifty thousand Polish residents, many of them émigrés who attend St. Stanislaus Kostka Roman Catholic Church and the Polish National Catholic Church of the Resurrection (Howe 1984). Despite dwindling and aging local communities, the Holy Ghost Ukrainian Catholic Church, the Russian Orthodox Cathedral of the Transfiguration, and the (Lithuanian) Roman Catholic Church of the Annunciation survive, in part with the help of suburban parishioners who return to Williamsburg's Northside to attend Sunday mass celebrated in their respective native languages. Latinos (Puerto Ricans, Dominicans, Mexicans, and Central Americans) constitute the majority of residents in the Southside, or Los Sures, located south of Grand Street and west of Union Avenue. Protestant Puerto Rican worshipers frequent local storefront churches, while Mexicans and Dominicans have established a strong presence in All Saints Roman Catholic Church and Transfiguration Roman Catholic Church respectively (Marks 1989:12–14). Lithuanian, Polish, and Russian Muslims founded New York's first mosque in 1907, and their descendants and recent Filipino immigrants from other parts of the city maintain the building on Powers Street (Ferris 1993:54). Farther south along Division and Lee Avenues, synagogues and yeshivas (parochial schools) cater to the Satmar and other groups of Hasidic Jews. Latinos and African Americans live together in Williamsburg south of Grand Street and in the adjoining neighborhoods of Bushwick and Bedford Stuyvesant.

Italian Williamsburg

Williamsburg's Italian community resides on both sides of the Brooklyn-Queens Expressway (BQE). The ethnically mixed Northside is home to a number of working-class groups, including Italians, Latinos, and Poles. Italian Americans live east of Bedford Avenue, for the most part, interspersed with these groups. The expressway constitutes such a psychological barrier that those Italians I spoke to, who live in the triangular area formed by Union Avenue, McCarren Park, and the BQE, consider themselves part of the Northside. But the vast majority of Italians reside in that section known by its neighbors as "Italian Williamsburg." Its approximate boundaries are Grand Avenue to the south, Bushwick and Kingsland Avenue to the east, and the expressway to the northeast. The population of this ten-by-six-block area consists of second- through fourth-generation Americans as well as a large foreign-born contingent hailing from the southern Italian region of Campania. It is also home to a few African, Irish, and German Americans, as well as immigrants from Asia, Latin America, Poland, and the former Yugoslavia. As with their ethnic neighbors, the Italian population consists of both blue- and white-collar workers.

For Williamsburg's Roman Catholic Italian Americans, religious processions and street feasts have been predominant performance modes for more than a century. A contemporary calendar of religious feasts celebrated publicly in the streets by the area's Italian residents reveals a profusion of processional events in the six-month period from Good Friday to late September.[1] Approximately twenty-five processional performances are presented annually in commemoration of Christ's martyrdom and in honor of four male saints and four aspects of the Virgin Mary. Two organizations, for example, sponsor three separate processions to celebrate St. Cono; twelve separate processions were held during the 1992 church-

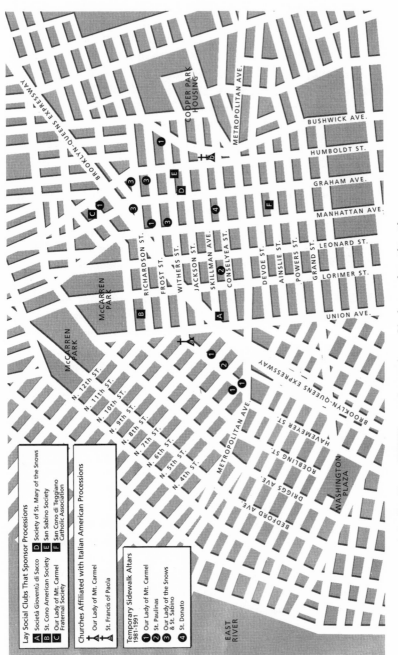

Lay Social Clubs That Sponsor Processions

A Società Gioventù di Sacco
B St. Cono American Society
C Our Lady of Mt. Carmel Fraternal Society
D Society of St. Mary of the Snows
E San Sabino Society
F San Cono di Teggiano Catholic Association

Churches Affiliated with Italian American Processions

✠A Our Lady of Mt. Carmel
✠A St. Francis of Paola

Temporary Sidewalk Altars
1981–1991

❶ Our Lady of Mt. Carmel
❷ St. Paulinas
❸ Our Lady of the Snows & St. Sabino
❹ St. Donato

8.2. Italian Williamsburg's religious institutions. Map by Michelle A. Sciorra.

sponsored feast of St. Paulinus and Our Lady of Mount Carmel. Included among the celebratory activities for St. Paulinus and Mount Carmel were the *questua* (the selling of blessed bread through neighborhood streets by three separate marching groups) and the "Line of March," a parade that picks up dignitaries of the feast at their homes in time for 11 A.M. mass at Our Lady of Mount Carmel Church. Individual devotees of St. Paulinus sponsor their own celebrations on occasion. In 1990 and 1991, brothers James and Joseph Nunziata spent a reported $19,000 for a "block party" in honor of the fifth-century bishop. Williamsburg's Italian residents demonstrate a special appreciation for the aesthetic and social aspects of community-generated pageantry through the staging of these religious processions.[2]

Two places of worship serve as the major foci for neighborhood processions.[3] Our Lady of Mount Carmel Shrine Church was established in 1887 as Brooklyn's second Italian "national" or "ethnic" parish. The original wood structure was destroyed in 1920 to make room for a larger building, which was completed in 1930. Seventeen years after its dedication, the new church was demolished to make room for the BQE. Our Lady of Mount Carmel was eventually rebuilt at the corner of North 8th and Havemeyer Streets in the Northside. The parish, designated a "shrine" church in 1981, celebrates an annual Good Friday procession as well as a two-week "street feast" each July in honor of St. Paulinus of Nola and Our Lady of Mount Carmel. A second national parish, St. Francis of Paola Church, was established in 1919 to meet the religious needs of the growing Italian "colony." Twenty years later, a larger building was constructed at its present-day site at Conselyea Street and Woodpoint Road. St. Francis of Paola initiated a procession in honor of St. Anthony of Padua in 1993.

There are also a number of lay "societies," or associations, in the neighborhood that organize religious processions independently of the two parishes. The San Cono di Teggiano Catholic Association, the Society of St. Mary of the Snow, the San Sabino Martire Mutual Aid Society, and the Societá Gioventú di Sacco are hometown voluntary associations that sponsor religious processions for their respective patron saints from club-owned meeting halls. The Societá dei Cittidini di Fontanarosa, which puts on an annual procession to the Madonna della Misericordia (Our Lady of Mercy), has no permanent home and holds its monthly meetings in the Mount Carmel basement. Membership in the Our Lady of Mount Carmel Fraternal Association, housed in a storefront hall on Graham Avenue, is not restricted by hometown origins and is theoretically, although not in practice, open to non-Italians. Operating out of a private home, the American St. Cono Society, as its name implies, considers itself a non-ethnic religious organization and marches in processions with American and Vatican flags. Although the Our Lady of Mount Carmel Knights of Columbus is not a sponsoring organization, its members are deeply involved in the planning and production of the Mount Carmel Church's summer festa.[4]

The paraded image of a saint or the Madonna encapsulates a sacred narrative of heavenly intervention or a Marian apparition and superimposes this mytho-historic time onto the everyday world of sidewalks and street corners. Ancient legends and hagiographies depicting the miraculous salvation of southern Italian towns from enemy attack, slavery, or earthquakes are evoked rather than dramatized in the vast majority of neighborhood events by the grandchildren and great-grandchildren of immigrants from these villages. Accounts of inter-town rivalries for control of sacred objects (St. Cono's bones, for example), and ultimately of the cult itself, serve as origin myths that situate southern Italian villages temporally within the context of a non-pagan, Christian history. The symbolic invocation of the historic and the miraculous attests to the procession's power to convey in simple and direct fashion disparate meanings and ideas in a unified aesthetic whole.

Only two processional events attempt to reenact the sacred narratives of southern Italian villages in the streets of Williamsburg. The dramatization of St. Paulinus's return by ship to Nola's shores is one of the most spectacular celebrations held each year in New York City. According to the story, Paulinus secured the freedom of his compatriots, who were enslaved by Mediterranean pirates, and upon his return to Nola was greeted by townspeople waving lilies. The "flower" used in Brooklyn to welcome home the bishop-saint is a multi-story tapering spire known as the *giglio* (lily). The giglio, along with a singer and a brass band, is lifted and carried on the shoulders of approximately 125 straining young men. The acknowledged highlight of the two-week feast is the encounter between the giglio and a replica of Paulinus's ship, manned by a bearded "Turkish sultan" and his crew of three schoolboys, in a compelling dramatization of the legend's climax.[5]

The Passion of Christ, produced by the parishioners of Our Lady of Mount Carmel Church on Good Friday each year, is considerably more theatrical than the other neighborhood events. The procession stops at a number of "House Stations," marked with a black cross, where costumed children strike the appropriate passional tableau on the sidewalk. The players recite no dialogue in the course of the three-to-five-minute scenes, although hymns, prayers, and a descriptive narrative (in English and Italian) are sung and read over a sound system anchored to a car roof. The marchers, joined by residents from the "House Station" carrying their black cross, regroup in the street and proceed to the next location.

8.3. The meeting of the giglio and boat at the intersection of Havemeyer and North 8th streets, 1981.
Photograph by Martha Cooper.

8.4. The Eighth Station of the Cross on Lorimer Avenue, 1985. The public gathering of parishioners reroutes vehicular traffic, as with the city bus seen in the background. Photograph by Joseph Sciorra.

Marching toward Consensus:
The Performance of Intra-ethnic Difference

For Williamsburg's Italian Catholics, religious processions are dramatic demonstrations and confirmations of group identity organized around the display of a central religious statue. An "affirm[ation] of sacred membership in community" (Turner 1980:6), processions are ceremonial gatherings of people with shared interests, beliefs, and histories. In his examination of such perambulatory events, Louis Marin noted, "To parade or to form a cortege or procession implies that the individuals constitute a totality and collectively 'take shape,' whatever the modalities of this coming together or the characteristics of the constituted product may be" (Marin 1987:222). But celebratory activities such as processions not only express preexisting community affiliations; they are themselves collective experiences that engender a heightened sense of belonging, what anthropologist Victor Turner called *communitas* (Turner 1982:96–97). The Italians of Williamsburg who organize and march in annual religious processionals create powerfully charged cultural occasions in which they generate and maintain a variety of intra-ethnic and religious identities.

The collective experience of festive display is achieved by properly employing a repertoire of malleable religious festival objects and practices created in common over the course of time that arouse intense emotional response (Abrahams 1982:161; Davis 1988:159–60). Exploding mats of firecrackers and aerial shells in Williamsburg herald the arrival of a religious procession or aurally mark the opening of the feast. A uniformed brass band parades to the rhythms of religious hymns, symphonic marches, and Italian and American pop standards, bringing neighborhood residents to their windows and doorways. The streets are transformed by society standards, colorful banners, and national flags paraded by bearers. Marchers dress in matching uniforms or in their Sunday best, association dignitaries sport lettered sashes, and general members wear society badges. Participants process in orderly fashion as they chat casually among themselves and wave to neighbors watching. The statue of the Virgin Mary or saint is carried on a litter by a crew of men or is pulled on a float by men or an automobile.[6] The success of any processional performance depends to a large degree on the proper combination of these familiar elements.

The Good Friday procession and the lifting of the giglio are exceptions to this general description of Italian Brooklyn celebrations. The giglio feast is considerably more boisterous in tenor, the Good Friday procession more solemn, than other processions. Although statues are paraded through the streets in the dramatization of Christ's Passion, costumed marchers remain the focus of attention on Good Friday. With its own unique history, the façade of the giglio (called a "statue" by some feast attendants) is bedecked with a number of religious personages, including St. Paulinus, Our Lady of Mount Carmel, and St. Anthony of Padua.

Italian Williamsburg's processions are "public dramas of social relations" (Davis 1988:6) that articulate local notions regarding group organization through the display of religious symbols. As rites of intensification (Falassi 1987:3), these processions are also public representations of the family, with separate marching units consisting of men, women, and children on display (Gambino 1975:1–41; see also Orsi 1985:75–106, 107–49). The order of the individual units varies from procession to procession. Children either march at the front of the processional line or are seated on the flower-adorned float, which also bears the sacred image. Sometimes children parade dressed as angels, as medieval courtiers, or as the monk St. Cono. Teenage males are an integral part of the Good Friday procession and the giglio feast, while their presence is minimal in the other religious events. It is no surprise to see men and women marching separately, because the lay societies that sponsor these events are social clubs

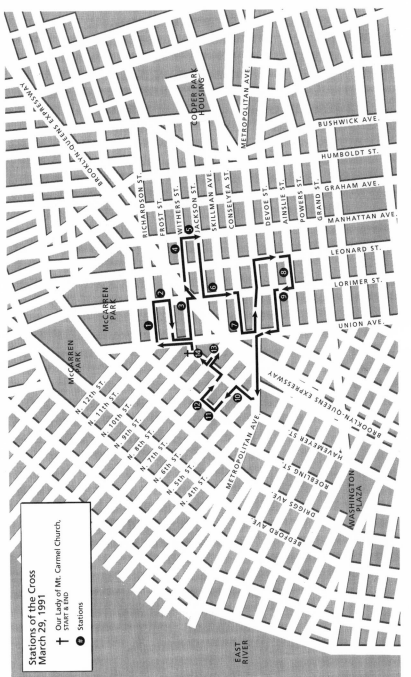

8.6. OLMC Church Stations of the Cross Route. Map by Michelle A. Sciorra.

8.5. The women's contingent of the 1985 Our Lady of the Snow procession on Graham Avenue. Photograph by Joseph Sciorra.

where men gather in the evenings to play cards away from the domestic space. While the hierarchical Italian American family formation is laid out horizontally in the processions, the male-dominated giglio event dramatizes a similar pattern vertically in its organizational structure. The festival's pyramidal chain of command (devoid of women) begins at the bottom, with the lifters organized into crews of thirty men led by "lieutenants," and continues upward with several "apprentices," topped finally by five *capos*, or "leaders," with "Capo Number One" serving a two-year reign.[7]

Williamsburg's processions are purposely designed to pass and sometimes to stop at locations significant to local history and community life. These sites are points of affiliation in a network of family members, *paesani*, neighbors, and believers (Hannerz 1980:162–201). A giglio capo, for instance, may lead the ceremonial spire in front of a grandparent's former home or business. The San Cono di Teggiano Catholic Association's procession makes an honorary stop at the house where the saint's feast day was celebrated privately during the 1950s and 1960s after local clergy prohibited public festivities, and where the members of the American St. Cono Society currently meet. The black crosses displayed along the route of the Good Friday procession identify the homes of parishioners of Our Lady of Mount Carmel Church. Processions stop at family altars temporarily erected for the feast day in front of individuals' homes, where scores of relatives, friends, and neighbors congregate for all-night vigils. The band plays a hymn, a priest (if one is traveling with the procession) blesses the altar, and marchers break for refreshments.

The power of these annual festive celebrations arises from their ability to imbue urban space with shared memories, emotions, and meaning, and to reinforce residents' prevailing attachments to place. This ongoing humanization of the city, or a section of it, renders a locale more familiar and cherished over time. Cultural geographer Yi-Fu Tuan has noted that the city dweller's comprehension of even a small urban unit such as the neighborhood is not immediate but involves a process of cognitive and empathic mapping: "A neighborhood is at first a confusion of images to the new resident; it is blurred space, 'out there.' Learning to know the neighborhood requires the identification of significant localities, such as street corners and architectural landmarks, within the neighborhood space. Objects and places are centers of values" (Tuan 1981:17–18). Transforming space, that "changing field of tensions and contradictions" (Abbas 1994:442), into place means establishing an emotional and psychological union with the "neighborhood" and infusing that urban entity with

8.7. The church-sponsored procession for Our Lady of Mt. Carmel stops to bless a sidewalk altar on Havemeyer and North 5th streets, 1985. Photograph by Joseph Sciorra.

an accessible "geometric personality" (Tuan 1981:17). Urban residents' collective inscription of meaning and value on city space through public display instills a sense of situatedness, the feeling of intimacy and identification with one's immediate surroundings (Abbas 1994:442; Lynch 1975:9–13). "Identity of place," Tuan says, "is achieved by dramatizing the aspirations, needs, and functional rhythms of personal and group life" (Tuan 1981:178). These activities and venues provide neighborhood residents with opportunities to reconfirm their involvement in, commitment to, and identification with their immediate area (ibid.:47).[8]

In Italian Williamsburg, social and emotional investment in the neighborhood through public religious dramatization is not achieved easily or without tension. Collectively, local religious processions reveal historical and contemporary differences existing between religious and social groups within the Italian community, and indeed contribute to further promoting the estrangement. The most common differences displayed in local processions are regional. Williamsburg is a community where religious devotion is strongly tied to its Old World settings in Campania: St. Cono of Teggiano, for example, in the province of Salerno, and Our Lady of Mercy, from the town of Fontanarosa, in Avellino.[9] Sentiments of social cohesion and identity are inextricably affixed to the disparate historical periods conjured up, juxtaposed, and celebrated within the feast's temporal frame (Zerubavel 1985:70; Turner 1982:95–96). The San Cono di Teggiano Catholic Association's June procession commemorates not only the monk's death and his miraculous rescue of Teggiano, but also the formation of the organization in 1888, the establishment of the women's auxiliary in 1935, and the association's revival by immigrants in 1973. As an "apparatus in the art of memory" (Marin 1987:227), the ceremonial movement through space reveals historical ruptures and points of contention regarding claims by various groups to sponsor a specific event.

While devotees consider Our Lady of the Snow and St. Sabino to be siblings, these sacred personages are honored in Williamsburg by two different societies tracing their roots to the town of Sanza. In 1933, there was a split in the Society of St. Mary of the Snow, and a faction formed a separate organization in honor of St. Sabino.[10] Tensions between the two groups were not resolved until the 1970s, when the San Sabino Martire Mutual Aid Society was invited to participate in the Our Lady of the Snow procession. Each August 5, the statue of Sanza's patron saint is paraded from the society's hall on Withers Street to the Our Lady of Snow headquarters on Graham Avenue in recollection of the ceremony in Sanza. Members of the Society of St. Mary of the Snow have reciprocated since 1991, when the St. Sabino Society amended its constitution to sponsor its own procession. These tensions have abated, to a large degree, because

8.8. Returning the statue to the St. Cono Catholic
Association after the procession, 1985. Photograph
by Joseph Sciorra.

post–World War II immigrants, who often share dual membership, are unconcerned with a feud that occurred more than half a century ago. But the historical break reverberates in the separate processions organized each August and September.

One past conflict that continues to have repercussions is evident in the public devotion to Our Lady of Mount Carmel. According to older neighborhood residents, the priests of Our Lady of Mount Carmel Church attempted to wrest control of religious feasts from the different lay societies in the 1940s and 1950s. The neighborhood story is that clergy wanted to be the sole recipient of money collected during the celebrations.[11] One of the many religious organizations affected by this conflict was the original Mount Carmel Society, which disbanded and reestablished itself in 1945 as the Our Lady of Mount Carmel Fraternal Society. By tacit agreement between the church and the local police precinct, required parade permits would not be issued to sponsoring societies without the prior approval of Mount Carmel's pastor—which he refused to grant, of course. The police stopped the 1949 procession and arrested the Fraternal Society's president for marching without a permit. As a result of this and other forms of harassment, the Mount Carmel Society and the groups affiliated with Our Lady of the Snow, St. Sabino, and St. Cono moved the celebrations of their respective panegyric masses to St. Francis of Padua Church. Today, representatives of Mount Carmel Church, on the one hand, and of the lay society in honor of the Madonna, on the other, skillfully avoid crossing paths as they march in two rival processions on July 16.

Another intra-ethnic difference is found among immigrants and their American-born counterparts. The attempt by clergy to control community celebrations resulted in the demise of the St. Cono procession after World War II. A statue of the twelfth-century saint was not paraded again until the society was revived in 1973 by more recent immigrants, who honored the family that maintained St. Cono's feast days during the 1950s and 1960s by routing the procession to stop at the house where annual novenas, open to the public, had been prayed. Differences soon developed between the American-born Teggianesi and the Italian-speaking devotees around the issue of language use during society meetings.[12] Society membership, furthermore, was open only to those who could trace their roots to Teggiano, despite the fact that devotion to St. Cono had become popular among non-Teggianesi.

The American St. Cono Society was founded in 1988, with membership open to non-Italians. (The society president boasted of having a Jewish member.) The society sponsors a candlelight procession on the eve of St. Cono's June and September holidays. Reconciliation seemed imminent in June 1992 when the Italian-born devotees resumed their previously canceled stops at the Quonset hut–cum–chapel located in the back-yard of the self-proclaimed "Casa di San Cono." When the American St. Cono Society staged its first daytime march that September, the marchers went out of their way to present the immigrant organization with a bouquet of flowers. Unfortunately, no one was present at the hall to receive the gift or acknowledge the gesture.

Two public events in the area consciously attempt to embrace all Italians. Several lay organizations join the scores of believers in the annual Good Friday procession, marching with their society banners. But this church-sponsored Passion does not host the parishioners of St. Francis of Padua Church or affiliated lay societies. The nonreligious Columbus Day parade is the area's most inclusive Italian celebration. Six out of the ten groups that made up the Federation of Italian American Organizations of Greenpoint/Williamsburg, the event's sponsor in 1992, are lay societies. But associations such as the American St. Cono Society and the Mount Carmel Fraternal Society are not federation members, and as a result they do not march in separate parade units, although unidentified members do. The one celebration that has come to represent the Italian Williamsburg community as a whole is the church-sponsored giglio festa, which attracts thousands of visitors each year and consistently receives citywide media attention.

Parading the Boundaries/Mapping the "Neighborhood"

While they articulate intragroup dynamics, processions sponsored by Italian Americans are informed by the area's diverse ethnic communities, and their circumnavigations constitute a performance of collective subjec-tivity staged topographically. When I asked the president of the Società dei Cittidini di Fontanarosa what the route of the 1985 procession would be, he answered, "We go where the Italians live. It would feel funny to go where people don't understand what's going on, what the tradition is." While church-sanctioned religious processions do not trace preestablished parish boundaries (the two "national" churches are technically open to all Italians in the United States), they do extend a "sacramental template" (McGreevy 1996:170) onto a specific urban area understood as distinct and recognizable. Processional routes map out "a territorial unit of mean-ing" (Kirshenblatt-Gimblett 1983:203; see also Marin 1987:223) compris-ing the geographic range of Italian influence considered to be the "neigh-borhood." In northern Brooklyn, where territorial units are defined by ethnicity, the public display of religious sentiment and ethnic affiliation are inextricably linked geographic identities (Tuan 1981:178; Marin 1987:222–23; Suttles 1974:50–52).

Ceremonial display is a dramatic way of delineating the edges of community domain (Turner 1980:7; Abrahams 1987:178) for urban residents who often disagree about the precise location of "neighborhood" borders (Hojnacki 1979:49; Kasinitz 1988:164).[13] Local perambulatory events reveal points of neighborhood contact and division. Italian American marchers rarely travel down what one Latina resident called the "invisible borders," those streets dividing the Italian section from the Latino and African American communities, such as Grand Street, Kingsland Avenue, and Bushwick Avenue. Instead, procession organizers acknowledge and reinforce these urban boundaries by passing down the closest parallel block. Processional paths also demarcate the areas where the Italian population gradually fades into other European communities in the Northside and around Bayard and Richardson Streets to the north. Processions are routed in a number of cases to the edges of the Italian section (as well as where nonresidential structures dominate) to recognize and involve families who have assembled domestic sidewalk altars for the feast (Sciorra 1989b). Marchers in this way symbolically renew the ties between the margins of the community and the vibrant "power stations" of the local "national" churches and/or the lay society headquarters by incorporating the former sites and individuals into the ceremonial order of religious pageantry.[14]

For many of New York's Italian American communities, self-representation has developed in symbiotic relationship to what Robert Orsi, in his chapter in this volume, has termed the "proximate dark-skinned other." The perceived threat and resulting negative assessment of Italian Williamsburg's neighbors of color emerged most strongly during the thirty years following World War II, as African Americans and Puerto Ricans migrated in increasing numbers to the area and surrounding neighborhoods. Italian Americans, along with other white New Yorkers, ascribed poverty, criminality, promiscuity, uncleanliness, and other urban pathologies as inherent and exclusive traits to the newly arrived migrants in racist mythologies shaping their notion of ethnic difference (Rieder 1985). Contemporary Williamsburg has evolved into a less threatened and more publicly tolerant neighborhood, although this construal of the dark-skinned other remains an underlying factor for residents who have viewed their locality as a "defended neighborhood." Sociologist Gerald Suttles, in *The Social Construction of Communities*, defines the defended neighborhood as "primarily a response to fears of invasion from adjacent community areas. It exists, then, within a structure of parallel residential solidarities which stand in mutual opposition. And it is this mutual opposition rather than primordial

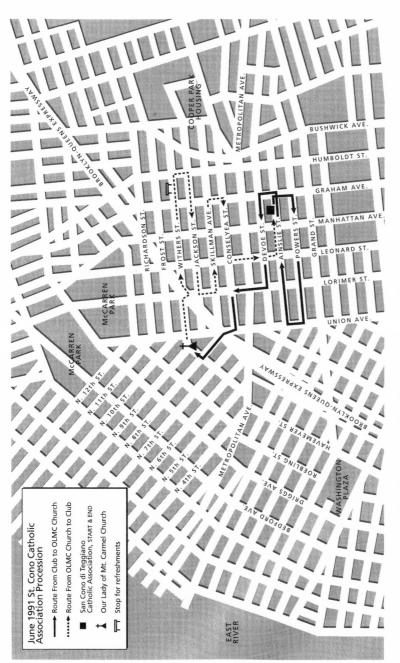

8.9. St. Cono Catholic Association's 1991 procession route. Map by Michelle A. Sciorra.

solidarity alone which gives the defended neighborhood its unity and sense of homogeneity" (1974:58). While I did not record the specifics, I remember vividly the school crossing guard who indicated the exact streets dividing the "good" (safe) area from the "bad" (dangerous) one when I was looking for an apartment in 1982. This cognitive mapping marks the confluence of ethnicity, race, and class on a constructed landscape of fear and difference.

The ceremonial retaking of the streets from early spring till fall communicates a public message of territorial proprietorship and local power to performer and spectator alike: "The restoration of some predictability to one's environment is a prescription for a territorial imperative. To define a small space of one's own permits a higher level of social control to be maintained. . . . Establishing the territory generates security; maintaining or embellishing it guarantees status" (Ley and Cybriwsky 1974:505). The processions reinforce the prevailing social order by ceremoniously asserting the ethnic hegemony of the area as well as extending popular notions of a religious moral imperative to the city streets (Suttles 1974:156–61; Orsi 1992:336). The collective claim to urban space of Williamsburg's cycle of processions is a powerful message: the streets are safe because we use them, and we use them because they belong to us. The giglio event is by far the most dramatic statement of ethnic strength and apparent unity; the display of male virility in the coordinated carrying of the ceremonial object is a masculine image of a powerful community united in faith.

Maintaining a highly visible corporate identity by means of a very public religious life is crucial for an area and city in which ethnicity plays such a predominant role in the political sphere. This is well understood by local politicians, who prominently march as invited guests at the head of a number of neighborhood processions. Writing about a multi-ethnic neighborhood in Queens, anthropologist Roger Sanjek notes that public ceremonial events are a "parapolitical means to voice community needs" by making visible voting blocs and reinforcing the ties that bind elected officials to their constituents (Sanjek 1992:136). "Public events," says Sanjek, "are not simply tangential to local politics. They *are* local politics" (ibid.). In Italian Williamsburg, lay societies are actively involved in area politics through the coordinated actions of the Federation of Italian-American Organizations. Federation members, as well as parish priests, sit on the local community board. When city council districts were reconfigured to reflect changing demographic factors throughout the city in 1992, the federation fought to have the lines redrawn in order to minimize the degree to which the Italian community was divided from itself and the predominantly "white district" of Greenpoint. The procession's circuitous course through the streets is the Italian community's ceremonial proclamation of its continued involvement in civic affairs.

Italian Americans' attempt to forge a unique geographic identity is both impelled and hampered by the confusion over whether they live in Williamsburg or Greenpoint. Italian residents, especially older ones, refer to the neighborhood as "Williamsburg" in casual conversation and "Greenpoint" when talking to outsiders, especially the media. This territorial schizophrenia is illustrated by the federation's name and by real estate agents' advertisements that identify the Italian community as "GRPT/ WMSBURG." In this way, a small portion of Community Board Number One (the Italian section) is redefined and reconfigured as the whole (Greenpoint and Williamsburg). City newspapers for the past twenty years have located the giglio feast in either of these two neighborhoods. Indeed, when the *New York Times* publicized Williamsburg and Greenpoint in two separate articles for the paper's weekly real estate column, the Northside and Italian Williamsburg were mysteriously excluded from either area (Dorian 1986:9; Wellisz 1982:9).

Adding to this ambiguity is the use of the term "Southside," which generally refers to the Latino section, Los Sures. But it is also used by some Italian Americans to refer to the area east of the expressway, especially in conversations about the relationship between it and the Northside. This is most evident in the Our Lady of Mount Carmel Church feast program,

8.10. Participants in the 1985 Stations of the Cross pass under the Brooklyn-Queens Expressway from the Northside. Photograph by Joseph Sciorra.

which lists the July 16 procession to the Madonna as taking place "through-out Northside Streets [and] Southside Streets." The fuzzy geographic identity is further complicated by the fact that local Italian Americans themselves have no name for their neighborhood; non-Italians have dubbed the area "Italian Williamsburg."

This identity crisis can be attributed to a number of sources. One is the way in which the various borders of political districts (such as those for Congress, the New York State senate and assembly, city service areas, and city police precincts) dissect Italian Williamsburg and the Northside. Another factor contributing to this confusion is the image of Williamsburg as a "stigmatized place" (Krase 1979) in the eyes of residents and outsiders alike, an image that was strengthened in the post–World War II period. One woman, who has resided in the Northside for the past forty years, told me that newspapers refer to her area as Williamsburg "only when some-thing bad happens." Italian Americans distanced themselves from this historical geographic appellation and, consequently, from identification with Williamsburg in the forty years following the end of the war.

This aura of negativity has not been lost on the organizers of the annual feast of St. Paulinus and Our Lady of Mount Carmel. When I began researching the community celebrations in 1981, the event invari-ably avoided naming the neighborhood for outsiders. One feast official told me in 1984, "When you say that the feast is in Greenpoint, people think Polish. When you say Williamsburg, they don't want to come." But this view is changing. Since 1991, Our Lady of Mount Carmel Church has advertised the feast with billboards placed throughout the neighborhood and city clearly identifying the feast site as Williamsburg. This is equally true for the parochial "middle school" that opened the following year. This turnabout can be attributed, in part, to a series of publications and the related exhibition in 1989–90 on the giglio celebration by folklorist I. Sheldon Posen and me that consistently located the feast in Williamsburg and portrayed the community in a favorable light. Equally important is Williamsburg's recent metamorphosis into New York City's "New Bo-hemia" (Gooch 1992; Carr 1992) with the influx of artists into the area during the 1980s. In an updated article in 1996, the *New York Times* suddenly redrew the borders of Williamsburg to include the displaced Italian section (Cohen 1996:5).

Border Crossings

While the concept of the "defended neighborhood" is a useful analytical tool for exploring the ceremonial maintenance of ethnic and territorial boundaries, its militaristic imagery of fortified barricades and ethnic combat, developed to address a specific moment in American urban history, is a misleading and inappropriate description of the current conditions in northern Brooklyn. Italian Williamsburg of the late 1990s in no way resembles New York City's embattled white communities of thirty years ago resisting the "invasion" of African American and Puerto Rican migrants; nor is it like the media's demonized portrayal of a contemporary apartheid-like Bensonhurst. There are no open ethnic hostilities such as those that currently exist between Williamsburg's Hasidic Jews and Latinos to the southwest. Male adolescent "street corner" activity typical of the District One neighborhood studied by Suttles in the early 1970s (1974: 188–229), is negligible, and Italian youth gangs, such as the "Jackson [Street] Gents" and the "Northside Twilights," who waged pitched battles with their Puerto Rican counterparts in the 1960s, are history.[15] On occasion, one finds prepubescent Italian, Latino, and African American boys neatly attired in hip-hop gear together on someone's parents' front stoop.

Geographic boundaries are symbolically reinforced to a large degree because of the continual flow of individuals across them. People of color walk, shop, and live in the "Italian" section unmolested. Ethnically marked cultural and religious expression is rich and varied: Puerto Rican flags fly from apartment windows and car antennas with the approach of Manhattan's Puerto Rican Day parade in June; the lively rhythms of Dominican *merengue* boom from passing cars year round; and African American worshipers' joyous praise of God's moving spirit permeates the entrance and stained-glass windows of the Devoe Street Baptist Church. Spanish-language billboards advertising tobacco and alcohol products loom over Metropolitan and Graham Avenues. Street designations such as Avenue of Puerto Rico, Boriquen Place, the Jaime Campiz Plaza/Playground, and the Thelma Martinez Playground are daily reminders of the Latino presence in the neighborhood and surrounding areas. In the summer of 1993, the sounds of a *tassa* drum band and *soca* recordings reverberated at a three-day Indo-Guyanese wedding celebration held in a neighbor's backyard on Metropolitan Avenue off Lorimer Street.[16]

Grassroots multicultural organizations such as the National Congress of Neighborhood Women and the St. Nicholas Neighborhood Preservation Corporation (to name just two) work across ethnic divisions to address the common concerns of community residents. Working-class women's formal and informal efforts to forge multicultural alliances in the area have been well documented (Susser 1982; Norchese 1985). Williamsburg's Italian residents, who did not flee the area their ancestors settled more than a century ago for other neighborhoods and enticing suburban townships, have learned how to deal with difference in the larger multiethnic, albeit divided, community.[17]

The ceremonial gathering of Italians and people of color is evident, to some degree, in at least one religious celebration staged in recent years. During the 1980s, Haitian devotees to Our Lady of Mount Carmel began marching in the church-sponsored procession, first on the sidewalk and eventually alongside their Italian counterparts. The procession is the only neighborhood event that is not organized with individual marching units, so that devotees form an interracial mass of believers surrounding the sides and back of the flower-adorned float bearing the Madonna as she is pulled by a car through neighborhood streets. This coming together can be accounted for in part because the cult of Our Lady of Mount Carmel in New York City has historically served to cut across regionally based Italian devotion (Orsi 1985:xix), and church-sponsored feasts in general tend to be open to a wider range of people (Giuliano 1976:49). Women's predominance in this event both as participants, with their history of local multiethnic coalitions, and as the central venerated figure of the Madonna, imbued with the "inclusive power of the Mother" (Turner 1980:15), established a parturient environment of acceptance and welcome. In addition, Haitians do not live in Williamsburg and thus are not perceived as a threat in the same way that neighborhood Puerto Ricans have historically been viewed.[18]

Haitians, who actively sought involvement in and incorporation into the procession honoring their spiritual patroness, helped usher in a series of significant changes in the parish vis-à-vis non-Italian devotees. Monsignor David Cassato began offering a Cantata mass in Creole on the Madonna's July 16 feast day in 1986, adding one in Spanish the following year, and another in Polish in 1992. These gestures of linguistic and religious inclusion flowered in December 1993, when weekly Sunday mass in Spanish was offered at the Italian "ethnic" parish for the first time. This belated outreach to the area's growing Latino community is dampened by the fact that services are held in the auditorium basement, the lower tier where Irish and German Catholics regulated Italian immigrants a century ago.

But focusing exclusively on the religious celebrations of a community as diverse as Italian Williamsburg creates a limited and ultimately distorted view of a place and its people. It is only by taking into account the "local ensemble of linked events" (Sanjek 1992:123), including nonreligious public gatherings, that one begins to gain a more complete picture of the area. Recently invented ceremonies bear testimony to and provide symbolically potent occasion for the coming together of the multi-ethnic communities of Williamsburg and Greenpoint. These attempts at ceremonial inclusiveness have been motivated by commercial interests (the Grand Street District Management Association's Easter parade held on the commercial strip since 1988) as well as concerns about crime (the coalition-sponsored National Night Out parade since 1983) and the environment (Autumnfest and the Harvest Procession, held at McCarren Park since 1990). Since 1992, organizers of the Winter Tree Festival have brought together different Christian communities around the decorating of a Christmas tree donated each year by former area resident and television personality Geraldo Rivera. Some new traditions can be attributed to the involvement of members of the recently arrived artist community. But long before Manhattan-centric painters and sculptors began moving to the area in search of low rents, the Greenpoint/Williamsburg Coalition of Community Organizations was formed in 1976 to fight cuts in services during the city's fiscal crisis and continued until reductions in funding brought about its demise in 1982. For four years the coalition sponsored a "Youth Olympics" at McCarren Park, providing the area's teenagers with organized recreational activities and a public face to its inter-ethnic political action (DeSena 1993). In 1993, Community Board Number One honored that history by holding its first "Unity Day" parade and feast in celebration of the area's multiculturalism.

Italian American participation in multi-ethnic gatherings in northern Brooklyn demonstrates that a single type of ceremony does not meet the complex needs of these urban residents. The religious procession is a familiar form of public culture expressing collectively a changing notion of faith and subjectivity. Local politics reinforces the ethnically marked character of religious celebrations, wedding Old World referents to contemporary territorial identities. Religious ceremonies are not considered the appropriate medium for reflecting and changing new realities. As Italian American residents march alongside their Latino and African American neighbors in the struggle for safe streets and a clean environment, the invented traditions of recent parades and marches become instrumental in the "very building and challenging of social relations" (Davis 1988:5). Border crossings are not only possible but, as residents of northern Brooklyn have long since discovered, necessary for survival.

Notes

1. While the number of street feasts has diminished in the past thirty years, processions have increased since I began my research in 1981: the Societá Gioventú di Sacco (1985); the American St. Cono Society (1988); the San Sabino Martire Mutual Aid Society (1990); and the St. Francis of Paola Church's procession to St. Anthony of Padua (1993).

According to members, one neighborhood feast was moved indoors in order to avoid their having to deal with the mob-controlled concession stands that monopolize

Italian street feasts citywide. Another society followed suit because of differences with residential neighbors who complained to police and the community board about noise, garbage, fights between youths, and parking problems resulting from the feast. This situation was aggravated by tensions between American-born home owners and the Italian-born society members. See Sciorra (1985) for the history of Williamsburg organizations and synopses of hagiographies.

2. Nonreligious, ethnic parades constitute another genre of perambulatory events held in the neighborhood. Since 1987, the Federation of Italian-American Organizations of Greenpoint/Williamsburg, a consortium consisting primarily of lay religious societies, has staged an annual Columbus Day parade. One-time events may also be planned, such as the neighborhood celebration of the Neapolitan soccer team's victory in the 1987 Italian championships. Marchers paraded through the streets with, among other things, a donkey (the team mascot), a coffin symbolizing the defeated Juventus team, and a huge cake depicting Naples' San Paolo Stadium. Even the opening ceremonies for a new parochial school at Our Lady of Mount Carmel Church were structured around several perambulatory events. A flyer announcing the September 8, 1992, event read "Festival Evening Prayer followed by a procession to the school for the momentous Ribbon-Cutting Ceremony, including a walk through the school."

3. Italian American Roman Catholics are also active in three other churches as part of multi-ethnic congregations: St. Vincent de Paul Church, St. Nicholas Church, and St. Cecilia's Church. A handful of elderly Italian American Baptists attend the Devoe Street Baptist Church.

4. A separate study on neighborhood voluntary associations is much needed. Two lay associations, the Pier Giorgio Frassati Catholic Association and the St. Joseph Society, do not sponsor a public procession in honor of their religious namesakes. A sign on one neighborhood building falsely proclaims the presence of a saint society. The organization held a religious feast the year after its founding in the late 1940s and was dissolved some forty years later. *Vox populi* maintains that the building's new owner is a well-known gangster. Several unnamed storefront clubs, some with bars, serve as hangouts for local mafiosi. For discussion of one mob club, see Pistone (1989:227–28; 283–84).

5. For more on the lifting of the giglio, see Posen (1986), Posen and Sciorra (1983), and Sciorra (1989a).

6. In the opening ceremony, members of the women's auxiliary of the Society of St. Mary of the Snow briefly carry the statue of the Madonna from the foot of the hall's exterior staircase to the float.

7. See Darnton (1984:107–43) for a discussion of the dramatization of social hierarchies in perambulatory events in eighteenth-century France.

8. Local religious life has been literally inscribed as a permanent feature of the urban landscape through municipal designation. Small triangular shards of public space resulting from the construction of the BQE have been officially christened Mt. Carmel Square (Meeker Ave./Union Ave./Jackson St.), Our Lady of the Snows Square (Meeker Ave./Graham Ave./Herbert St.), and Father Giorgio Triangle (Meeker Ave./Withers St./Lorimer St.). Richardson St. between Union Ave. and Lorimer St. has been renamed St. Cono Strada [*sic*]. Secular icons representing ethnic affiliation have also been formally marked in the area as with Via Vespucci and Christopher Columbus Way (Havemeyer St. between North 8th and North 9th Streets) in front of Our Lady of Mount Carmel Church.

9. Regional identity remains quite strong among Williamsburg's Italians, who

continue to employ traditional collective nicknames. Teggianesi are known as *cervi* ("reindeer"), because of the town's mountain location, and the Sanzese are *piedi bruciati* ("burnt feet"), because they were considered peasants too poor to own shoes.

10. Members of both societies attribute the fissure to a disparaging remark made by the then-pastor of Our Lady of Mount Carmel Church regarding the plaster visage of the Christ Child held by the original society's statue of the Madonna.

11. See Sciorra 1993 for an example of tensions between the local clergy and an Italian lay society in contemporary Staten Island.

12. The proposal to rename a stretch of Graham Avenue "Via Vespucci" was delayed for twelve years after the Puerto Rican community successfully lobbied for the change to "Avenue of Puerto Rico" in 1976, in part because of disagreements within the Italian community about the use of the Italian "via" versus the English "street." Language use during the panegyric mass for St. Cono at St. Francis of Paola Church was at the heart of the San Cono di Teggiano Catholic Association's decision to return to Our Lady of Mount Carmel Church, where services in Italian were allowed.

13. William Christian, Jr. (1972), explored the ways Catholic devotion and shrines topographically mark local, regional, and national identities in northern Spain.

14. The one perambulatory event that ventures beyond the Italian area, the *questua*, parades through the streets of predominantly Polish Greenpoint. In 1981, one *questua* leader explained why the marchers did not visit the Latino Southside by simply stating, "That's Zululand."

15. Ida Susser describes violent street-corner gang behavior among white youth directed against African Americans and Latinos (1982:120–24) in an unidentified part of the area during the mid-1970s. Author Daniel Fuchs (1972) provides a powerful account of gang activity among the teenage children of European immigrants in Williamsburg in his semi-autobiographical account from the 1930s, "Summer in Williamsburg."

The area's safe or forbidding reputation, depending on one's perspective, is reinforced through the presence of active voluntary associations, bastions of vibrant community life, scattered throughout the neighborhood. Storefront social clubs and bars commonly understood to be hangouts for local mafiosi ironically contribute to the popular perception held by insiders and outsiders alike that the presence of mobsters serves as a deterrent to street crime. The difference between those clubs associated with criminality and those that are not is often invisible to outsiders.

16. Non-Italians are less inclined to engage in such an array of perambulatory display as Italian Americans. Parades are staged as one-time events, as in 1990, when African American residents of the Cooper Park Housing Project celebrated the tenth anniversary of the state's designation of Grandparents' Day, a local initiative, by marching along Kingsland (Grandparents') Avenue to the accompaniment of Manhattan's Loisaida Samba Band.

When area residents do stage events, they tend to be far from where Italian Americans are concentrated. Four Roman Catholic churches sponsor separate processions on Good Friday for Latino parishioners in the Southside and in the area south of Grand Street. Each spring, the links between the Polish immigrant communities residing in the Northside and Greenpoint are dramatized in a Corpus Christi procession.

In 1994, the Puerto Rican community staged a massive Fifth Avenue–style ethnic pride parade that made its way down Graham Avenue and along Italian Williamsburg's main thoroughfare. The route was subsequently changed to turn on Grand Street, avoiding the Italian section.

17. Marriages have produced families that are living testimony to border crossings that are not heralded in public pageantry: on my block alone live an Italian immigrant husband and dark-skinned Brazilian wife whose preschooler speaks a mix of Neapolitan and Portuguese, as well as a trilingual Italo-Argentinean woman who babysits the ten-year-old son of Italian/African American parents who understands spoken Italian and marches in the St. Cono procession.

18. The recent inclusion of non-neighborhood Haitian immigrants in the church's procession and the historic exclusion of local Puerto Rican Catholics from it follows similar patterns in Harlem, as described by Robert Orsi in this volume.

Bibliography

Abbas, Ackbar. 1994. "Building on Disappearance: Hong Kong Architecture and the City." *Public Culture* 6, no. 3: 441–59.

Abrahams, Roger D. 1982. "The Language of Festivals: Celebrating the Economy." In *Celebration: Studies in Festivity and Ritual*, ed. Victor Turner, pp. 161–77. Washington, D.C.: Smithsonian Press.

———. 1987. "An American Vocabulary of Celebrations." In *Time Out of Time: Essays on the Festival*, ed. Alessandro Falassi, pp. 173–83. Albuquerque: University of New Mexico Press.

Carr, C. 1992. "The Bohemian Diaspora." *Village Voice*, February 4, pp. 26–31.

Christian, William A., Jr. 1972. *Person and God in a Spanish Valley*. New York: Seminar Press.

Cohen, Joyce. 1996. "If You're Thinking of Living In: Williamsburg." *New York Times*, October 6, p. R:5.

Darnton, Robert. 1984. *The Great Cat Massacre and Other Episodes in French Cultural History*. New York: Vintage.

Davis, Susan G. 1988. *Parades and Power: Street Theatre in Nineteenth-Century Philadelphia*. Berkeley and Los Angeles: University of California Press.

DeSena, Judith. 1993. "Community Co-operation and Activism: Italians and African Americans in Williamsburg, Brooklyn." In *Italian Americans and Their Public and Private Life*, ed. Frank J. Cavaioli, Angela Danzi, and Salvatore J. La Gumina, pp. 116–24. Staten Island: American Italian Historical Association.

Dorian, David. 1986. "If You're Thinking of Living In: Williamsburg." *New York Times*, June 16, p. R:9.

Eliade, Mircea. 1959. *The Sacred and the Profane: The Nature of Religion*. Trans. Willard R. Trask. New York: Harcourt Brace Jovanovich.

Falassi, Alessandro. 1987. "Festival: Definition and Morphology." In *Time Out of Time: Essays on the Festival*, ed. Alessandro Falassi, pp. 173–83. Albuquerque: University of New Mexico Press.

Ferris, Marc. 1993. "The Crescent in the Apple." *New York Newsday*, April 8, pp. 54, 100.

Fuchs, Daniel. 1972. *The Williamsburg Trilogy*. New York: Avon.

Gambino, Richard. 1975. *Blood of My Blood: The Dilemma of the Italian-Americans*. Garden City: Anchor.

Giuliano, Bruce B. 1976. *Sacro o Profano? A Consideration of Four Italian-Canadian Religious Festivals*. Canadian Centre for Folk Culture Studies Paper No. 17. Ottawa: National Museums of Canada.

Gooch, Brad. 1992. "The New Bohemia." *New York Magazine*, June 22, pp. 24–31.

Hannerz, Ulf. 1980. *Exploring the City: Inquiries toward an Urban Anthropology*. New York: Columbia University Press.

Hojnacki, William P. 1979. "What Is a Neighborhood?" *Social Policy* 10, no. 2: 47–52.

Howe, Marvine. 1984. "Polish Newcomers Revive Dying Greenpoint Customs." *New York Times*, June 22, pp. B:1–2.

Kasinitz, Philip. 1988. "The Gentrification of 'Boerum Hill': Neighborhood Change and Conflicts over Definitions." *Qualitative Sociology* 11, no. 3: 163–82.

Kirshenblatt-Gimblett, Barbara. 1983. "The Future of Folklore Studies: The Tradition and the Future." *Folklore Forum* 16, no. 2: 175–234.

Krase, Jerome. 1979. "Stigmatized Places, Stigmatized People: Crown Heights and Prospect-Lefferts Gardens." In *Brooklyn USA: The Fourth Largest City in America*, ed. Rita Seiden Miller, pp. 251–62. New York: Brooklyn College Press.

Ley, David, and Roman Cybriwsky. 1974. "Urban Graffiti as Territorial Markers." *Annals of Association of American Geographers* 64, no. 4: 491–505.

Lynch, Kevin. 1975. *The Image of the City*. Cambridge: MIT Press.

McGreevy, John T. 1996. *Parish Boundaries: The Catholic Encounter with Race in the Twentieth-Century Urban North*. Chicago: University of Chicago Press.

Marin, Louis. 1987. "Notes on a Semiotic Approach to Parade, Cortege, and Procession." In *Time Out of Time: Essays on the Festival*, ed. Alessandro Falassi, pp. 220–28. Albuquerque: University of New Mexico Press.

Marks, Morton. 1989. *Brooklyn's Hispanic Communities*. Brooklyn: Brooklyn Historical Society.

Miska, Maxine, and I. Sheldon Posen. 1983. *Tradition and Community in the Urban Neighborhood*. Brooklyn: Brooklyn Education and Cultural Alliance.

Norchese, Christine, dir. 1985. *Metropolitan Avenue*. Documentary film.

Orsi, Robert A. 1985. *The Madonna of 115th Street: Faith and Community in Italian Harlem, 1880–1950*. New Haven: Yale University Press.

———. 1992. "The Religious Boundaries of an Inbetween People: Street *Feste* and the Problem of the Dark-Skinned Other in Italian Harlem, 1920–1990." *American Quarterly* 44, no. 3: 313–47.

Pistone, Joseph D., with Richard Woodley. 1989. *Donnie Brasco: My Undercover Life in the Mafia*. New York: Signet.

Posen, I. Sheldon. 1986. "Storing Contexts: The Brooklyn Giglio as Folk Art." In *Folk Arts and Art Worlds*, ed. John Michael Vlach and Simon Bronner, pp. 171–91. Ann Arbor: UMI Research Press.

Posen, I. Sheldon, and Joseph Sciorra. 1983. "Brooklyn's Dancing Tower." *Natural History*, June, pp. 31–37.

Rieder, Jonathan. 1985. *Canarsie: The Jews and Italians of Brooklyn against Liberalism*. Cambridge: Harvard University Press.

Sanjek, Roger. 1992. "The Organization of Festivals and Ceremonies among Americans and Immigrants in Queens, New York." In *To Make the World Safe for Diversity: Towards an Understanding of Multi-cultural Societies*, ed. Ake Daun, Billy Ehn, and Barbro Klein, pp. 123–43. Helsingborg, Sweden: Schmidts Boktryckere AB.

Sciorra, Joseph. 1985. "Religious Processions in Italian Williamsburg." *Drama Review* 29, no. 3: 65–81.

———. 1989a. " 'O' Giglio e Paradiso': Celebration and Identity in an Urban Ethnic Community." *Urban Resources* 5.3: 15–20, 44–46.

———. 1989b. "Yard Shrines and Sidewalk Altars of New York's Italian-Americans." In *Perspective in Vernacular Architecture, III*, ed. Thomas Carter and Bernard L. Herman, pp. 185–98. Columbia: University of Missouri Press.

———. 1993. "Multivocality and Vernacular Architecture: The Grotto of Our Lady of Mount Carmel in Rosebank, Staten Island." In *Studies in Italian American Folklore,* ed. Luisa Del Giudice, pp. 203–43. Logan: Utah State University Press.

Susser, Ida. 1982. *Norman Street: Poverty and Politics in an Urban Neighborhood.* New York: Oxford University Press.

Suttles, Gerald D. 1974. *The Social Construction of Communities.* Chicago: University of Chicago Press.

Tuan, Yi-Fu. 1981. *Space and Place: The Perspective of Experience.* Minneapolis: University of Minnesota Press.

Turner, Kay. 1980. "The Virgin of Sorrows Procession: A Brooklyn Inversion." In *Folklore Papers 9,* ed. Kay Turner, pp. 1–26. Austin: Center for Intercultural Studies in Folklore and Ethnomusicology.

Turner, Victor. 1982. *The Ritual Process: Structure and Anti-Structure.* Ithaca: Cornell University Press.

Wellisz, Christopher. 1982. "If You're Thinking of Living In: Greenpoint." *New York Times,* December 12, p. R:9.

Winkleman, Michael. 1986. *The Fragility of Turf: The Neighborhoods of New York City.* Albany: State Department.

Zerubavel, Eviatar. 1985. *Hidden Rhythms: Schedules and Calendars in Social Life.* Berkeley and Los Angeles: University of California Press.

The Stations of the Cross

Christ, Politics, and Processions on New York City's Lower East Side

Wayne Ashley

To see [how the] system touches our own lives and to see if we can extricate ourselves . . . with the help of God. . . . And . . . when you do, you are in the place of Jesus. You then become the outcast, because if you free yourself from the structure, you can't be rich and powerful. And if you're not rich and powerful, you're poor and powerless, and then you become identified with Jesus. . . . The idea is to unite and resist, support one another in the struggle to say no to the evil of the system.

— Interview with Father George Kuhn, March 24, 1989

Since the early 1960s, St. Brigid's parish, like other Hispanic parishes on Manhattan's Lower East Side, has been performing an outdoor Stations of the Cross procession on Good Friday each year. An emotionally charged and religiously potent day in the Catholic liturgical cycle, Good Friday is the center point of a week-long celebration that commemorates the last days of Christ's life. Holy Week, as this time is called, includes Palm Sunday, the day Jesus entered the city of Jerusalem, and Holy Thursday, when Jesus was said to have transformed the bread and wine of his last meal with his apostles into his own body and blood so that friends and followers could experience his presence after his death. Good Friday marks the day Jesus died on the cross. It is followed by Holy Saturday, the day Jesus' followers held a special vigil at his tomb, and finally Easter Sunday, when Jesus rose from the dead.

The ritual of the Stations of the Cross enacts fourteen incidents in Christ's journey across Jerusalem on his way from condemnation to crucifixion. This chapter examines one expression of this tradition on New York's Lower East Side in 1989 and 1990. In the streets within the boundaries of St. Brigid's parish, participants enacted each of the Stations in front of strategically chosen, and extremely volatile, problem areas: a controversial health clinic, a deteriorating public school, a street corner where drugs were sold, a luxury condominium, and a park associated with danger and vice. Performed only months after the 1988 anti-gentrification protest in Tompkins Square Park that quickly became a riot, St. Brigid's procession was both public prayer and political critique. It emerged during one of the most explosive conflicts on the then "new urban frontier," as the Lower East Side was becoming increasingly emblematic of a widespread political and economic polarization of the city. As social critic Neil Smith remarked, "Apartment rents [were] soaring on a par with the numbers of homeless; record levels of luxury condo construction [were] matched by a retrenchment in public housing provisions; a Wall Street boom generate[d] seven and eight figure salaries while unemployment [rose] among the unskilled; poverty [was] increasingly concentrated among women, Hispanics and African Americans while social services [were] axed; and the conservatism of the 1980s brought us the recrudescence of racist violence from Howard Beach to Eleanor Bumpers."[1]

In symbolically retracing Christ's journey through Jerusalem, participants in the procession shifted the biblical text to a visual/spatial referent located in their neighborhood. They allegorized particular places and made them resonate with Christ's journey. Parishioners attempted to invest these places with "precise historical meanings" and "narrative sentiment," fashioning them into artifacts of collective action.[2] As participants traversed the neighborhood, two overlapping narratives emerged: one about Christ's suffering, the other about the topography of the East Village and its residents' suffering.

As historian Susan Davis has noted, dramatic representations, parades, and public ceremonies are political acts. They have pragmatic objectives and concrete, often material, results. People use these public displays as tools for building, maintaining, and confronting power relations.[3] St. Brigid's reworking of the Passion was not a subtle argument in political discourse; nor did it present complex plans for change. Rather, the clergy manipulated rhetorical strategies and religious symbols of the Passion for the purpose of creating new meanings that dramatized the difficult conditions of their parishioners' lives. This raises questions about the nature of ritual improvisation on a specific social field and about the relationship between ritual and neighborhood life. How are traditional texts and performances repositioned and inserted into new discourses? How were the ongoing debates and conflicts surrounding housing, welfare, and morality assimilated into the Christian narrative? How did the church employ a circumambulatory event in an effort to shape its congregants' experience and knowledge of the city?

Although St. Brigid's procession represented a church-based response to social injustices in civil society—"the efforts of the politically and economically weak to resist conditions they consider unjust"—the issue of who was speaking in this procession and the content and style of that enunciation were hotly contested by priests and parishioners.[4] Were the social issues articulated in the performance relevant to parishioners? Or were the clergy subsuming parishioners' voices within their own discourse?[5] To an outsider like me, St. Brigid's politicization of the Christ narrative appeared empowering. Fathers George and Frank spoke of giving the parks to the homeless and reclaiming abandoned buildings, and they prophetically denounced inadequate health care and misplaced military spending. Some parishioners, however, offered a more contentious reading of the procession, claiming that the church's attempt to re-edify their devotion toward social and political ends exemplified official intervention and control. Moreover, the event revealed a complex discourse on the relationship of bodies to urban space, and one fraught with many tensions. How do we interpret an event such as St. Brigid's Good Friday procession, situated as it was in the confluence of such contradictions and conflicts?

St. Brigid's Church is located in what is now called the East Village, the northern part of the Lower East Side, an area roughly east of the Bowery, stretching from about Houston Street to 14th Street. During the period of its earliest settlement in the 1800s, the Lower East Side was the site of the mansion homes of well-to-do English and Dutch traders. After 1840, the wealthy moved north to what is presently 14th Street; their mansions were split into multi-unit dwellings, and vacant land was in-filled with tenement buildings. Irish immigrants began arriving in the mid-nineteenth century, followed by Germans, many of whom were skilled workers with a background of labor organization. They occupied the area along St. Mark's Place and on 6th and 7th Streets before being joined by Jewish, Italian, and Polish immigrants at the turn of the century. After World War II, Latinos and Asians followed, and by the mid–1970s there were so many Puerto Ricans living in the East Village that local residents dubbed the area Loisaida (low-ees-SIDE-ah), the Puerto Rican pronunciation for "Lower East Side." The city partially recognized the Puerto Rican community's significance when it officially gave Avenue C the additional name Loisaida Avenue in 1986.

The area around St. Brigid's was once considered just a part of the Lower East Side, but it was renamed the East Village after hippies from the nearby West or Greenwich Village took up residence there. According to Neil Smith, the real estate industry imposed the new name to capitalize on the neighborhood's geographical proximity to the respectability, security, culture, and high rents of Greenwich village.[6] The major point of entry to the East Village is St. Mark's Place, the street running from Astor Place to Tompkins Square Park and beyond to cheap tenements as far east as Alphabet City, where Manhattan's north-south avenues are designated by letters rather than numbers.

Working-class for the past 160 years, the East Village has been the site of an ongoing struggle involving the real estate industry, social services, community groups, artists, and squatters, all with competing interests in how the neighborhood should develop and in what should be made of the numerous deteriorated and underutilized city-owned properties. Smith interprets the history of the Lower East Side as a series of "stalled attempts to reinvest and reconstruct the area in order to house late capitalism's labor force, a professional white middle class."[7] Sporadically since 1929, developers have sought to displace an increasingly redundant working class by taking control of neighborhood property, allowing it to become run-down, and "turning it over for large profits based upon its potential price (the price land could command if the area were redeveloped or the neighborhood gentrified)."[8] The city's Artist Homeownership Program, which resulted in subsidized housing opportunities for visual artists, tax abatement for luxury housing, and landlords' systematic abandonment of their properties, managed to drive many local families from their homes. Parishioners from St. Brigid's spoke about the steady deterioration of the East Village during the late 1960s and 1970s, which led to the forced migration of Puerto Ricans to other boroughs, to different states, and even back to Puerto Rico.

By 1985, developers had "restored" properties—which is to say they had readied them for upper-middle-class consumption—all the way to the East River, "leaving only city-owned buildings unaffected by reinvestment."[9] At the time of my research, the housing projects located on 7th Street and FDR Avenue were among the few remaining strongholds for working-class families. Many of St. Brigid's parishioners lived there.[10]

To understand the debates surrounding Good Friday processions at St. Brigid's during the late 1980s and early 1990s, it is important to recognize that they were part of a much larger discussion that had been ongoing since at least the early 1960s: Where was the "vigor of priestly and religious commitment" to be centered? On the church or on the world?[11] In other words, would the clergy focus their attention primarily on the particular spiritual and ethical needs of their Puerto Rican constituency, or attend to the structures outside of the church, to social and political causes divorced from any specific Puerto Rican agenda?[12] Over the next thirty years, these questions continued to be debated at St. Brigid's, but the intensity with which parishioners and clergy sought to find resolution appeared to fluctuate depending upon the particular church leadership at the time, the goals of the Archdiocese, and a number of other social and economic constraints. During my interviews with parishioners about past processions, many spontaneously evoked the situation at St. Brigid's in the 1960s as the originary moment of a great chasm, which appeared never to have fully disappeared.

During the 1960s, against the backdrop of official neglect that Smith describes as the planned deterioration of the Lower East Side, New York's Catholic Church sought to make religion a more vital force in what had become a slum neighborhood. Church leaders aimed to reinvolve young people in community and parish activities and to find ways of reversing the decline in church attendance.[13] Inspired by the spirit of the Second Vatican Council (1962–65), the Archdiocese of New York initiated a broad range of innovations. These included directly involving parishioners in religious leadership and ministry, more attention to the promotion of justice particularly for the poor, and more effective evangelization among the people in the neighborhood. These changes in religious practices intersected historically with shifts in social values in general occurring in the United States during the 1960s.

In 1967, the Archdiocese of New York designated St. Brigid's and St. Rita of Cascia in the Bronx as experimental churches. In place of the traditional organization of a senior pastor aided by associates, St. Brigid's had a team of three priests—Dermod McDermott, John Calhoun, and Matthew Thompson—working together as equals to help break down the perception of the church as an authoritarian hierarchical structure with little personal involvement in the lives of its parishioners. Together, the three pastors attempted to bridge the gap between the church and the community by sponsoring block parties and neighborhood clean-up programs, and by opening the rectory to help drug addicts and troubled teenagers. They brought the Spanish Mass out of the basement into the main church, added folk instruments and Puerto Rican songs, and made many innovations in the liturgy and festival life of the parish.

One of these innovations was Father McDermott's Stations of the Cross. In Puerto Rico, outdoor processions were a common part of religious life, and McDermott felt that the institution of such a celebration on the Lower East Side would help make the church more available and recognizable to its growing Puerto Rican constituency. Because of the scarcity of Puerto Rican clergymen ministering in the homeland, few indigenous priests were able to accompany the immigrants to their new destinations.[14] Unlike Polish and Italian immigrants, who had their own national churches, and who employed priests from their countries of origin and preached in their native languages, the Archdiocese insisted that the Puerto Ricans join established neighborhood churches. The consequences of this convergence of factors were enormous. Parishes had to operate bilingually and biculturally, recruit Spanish-speaking clergy, and direct some of their existing resources to the needs of the new immigrants.[15]

When Puerto Ricans began coming to St. Brigid's, Polish and Italian

Americans dominated the decision-making processes in the parish, ran the various church organizations, and provided most of the help to the new-comers. Because the old-timers refused to establish a Spanish-speaking society among their organizations, McDermott organized the Puerto Rican parishioners into their own devotional society, called Los Caballeros de Santa Brigida. Los Caballeros held monthly meetings, ran one or two dances a year, helped out at bingo, collected and counted the weekly donations, held a feast on San Juan Day, and were available to help make repairs or clean up the church.[16] Together with the women's society, the Damas (Christian Mothers), they went on religious retreats and eventually took responsibility for the Stations of the Cross, which they enthusiasti-cally organized until 1985 (when, for reasons that are still unclear, they refused further participation). Under the guidance of Father Frank Scan-lon, and later with the assistance of senior pastor Father George Kuhn, the church youth group took over the Stations, performing the procession until 1991, when Father Frank moved to another parish, leaving Father George as the church's sole administrator and religious leader.

The first year, McDermott staged the procession in the traditional devotional style, mildly contemporizing the prayers by forging connec-tions between Christ's suffering and the parishioners' own grievances. The Puerto Rican parishioners stopped at various places along a pre-established route and recited prayers expressing a muted social message. Simple analogies were made between, for example, Christ being crowned with thorns and the community being metaphorically crowned by the thorns of poor education and inadequate social services. Participants chose sites based on distance and location and assigned no special significance to them.[17] McDermott recalled that people were ambivalent about the pro-cession, charging him with "bringing politics into the church," an issue that parishioners continued debating during the time of my research.[18]

McDermott interpreted this negative response as the inability of older and more "traditional" Puerto Ricans to accept innovation. Believing that younger folk would be more receptive to his changes, he channeled his energy toward the church youth, involving them in social action and "political consciousness-raising."[19] In order to fulfill parishioners' needs for devotional expression while simultaneously inflecting the Passion with social concerns, McDermott divided parishioners along generational lines the following year. Adults would stage half the Stations in the traditional devotional style, while the parish youth would stage the other half as a series of short social dramas.

Young men and women in the neighborhood scripted these dramas from their own personal life biographies and performed them with the help of a sound system atop a flatbed truck. The small sketches focused on abortion, drugs, and relationships among racial groups. In the Station "Christ Meets His Mother," for example, actors depicted a pregnant sixteen-year-old girl deciding whether she should marry her boyfriend or have an abortion. Her mother and father argued different positions, until finally her father insisted that she have the abortion. At the last moment, a friend complicated the decision by pointing out that the girl would be *killing* her baby if she went through with the abortion. There was no ending to the skit and no final resolution, just an explication of the turmoil.[20] Meanwhile, the Caballeros and Damas organized the adult component of the Passion. Wearing costumes meant to evoke biblical times, men and women of the society arranged themselves into various tableaux and recited the traditional text from St. Alphonsus Liguori's "The Way of the Cross."

By focusing on the experiences and ideas of youth, the clergy hoped to increase the young people's involvement in the church and the neighborhood. The result of this plan, however, was to create a generational conflict within the parish. This old dissension prefigured the exodus of adults from the church in the late 1980s and early 1990s, particularly those associated with the traditional devotional societies on similar grounds. Father Birkle, a priest at St. Brigid's during part of McDermott's tenure there (1969–72), remembered tensions rising several times between the younger generation and their parents over changes in liturgical practice. Many older parishioners objected to the new music introduced into the Mass (which included songs such as "The Age of Aquarius" from the musical *Hair*), liturgical dancing, and what Birkle described as a shift away from the "awesome, mysterious element of the divine toward the humanistic."[21]

In his zeal for social criticism, however, McDermott pushed many parishioners even further away when he staged "The Death of Santa Claus" during a Three Kings procession, a traditional Puerto Rican festival performed the week after Christmas. McDermott's idea was to demonstrate how commercialism had destroyed the meaning of Christmas, so he paraded a coffin containing a dead Santa Claus shot by a boy dressed up as a television set. Another youth dressed in a costume symbolizing "a capitalist pig" was shown poisoning another Santa Claus. When McDermott saw children in the crowd crying at these terrifying images, he realized that he had gone too far, and he never repeated the drama. But he carried his rebellious style into his personal life, creating an enormous scandal when he revealed to parishioners that he had become romantically involved with a woman and still wanted to continue as pastor of the church. The Caballeros angrily forbade him from performing the Mass and declared that the priest would have to kill them before he could minister to them again.[22]

McDermott was not the only provocateur. Trouble had started much earlier in the period of liturgical experimentation and change when Father Calhoun, taking his cue from the new Vatican orientation, ordered the removal of the saints from the front of the church. Calhoun wanted to emphasize the liturgy and the sacrifice of the Mass as the community's central act of worship, and to simultaneously minimize parishioners' devotion to the saints, which he felt competed for their attention. Without the people's knowledge, Calhoun arranged for the destruction of the altar's ornate structure and removed the saints out onto the streets. People were shocked. As a result of this act, many of the Polish congregation left for other churches.[23] Ray Acevedo, an altar boy at the time, told how he and other church members used a dolly to cart the statues to their homes, where parishioners continued to make offerings and light candles before them.[24] Older Puerto Rican parishioners still recalled the incident with bitterness, and during some of my interviews they used it to account for the mistrust they felt toward the clergy.

In an effort to contain what the Archdiocese realized had become a chaotic situation at St. Brigid's, Father Tom Leonard was assigned to the church for three months, essentially to "clean up the mess" and end the pastoral experiment. By the time the Archdiocese had made Father Ed Keehan senior pastor at St. Brigid's in 1972, and reinstituted the hierarchical system of administration, the Passion procession had already taken on a more devotional quality, without the overt political and social content of Father McDermott's performances. Father Juaquin Beaumont, a Spaniard who ministered the church from 1980 to 1986, also reported a reluctance on the part of parishioners to link the teachings of the Bible with social and political conditions in their lives. "As soon as you made a social connection between the teachings of Christ and the parishioners' everyday life, they evoked the specter of Communism," Beaumont told me in a conversation. "They were suspicious and hurt by the previous experiments." He recalled that the Caballeros were very difficult to get along with. "They thought they were the owners of the church and told me what to do."[25]

My point in narrating these incidents is not to fault the clergy or to belittle their attempts at social activism. Parishioners I interviewed also talked highly of the priests' innovative ideas, commitment to the neighborhood, and efforts to create a sense of community among newly arriving Puerto Ricans. What I want to establish is the existence of a fluctuating tension, which began at least thirty years prior to my research, between what Patrick McNamara refers to as pastoral care and social action.[26] In other words, clergy and parishioners at St. Brigid's debated how much emphasis should be given to the faith dimension of Catholicism (e.g., creed, rules of conduct, precepts, and forms of worship including the sacraments, liturgy, and devotion), and how much to its social concerns (e.g., the material needs of the people). On the basis of my research, it is apparent that most of the lay leadership, when left to their own choices, preferred the spiritual dimension of the ritual to the political and social. And at times the clergy made decisions about the focus of the church without seriously taking into account the aspirations of their congregants. I do not mean to suggest that parishioners were not otherwise involved in social action, did not exercise their franchise, or did not participate in other available political alternatives. But many questioned the extent to which the church should take on this role.

The Caballeros and Damas continued to perform the procession on the streets until the early 1980s, when the new pastors, Fathers Beaumont and Carlos Acosta Lopez, moved it back inside the church.[27] Beaumont thought the streets were too distracting and disordered and that parishioners would have a more focused religious experience within the confines of the church. He also wanted to avoid being charged with "forcing our religious views on other people" through public evangelization.[28]

Taking over from Father Keehan, Beaumont and Lopez attempted to negotiate between the radical impulses of Father McDermott, on the one hand, and what Father Beaumont described as Keehan's exclusively spiritual emphasis, on the other.[29] Members of the Caballeros and Damas organized the production and staged it in the tradition of a Passion rather than a procession. The groups took great pride in the production, vied for particular roles, and rehearsed for months. The staging was elaborate and included sound effects, lighting, the addition of many characters to the scriptural cast, hand-sewn costumes, and special crosses built to simulate actual crucifixion.

"I saw people in the audience crying," Beaumont recalled. "When Jesus fell down and was crucified, parishioners really gasped. That day people were ready to spend as many hours to watch as it took to complete the Passion. The church was filled and the balconies were crowded. People were more present and excited by the Passion than the celebration of the liturgy."[30]

By 1985, the Caballeros and Damas had discontinued organizing the Passion and become less involved in church activities. Father Frank, who came to St. Brigid's in 1982, believes that the reason was intense infighting among the society's members and an absence of leadership.[31] But Father Frank also alluded to an ongoing struggle between Father Carlos and the Caballeros over the role of the church in society and the function of the Caballeros and Damas in the fulfillment of that role. Father Carlos Lopez was very concerned about evangelization, public outreach, and home visitation, while the parishioners wanted to continue to "run the dances, do the Passion. Leave us alone; let us do what we've always done."[32]

Father Frank took over responsibility for organizing the procession in

1985, and a year later, with permission from Father George, the new senior pastor who replaced Father Juaquin, he brought it back out into the streets, reviving its political and social dimension. Parish teenagers had completely taken over the event; although some Puerto Rican church elders could be seen walking in the procession, they would never fully participate again.[33] This is significant, because beginning in the 1960s, the outdoor religious processions had been organized mostly by the laity, and they were considered, at least by most clergy, a Latino expression lying outside the domain of "official" religious practice.[34] Now the impetus and leadership of the procession were coming from the clergy.

Possibly reacting to what he felt was the Caballeros' over-produced, sentimental presentation of the Passion, Father Frank structured his procession to downplay aesthetic virtuosity in favor of minimal action and costume and an almost didactic style of recitation. The ritual required very little rehearsal and almost no preparation. Although youth group members donned costumes, arranged themselves into various tableaux, and invoked biblical personages, Father Frank's procession was less a dramatic reenactment and more a public prayer.

The Procession

Father Frank revived the idea of the outdoor procession during a regular weekly youth meeting at the church. He composed the text by piecing together prayers from a pamphlet entitled *Aqui Estoy Senor*, a religious workbook published by the Hispanic Catholic Center to instruct young people in the teachings of the Gospel, with particular attention to their political, social, and economic importance. Father Frank added his own prayers and reflections to speak to local issues and grievances.[35] The procession mapped out the last days of Jesus' life, beginning in Pilate's praetorium, where Christ was condemned to die, and ending with his crucifixion and death at the hill of Golgotha. The final Station, Christ's burial, took place back in the church. Lasting just over two hours, the Good Friday procession traversed the area between 3rd and 9th Streets and between Avenues B and D, the rough boundaries of the parish.

At the head of the procession, Fathers Frank and George led the congregation through a preestablished route of boarded-up buildings, little bodegas, city rubble, and tiny clearings of reclaimed land converted into parks. They moved past graffiti-covered walls, squatters' buildings, and newly renovated apartments. At each stop, Father Frank read a description of the Station in both Spanish and English, and recited a prayer and a short homily relating the biblical incident to a specific local social problem. The congregants were invited to meditate on the details of Christ's Passion and use them to focus on their own social conditions. Meanwhile the young people of the church arranged themselves in the appropriate configurations to illustrate the Stations. Father Frank broadcast pre-recorded Spanish liturgical music over a loudspeaker mounted on top of a car that accompanied the procession as it moved between Stations.

I followed the route, too, noting the particular sites, recording the prayers and reflections, and describing the numerous tableaux. But it was only later, during scheduled conversations with clergy members and parishioners, that I came to understand the implications of the places where we stopped and their resonance with specific Stations. I have not included a description of the entire route because some of the Stations repeated themes introduced at earlier stops. Here is the journey we made through Loisaida:

Station one: *Parishioners performed the first Station in front of a pharmacy located in a newly renovated building on Avenue B between 6th and 7th Streets. Standing in the middle of the street in front of the store, Father Frank announced the Station over the loudspeaker: "Pilate condemns Jesus to die. Jesus has been flogged and crowned with thorns. Now Pilate unjustly condemns him to die on a cross." Two young men stood apart from the line and moved into their tableaux. Pilate, a dark bearded youth dressed in a maroon velvet robe, accusingly pointed his finger at Jesus, another youth draped in a white robe with a crimson cloth wrapped around his shoulder that trailed down to his feet. The action was spare. Father Frank lowered his head and prayed, enunciating each word carefully: "Lord, help me to realize that you live inside all of us. . . . Many times we look for peace and contentment outside of you. Many times we try to escape from our problems by abusing prescription drugs. This abuse leads us astray and further away from you, our source of peace and contentment." This opposition between inside and outside, between Christ/the interior and a dangerous exterior, would be further elaborated upon in the course of the procession and made manifest in spatial terms. Order is located in Christ, within the Church; chaos exists outside on the street, in the public domain.*

In a later conversation, Father George explained that he and Father Frank suspected one of the pharmacists of giving out prescription drugs to addicts who either used them without supervision or resold them on the street to buy deadlier illegal drugs such as crack. The priests believed the pharmacist had already been run out of another neighborhood in Harlem for cheating patients on Medicaid and giving doctors financial kickbacks for prescribing large quantities of unnecessary drugs.[36]

Station two. *The procession stopped frequently at sites of displacement and homelessness, vividly calling attention to the absence of adequate* domestic space in New York City, and to the failure of city officials to provide housing for poor people. Parishioners staged the second Station in front of the Trinity Shelter on 6th Street between Avenues B and C. Two younger boys dressed in the attire of Roman soldiers hoisted a large wooden cross onto the shoulder of the boy portraying Christ as Father Frank announced, "Jesus receives a cross to carry on his bleeding and bruised shoulders." Then he prayed: "Lord, your fall strikes my heart and brings out my compassion. Let the fall of my brothers without homes strike my heart and move me to do something for them."

Station five. Father Frank intoned the fifth Station at the federally subsidized Nena medical clinic: "Simon helps Jesus carry the cross. Jesus becomes more weak. Fearing that he won't be able to continue, his executioners force Simon of Cyrene to help him carry the cross." The procession stopped here, according to Father George, to remind parishioners of their successful struggle to keep the clinic operating after investigators, having discovered that the hospital's board of directors had been illegally investing grant money in East Village real estate, had threatened to close it down. When members of the board refused to resign, the government cut off its financial support, jeopardizing the clinic's future. Father George organized demonstrations in front of the clinic, obtained parishioners' signatures in support of keeping it open, and together with members of the Lower East Side Area Conference put pressure on the district attorney to get the closing decision reversed. The issue finally went to court. The judge assigned a new temporary manager to oversee the clinic, and the city government reallocated the frozen funds.

As a boy dressed in a white robe took hold of Jesus's cross and lifted it onto his own shoulder, Father Frank recited the following prayer: "Jesus suffers today in all the sick who are not receiving proper medical care. The sick are among the weakest in our community, and like Simon, we are asked to help carry their crosses. We ask for forgiveness for all who use the medical profession for their own financial gain and do not give themselves selflessly to heal and comfort the sick. We pray for all who work in the medical profession here in our neighborhood. We ask God to give them the patience and compassion that is necessary to help the sick."

Station six. Parishioners performed the sixth Station, "Veronica wipes the face of Jesus," in front of the old women's shelter across the street from Nena Clinic. Father Frank read, "The face of Jesus is covered in sweat and blood. Out of piety, Veronica moves to wipe his face with her veil, and the image of his sacred face is imprinted on the cloth." The girl playing Veronica approached Jesus and touched his face with a cloth. Standing back from him, she opened the crumpled fabric to reveal the scrawled image of Christ's face. Father Frank spoke: "Many times we withhold from women their *dignity as daughters of God. Jesus fought hard so that there would be respect for women, and he suffers today when others take advantage of them. Jesus suffers when women are exploited for sexual pleasure. Jesus suffers when women are forced to have abortions for economic reasons. Jesus suffers when women have to give up their children.*"

Station seven. *On Avenue D and 4th Street, the procession stopped in front of a public school. Father Frank announced the Station: "Jesus falls a second time. Jesus falls under the weight of the cross. His executioners drag him by the feet and force him to continue onward to Calvary." The boy portraying Jesus dropped to his knees and bowed his head as Father Frank recited, "Just as Jesus fell under the width of the cross, our children are falling under the lack of values being taught in the public schools of our neighborhood. How is it possible that in our public schools birth-control pills can be distributed and twelve-year-olds can be sent for abortions without their parents' permission? Shame on our public school system. Jesus is truly suffering in the children of our neighborhood."*

Station ten. *After winding through abandoned lots, past pop figures of Batman and the Joker painted on vacant buildings together with murals memorializing drug overdoses and motorcycle accidents, the procession stopped at a deserted building on the corner of Avenue C and 10th Street. The place had been used for selling drugs. A red devil with a spiked tail and pointed ears was painted prominently over the doorway, warning prospective dealers to leave the area. Next to this image was a scrawny cartoon figure of a man holding a crack pipe, under which someone had painted the numerical sign for Satan, "666," in bold black strokes emerging from a sooty smoke-filled mouth. The drawing was captioned "Just saying no is not enough." In front of these harshly cartooned walls, parishioners performed the tenth Station. Father Frank announced, "Jesus is coming closer to the summit of Calvary, the place of his execution. He is stripped of his clothing, which reveals new bleeding wounds." The youth depicting Jesus fell to his knees clasping the heavy cross in his arms, while Veronica stood by his side displaying the image of his face on the white cloth. Father Frank prayed: "Father, for all those who find themselves falling into the hands of drugs and alcohol, help me, Lord, not to be one of those who sit back to watch, criticize, and without making an attempt to help the alcoholics and drug addicts of this world. May I learn and believe that whatever I do to and for my neighbor, I do for you. Lord, give me strength and wisdom not to push them aside, put them down, or hurt them. Let me make a difference in their lives, so that they may one day experience your compassion and know that they are not alone."*

Station twelve. *For some residents living in the East Village, Christadora House, a sixteen-story luxury condominium on Avenue B and 9th*

Street, had become the symbol for anti-gentrification sentiments and protests. During the Tompkins Square Park riot in the summer of 1988, a group of demonstrators blocked the art deco door, flung garbage into the lobby, and chanted "Death to yuppie scum!"[37] On another occasion, demonstrators hurled bricks through the glass door of the marble-floored lobby in an act of retaliation after the demolition of the squatters' building at 318 East 8th Street. Allegorized as the hill of Golgotha, Christadora House was the site of the twelfth Station, "Jesus dies on the cross."

Father George positioned three crosses, each bearing a boy with bowed head, so that their tableau was perfectly framed by the doorway of Christadora House. The word CHRIST embedded in the name of the building—CHRISTADORA—ironically announced the Station. Father Frank read a prayer in Spanish: "The weight of the cross is shared by many people in our community who are uprooted from their family life by gentrification. Look around you at the construction of new buildings, luxury buildings that are built throughout the city, out of greed, not out of necessity. All of this goes on while people in our community live crowded in the same apartment. . . . It is not considered a luxury but a right that we can have." One of the girls approached Jesus and touched his face as if to wipe away his tears. It started raining again. The red paint from the crown of thorns began to drip and streamed down his face.

Station thirteen. Parishioners performed the thirteenth Station in Tompkins Square Park. During the last couple of years, this city park had become the site of an ongoing struggle among community groups, homeless persons, self-styled anarchists, and neighborhood residents over how it was to be used and by whom. The conflict intensified as numerous homeless men and women began setting up tents and permanently occupying the park. A riot erupted in the park in the summer of 1988 over a one A.M. curfew enforcement imposed on the pretext of clearing out the growing number of homeless, the kids who played their boom boxes until late at night, and drug buyers and sellers who used the site for business.[38] Father George rallied for the homeless and fought to keep the park available as a place for them to live.

Amid garbage and fires burning to keep a group of homeless families warm, Father Frank read out, "Jesus is taken down from the cross." The boy playing Jesus lay down, while his mother nestled his head in her arms and caressed his face. Parishioners and other passersby encircled the couple as Father Frank spoke in the same unaffected voice: "Although there is wood for crucifying Jesus, thousands of people in our community don't have wood for housing. They share the passion and death of Jesus on our walkways and park benches. After Jesus was let down from the cross, he received the arms of his mother. Whose arms are waiting for the displaced?" The men lifted Christ onto a stretcher and carried him from the park into the church, where they performed the last Station, "Jesus is buried."

In addition to the Stations described above, Father Frank led the procession to a check-cashing service, a homesteader's building, a corner where unemployed men regularly hang out, and another location where illegal drugs could be bought.

Representations of Place and Maintaining Boundaries

For many years now, anthropologists, urban folklorists, cultural geographers, and social psychologists have increasingly turned their attention toward understanding the meaning of urban spaces through the knowledge and practices of the people who live within them. They view the ways individuals ascribe social and cultural value to the cityscape and built environment, and the emerging discourses about these spaces, as important processes in the constitution of social reality. As Matthew Cooper notes, spatial discourses enable people to elaborate ideologies of place "which variously and ambiguously help/lead/force them to think and act in certain ways. . . . Using ideologies of place, people describe the kinds of places that exist, explain their nature, evaluate them (employing cognitively and emotionally salient imagery to create a symbolic landscape), identify with them, and imagine places as they ought to be (thus creating moral landscapes)."[39]

Sociologist M. Gottdiener, echoing Cooper, suggests that emphasis be given to the way "urban artifacts, discourses about the city environment, and locationally oriented ideologies comprise factors in the determination of urban processes and activities."[40] He asks, Which ideological representations of the city do varying social groups use in their struggles for control of space? In seeking answers to this question, Gottdiener recommends exploring not only the symbolic conception of objects such as buildings, but also those signifying practices that imbue such objects with oppositional or alternative meanings, such as graffiti, for example. He also suggests examining both written and verbal discourses — planning commission reports, as well as metaphors of novelists, for example — as "significant symbolic referents in the organization of behavior."[41] I would also include extra-textual discourses such as rituals, festivals, parades, street performances, and other forms of public display as important occasions through which to explore the social production of space.[42]

More important, Gottdiener reminds us that meaning in the city is multi-coded. Different social groups possess varying conceptions of urban space, just as the "different interests in the city compete with each other over control of the social surplus. Gender, age, and status groups as well as classes hold fundamentally different images of the city and base the organization of daily life on these differently conceived symbols."[43] What is useful about these perspectives is that they problematize any essentialist notions of place and draw our attention to ways in which spatial meanings are always historically and socially contingent. At any given moment, competing images may emanate from antagonistic social fields, contributing to contradictory perceptions, feelings, and consciousnesses about the spaces we live in. Thus, during the late 1980s and early 1990s, St. Brigid's representation of the East Village as the suffering body of Christ in need of redemption was countered by two other potent but more widely circulated images: the real estate business's image of the East Village as a "dangerous frontier" in need of civilizing, and the art establishment's image of the neighborhood as a site of the new avant garde, individual liberation, and adventure.[44] Both of these images were deployed to help legitimize gentrification processes in the Lower East Side.

Given the polysemous nature of urban life, the need of some groups, under particular conditions, for more stable, uniformly conceived representations of place can be great. Managing and negotiating boundaries and representations of place is a constant cultural and political struggle. Seen in this light, the Good Friday procession of St. Brigid's was an assertion of limits. Not only did it trace the physical boundaries of the parish, it attempted to ritually maintain and bound the collective body by linking and purifying those sites of disorder and deficiency that threatened its integrity. Each Station was continuous with Christ's suffering; each was an open wound in need of healing. The procession posited an ideal collective body that could consolidate itself in the body of Christ, which was literally mapped out onto the urban landscape.

The procession aimed to resemanticize the urban environment, constructing a sanctuary, a refuge, from which to articulate a resistant voice. As opposed to the plethora of media representations of the East Village and its ills, the voice of the Passion was in a language known to the parishioners, even though this speaking was initiated and created by church leaders. It was a critical voice, denouncing the excesses of capitalism, real estate development, and corruption. To some parishioners, it was redemptive, mobilizing action, finding sanction in the performed image of a self-sacrificing Christ.

The procession attempted to reorganize people's perception of those problems as collective by enacting a shared, morally resonant narrative. For Nilsa Fiol, a parishioner at St. Brigid's for eight years, the procession transformed an often privatized, fragmented, and isolated experience of the city into a public experience. Speaking about one of the Stations where she encountered a group of homeless men and women living in cardboard boxes, Nilsa recalled,

> It was sad, because this is the Big Apple, one of the richest cities in the world, supposedly, and you can even walk to the Stock Exchange—and here we have people living in cardboard boxes and tents. But that's not what affected me so much. It was the people's reaction when they saw us. . . . They saw a little dim light of hope. . . . It's a reminder that everybody has a cross to carry, and they were carrying their cross. And we were telling them that they hadn't been forgotten. They're not carrying the cross alone; we're helping them along the way. . . . We see, and hear, and we feel their sufferings. We're trying to do our best to rectify what the system has screwed up years and years ago.[45]

Urban space had been recodified for Nilsa and other parishioners who "heard" and "saw" the possibility for the betterment of the oppressed in their readings and visualizations of these texts.

As Louis Marin has pointed out, processions play on a spatial tension produced by the process of moving anomalously through preexisting spaces already articulated by certain named or marked places: neighborhoods, buildings, streets, monuments, corners, and boundaries within the city. These places already have varied and sometimes conflicting resonances and meanings in people's everyday lives. The stops along St. Brigid's Passion route did not have the same significance to all parishioners, and at times they were the object of a great deal of contention, not only among various groups in the neighborhood but among the parishioners themselves. How these places were to be used, by whom, and for what purposes continued to be argued in community board meetings, among neighborhood action groups, and at St. Brigid's.

Participants in the procession constructed the stage and decor of their religious performance out of this hostile, contested space. Certain parts of the route were privileged over others; some places were included and others not; some buildings or areas were visited and others ignored. A procession thus manipulates space and the places that already exist, giving space a meaningful structure. Places chosen for the route articulate what Marin identifies as "sentences of a spatial discourse," whereas "those places bypassed or avoided by the procession deploy a counter-discourse which helps to form the background of the first discourse, thereby giving it another dimension of meaning."[46]

The spatial discourse that emerged in this procession articulated sites of excess (drugs, alcohol, money, sex) and sites of deficiency (lack of food, lack of health care, lack of housing, lack of values). They were all places implicating the body. Shelters, health care centers, schools, pharmacies, shooting galleries, liquor stores, and abortion clinics (all stops along St.

Brigid's procession) constitute various social fields in which individuals come to manage and experience their bodies. These are sites where struggles over the corporeal are an everyday process, and where definitions as to what counts as a legitimate body, and a legitimate use of the body, are asserted, undermined, put into question, or enforced. The physical space of the city and the territory of the body were related to each other by the procession. Moreover, the procession posited these sites as disorderly—in need of physical, spiritual, and moral repair. A disordered space was analogous to a disordered body. The procession was an act of ordering the space and thereby analogous to ordering the body.

But just who was ordering this body? Fathers George and Frank chose the specific places on the procession route, linked those places to political struggles they themselves had often initiated, and shaped the terms and styles of those struggles. In fact, many of the stops along the procession route were organizations that either sympathized with the clergy's political views or had actually worked with them on various causes. While the procession succeeded in dramatizing important issues, it simultaneously inscribed the experience of participants within the specific political discourse of the clergy. To what extent, then, can we talk about a truly collective body? What kind of cohesive body can the Christ allegory sustain?[47]

The procession was inseparable from Father George's and Frank's theology, which viewed religious values and symbols as the impetus for "economically disempowered individuals to mobilize against immoral social structures."[48] But this view was not always consonant with popular desire.

I was initially drawn to St. Brigid's parish because of the clergy's commitment to social action, and by what I initially mistook as parishioners' unbidden, spontaneous commitment to change. My own impulse had been to support the clergy's political initiatives and view the Passion as an important critical voice emerging from among the parishioners. But after spending time at St. Brigid's and talking to priests and parishioners, I had to confront a paradox. Father George's commitment to bringing about a more just and egalitarian community in the neighborhood was countered by some parishioners' assertion that they were being simultaneously erased from the center of church activities. These parishioners linked Father George's political agenda to a trivialization of their own cultural and spiritual desires. Their feelings of marginalization emerged during my interviews, not only around key concerns such as whether the church should become a shelter for the homeless or a sanctuary for anti-war activities, but also around more everyday activities such as church music, social dances, and the dissolution of the Holy Names societies, the Caballeros and the Damas. "When Father George came, everything changed," remembered a long-time parishioner. "The Caballeros and the Christian Mothers [Damas] broke up. A lot of people moved away from the church because of his other involvements. . . . The parishioners felt that a priest should attend to the concerns of his parish, but Father George had become too involved in political issues like the homeless in the park, and the anarchists."

One thing Father George did to upset many parishioners was to bring in a Dominican organist to direct the church music. This Sister introduced new songs and rhythms; her more subdued musical style could not accommodate the exuberant Puerto Rican ensemble of guitar, maracas, and guido. One parishioner lamented,

> When [Father George] first came in, we had a nice choir. I loved it. It was very nice. And then he decided to buy an organ and have a Sister, a nun, play the organ and just the organ. So the choir was gone. . . . We used to play beautiful songs, Spanish songs. Everybody knew the songs . . . oh my God, and you'd see the people clapping and everything; it was wonderful. And then he brought the Sister. . . . She had a beautiful voice, there was no denial of that. But some of the songs she was singing, nobody knew. And there was only the organ. So the music sounded so sad. Nobody liked the music. [Father George] said that the guitars, maracas, and guido music didn't sound spiritual [enough].

Another parishioner was so upset about the change in music that he left the parish:

> And I went and sat there, and it was like going back with the old requiem. And there was no pizzazz. No guitars, no congas; the spirit was dead. I said, "I'm not going to go back there." Because I really felt upset.[49]

The ensemble was eventually reinstated when the organ player left, but some of the older repertoire was abandoned, and many of the previous players did not return.

Carmen, a parishioner who had long since left the neighborhood, believed that one of the most serious things that had happened to cause friction in the parish was Father George's dissolution of the Caballeros and Damas, the two religious and social organizations in charge of raising money for the church and of organizing many of the festivities throughout the year. Although the societies had become less important by the time Fathers George and Frank arrived, they still held monthly meetings and conducted the popular social dances. The dances were special occasions when the organizations took full control. They made all the preparations, cooked the food, bought drinks, hired bands, sold tickets, and collected money for the church. But Father George stopped the dances after an incident brought the police and complaints from the neighbors. A member of the Caballeros remembered:

> Then he stopped the group organizations in the church. He said he didn't want no groups in the church . . . like the men's group, the women's group, that used to celebrate dances. We used to bring good music, big orchestras, to the social hall, and we used to have big dances. We used to make at least three or four thousand dollars in one night. And he stopped that. No dances in the church. . . . He [is] a spiritual man, you know; he says people drink alcohol. Of course in a dance like that you got to sell alcohol.[50]

At times, those activities that parishioners initiated, felt in control of, or could shape to their own sensibilities and aesthetics seemed to be subordinated to the clergy's vehement public involvement in socal transformation. Susan Eckstein has alerted us to the ways in which religious values and new religious activity may stir conflict, not only within religious hierarchies but within the societies in which they are embedded.[51] She cautions us to be aware that the outcome of defiance may differ from its intent. While the clergy's Stations of the Cross appeared to promote change and legitimate popular protest in the neighborhood, parishioners' reception of these strategies was conflictual. Some of the stops along the route were as much sites of contention as they appeared to be rallying points for solidarity and collective action, although this divisiveness was absent from the public level of the Passion.

One site of intense local debate was Tompkins Square Park, across the street from St. Brigid's. As previously mentioned, the park had become the focus of a bitter dispute over how it should be used, and by whom. The debate pitted various neighborhood groups and government agencies against one another. Much of the liberal media linked the police crackdown in Tompkins Square Park to upwardly mobile professionals who were concerned more with elevating their property values[52] than with social and economic equity (as if enabling people to live in squalor in the park was any more noble and redeeming). Cleaning up the park, and clearing out the homeless, was simply one more attempt by the city to "tame and domesticate the park as a lubricant for already rampant gentrification on the Lower East Side."[53] But protest against people living in the park did not emanate only from upwardly mobile residents. Poor working-class families, especially those living in the projects, also expressed concern about the homeless presence in the park, and thought the city should come up with other solutions. Explaining why so many people had stopped going to St. Brigid's, one devoted parishioner pointed to this conflict:

> Because something's been happening at St. Brigid's since Father George took over. Some of the things he has done, the people don't like. But he's a

good priest; he's very spiritual. In other words . . . I give you an example. When the homeless used to live in Tompkins Square Park, I didn't have a car then. I used to walk from here to 1st Avenue. And there were about three or four hundred homeless people there. And it was dangerous because they were doing nasty stuff in there—drugs, and they were engaging in sex and everything—and it was pretty dangerous. And when the police stormed the park to get them out, Father George was against the police. We got into an argument, me and him. Because he says, "The homeless belong in the park." I said, "How about the rest of the people? How about the rest of the people who have children, who want to bring the children to the park, and they don't want to because they're afraid of the homeless people? You know they throw needles in there; might get spiked by a needle and catch AIDS, and stuff like that." So I told him, "Look, it's not us that has to do anything for the homeless; it's the city, it's the mayor. This park belongs to the community, not to the homeless."

Another parishioner explained her dissent from Father George this way:

Most of the people living in the park are not from the community. Most of them are from outside, selling drugs. The park belongs to the people, not only to the homeless. I think that it was right that the people were removed. They shouldn't have been removed by force. They should have their own individual rooms, not shelter, and not in the park. They bring sickness to the neighborhood. Father George wanted the park for the homeless. It used to be such a beautiful park. Of all the parks in New York, it made me feel so good to walk in that park. More beautiful than the park by the river. I used to bring my children there. But not anymore.

Besides supporting the right for the homeless to occupy the park, Father George came up with an idea for turning the dining room downstairs in the Catholic school into a shelter. This evoked an extremely volatile response from many parishioners. An older church member explained,

That's when people started leaving. They started taking their children out of the school. And again I told him it wasn't fair. It's dangerous. . . . And it's not that I have anything against the homeless, because I know they need shelter. I know they need food and clothing. But how can you bring people from the street into a place where the children are going to have their food? So a good amount of people left St. Brigid's since he took over. He's good, he's a priest. If you need a favor from him, he'll do it.[54]

Enough parishioners finally conceded to having the shelter in the school, and some even took an active role in cooking for the homeless, as well as managing the shelter during the night. But the conflict between the priest and congregation on this issue had run deep.

Another fierce debate was provoked by the performance of the ninth

Station in front of a Mobil gas station during the 1991 Passion. The presentation was organized and scripted solely by Father George. The Gulf War was under way; earlier in the year, Father George had attempted to turn the church into a sanctuary for anti-war activities. He hung a large banner on the front of the church displaying the Iraqi and American flags side by side and captioned with the words "Never again war. Adventure without return: never again war. Spiral of struggle and violence, never this war in the Persian Gulf; threat to your creatures in the sky, on earth and in the sea." The banner was meant to criticize the U.S. government for intervening in the Middle East, and to show that an alliance between the Iraqi and American peoples was possible despite official hostilities.

As the Stations of the Cross procession came to a halt in front of the Mobil station, Father George prayed:

> Lord, one of the deadliest routines we fall into when we leave out the most important things is warfare. Time and time again we approve of and rejoice in the shedding of your blood when we support our nation's war-making policies. This latest venture was undertaken so that we might have inexpensive gasoline to fuel an important American idol, the automobile. To ensure that a barrel of oil would cost between eighteen and twenty-one dollars, we accept massive loss of life, environmental destruction, and a further loss of humanity. And we call this "Peace," we call this "victory." Lord, have mercy on us! We place this cross on you, the cross of accepting the lie that wars can be "just." Give us the courage to begin, or continue in, our struggle to arrive at the day when we will love one another, including our enemies, as you love us.[55]

But few parishioners shared this vision. There was great resistance to Father George's sanctuary plan. Some feared they would be thrown into jail. As one parishioner told me angrily, "When the war in the Persian Gulf started, Father George started fighting in the church with the people. He say he going to open the church to keep some people who don't want to go to war in the church. . . . And what happen is the government come and take all inside the church, and he say, 'Oh we could get arrested, and we could be three years in jail.'" People with friends and family members in the Gulf found Father George's protests insensitive and hurtful. A woman who vehemently disapproved of the pastor's tactics and values reflected on why people had begun to leave the church again:

> People left [St. Brigid's] because they were depressed, you know. Because they have family in the war. . . . That's why they get depressed. They don't want to hear about the war. They want to go to church to pray for the soldiers in the war, not to hear about . . . the problems to make a refuge for the ones that don't want to go. To make a vigil, you know, to pray, that's a good idea. But the priest don't want to do that. In Puerto Rico they make a vigil. . . . They

put a big tree in the plaza, and they put the names of all the people that gone to the Gulf, and light candles. And nobody died from my town. They came home safe. That's what we wanted in the church, but he wouldn't.

Unable to get a clear endorsement from the parishioners for his protests, Father George eventually dropped the idea of the sanctuary.

As Susan Eckstein writes, "Privileged individuals do not always channel ordinary people's grievances in ways that effectively bring about change. Their visions may be imperfect, and their self-interest may stand in the way."[56] Some parishioners evidently believed that the church's attempt to re-edify their devotion toward social and political ends exemplified "official" intervention and control. While the clergy seemed to be concerned with bettering their mostly working-class congregants, some parishioners felt that they were being made responsible for an even poorer population of the community who had been lured to the East Village by an array of social services, ineffective shelters, and squatter settlements. And finally, some came to believe that Father George was neglecting their spiritual needs in favor of political and sociological agitation. As we saw, the clash of popular desire for liturgy with activist stress on "useful" collective action had been an ongoing feature at St. Brigid's since the early 1960s.[57] Some parishioners believed that the attempt by their pastors to politicize their aspirations had done more to engender conflict and divisiveness among the community than to mobilize collective action. An angry husband and wife who left the parish spoke bitterly to me about this problem:

> The argument I have with the priest . . . is that he is too much into politics. He always talks about Bush and what is wrong with this country. . . . So I get mad with him. I told him in a meeting that I believe . . . Jesus Christ loves community together in love. I believe in that. Not to make people fighting because some people have different opinions. In every meeting they have a fight. I didn't like that. That's why I left St. Brigid's. He was dividing people. I know one husband and one wife, they break up because of this. . . . I believe when he get politics and church there's a lot of problems. That what I object to. I believe we should talk about the problems of our country, we should have meetings to talk about that, but I don't believe it should mix [with religion]; it's going to cause problems. People have different opinions. . . . At this moment, I'm sure that most, a lot of people disagree with him, but they don't want to get in trouble.[58]

Another parishioner echoed this sentiment:

> We Puerto Ricans have real religion. We do not involve politics with religion. . . . He [Father George] talks a lot about politics. We want to hear religion. He talks a lot about abortion, all right. Say a little piece, [but] talk to us about the Lord. . . . He talks about the Iraqi war, we read about it in the paper, we see

it in the news. We don't want to see it, [or] hear it in the church; we want to hear the meaning of the lecture, of the Bible, what was written in the church.[59]

There are not isolated feelings. In an extensive survey conducted by the Office of Pastoral Research and Planning, the majority of Puerto Ricans interviewed opposed any church intervention in politics for the sake of social justice and defense of the poor.[60]

As the attendance at St. Brigid's continued to drop in the early 1990s, as more Puerto Ricans moved away from the neighborhood or "defected" to other parishes, and as the Archdiocese debated the future of St. Brigid's Catholic School, St. Brigid's Stations of the Cross appeared more and more like the single vision of a deeply committed pastor whose effectiveness had been extremely ambivalent. It seemed less an act of empowerment and more a gesture toward removing the traditional Puerto Rican leadership from the church, a process that had been going on since the saints' removal from the altar nearly thirty years ago. In my opinion, the church leadership's attempt to provide a religious motivation for change and solidarity among all classes, and to achieve unity in its fight against poverty, war, and the deteriorating conditions in its neighborhood, fell short. Finally, the Stations of the Cross procession could not mobilize a unified collective body; and no singular congregation could be sustained by the Christ allegory.

Notes

I am indebted to Allen Feldman for his insights and assistance in the preparation of this chapter. I also want to thank Robert Orsi for his persistence and editorial generosity.

1. Neil Smith, "Tompkins Square Park: Riots, Rents and Redskins," *The Portable Lower East Side* 6, no. 1 (1989): 3.

2. Allen Feldman, *Formations of Violence: The Narrative of the Body and Political Terror in Northern Ireland* (Chicago: University of Chicago Press, 1991), 27.

3. Susan Davis, *Parades and Power: Street Theatre in Nineteenth Century Philadelphia* (Philadelphia: Temple University Press, 1986), 2–22.

4. Susan Eckstein, "Power and Popular Protest in Latin America," in *Power and Popular Protest: Latin America Social Movements* (Berkeley and Los Angeles: University of California Press, 1989), 9.

5. I am thankful to Lynn Tiefenbacher for drawing these points of conflict to my attention.

6. Smith, "Tompkins Square Park," 13.

7. Ibid., 22.

8. Rosalyn Deutsche and Cara Gendel Ryan, "The Fine Art of Gentrification," *October* 31 (Winter 1984): 91–111.

9. "Smith, "Tompkins Square Park," 25.

10. Interviews with parishioners Carmen, Jerry, Thomas, Carmen S., and Father Frank confirmed this.

11. Ana Maria Diaz-Stevens, *Oxcart Catholicism on Fifth Avenue: The Impact of the Puerto Rican Migration upon the Archdiocese of New York* (Notre Dame: University of Notre Dame Press, 1993), 158.

12. Ibid., 161.

13. Eleanor Blau, "Church's Slum Experiment Ends in Dissent," *New York Times*, April 11, 1972, 43.

14. Robert Stern, "Evolution of Hispanic Ministry in the New York Archdiocese," in *Hispanics in New York: Religious, Cultural and Social Experiences*, ed. Ruth T. Doyle and Olga Scarpetta (New York: Office of Research and Planning, Archdiocese of New York, 1989); see also Diaz-Stevens, *Oxcart Catholicism on Fifth Avenue*.

15. Stern, "Evolution of Hispanic Ministry," 306.

16. Interview with Carmen Guillermo, September 25, 1991.

17. Interview with Carmen and Tomas, 1991.

18. Interview with Dermod McDermott, January 10, 1992.

19. Ibid.

20. Ibid.

21. Interview with Father Birkle, January 6, 1992.

22. Interview with Ray Acevedo, January 2, 1992.

23. Interview with Tom Leonard, June 17, 1992.

24. Interview with Ray Acevedo, January 2, 1992.

25. Interview with Father Juaquin Beaumont, January 18, 1992.

26. For a discussion of the interplay between pastoral care and social action see Diaz-Stevens, *Oxcart Catholicism on Fifth Avenue*, 30–34.

27. Interview with Father Juaquin Beaumont, January 18, 1992.

28. Ibid.

29. Ibid.

30. Ibid.

31. Interview with Father Frank, October 17, 1991.

32. Ibid.

33. Ibid.

34. Interview with Sister Patricia, May 1991. Also see Jeanette BeBouzek, "Ritual and Theater in the Way of the Cross Procession" (unpublished paper).

35. *Aqui Estoy Senor* (New York: Centro Catolico Hispano Del Nordeste, 1989).

36. Interview with Father George, March 28, 1989.

37. Peter Alson, "The Building That Ate Tompkins Square Park," *Village Voice*, July 18, 1989, 26.

38. Neil Smith, "New City, New Frontier: The Lower East Side as Wild, Wild West," in *Variations on a Theme Park: The New American City and the End of Public Space*, ed. Michael Sorkin (New York: Hill and Wang, 1992), 61.

39. Matthew Cooper, "Spatial Discourses and Social Boundaries: Re-imagining the Toronto Waterfront" in *City and Society* (Annual Review, Society for Urban Anthropology, 1994), 94.

40. M. Gottdiener, "Culture, Ideology, and the Sign of the City," in *The City and the Sign: An Introduction to Urban Semiotics*, ed. M. Gottdiener and Alexandros Ph. Lagopoulos (New York: Columbia University Press, 1986), 203.

41. Ibid., 206.

42. See also Mona Ozouf, *Festivals and the French Revolution* (Cambridge: Harvard University Press, 1988), 126–96; Robert Rotenberg and Gary McDonogh, eds., *The Cultural Meaning of Urban Space* (Westport, Conn.: Bergin and Garvey, 1993).

43. Ibid., 206.

44. For a fuller discussion of these two other images see Smith, "New City, New Frontier," 61–93. See also Deutsche and Ryan, "The Fine Art of Gentrification," 91–111.

45. Interview with N.F., January 11, 1992.

46. Louis Marin, "Notes on a Semiotic Approach to Parade, Cortege, and Procession" in *Time Out of Time: Essays on the Festival*, ed. Alessandro Falassi (Albuquerque: University of New Mexico Press, 1987), 223–28.

47. I am grateful to Marilyn Ivy, Columbia University, for her comments and questions regarding my discussion of the body and its relationship to the procession.

48. Eckstein, "Power and Popular Protest in Latin America," 1–60.

49. Interview with Ray Acevedo, 1991.

50. Interview with J.D., January 18, 1992.

51. Eckstein, "Power and Popular Protest in Latin America," 1–60.

52. Smith, "New City, New Frontier," 61.

53. "Smith, "Tompkins Square Park," 3.

54. Interview with J.D., January 18, 1992.

55. This passage is excerpted from Father George's unpublished script of the *Via Crucis*.

56. Eckstein, "Power and Popular Protest in Latin America," 38.

57. Daniel Levine and Scott Mainwaring, "Religion and Popular Protest in Latin America: Contrasting Experiences," in *Power and Popular Protest*, 13.

58. Interview with J. C. and N. C., January 11, 1992.

59. Interview with J. D., January 18, 1992.

60. Ruth T. Doyle and Olga Scarpetta, "The Survey: Religious Experience of the Hispanic in the Archdiocese of New York," in Doyle and Scarpetta, *Hispanics in New York*, vol. 1, 42.

"The Cathedral of the Open Air"

The Salvation Army's Sacralization of Secular Space, New York City, 1880–1910

Diane Winston

"An Army for Missionary Purposes"

Gray skies and winter winds greeted passengers disembarking at Castle Garden, the immigrant reception station at the southernmost tip of Manhattan, on March 10, 1880. Among those leaving the ocean liner *Australia*, which had sailed from London four weeks earlier, were seven somberly dressed young women and their blue-uniformed male leader. Those eight, the official landing party of The Salvation Army, marched down the ship's gangplank under a crimson banner bearing a blue border and a bright yellow sun in the foreground.[1] On one corner, a small American flag had been affixed. Kneeling on the cold ground, the members of the group planted their flag, sang a hymn, and claimed America for God.[2]

This unexpected sight sparked the curiosity of reporters who frequented the spot looking for colorful copy. Commissioner George Scott Railton, the group's leader, did not disappoint. Making himself available for interviews, he told the press that his party represented an "army of men and women mostly belonging to the working class" who had been saved from "lives of immorality and ruffianism." They worshiped like the early Methodists, but instead of employing regular preachers, they encouraged new converts "to speak from their own experience." This "was not a society of unruly religionists defying or rushing into conflict with order, law and society," he averred, "but an army for missionary purposes."[3]

From its first steps on American soil to its subsequent parades, open-air services, and visits to slums, brothels, and saloons, The Salvation Army sought the unchurched, "heathen" masses on their own ground—the city's streets and its commercial attractions. Hoping to compete with secular

10.1. Although this illustration of The Salvation Army's arrival in New York frequently appeared in the *War Cry,* it romanticizes the actual event. The lassies in the landing party wore plainer bonnets and uniforms, and contemporaneous illustrations indicate that they were neither as delicate nor as comely as the picture suggests. Yet the image of the party praying in a circle and Railton's arm raised to the heavens created an iconographic image of the mission to the city. "The Landing of Commissioner Railton and the 'Hallelujah Lasses,'" *War Cry,* March 19, 1904. Source: The Salvation Army National Archives.

amusements, Army leaders used popular music, lively pageantry, and dramatic testimonies to express themes of love, service, and salvation. Yet the Army's underlying aim was more than just saving individual sinners. Fired by a postmillennial fervor that was itself the legacy of American revivalism, Salvationist leaders planned to spiritualize the world and, in the process, to "sanctify the commonplace."[4] Their crusade to hallow the city—its buildings, streets, and public squares—was part of their attempt to establish the Kingdom of God. An 1896 editorial in the *War Cry*, the weekly Salvationist newspaper, explained:

> The genius of the Army has been from the first that it has secularized religion, or rather that it has religionized secular things.... On the one hand it has brought religion out of the clouds into everyday life, and has taught the world that we may and ought to be as religious about our eatings and drinkings and dressing as we are about our prayings. On the other hand it has taught that there is no religion in a place or in an attitude. A house or a store or factory can be just as holy a place as a church.[5]

In its early years in New York, The Salvation Army's greatest triumphs frequently occurred, as the Castle Garden landing illustrated, during open-air services and colorful parades. Believing they could "purify the moral atmosphere," Salvationists marched down the avenues and up the boulevards, crisscrossing New York's east/west and north/south axes.[6] When they ceased parading, officers led street-corner services that they called "the cathedral of the open air." The open-airs were part of a campaign to spiritualize social, moral, and urban space in preparation for the Second Coming, and the cathedral signified a sacred space large enough to encompass the entire city. Moreover, it signaled the belief in God's centrality by evoking the medieval cathedrals—material archetypes for the theological model of Christendom.

Postmillennial perfectionists in the first half of the nineteenth century had held similar notions, but their zeal had since waned. Their triumphalist dreams died on the blood-soaked fields of Gettysburg and Antietam, while new currents in biblical scholarship, natural science, and the social sciences displaced the preeminence of religious truths. Resigned to a shrinking portion of the social discourse, many religious leaders retreated to their bailiwicks, contenting themselves with bigger steeples and building programs. The commercial culture of advanced industrial capitalism filled the breach with its own normative set of meanings, signs, and symbols.

A new commercial aesthetic made possible by the rise of mass production reshaped culture and society in the century's final quarter. Animating this culture was a set of beliefs antithetical to republican political philosophy, traditional Christian values, and the economic axioms of an earlier producer-oriented era. The new beliefs hallowed acquisition as the key to happiness, the new as superior to the old, and money as the measure of all value. It predicated a society where democracy did not mean equal opportunities for owning land or for wielding political power, but rather equal opportunities for desiring and obtaining commodities and goods.[7]

The Salvation Army, whose postmillennial theology held that all aspects of everyday life could be sacralized, had an expansive spirit similar to that of the commercial culture of advanced industrial capitalism.[8] Both sought to saturate public space and control public discourse through a vision of individual transformation that would lead to a corporate utopia. The Army's means was the internal experience of salvation; the commercial culture offered fulfillment through external experiences of self. Each directed its message to the individual, yet both had important consequences for urban, social, and moral space.[9]

The Army's desire to "secularize religion" or to "religionize secular things" meant hallowing all space, activities, and relationships—in other words, saturating the secular with the sacred.[10] Parades provided a visual metaphor of the saturation campaign. Marching through commercial and residential areas, rich and poor neighborhoods, Salvationists blurred boundaries that urban Baedekers had studiously drawn by proclaiming that all space belonged to God. Not content to transgress geographic boundaries, Salvationists defied symbolic borders, too. The spectacle of a religious parade with brass bands and marching women struck many New Yorkers as a violation of Christianity. These critics perceived the Army as a threat to organized religion because it did not adhere to conventional notions of sacralized—that is, ecclesiastical—space.

"Soup, Soap, and Salvation"

The Salvation Army began in London in 1865 as the Christian Mission, a religious outreach run by William Booth, an independent evangelist determined to reach the unchurched masses. Booth, who began his ministry in the Methodist New Connexion, was greatly influenced by American revivalists Charles Finney and James Caughey, as well as by Phoebe Palmer, the revered Holiness teacher. Shaped by Wesleyanism and Holiness, the Army's theology, especially in its early years, had a postmillennial dimension akin to antebellum evangelicalism. Unlike their premillennialist contemporaries who focused on the world to come, Salvationists planted themselves in this world, seeking both to save souls and to redeem society.

Booth and his wife, Catherine, an early proponent of women's right to preach, delivered the gospel message to poor and working-class people in tents, graveyards, theaters, and city streets. In 1878, when Booth changed the name of his organization to The Salvation Army, he was already called "The General," and his new "army" rapidly adopted a military look and language. Its newspaper was the *War Cry*, its ministers were "officers," and its members were "soldiers." Early Salvationists wore plain dark clothes that varied from soldier to soldier until Booth standardized a simple blue uniform in the early 1880s.[11]

To attract notice from the "heathen masses," early Salvationists employed sensational tactics. They marched through the city streets with bass drums and waving banners. Their determination to pursue the unchurched public on its own territory seven days a week meant that the secular marketplace and its entertainments, not the churches, were a main source of competition. Thus, Salvationists adopted a self-consciously dramatic flair. Booth advised his followers to "invent for yourself," encouraging them to employ creative means—bold posters, theatrical handbills, dramatic presentations—to advertise their campaign.[12]

Early on, Booth discovered that the people he aimed to save were too distracted by physical need to hear the gospel message. Soup and soap were, indeed, the handmaidens of salvation. When "slum angels," Army women who lived and worked among the poor, went out in London in 1884 and New York in 1889, they cooked and cleaned, nursed and nurtured before they even mentioned religion. Booth's interest in social Christianity was further encouraged by two fellow Britons, W. T. Stead and Frank Smith. Stead, a crusading journalist, had enlisted Booth's aid in a campaign to raise public sentiment against sexual traffic in young girls.[13] Smith, a Salvationist and socialist who headed the American Army from 1884 to 1887, was a follower of Henry George.[14] Smith and Stead helped Booth devise a scheme to regenerate society's "submerged tenth." The plan, published in 1890 as *In Darkest England and the Way Out*, proposed setting up "salvage stations" where the urban poor could work, and from which, once saved and skilled, they would move on to farm settlements in England and abroad.[15] After the book's publication, Salvationists in Britain and the United States established an array of social services, including rescue homes, cheap lodging houses, salvage stations, nurseries, workingmen's hotels, cheap restaurants, and labor bureaus.

"The Cathedral of the Open Air"

Even before Booth's social programs began in New York, residents saw The Salvation Army on the city's streets. Army incursions most frequently took the form of parades and open-air services. Each corps was expected to hold several open-airs weekly. Officers and soldiers marched through the neighborhood booming their music on bass and brass. When a crowd gathered, Salvationists would sing, pray, and offer their own testimony before asking sinners to kneel at the drum and seek repentance. Salvationists then invited converts to their meeting hall—a local storefront or an auditorium in an Army garrison, lodging, or slum post—for a full service. For Army officers, open-airs were the latest incarnation of religious reform. Casting themselves as latter-day heirs to the open-air tradition of the Hebrew prophets, Jesus and the apostles, and the leaders of the Reformation, Salvationists saw their work as an alternative to the established churches.[16] Major Frank Smith, the Salvationist-socialist, emphasized the importance of outdoor services as a means "to get religion back on the streets," away from "the corrupting influence of the commercial classes."[17]

The open-airs seemed to provide a social function as well, serving as public rituals of an increasingly privatized faith. By the late nineteenth century, many Christians observed their religion privately in churches and within their own homes.[18] Religion was a refuge from the world, not a way into it. Catholics held processionals on special feast days, but their odysseys were confined to a particular neighborhood.[19] Jews, too, went outside for annual rituals, such as *tashlich* during the New Year and *Sukkot* later in the fall. But again, this was not the norm. Only the Army marched regularly through the local streets and routinely traversed long stretches of the city. These large-scale parades, spanning residential and commercial sections of Manhattan, always surprised spectators, who did not expect the tramping columns and braying horses to be part of an evangelical movement.

But to take part in the nascent debate on morality, poverty, and the role of religion in civic life, Salvationists had to occupy the "battlefield," specifically the city streets and the public presses. Their most effective weapon was the extended military metaphor by which the small evangelical group originally known as the Christian Mission had already transformed itself into a Salvation Army. The meanings embedded in Army dress, language, and ethos communicated two compelling messages to commentators and spectators alike. On the one hand, the Army represented obedience, discipline, and uniformity. William Booth had modeled his troops on the fighting forces of the British empire, and the gravity of their crusade was underscored by the pious dedication of his marching squadrons.[20] On the other hand, the Army was subversive, sensational, and dangerous. It ignored propriety and defied convention. Its women preached on street corners, and its bands played hymns set to popular ditties. Its converts testified publicly about private matters, and its accoutrements—circus-type posters, theatrical handbills, a newspaper that resembled the penny press—all seemed to mock Christian respectability.

10.2. The "Cathedral of the Open Air" was more than an Army metaphor. When Salvationists knelt and prayed in the city's streets, an ethereal church hovered above. Note the stars and clouds at the top of the page, contributing to the open-air theme. "The Army's Great Open-Air 'Cathedral': Arlington Square, New York City — a Historic Spot," *War Cry*, October 7, 1893. Source: The Salvation Army National Archives.

The contrasting images compelled public attention. New York elites criticized the "Jesuitical" discipline of Booth's adherents and lambasted their "vulgarizing religion," but they could not ignore it.[21] The Army's flamboyant displays and its aggressive evangelism quickly became part of the public culture. New Yorkers saw the Army downtown at the city's piers and uptown at its concert halls. In addition to holding local open-air services, the Army could marshal hundreds of supporters for special occasions.[22] These large-scale parades occurred either when the Army held a "War Congress," its annual interstate gathering, or when movement luminaries, such as William Booth, came to town.

Parades were a familiar sight on the New York City streets. Before the Civil War, marches were held to mark civic accomplishments such as the completion of the Erie Canal, to celebrate holidays such as Christmas and the Fourth of July, and to honor local militia units, trade associations, reform groups, and political parties. In the latter part of the century, parades continued to commemorate civic, military, and work-related achievements. In 1882, the city's first Labor Day parade rallied several thousand workers, including a squad of flag-waving Socialists, in a march from City Hall to Fifth Avenue. Large crowds also paraded at the 1885 funeral of Ulysses S. Grant, the 1889 centennial of George Washington's inauguration, and the quadricentennial of Columbus's voyage in 1892.[23]

Although parades were commonplace, they usually were not mounted by churches. Even the Easter parade, occasioned by a religious holiday, celebrated consumer culture rather than spiritual ideals. While parading in the new season's finery was a socially acceptable expression of Christian behavior, marching with Salvationist banners, bands, and uniforms was not. In the commercial culture of advanced industrial capitalism, the contestation for public space favored spectacles whose message coincided with market values. The Army's parades, signifying the sacrality of everyday life and celebrating the Kingdom of God, could be perceived as potentially disruptive because they advocated an alternate meaning system. Their challenge was writ clear in the visual text of the parade: Salvationist marches simulated military processions. Mounted leaders, flying banners, and disciplined battalions filled city streets with the sights and sounds of a conquering army. Not surprisingly, spectators stopped to watch this uncharacteristically aggressive display of the Christian faith.

During an 1885 War Congress, Major Frank Smith headed a parade, in a "blinding snowstorm," from the Army barracks on 18th Street and Eighth Avenue to the Academy of Music on 14th Street near Sixth Avenue. Trailing behind him were six mounted aides, one hundred tambourine-"thumping" young women with red jackets under their cloaks and red ribbons on their bonnets, a brass band, a "War Chariot," and thirty men dressed like "volunteer firemen." Sightseers thronged the parade route, and many marched along to the final destination.[24] Over time, Salvation Army parades became more elaborate still. In June 1892, en route up Lexington Avenue to Carnegie Hall, the half-mile-long march included men on horseback, standard bearers with banners of Booth family members, several carriages of dignitaries, floats demonstrating Army work in the slums and salvage centers, numerous bands, and soldiers representing foreign countries in their native dress.[25] Newspaper accounts indicate that passersby were intrigued by the proceedings. Some heckled, others gawked, and a few even followed.[26]

The Army also held what it referred to as "monster" open-air meetings at city landmarks such as Wall Street, Union Square, and even the steps of City Hall. Hundreds gathered for an evening's entertainment, because Salvationists provided, as an added inducement, a novel application of the latest technology. An 1896 midnight open-air meeting at City Hall began with a torch-lit procession featuring an illuminated wagon. The parade wended its way from the Army's 14th Street headquarters through the Bowery to lower Manhattan. When a large crowd had gathered on the steps of City Hall, they were treated to a stereopticon display of Salvationist leaders and Salvationist work to relieve urban squalor.[27]

Writing in the War Cry, Army officers emphasized the importance of open-air services as a way to attract non-believers. But the open-airs rallied stalwarts, too. In the 1880s, William Booth discontinued the use of sacraments, reasoning that these outward signs should not be confused with the reality of a changed heart.[28] According to Booth, a changed heart was effected by a personal spiritual experience that, to outside observers, resembled the frenzied fervor of a revival service or a camp meeting. At one service a New York Times reporter witnessed "whooping," "shouting," and "shrieking" as well as women "jumping into the air," an officer "bumping her head on stage," and three prostrate men.[29] Even the War Cry referred to the "Pentecostal waves" and the "showers of fire" that accompanied a Salvationist holiness meeting.[30] It was in this context—Army worship services focused on individual conversions—that open-airs became an expression of corporate solidarity and religious affirmation among Salvationist ranks.

By the early 1890s, mindful of their need for financial support, Army leaders toned down the excesses of their spiritual zeal: less holy-rolling and more hymn-singing. Moreover, the public had grown accustomed to its self-promotional campaigns, and what had once seemed profane was now merely humorous. The blue uniforms, signs of social and spiritual service, were part of the urban landscape—equally familiar on Fifth Avenue and in the Bowery. As Robert H. Bremner wrote in From the Depths, "The Army's dramatic and apparently successful methods of dealing with the dangerous classes aroused new support for slum evangelization in the old-line churches. . . . This work had not been wholly neglected before General Booth's organization came to the United States, but never before had the need and the opportunity been so successfully publicized."[31]

"Doing the Devil's Business"

The Army's drive to sacralize secular space extended indoors as well, to the most profane spots in the city. During his first days in New York, Salvationist leader George Scott Railton looked for halls to hold religious services. He found what he wanted at Harry Hill's Variety Theater, a notorious saloon in lower Manhattan. Unlike the many downtown dives whose dark interiors guaranteed their clientele anonymity, the well-lit Harry Hill's was an 1880s tourist trap, a spot where cabbies deposited out-of-town customers who wanted a taste of New York nightlife. Appearing there garnered Railton the press attention that might not have accompanied a Salvationist service at a storefront mission or even a rented hall. Harry Hill's, a series of crowded, smoky rooms, provided free entertainment. At one end of the saloon was a stage that featured musicians, boxing matches, puppet shows, and short plays. It was there, on a cold, damp Sunday night, that the Army held its first official American meeting. Railton led a service that alternated between hymn-singing and exhortations. Kneeling in prayer with the Hallelujah lassies, Railton surprised spectators with his swaying torso, flailing arms, and frequent cries of "Amen!" and "Hallelujah!"

Earlier in the day, Railton and the women had plastered the city with posters reading "The Salvation Army will attack the kingdom of the Devil at Harry Hill's Variety Theatre." But the packed crowd of curiosity-seekers did not warm to the performance. Some were annoyed when Hill, at Railton's request, stopped selling liquor during the service. Others were put off when Railton asked them not to smoke. Still others were bored by the religious sentiments. After more than two hours and no penitents, the Army left the stage, followed, to the audience's relief, by a panorama of *Uncle Tom's Cabin.*[32]

At a prayer breakfast the next morning, Railton's more orthodox sponsors were displeased by the group's appearance at the saloon. But one supporter, impressed by their spunk, offered them his own hall.[33] This site, the Hudson River Mission Hall at Ninth Avenue and 29th Street, became the Army's regular meeting place for the next few weeks. But as their movements that first Monday revealed, the English crusaders did not confine their missionizing to one spot. After the early morning prayer meeting on Fulton Street, Railton and his band headed north to the Baxter Street Mission, a converted brothel in the city's Five Points slums where Phoebe Palmer had proselytized thirty years earlier.[34] The walls in the meeting room were cracked and peeling; Bible verses hung askew. Most striking, however, was the diversity of the congregation. Seated along the straight-backed, wooden benches were many African Americans. While it was not unheard-of to find black worshipers at slum mission meetings, the Army encouraged their participation.[35] A reporter from the *New York Herald*, describing the Baxter Street meeting, noted the unusual mix of worshipers:

> A more motley, vice-smitten, pestilence-breeding congregation could seldom be found in a house of worship. There were Negroes, dancing girls, prostitutes, and station house tramps sandwiched between well-dressed visitors who had sauntered in out of curiosity. . . . The floors were as clean as a deck of a man-of-war, but in a few minutes they were frescoed with tobacco juice, the stench became overpowering, and a yellow-fever pest-house could not have been less attractive.[36]

From Baxter Street, the group went west for a noonday prayer meeting of businessmen on a lower Manhattan street corner.[37] At the day's end, the Salvationists held an outdoor service uptown, on the steps of the Hudson River Hall at 29th Street. Their enthusiastic praying and singing attracted the notice of residents and drew many inside. At the indoor service, which was "crowded to overflowing," some listened out of curiosity, but many others displayed a "sincere interest" in the Army's message.[38]

Earlier in the day, Railton had applied to Mayor Edward Cooper for a permit allowing The Salvation Army to preach outdoors and to hold religious services in the streets.[39] Stringent city laws had restricted street preaching since an 1810 incident when two evangelists, Johny Edwards and Dorothy Ripley, held an outdoor revival that ended in mob violence. Rather than control spectators, city authorities chose to prohibit outdoor services, passing a law that prevented "disorderly assemblies of persons in the City of New York." When Ripley sought to test the stricture, city officers dragged her off to jail. Aware that their concern for order came close to abrogating constitutionally guaranteed religious freedom, municipal leaders mediated their stance and allowed licensed clergymen to preach publicly after receiving legal permission. This compromise safeguarded religious tolerance while allowing officials to rebuff zealots with an incendiary message.[40]

Salvationists were just the kind of zealots that city leaders wished to discourage. Advance word from England had described their skirmishes with local magistrates as well as with rowdy mobs.[41] New York authorities did not want riots on their own streets, so when Railton sought permission to hold outdoor services, he was told that each member of the group would need to apply for a permit each time they planned an outdoor meeting. Railton was also asked if he was an ordained clergyman, the prerequisite for obtaining a license. He said he was not. The mayor explained that under the existing law, Railton could not receive a permit, but he was welcome to petition the Common Council to modify the ordinance.[42]

The next day, Railton announced that if the law was not changed, he would move the Army's national headquarters to Philadelphia. Railton's public proclamation was an empty threat. City officials did not care whether or where he moved his Army, but his brazen tactics kept Salvationists in the news.[43] When Mayor Cooper turned down Railton's request, the English evangelist did move Army headquarters to, as he noted, the "City of Brotherly Love." But several lassies stayed behind to continue the outreach work in New York. In the weeks that followed, they rented halls throughout the city and appeared at local missions. On weekends they held open-airs on the downtown piers followed by indoor services.

Even as the Army became more established, setting up corps (the equivalent of local churches) throughout the city, soldiers repeatedly returned to secular sites where sinners congregated. Salvationist lassies visited saloons nightly, proselytizing patrons while peddling the *War Cry*. An 1891 article in that paper saluted a group of ten female cadets (officers in training) who visited 1,025 saloons in one week. Lassies themselves described patrons whose hearts were stirred by the word of God. Recounting a Sunday visit to an illicit saloon, one officer wrote,

> When we distributed the tracts we announced that we would sing a song for them, which we did, and when they discovered it was a religious song some of the men sitting around, in a shamefaced sort of way, slipped their caps off. At the end of the song, I told them that we wanted to pray with them, so we got down on the filthy bar-room floor, and I noted that the head of almost every man and woman in the place bowed and the hats of the men came off when they saw us kneel. At the end of the prayer we told them that we wished to leave so the door was again carefully unlocked and we went out, but we saw tears on many faces.[44]

By the early 1890s, Army leaders recognized the explicit need to save the city's wealthiest as well as its poorest residents. Maud Booth, who commanded the American forces alongside her husband, Ballington, from 1887 to 1896, began reaching out to the well-to-do at Fifth Avenue parlor meetings and by-invitation-only lectures.[45] But it was one thing when Mrs. Booth, the refined daughter of an Anglican clergyman, addressed a private audience of the Social Register. It was quite another when the rank and file decided to share the message with the city's genteel classes, as did soldier

Jenny Skanberg when her employer gave her two tickets for a masked ball at Madison Square Garden. The young girl seized the opportunity to bring a spiritual presence to a key node of urban immorality.

Sponsored by the Cercle Française de l'Harmonie, the masquerade ball was, according to historian Timothy Gilfoyle, "probably the most significant event for testing the boundaries of urban sexual behavior."[46] Held annually, it was a notorious occasion of licentious excess. Skanberg asked another Salvationist lass to accompany her to the Garden, and the two brought along a hundred copies of the *War Cry* to sell to revelers. Once inside the festooned hall, the pair were asked if they were indeed Salvationists or just in clever costume. When the girls replied that they were the real thing, the ball's organizers asked why they had come. Said Skanberg, "Our place is here just as much as in the saloons, for you are doing the devil's business in both places."

By the late 1890s, Army leaders were also commandeering commercial theaters in their quest to spiritualize the profane and reach the unchurched. The Army often held its own internal meetings on secular stages, but now it mounted theatrical spectacles targeted to different audiences: revues for the lower classes and lectures with living tableaux for the more sophisticated. Theater had become big business; New York's seating capacity doubled between 1890 and 1900. The advent of vaudeville, offering a variety of decent entertainments for "respectable" people, had won over women from shop girls to society matrons. Catering to newfound customers, popularly priced houses featured melodramas and musical comedies as well as the successful vaudeville revues.[47]

Although The Salvation Army did not approve of the theater per se, it did appreciate the need for latitude when it came to saving souls. So when Consul Emma Booth-Tucker, who headed the American Army alongside her husband, Frederick, from 1896 to 1904, launched the "Red Crusade," an Easter-time campaign featuring medieval costumes, the opening salvo looked a lot like a theatrical performance. On Easter Sunday 1900, Salvationists paraded down the Bowery and into the London Theatre. There the consul, wearing a "scarlet scarf across her forehead, bearing the imprint of a Maltese cross," told stories of salvation while presenting the religious equivalent of vaudeville acts:

> The program was very varied and teemed with specialties such as were sure to captivate an audience of this character. There was first our excellent Staff Band, which, of course, was invaluable. The duets of Comrades Lackner, our saved variety actors, struck home and were greeted with deafening applause. Brigadier Hicks' style of delivery provided the missing link. Major Ferris, the "tamest Tammany Tiger," stood on familiar ground. . . . Everything, in fact, was fine; every "turn" seemed better than the previous one.[48]

The Easter Sunday service at the downtown theater was the "revival" portion of the evangelical campaign. During the five years that the Red Crusade toured the country, it was usually preceded by "Love and Sorrow," an illustrated lecture on the Army's burgeoning social program. Accompanied by a series of stereopticon views of Salvationist social work at home and abroad, the two-hour lecture was punctuated by living tableaux and choral numbers from the Yankee Songsters and the American Staff Cowboy Band. To build an audience, the Army placed articles and advertisements in local newspapers. On the day of the lecture, a brass band paraded through the streets playing a repertoire of loud military music. The tactics worked: frequently several thousand people sought admission to the Army performance.[49]

"Love and Sorrow" continued the Army practice of suffusing theatrical styles with spiritual meaning. But this presentation was particularly noteworthy because it separated the evangelical side of the work from the social ministry. Ideally, the lecture laid the foundation for the revival work of the Red Crusade, but those who chose not to attend the second meeting at least were exposed to the Army's outreach to the poor. For those who questioned whether helping the poor was a worthwhile activity for a religious group—social workers and charity societies claimed to have a better understanding of the causes and remedies for poverty—"Love and Sorrow" valorized the Army's vision of the problem and solution. The message was simple: Only the power of God's love could help. That power was twofold: manifest in the selfless ministries of social service (made possible by the second baptism of sanctification) and in the gift of salvation, the only sure way to turn one's life around. In this sense, social service delivery was a new tactic in the Army's ongoing sacralization campaign. Neither parading through the streets nor storming the citadels of sin had brought the Kingdom any closer. Concerned that their message could not penetrate the barriers of hunger, homelessness, and unemployment, Salvationists began responding to material needs. The Army's social missions, safe havens in a dangerous city, sanctified the urban landscape not just by their work but by their very presence.

"Love and Sorrow," a dramatic form of fundraising, illustrated the Army's efficient delivery of social services. Before the mid-1890s, Salvationists had opened shelters, food depots, slum posts, and rescue homes, but the Booth-Tuckers quickened the pace and increased the numbers. Within a year of their arrival, the number of social institutions that the Army operated rose from nine to twenty-one, and accommodations for the homeless tripled.[50] The Army may have failed at saving slum dwellers' souls, but it could meet some of their physical needs and allay the worst ravages of a rapidly advancing industrial economy beset by severe cycles of unemployment and depression. By the late 1890s, the Army began to describe itself as a religious and philanthropic organization rather than as an evangelical mission that also attended to dire physical needs.

It is possible that the emphasis on social programs represented a tacit admission of the Army's lack of success at slum evangelism. Contemporary Army sources celebrated their soul-saving work, but the numbers of conversions varied. Actual success at winning the unchurched masses, especially those in urban slums, appeared small. *War Cry* accounts typically profiled converts from rural communities or small towns who tended to be tepid or lapsed Protestants from petit-bourgeois homes. An occasional article described a converted, slum-dwelling Jew or Catholic, but these "trophies," as converts were called, were rare. Even Salvationists had noted that their slum work typically set an example for neighbors rather than spurred a conversion.[51]

Christian social critics increasingly considered the city to be their most important mission field.[52] Dubbed by Josiah Strong, an influential minister and social critic, as "the Gibraltar of civilization," it was seen as key to the development of culture and society.[53] Encompassing elements of both good and evil, the city required a strong Christian influence lest potential Jerusalems erupt into Babylons. When ascribing blame for the city's sinful state, religious rhetoric focused on the corrosive influence of foreign immigrants. Unfamiliar with American culture, language, and mores—not to mention Protestantism—Catholic newcomers, in particular, were charged with rending the fabric of Christian civilization.

The Army aimed to reach these masses by battling on two fronts. First and foremost, they sought souls, but they cared for bodies, too. Other groups, such as city missions, institutional churches, and social settlements, did similar work, but the Army operated on a larger scale, serving a broader spectrum of needs. Emphasizing its nonsectarian character, it spoke to a wider audience than either Catholic or Jewish charities that offered comparable services. By the late 1890s, many Christian leaders considered the Army to be the church's best hope for the city, combining the can-do spirit of the times with the Protestant zeal to build the Kingdom of God.

Army leader Booth-Tucker believed that once men had work, family, and religion—the classical evangelical trinity—God would step in and bring redemption. That difference in emphasis, or agency, has led many historians to distinguish the Salvationist social vision from that of the Social Gospel, describing the former as conservative and ameliorative while the latter was progressive and comprehensive. But Booth-Tucker's ideas were similar to those of contemporaries such as Josiah Strong, Washington Gladden, and Lyman Abbott. These socially active clergymen also believed that Christians had a duty to help the poor, and that such efforts would revolutionize the social order by initiating the Second Coming. It was the later Social Gospelers, such as Walter Rauschenbusch, who parted company with the original mission that the Army shared with other socially minded evangelicals.

At the center of the Army's urban strategy was its salvage operations. Collecting discarded household items for reuse and resale was already a familiar operation. William Booth had proposed it in *In Darkest England,* and a San Francisco shelter had dealt in salvage for a short period during the Ballington Booths' tenure. But Booth-Tucker seized upon the idea—which had the potential to subsidize Army activities, employ men willing to work, and provide cheap goods for the poor—and turned it into a national strategy.

The first salvage brigade operated out of the basement of an Army shelter for men in Manhattan. Workers supplied with a yellow wagon emblazoned with the red "Salvation Army" logo went door to door picking up household junk: old clothing, furniture, paper, scraps, and waste. Since municipal street cleaning had begun only in 1895, trash collection was at a rudimentary stage, and housewives had many items to give away. While one group of workers collected junk, a second crew sorted the take—mending, repairing, and baling the haul. Rags and paper were sold to dealers; clothing and household items were offered at minimal prices to the poor. The business proved so successful that the Army soon transferred its salvage operations to a site near a Lower East Side slum post. As business grew, this site proved inadequate, too.[54]

Salvage workers were recruited from the shelters that Salvationists established near local corps. Officers encouraged men housed in the shelter to attend worship services at the corps, since conversion was, after all, the Army's explicit goal. But by the end of the 1890s, officers were admitting that the shelter clientele and the corps soldiers did not mix. The latter tended to be members of the respectable poor and the working class, while the former were vagrants, tramps, and drunks. The decision was made to separate the shelter and corps, but a problem remained: since conversion was still paramount, a new model for integrating the social and spiritual work was needed.

The solution was the "Industrial Home," a center that provided food, lodging, work, and evangelistic activities under one roof and would eventually supersede shelters, workingmen's hotels, wood yards, and salvage brigades.[55] Residents at the homes were put to work. An excess labor force, they were employed at subsistence wages to cart off upper-class waste and to recycle it for businesses and for sale to the poor. In this tidy ecology, the victims of the new commercial society found their place as scavengers and bottom-feeders. As opportunistic and exploitative as this scheme may sound, it dispatched with the moralizing attendant upon distinguishing between the deserving and undeserving poor—the custom of most charitable institutions of the era.[56] If a man was willing to work, then investigating his past or present circumstances was unimportant. From the Salvationist perspective, converting to a profitable life, like a spiritual conversion, wiped the slate clean. It also provided a religious purpose for the human and material waste of advanced industrial capitalism.

Keep the Pot Boiling

Although Salvationists believed that a man should work for what he received, there were times when even they provided free relief. Weather emergencies were one such occasion; summer excursions, organized for women and children, were another. But the biggest giveaway in the Salvationist year was the annual Christmas banquet. Whether because of shrewd public relations or because they believed that everyone deserved a chance for Christmas cheer, the Booth-Tuckers institutionalized and expanded the free holiday meals that were provided at local corps and slum posts. The resulting extravaganza was criticized by some charity movement leaders as redundant, pauperizing, and little more than a staged spectacle for Army contributors. But the banquets were popular with the public, and the Army's fundraising apparatus, the Christmas kettle, became emblematic of its vision of service. As one newspaper noted, "Three gallon pots of money appeal to the imagination. None of the plans for raising funds for the Christmas of the city's poor seems to be more effective than these kettles on tripods with Santa Claus on guard, which the Salvation Army has placed in many conspicuous sidewalk positions."[57]

The kettles' appeal worked on several levels. The pot itself reminded passersby of hearth and home, conjuring up warm images of winter nights, sturdy stews, and an older frontier generation. Moreover, it was not associated with a particular religious group, and its nonsectarian identity was reinforced by the presence of Santa Claus. The kettle also acted as a corporate logo; it standardized giving across space and time, so that donors knew where their money was going whether they contributed in 1898 New York or 1998 San Francisco. Army leaders appreciated the fact that the kettles operated as a multivalent symbol. In a 1916 article, "At the Sign of the Tripod," the author observed that "the boiling kettles, signifying plenty," served as a "symbol" for the poor, for the rich, and for the spirit of Christmas. "In the tripod is focused the genius of The Salvation Army; in it concentrate all the high and holy impulses and moods in which the Spirit has manifested Himself in us."[58]

Contributions of nickels, dimes, and quarters fed some twenty thousand people at the Army's first Christmas gala. The dinner, "the largest Christmas feast ever in New York City," was held at Madison Square Garden.[59] Chosen for its size and reputation ("the reputation of the Garden will give the scheme a certain dignity," noted the War Cry), the midtown hall encompassed all the holiday banquets that had previously been held at local corps and slum posts.[60] Several thousand diners sat at long tables splendidly appointed with crisp linen and fine china. Served by Army soldiers and officers, the guests enjoyed a hearty meal of turkey, beef, mutton, pork, chicken, potatoes, celery, turnips, onions, plum pudding, oranges, bananas, and coffee.[61]

For the evening's entertainment, the Army staff band went through its paces, and a stereopticon show, illustrating Salvationist social work and the Oberammergau Passion Play, was screened. Yet even as the city's poor were treated to a festive holiday performance, they themselves provided entertainment of a similarly uplifting variety, to spectators whom the Army invited to fill the hall's upper tiers. Whether the Army intended the banquet as a religious spectacle or a spectator sport is debatable. Most likely it was the confluence of so many themes—sacralizing secular space through a religious performance (the banquet itself), creating an opportunity for spiritual entertainment (the stereopticon presentation), meeting material needs, advertising its own work, and soliciting donations—that appealed to Salvationist leaders.

In a front-page story the following day, the New York Times noted the thousands of "well-fed and prosperous" onlookers, bedecked and bejeweled, "who looked on in happy sympathy" at the festivities.[62] Some of these invitees, who included politicians, philanthropists, clergy, and society folk, were solicited by "pretty lassies" for donations. Salvationist leaders hoped that the Christmas spectacle would arouse sympathy for the poor and support for the Army's particular method of philanthropy. Yet in some quarters, it raised mostly criticism. In 1906, charity official Edwin D. Solenberger faulted the Army for reducing Christmas to a crass public-relations ploy.[63] His criticisms were anticipated in a New York World article describing the very first banquet. Describing the five thousand to six thousand comfortable-looking spectators, the reporter notes, "The contrast between their well-fed satisfaction and the hungry, bustling crowd was sharp. Some seemed to look upon this feeding of the ravens as spectacle and whispered and pointed at poorly clad men and women who ate ravenously, or smiled when a piece of turkey was surreptitiously slipped into a capacious pocket."[64]

The annual Christmas banquet was replaced around the time of World War I by more private forms of seasonal charity, but the Booth-

Tuckers' positioning of the Army as a Christmas charity was a strategic coup. The bell-ringing lassie and the kettle and tripod symbolized love, service, and compassion amid the consumer frenzy. It was not coincidental that the Army stationed soldiers and kettles near stores, theaters, and commercial centers. What better locations to display spiritual values? On one level, the Army's presence was an attempt to redeem the holiday marketplace by projecting religious claims alongside the acquisitive spirit

10.3. The Army lassies mesh with the costumed revelers, underscoring the uniform's function as a form of masquerade. "Selling *War Cry* in Madison Square Garden, NY," *War Cry*, March 14, 1896. Source: The Salvation Army National Archives.

that marked the season. But on another level, the Army sought to profit from that very spirit of acquisition. The humble kettle was a silent reminder of what the holiday was really about. Tossing in a few coins was an easy way to assuage an uneasy conscience.

Sanctify the Commonplace

The Army's creative appropriation of contemporary ideas, ideologies, and tools enabled it to grow as a cultural force when other religious crusaders were marginalized. Inspired by the postmillennial hope of ushering in the Kingdom of God, Salvationists set about to spiritualize the profane. Steeped in William Booth's dictum to attract attention, The Salvation Army used the tools of popular culture to express its message and was willing in turn to be used by secular wielders of those same tools. Neither rejecting nor succumbing to the secular culture, the Army sought to subvert its forms. When it became apparent that the goal of sacralizing secular space had not been successful, Salvationists focused on the more modest task of hallowing specific activities. A 1909 article in the *War Cry* explained their mission to "sanctify the commonplace":

> Get rid forever of the idea that the affairs of human life are divided into things secular and things sacred; that business is separate from religion and religion separate from business; that the consecration of certain hours to meetings, to Bible readings or to religious work is different from the devotion of the hours to labor or eating or physical necessities. . . . For the consecrated there is only one thing: "Holiness unto the Lord."[65]

Salvationists believed that Holiness was attainable here and now, and that its presence had practical ramifications in the conduct of one's life. The pragmatism inherent in this theology mirrored the bottom-line orientation of corporate capitalism. The Army's activist and pragmatic theology had strong affinities with the era's social ideology. On the one hand, the Army was part of the old evangelical consensus; it honored the family, held to a fundamentalist faith, and worked for the Second Coming. Yet even as Salvationists cleaved to these principles and asked others to do the same, they acted on a more pluralist and modern vision. Slum workers were taught to be tolerant of other faiths, and the need for public fundraising made Army leaders inclusive in their delivery of services and circumspect in sharing their witness. Aware of the need to distinguish one's private faith from a public religion, the Army modeled a new form of Christianity, which, as the twentieth century progressed, became increasingly attenuated from its evangelical roots.

Salvationists pioneered a new way of doing religion. Interpreting

10.4. In its early years, The Salvation Army kettle was a modest black pot suspended from a tripod. In this scene, each of the three females carries symbolic weight. The matron gives, the child will receive, and the lassie is the bridge between the two. In the background, the spectator, like the viewer, watches this cross-class display of charity. "Keep the Pot Boiling," *War Cry*, December 13, 1902. Source: The Salvation Army National Archives.

Holiness theology as a way of being in the world, they initially made the entire city their mission field. Later, as the Army expanded its mission to include humanitarian aid, New Yorkers encountered its network of social services in diverse neighborhoods. Salvationists sent out ice carts in summer, coal wagons in winter, and salvage crews year-round. They set up soup kitchens, rescue homes, employment bureaus, hospitals, shelters, and thrift shops. Along with the annual Macy's Thanksgiving Day Parade, the Army's annual kettle drive marked the onset of the Christmas holiday season, and each spring its fundraising appeal was heralded in posters plastered all over town.

Salvationists could be heard throughout the town, too. In the early days, their brass instruments, jingling tambourines, and resonant bass drums clamored over the din of horse-drawn carriages and noisy peddlers. Their testimonies, shouted from street corners, captured curious souls, while their renditions of popular music—"Sewanee River" or "Tramp, Tramp, Tramp" rewritten as hymns—roused critics to decry such blasphemous stratagems. Over the years, the music acquired more sophistication and the testimonies were toned down, but the open-air outreach continued. Well into the 1950s, Salvationists still played lunch-hour concerts on Wall Street and pounded their drums while curtains rose along the Great White Way. In winter, the tinkle of their bells was an unmistakable call to help the poor—just as their radio broadcasts were a reminder to send in a donation.

Rather than depend on buildings, hierarchies, or congregations, the Army built from the ground up. The city was their space, the citizens were their congregants, the public provided financial backing. Supporters were wooed not because they supported Salvationist doctrine but because they believed in Army practices. People purchased different things. Some threw money into the kettle because it was there; others wanted to help the poor. Still others salved their conscience, and some hoped to propagate Christianity. The Army attracted support disproportionate to its numbers because it invented itself as an urban religion. It was a public faith that grew by interacting with the surrounding culture—in other words, by seeking to sacralize the secular city.

Notes

1. This "official" party was preceded by Salvationists who came to the United States on their own. James Jermy tried to spread the message of the Christian Mission, the Army's forerunner, when he emigrated from Britain to Cleveland in 1872. His mission ended when he returned to his homeland four years later. In 1879, the Shirley family, also British Salvationists, asked William Booth for permission to start the Army in Philadelphia, where Amos Shirley had taken a job. Booth reluctantly agreed to let them use the Army's name, but after their initial success, he decided to send his protégé, George Scott Railton, to start the American work in earnest. Railton was accompanied by seven women.

2. In 1942, one of seven women told a *War Cry* reporter, "I can still see the dear Commissioner [Railton] standing in our little ring, claiming America for God and speaking on the text, 'God so loved the world. . . .'" Robert Sandall, *The History of the Salvation Army*, vol. II: *1878–1886* (London: Thomas Nelson, 1950), 233.

3. *New York Tribune*, March 11, 1880, 8.

4. William Booth, "The Millennium; or, The Ultimate Triumph of Salvation Army Principles," *All the World* VII (August 1890): 337–43. *American War Cry*, July 31, 1909, 2.

5. *American War Cry*, September 23, 1896, 8.

6. Ibid., January 28, 1893, 1.

7. William Leach, *Land of Desire: Merchants, Power, and the Rise of a New American Culture* (New York: Pantheon, 1993), 3–12.

8. Scholars have argued that commercial culture was already in place by the late eighteenth and early nineteenth century. Yet the scope and elaboration of that culture, from visual spectacle to transportation networks, had vastly increased by the 1880s. One explanation for that increase is the economic and ideological changes spurred by advanced industrial capitalism. Richard L. Bushman suggests some linkages in the introduction to his book on the rise of gentility, *The Refinement of America: Persons, Houses, Cities* (New York: Vintage, 1993), xvii–xviii. On religion and commercial culture, see R. Laurence Moore, *Selling God: American Religion in the Marketplace of Culture* (New York: Oxford University Press, 1994), and Leigh Eric Schmidt, *Consumer Rites: The Buying and Selling of American Holidays* (Princeton: Princeton University Press, 1995).

9. See David Carrasco, "The Sacrifice of Tezcatlipoca: To Change Place," in *To Change Place: Aztec Ceremonial Landscapes*, ed. David Carrasco (Boulder: University of Colorado, 1991).

10. *American War Cry*, September 23, 1896, 8.

11. For histories of the Salvation Army, see Frederick Lee Coutts, *The Better Fight: The History of the Salvation Army* (London: Salvationist Publishing and Supplies, 1977); Edward H. McKinley, *Marching to Glory: The History of the Salvation Army in the United States, 1880–1992* (Grand Rapids: William B. Eerdmans Publishing Co., 1995); and Robert Sandall, *The History of the Salvation Army* (London: Thomas Nelson, 1947–86). On William Booth, see St. John Ervine, *God's Soldier: General William Booth* (New York: Macmillan, 1935); Richard Collier, *The General Next to God: The Story of William Booth and the Salvation Army* (New York, 1965).

12. Quoted from the Salvation Army's *Doctrine of Discipline* in *The Nation*, August 17, 1882, 126–27.

13. The "Maiden Tribute" campaign is wonderfully described in Judith Walkowitz, *City of Dreadful Delight: Narratives of Sexual Danger in Late Victorian London* (Chicago: University of Chicago Press, 1992).

14. Norman Murdoch, "European Sources of William Booth's Darkest England Scheme of 1890," paper presented at the International Conference of Utopian Thought and Communal Experience, New Lanark, Scotland, 1988.

15. William Booth, *In Darkest England and the Way Out* (Montclair, N.J.: Patterson Smith, 1975; orig. pub. 1890).

16. *The Conqueror*, December 1897, 289–90; Maud Booth, *Beneath Two Flags* (New York: Funk and Wagnalls, 1889), chap. 5.

17. Frank Smith, *The Salvation War in America for 1885* (New York: Headquarters and Trade Dept., 1886), 76–77.

18. For a discussion of the domestication of Christianity, see Colleen McDannell, *The Christian Home in Victorian America, 1840–1900* (Bloomington: Indiana University Press, 1986).

19. Robert Orsi, *The Madonna of 115th Street* (New Haven: Yale University Press, 1985).

20. Olive Anderson, "The Growth of Christian Militarism in Mid-Victorian England," *English Historical Review* 86, no. 338 (January 1971): 46–72.

21. *The Nation*, August 17, 1882, 126; ibid., January 25, 1883, 78.

22. For more on parades, see Susan G. Davis, *Parades and Power: Street Theatre in Nineteenth Century Philadelphia* (Philadelphia: Temple University Press, 1986); Paul A. Gilje, *The Road to Mobocracy: Popular Disorder in New York City, 1763–1834* (Chapel Hill: University of North Carolina Press, 1987), 253–60; Mary Ryan, *Women in Public: Between Banners and Ballots* (Baltimore: Johns Hopkins University Press, 1990), 22–24, 30–33, 43–44.

23. Ryan, *Women in Public*, 22–24; Thomas J. Schlereth, *Victorian America* (New York: HarperCollins, 1991), 52–53; William Taylor, ed., *Inventing Times Square: Commerce and Culture at the Crossroads of the World* (New York: Russell Sage, 1991), 71–72.

24. *New York Tribune*, March 20, 1885, 2; *New York Times*, March 20, 1885. 2.

25. *American War Cry*, June 4, 1892, 2.

26. Ibid., 2, 3, 5.

27. Ibid., September 12, 1896, 1, 9.

28. Sandall, *History of the Salvation Army*, vol. II, 129–34. The Army was among the first Christian groups to allow women to perform the sacrament of the Lord's Supper. Many Salvationists were reluctant to give up the sacrament and, for a time, attended churches where they could continue. Salvationists instituted a dedication service in place of baptism.

29. *New York Times*, March 20, 1885, 2.

30. Ibid., March 22, 1883, 8; *American War Cry*, December 24, 1887, 13.

31. Robert H. Bremner, *From the Depths: The Discovery of Poverty in the United States* (New Brunswick, N.J.: Transaction, 1992; orig. pub. 1956), 29.

32. See Luc Sante, *Low Life* (New York: Vintage, 1992), 109–10; Richard Collier, *The General Next to God* (New York: Dutton, 1965), 81–82; Herbert A. Wisbey, Jr., *Soldiers without Swords* (New York: Macmillan, 1955), 3–5; McKinley, *Marching to Glory*, 16.

33. McKinley, *Marching to Glory*, 16.

34. *New York Times*, March 16, 1880, 8; Collier, *The General Next to God*, 223; McKinley, *Marching to Glory*, 18.

35. Sallie Chesham, *Born to Battle: The Salvation Army in America* (Chicago: Rand McNally, 1965), 62; Bernard Watson, *Soldier Saint* (London: Hodder and Stoughton, 1970), 61.

36. Chesham, *Born to Battle*, 59.

37. *New York Times*, March 16, 1880, 8.

38. Ibid.

39. Ibid.

40. Gilje, *Road to Mobocracy*, 212–14.

41. *American War Cry*, March 9, 1912, 6; Sandall, *History of the Salvation Army*, vol. II, 233.

42. *New York Times*, March 16, 1880, 8.

43. *New York Tribune*, March 17, 1880; Sandall, *History of the Salvation Army*, vol. II, 234.

44. *Social News*, July 1911, 4.

45. William and Catherine Booth had eight children: William Bramwell (1856–1929), Ballington (1857–1940), Catherine (1858–1955), Emma Moss (1860–1903), Herbert Howard (1862–1926), Marian (1864–1937), Eveline Cory (1865–1950), and

Lucy Milward (1867–1953). All the Booth children, except for the sickly Marian, were Army leaders, although Ballington, Catherine, and Herbert all resigned. When they married, the Booth daughters and their husbands used hyphenated names—Booth-Clibborn (Catherine), Booth-Tucker (Emma), and Booth-Heilberg (Lucy). Eveline Booth was called Eva by her family and changed her name to Evangeline, at Frances Willard's suggestion, when she took command of the American Salvation Army.

46. Timothy Gilfoyle, *City of Eros: New York City, Prostitution, and the Commercialization of Sex, 1790–1920* (New York: Norton, 1992), 232–36.

47. See Sante, *Low Life*, 71–103; David Nasaw, *Going Out: The Rise and Fall of Public Amusements* (New York: Basic, 1993), 19–46.

48. *American War Cry*, April 28, 1900, 9.

49. Ibid., February 11, 1899, 4; February 25, 1899, 4.

50. Edward McKinley, *Somebody's Brother: A History of the Salvation Army Men's Social Service Department, 1891–1985* (Lewiston, Maine: Edwin Mellen, 1986), 37.

51. *The Conqueror*, October 1895, 468–72.

52. For example, see Thomas Dixon, Jr., *The Failure of Protestantism in New York and Its Causes* (New York: Strauss and Rehn, 1896); Samuel Lane Loomis, *Modern Cities and Their Problems* (New York: Baker and Taylor, 1887); W. T. Stead, *If Christ Came to Chicago* (Chicago: Laird and Lee, 1894); Charles Stelzle, *Christianity's Storm Centre* (New York: Fleming H. Revell, 1907); Josiah Strong, *The New Era* (New York: Baker and Taylor, 1893); Josiah Strong, *The Challenge of the City* (New York: Missionary and Education Movement of the United States and Canada, 1911); Josiah Strong, *Our Country: Its Possible Future and Present Crisis* (New York: Baker and Taylor, 1885).

53. Loomis, *Modern Cities and Their Problems*, 5.

54. *American War Cry*, July 17, 1897, 3; Information for "History of the Salvation Army," USA Salvage Work, Salvation Army Archives; McKinley, *Somebody's Brother*, 40–43.

55. For more on industrial homes, see McKinley, *Somebody's Brother*, chap. 3; *New York Tribune*, October 9, 1904, sec. II, 6–7; *New York Tribune*, October 5, 1902, sec. II, 8; *American War Cry*, March 21, 1903, 3; *American War Cry*, January 2, 1904, 2.

56. For The Salvation Army's ideas about philanthropy and Social Christianity in this period, see Frederick Booth-Tucker, *Our Future Pauper Policy in America* (New York: Salvation Army Press, 1898); Booth-Tucker, *The Salvation Army in the United States* (New York: Salvation Army Press, 1899); Booth-Tucker, *The Social Relief Work of the Salvation Army in the United States* (New York: Monographs on American Social Economics, 1900); Booth-Tucker, *Light in Darkness* (New York: The Salvation Army Printing and Engraving Dept., 1902); Frederick Booth-Tucker, *Farm Colonies of the Salvation Army* (Washington, D.C.: Bulletin of the Bureau of Labor, 1903); Frederick Booth-Tucker, "The Salvation Army as a Temperance Movement" (paper presented at the Chautauqua Assembly, New York, n.d.); and Frederick Booth-Tucker, "Commander Booth-Tucker on the Pauper Problem in America," *Review of Reviews*, January–June 1897, 728. See also *The Conqueror*, May 1897, 116–20; *Harbor Lights*, May 1898, 144–47; *Harbor Lights*, June 1899, 186–89; *American War Cry*, February 14, 1899, 8.

57. *American War Cry*, February 14, 1899, 3.

58. *Social News*, December 1916, 10.

59. *New York Times*, December 16, 1899, 1.

60. *American War Cry*, December 2, 1899, 9.

61. *The World*, December 26, 1899, 3.

62. *New York Times*, December 26, 1899, 1.

63. Edwin D. Solenberger, "The Social Relief Work of the Salvation Army" (paper presented at the National Conference on Social Welfare, New York, 1906), 349–66.

64. *The World*, December 26, 1899, 3.

65. *American War Cry*, July 31, 1909, 2.

Contributors

Wayne Ashley teaches at Antioch University of Seattle. His writings on ritual, theater, and urban culture have appeared in a variety of professional publications.

David Brown is currently Visiting Assistant Professor of Art History at the University of Texas at Austin. His forthcoming book on Afro-Cuban religion is *Thrones of the Orichas: Iconographic and Ritual Innovation in Afro-Cuban Religion*. He is currently researching an oral history of Cuba's Yoruba diviners of the Ifa Oracle.

Karen McCarthy Brown is Professor of Anthropology of Religion in the Theological and Graduate Schools of Drew University and Director of The Newark Project, a field-based education program that is preparing an ethnographic "map" of religious practices found in the city of Newark, New Jersey. She has been engaged in intermittent field research on Vodou in Haiti since 1973, and continuous field research on Vodou among Haitians in Brooklyn since 1978. She is author of *Mama Lola: A Vodou Priestess in Brooklyn* and *Tracing the Spirit: Ethnographic Essays on Haitian Art*.

Madeline Duntley is Associate Professor of Religious Studies at the College of Wooster in Ohio, where she teaches American Religions, History of Christianity, and Ritual Studies. A charter editor of the *Journal of Ritual Studies*, she has published several articles on ritual and American religion. Duntley grew up and attended public schools in the same inner-city Seattle neighborhood which is featured in her contribution to this volume. She is currently working on a monograph, *Japanese-American Christianity and Asian-American Solidarity in Urban Seattle*.

Jack Kugelmass is currently Professor of Humanities and Jewish Studies at Arizona State University in Tempe. His books include *The Miracle of Intervale Avenue: The Story of a Jewish Congregation in the South Bronx; Between Two Worlds: Ethnographic Essays on American Jewry; Masked Culture: The Greenwich Village Halloween Parade; Going Home: How Jews Invent Their Old Countries; From a Ruined Garden: The Memorial Books of Polish Jewry;* and *Let There Be Laughter: Jewish Humor in America*.

Robert A. Orsi is Professor of Religious Studies at Indiana University and author of *The Madonna of 115th Street: Faith and Community in Italian Harlem, 1880–1950* and *Thank You, Saint Jude: Women's Devotions to the Patron Saint of Hopeless Causes*. He has also taught at Fordham

University at Lincoln Center and the Università degli Studi di Roma. Orsi has held fellowships from the Fulbright Foundation and the National Endowment for the Humanities. His books have been awarded the Alpha Sigma Nu National Book Prize of the Association of Jesuit Colleges and Universities (1985), the American Catholic Historical Association's John Gilmary Shea Prize (1986), and the Merle Curti Award in American Social History from the Organization of American Historians (1998).

Joseph Sciorra received his Ph.D. from the Department of Folklore and Folklife at the University of Pennsylvania. He has written extensively on popular religion and vernacular culture in New York City and is author of *R.I.P.: Memorial Wall Art*, with photographer Martha Cooper. Sciorra produces web sites for iXL–New York.

Thomas A. Tweed is Associate Professor of Religious Studies at the University of North Carolina at Chapel Hill. He edited a collection of essays that challenged the standard historical narratives, *Retelling U.S. Religious History*. Most of his historical and ethnographic research has focused on Asian religions and Roman Catholicism in the United States, including *The American Encounter with Buddhism, 1844–1912* and (coedited with Stephen Prothero) *Asian Religions in America: A Documentary History*. *Our Lady of the Exile: Diasporic Religion at a Cuban Catholic Shrine in Miami* (1997) won the 1998 American Academy of Religion Award for Excellence. Tweed's contribution to this book is taken from research he did for that ethnographic study.

Joanne Punzo Waghorne teaches Hinduism in the Department of Religious Studies at the University of North Carolina at Chapel Hill. Her most recent book is *The Raja's Magic Clothes: Kingship and Divinity in England's India*. She returned to India in 1994–95 with support from the National Endowment for the Humanities to study new temples in Madras city and their connections to recent temples in the United States. Waghorne is now writing a book on new Hindu temples in a global context.

Diane Winston is a Visiting Fellow at the Center for the Study of American Religion at Princeton University. Her book on the Salvation Army is forthcoming from Harvard University Press.

Index

Fernández, Adolfo, 186–94, 199–205, 219*n.15*, 220*n.33*
Festa of Italian Harlem, 257–88
Folk groups, urban, 155–56. *See also* Ethnic identity; specific ethnic groups
Franciscans, 51, 62–63
Frank, Father, 349–55
Fundamentalists, Hindu, 106–107

Gang activity, in Italian Williamsburg, 337*n.15*
García, Josie, 205
Garvey, Marcus, 22
Gay men, urban mapping by, 52, 77*n.93*
Genesis Garden, 62–63
Gentlemen's Agreement, 290–91
George, Father, 350–52, 354
Giglio, in Italian religious processions, 317, 318f, 320, 322
Giles, Brother, 2–3
Gladden, Washington, 26
Glassie, Henry, 156
Goatee rock, 281–82, 288*n.66*
González Huguet, Lydia, 175
Good Friday, 341
Good Friday procession, 60; Italian American, 320, 327
Gospel of wealth, 23–24
Green Pastures, The, 10–11, 64*n.14*
Greenhorn and black man myth, 257–58, 280–83, 282*n.1*
Greenpoint: ethnic populations of, 311, 313–14. *See also* Williamsburg
Gurus, Hindu, 107–108

Haiti: geographical transposition of, 91–92; slave revolution in, 84, 101*n.13*; Tenth Department of, 80, 97
Haitians, 58, 79: first diaspora of, 79–80; in Italian Harlem, 273–76; in Italian Williamsburg, 334; racism and, 93–94, 96; religious crisis of, 81–82; religious transnationalism of, 96–98; second diaspora of, 80, 84. *See also* Vodou
Hall, Edward, 156–57
Hannerz, Ulf, 54–55
Harlem, 45, 65*n.15*; East versus West, 262–65; as exotic locale, 7; idea of, 263–64; middle-class attraction to, 9–

11; street culture of, 50. *See also* Italian Harlem
Highways, social impacts of, 33–35
Hindu temple: American versus Indian, 116–21; gender/generational issues, 121–25; middle-class Indian and, 119–20; non-Hindu community and, 126; role of, 108–11; sacred-secular separation in, 118–19; suburban, 111–21; technology and, 125–27
Hinduism: city in, 109; dance in, 121–22; deities of, 113–15; fundamentalist, 106–107; gurus in, 107–108; of middle class, 105–11; reconstruction of, 103–30
Home: migration as loss of, 80–81; separation from work, 15
Homelands: Cuban attachment to, 132–33, 149*nn.4,6*; and Our Lady of Charity shrine, 145; reinvention of, 157–58, 214
Homeless, 352. *See also* Poverty
Housing projects, 34–35
Huggins, Nathan Irvin, 7, 10–11, 65*n.14*

Identity: city religion and, 54–58; of Cuban exiles, 131–32, 147–48; defined against other, 277, 279–80; dual, 56; ethnic, 57; of exiled Cubans, 131–33; Italian American, 258, 261–62, 319–20, 322–24, 326–27; in Japanese Presbyterian Church, 298–302; spatial form and, 156–57; through religious processions, 330–32. *See also* Ethnic identity; National identity; Nationalism; Subjectivities
Igbodún, 161–70
Immigrants: light- versus dark-skinned, 258; and loss of home, 81; origins of, 16; in South Bronx, 2; urban growth and, 19–20; urban religion and, ix–x. *See also* specific groups
Indian immigrants, 58, 103; bond to mother country, 105–11; economic/social background of, 103–105. *See also* Hindu temple
Individualism, 42–43
Industrial Home, 382–83
Inouye, Orio, 291, 304

Urbanization: social-psychological consequences of, 5; U.S., 69n.37

Varela, Félix, 144, 153n.26
Virgin Mary, in Italian religious processions, 320
Virgins, national, 136, 151nn.12,13
Vlach, John, 156
Vodou, 49, 50, 58, 79–102, 100n.2; Catholicism and, 89–91; cosmology, 81–84; European view of, 93; hidden identity, 93–95; Italian American denial of, 275–76; libations in, 84–86; in New York, 95–96; ritual, 81–89, 101nn.14,15; social commentary in, 88; spirit transformation in, 92–93; transnational, 96–98; yam feast in, 86–89
Voluntary associations, Italian American, 316–17

Wesley Chapel, 25
Wesleyanism, Salvation Army and, 370

Wetli, Charles, 208
White City, 38–39
Wilkerson, David, 11–12, 65n.16
Williamsburg: ethnic and religious populations of, 311–14, 312f; ethnic boundaries in, 310; stigma of, 332. See also Italian religious processions; Italian Williamsburg
Women: exploitation of, 353; in Salvation Army, 370–72, 374, 376, 378–79, 385, 385f, 390n.28
Work, separation from home, 15
Working class: fear of, 15–16; reformers' assaults on, 67n.26
World Hindu Council, 106–107
World War I, urban change and, 21–22

Xenophobia, 29; Italian immigrants and, 261–62; post–Civil War, 23–24. See also Otherness

Yam ceremony, 86–89
YMCA, 24; reform strategies of, 18